# THE WORLD ENCYCLOPEDIA OF
# FOOTBALL
## A COMPLETE GUIDE TO THE BEAUTIFUL GAME

## TOM MACDONALD

LORENZ BOOKS

This edition is published by Lorenz Books,
an imprint of Anness Publishing Ltd,
Hermes House, 88–89 Blackfriars Road, London SE1 8HA;
tel. 020 7401 2077; fax 020 7633 9499

www.lorenzbooks.com; www.annesspublishing.com

Anness Publishing has a new picture agency outlet for images for
publishing, promotions or advertising. Please visit our website
www.practicalpictures.com for more information.

UK agent: The Manning Partnership Ltd;
tel. 01225 478444; fax 01225 478440;
sales@manning-partnership.co.uk

UK distributor: Book Trade Services;
tel. 0116 2759086; fax 0116 2759090;
uksales@booktradeservices.com; exportsales@booktradeservices.com

North American agent/distributor: National Book Network;
tel. 301 459 3366; fax 301 429 5746; www.nbnbooks.com

Australian agent/distributor: Pan Macmillan Australia;
tel. 1300 135 113; fax 1300 135 103;
customer.service@macmillan.com.au

New Zealand agent/distributor: David Bateman Ltd;
tel. (09) 415 7664; fax (09) 415 8892

Publisher Joanna Lorenz
Project editors Dan Hurst and Sarah Ainley
Copy editors Richard Rosenfeld and Peter Arnold
Editorial assistant Joel Simons
Production manager Stephen Lang

Original material supplied by Sport and Leisure Books Ltd.

ETHICAL TRADING POLICY
Because of our ongoing ecological investment programme, you, as
our customer, can have the pleasure and reassurance of knowing
that a tree is being cultivated on your behalf to naturally replace
the materials used to make the book you are holding. For further
information about this scheme, go to
www.annesspublishing.com/trees

© Anness Publishing Ltd 2001, updated 2009

PICTURE CREDITS
All images supplied by **Colorsport** except for the following:
t = top; b = bottom; c = centre; l = left; r = right
**Action Images** 31bl, 188t, 226t, 226b, 233t; **Allsport** 42, 43, 46t,
48, 49, 52, 182t, 209t, 224b; **Empics** 4t, 5tr, 32, 37, 38, 44, 45, 47,
49b, 50t, 51, 57b, 58t, 58b, 59, 60t, 60b, 61, 64b, 66, 67, 68t, 68b,
69, 70t, 70b, 71t, 95, 97t, 105b, 107t, 108t, 109t, 118t, 118b, 121b,
133, 139b, 143b, 145b, 146t, 151b, 160b, 161b, 168t, 170t, 179t,
179b, 185b, 186, 187t, 188b, 189t, 191b, 199t, 202t, 203b, 209b,
210, 211t, 211b, 213t, 213b, 217t, 219t, 223b, 230b, 233b, 234b,
237b, 243b; **Hulton Getty** 9t, 9b, 14t, 15cr, 19, 20r, 21t, 22, 24b,
33, 54t, 62t, 78b, 94b, 109t, 130t, 144b, 147b, 176b, 177t, 197t,
223b, 224t, 238b; **Offside** 1, 4b, 5tr, 5b, 46b, 53b, 71b, 72tr, 73t,
75b, 97b, 98b, 110t, 112b, 126t, 134b, 138t, 140b, 141t, 150t, 160b,
161t, 171t, 174b, 189b, 200t, 207t, 220b, 222b, 237t; **Popperfoto**
13t, 14b, 15b, 16, 17tl, 17tr, 17b, 21b, 23t, 23b, 25, 28b, 30t, 30b,
34t, 34b, 35, 63t, 90b, 92t, 99b, 103b, 117c, 120t, 125b, 149c, 153b,
174t, 176t, 238t, 242; **The Art Archive** 8.

# Contents

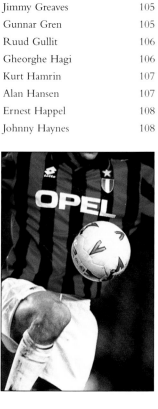

# Introduction

Football is big business in the 21st century. When a Russian billionaire can buy Chelsea Football Club and spend hundreds of millions on new players, a Gulf state sheikh can turn lowly Manchester City into the world's wealthiest club and Real Madrid can spend £30 million on buying a new "galactico" each season, it is clear that the sport is not the same as it was 100 years ago, when the maximum wage was £4 per week.

Yet the game itself has not changed. It is still the people's game, the beautiful game. More people play it, watch it and dream about it than they do any other sport in the world.

The great beauty of football is that it retains its ability to shock and surprise, to delight and astonish. The 2002 World Cup demonstrated the remarkable power of football. The tournament in Japan/Korea saw the emergence of new nations – such as Turkey, South Korea, Senegal – who challenged the established order.

Brazil may have overcome another traditional superpower, Germany, in the final in Yokohama, but the Turks and the Senegalese surprised many with their progress, while the South Koreans provided one of the most astonishing stories in the history of the World Cup

Above: Brazil's Ronaldo and Gilberto Silva kiss the World Cup trophy in 2002.

Below: Spain take the title of European Champions in 2008.

*Above: Cristiano Ronaldo became the world's most expensive player in 2009.*

finals. South Korea, willed on by some of the most amazing crowds ever seen in a World Cup, beat Portugal, Italy and Spain before losing to Germany in the semi-finals. Turkey finished in third place. Brazil's victory was sealed by two goals from Ronaldo, who finished as the player of the tournament.

*Below: The Italian team celebrate their victory in the 2006 World Cup Final.*

*Above: Chelsea celebrate their second league title – 50 years after their first.*

After the World Cup, Ronaldo was transferred from Inter Milan to Real Madrid, who had broken the bank to land a star name. This trend for spending breathtaking sums on star players is still on the rise, with Cristiano Ronaldo becoming the most expensive player in the world in June 2009, moving from Manchester United to Real Madrid for £80 million.

However, there is a downside to the business boom. As the few richest clubs prosper, others are unable to keep pace, and can overstretch themselves. Even in the richest football continent, Europe, big and long-established clubs such as Leeds United and Liverpool in England, Lazio and Parma in Italy, and Bayern Munich in Germany have had financial problems of varying degrees. There has also been growing tension between clubs and international federations over the use of their expensive players in friendly internationals. The club v country debate threatens to run and run.

Yet for the football lover, the game itself remains the real interest. Millions of people watched Italy winning the 2006 World Cup, and Euro 2008, with Spain deservedly becoming champions for the first time in several decades, while Barcelona's stunning demolition of Manchester United in the 2009 Champions League Final was a reminder to fans worldwide of why football continues to be the world's greatest game.

# THE GAME OF FOOTBALL

Football today is the most popular sport on the planet. It links nations, cultures and continents, and is one of the world's most profitable businesses. Yet it wasn't always so, and the story of football's development since its pre-13th-century origins is a tribute to its overwhelming, and ever-growing, popularity. First synonymous with violent street brawls, football was at one time banned by royal decree. But it re-emerged; rules were drawn up and leagues were formed. Once the game had become part of public consciousness, the passion spread: this chapter looks at how it happened.

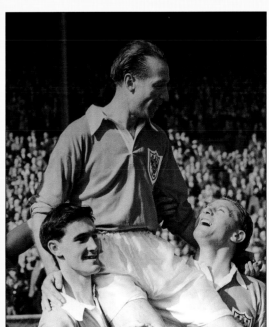

# Early Days

There is evidence from across the world that football is a truly ancient pastime. We know that ball games were played in China 3,000 years ago, and records in Japan refer to a 14th-century ball game called *kenatt*. The Toltécs of Central America are known to have played a ball game called *tlatchi* in the 9th and 10th centuries AD. There are contemporary drawings of the ancient Greeks playing with a ball, while the Romans played a proto-football game called *harpastum*. In 16th-century Florence, Italian aristocrats enjoyed a lively carnival game, which was played in the streets and involved pushing and kicking for possession of a ball (often a decapitated head). They called the game *il calcio*, and Italians use the same word for association football today. There may have been differences concerning rules and the number of players, but these

*Below: A painting of the Roman game* harpastum *from the 1st century* AD.

games all had the same aim, two opposing teams trying to propel a ball at a designated target. The basics of football have not changed.

Football as we know it was invented in England but the original idea does not seem to have been English. The game is known to have existed in England before the Norman Conquest in 1066, and was probably introduced by the Romans. Typically, two villages, or two teams from within one village, chased a ball through the streets, and each village had its own set of rules. The games were played with great gusto and vigour. With no referees to impose the rules, the sport became known for its aggression, with violent confrontations, injuries and even deaths. Householders who lived in the streets where a football match was being played had to barricade their lower windows in order to protect themselves from the hostile mob. The Shrove Tuesday carnival day before Lent was a favourite date for a

game. The village of Ashbourne in Derbyshire, northern England, still celebrates the event with an exhibition match featuring a heavy leather ball, the origins of which date back at least to the 13th century. The phrase "Derby match" derives from this Derbyshire game between two local teams.

The spread of football, with its serious danger to life and limb and threat to law and order, concerned the authorities so much that King Edward II banned the game by royal decree in 1314. He was worried that his soldiers would not be fit to serve, so much time did they spend "in such idle practices", brawling and scrambling over a football. Similarly, Richard II outlawed the game in 1389 because he feared it would prevent his army getting enough archery and javelin practice. Further prohibitive decrees were issued in 1477 by Edward IV and 20 years later by Henry VII. But the game continued to be played

*Above: Gentlemen playing football in the Strand in 18th-century London.*

throughout the Tudor and Stuart eras, and with increasing enthusiasm. By the early 17th century we know it was being played at the universities of Oxford and Cambridge. However, the Puritans strongly disapproved of football because it was played on Sundays, the sacred Christian day of rest, and because it aroused violent, non-Christian passions in its players. The game was suppressed by Oliver Cromwell and it did not reappear until the Restoration and the end of Puritan rule in 1660.

As football grew in popularity, the lack of common standards became more apparent, and in some cases the "matches" were little more than unconstrained brawls. Kicking, handling and carrying the ball were accepted, while the goals could be any size and the pitch might be a street or field. The number of players varied from 20-a-side to practically everyone in the village. In the 19th century, two

incidents in particular checked football's popularity. The Enclosure Act of 1852 reduced the amount of common land available for recreational use, while in the cities, the long working hours that

came with the Industrial Revolution restricted the amount of leisure time available. The increasing number of factories also meant that there was less public space available and the emphasis was now more on street football, which led many towns to ban or heavily proscribe the game as it was widely regarded as antisocial, rough and potentially dangerous.

What saved the game from its early 19th-century decline was its increasing popularity in the English public schools, where all kinds of variants on the game had been played since the 16th century. The schools thought football a laudable activity and excellent training, with its emphasis on teamwork and discipline. In fact, it was the public schools that kept the game alive. They were the crucial bridge between the old, shambolic, unregulated game and the highly organized one that is played today.

*Below: Supporters cheer a group of footballers playing in Crowe Street, an East London slum, in 1721.*

# The Game Takes Off

For all today's talk about football being a "working man's game", by the mid-19th century it was largely the preserve of the English public schools, each of which had its own particular version. At Charterhouse, they played 20-a-side and the players could dribble the ball but not handle it; Eton had its own peculiar Wall Game; Uppingham had goals the width of the pitch; and Rugby allowed handling but not if you ran with the ball (at least, according to legend, until William Webb Ellis decided otherwise in 1823, and created the game of rugby).

## The Rules

In 1848 came the first attempt to codify the rules of the game. Representatives of the major public schools met at Cambridge University and agreed that the ball could be handled, so long as it was immediately placed on the ground and kicked, and that kicking an opponent was illegal. An offside law was also drafted. These Cambridge Rules formed the basis of the modern game.

A further attempt to unify the many forms of the sport was made on

*Below: The Wall Game, an early version of football played by Eton schoolboys.*

26 October 1863, at the Freemasons' Tavern in Great Queen Street, London. Eleven clubs met to form the Football Association (FA), the aim of which was to establish "a definite code of rules for the regulation of the game". Mr E. C. Morley was the first secretary of the Association, and by the time the rules were published that December, the FA had decided that picking up and carrying the ball and "hacking" an opponent in order to win possession were illegal. Blackheath school disagreed and went on to form the rugby club that still plays today.

*Above: The Royal Engineers, who played in the first FA Cup final in 1872.*

> **Early Football Associations**
> **1863** England
> **1873** Scotland
> **1876** Wales
> **1880** Ireland
> **1889** Denmark; Holland
> **1893** Argentina
> **1895** Belgium; Chile; Switzerland
> **1898** Italy

## Professionalism

Despite the attempts to regulate football with a set of rules, one thorny issue remained. Most of the affiliated members of the FA were from relatively affluent areas in the south of England and they believed in the Corinthian ideal of amateurism, that players should not earn their money from football. However, the situation was different in the poorer north, where players were paid, and this attracted Scots who brought their passing game with them. Until that time the English game had focused on dribbling skills, and the novel but effective Scottish method of short, interconnected passing was much in demand. The FA's response, in 1882,

was to ban professionalism, which provoked an immediate and volatile outcry. Preston were banned from the FA Cup in 1884 for paying their players. But the protests continued and the FA was finally forced to legalize professionalism in 1885.

In Scotland, too, the FA were strongly anti-professional, but with so many Scots being lured to England, the clubs had to offer financial incentives to keep their best players. The Scottish FA capitulated to professionalism in 1893.

### The First League System

William McGregor, a Scottish director of English club Aston Villa, wrote to a number of clubs in 1888 suggesting the formation of a football league. A meeting was held on 23 March in Manchester, with no southern clubs present, and it was decided that a 12-club league be formed the next season. The original 12 clubs were Accrington, Aston Villa, Blackburn Rovers, Bolton, Burnley, Derby County, Everton, Notts County, Preston North End, Stoke City, West Bromwich Albion and

Wolverhampton Wanderers, thus making the English Football League the oldest in the world.

### Taking the Game Abroad

Through colonial links and the growth of industry in the 19th century, sailors, traders, railway workers, engineers, teachers and students from the United Kingdom travelled further afield, and they took the game of football with them. Games were played, interest generated and local teams formed. In continental Europe, the first organized association football took place in Switzerland as early as the 1850s; the game developed to such an extent that a national championship was held in 1897. In France, an early version of football called *la soule*, which can be traced back to the Romans and Celts, had been outlawed in the 18th century as a threat to law and order. Off-duty British sailors in France reintroduced the game in the 19th century and France's first association football side, Le Havre Athletic Club, was formed in 1872. Sailors also

*Below: Aston Villa, FA Cup winners 1895. In 1897 they won the "double".*

played football on the shores of Brazil in 1874, and by 1898 Brazil had its first mainly Brazilian club – the Associaciao Athlética Mackenzie College in Sao Paulo. The British influence can be seen in the names of some of the older European sides, such as First Vienna, Genoa Football and Cricket Club and Milan FC (later AC), all of which were founded by English expatriates homesick for the game.

---

### Formation of Famous Clubs

**1855** Sheffield FC (England), the world's oldest club
**1873** Rangers (Scotland)
**1878** Manchester United (England)
**1886** Arsenal (England)
**1887** Hamburg (Germany)
**1888** Celtic (Scotland)
**1891** Penarol (Uruguay)
**1892** Liverpool (England)
**1893** Genoa (Italy), FC Porto (Portugal), Sparta Prague (Czechoslovakia)
**1897** Juventus (Italy)
**1898** Marseille (France)
**1899** Barcelona (Spain), Eintracht Frankfurt (Germany), AC Milan (Italy), Nacional (Uruguay), Rapid Vienna (Austria)

---

### Landmarks

**1848** First code of rules written at Cambridge University.
**1866** Offside rule requires three players between a player and the goal.
**1869** Goal kicks introduced.
**1870** Clubs accepted 11-a-side as the norm.
**1872** Introduction of corner kicks; ball size standardized; England draw with Scotland 0–0 in the world's first international match.
**1873** Introduction of free-kicks.
**1874** Introduction of umpires.
**1875** Crossbar replaces tape.
**1891** Penalties introduced.

# World Developments

At the start of the 20th century, the social composition of football was changing dramatically. No longer exclusive to wealthy public schools, football was fast becoming the game of the working people. In England, where the organized game was at its most developed, there were over 10,000 clubs affiliated to the Football Association (FA), including Sunday teams and factory sides.

## Players' Revolt

Although football was becoming a lucrative business, the players were generally unhappy about their wages. A maximum wage of £4 per week had been established in England in 1901 but it was only paid to star players. The players, therefore, instituted a Players' Union in 1908 and applied to join the Federation of Trade Unions. Just days before the start of the 1909–10 season, the League and FA threatened to ban all union players. The star Welsh winger Billy Meredith

*Below: Villa Park, 1900. Capacity crowds were already a regular occurrence.*

*Above: Huddersfield Town, three-times winners of the English League, 1924–26.*

led a revolt among his Manchester United team-mates, and they formed a team called Outcasts FC. The day before the season kicked off, the authorities caved in. The next season the maximum wage was increased to £5 per week.

### Sport Becomes Business

As early as the 1904–5 season Newcastle United recorded a turnover of £25,000 in gate receipts. The transfer of players from one club to another for large fees was increasingly common, and football was becoming a lucrative business.

## International Impetus

Football was now thriving outside the United Kingdom and was particularly popular in central Europe, specifically in Austria, Hungary, Holland and Denmark. In South America, too, the early 20th century saw an expanding list of club sides formed, among them were Corinthians in Brazil and Newell's Old Boys in Argentina (both with British origins, as the names reveal), and Fluminense, which was founded by an Englishman, Arthur Cox, in 1902. In Argentina, the Boca Juniors were founded by an Irishman and a group of Italians in 1905.

The first international match to be played in South America was in 1901 between Argentina and Uruguay. A year later, Austria played Hungary in Vienna and won 5–0. It was the first European international match not involving an English team to be played outside the United Kingdom, and it marked a turning point in the story of football.

One key event took place in the early years of the 20th century that had a lasting effect on football. This was the founding of the game's international governing body FIFA (*Fédération Internationale de Football Association*) on 21 May 1904, by Robert Guerin, a French journalist. The founder members comprised of France, Holland, Belgium, Switzerland, Denmark, Sweden and Spain. One notable absentee was England, who

### Rule Changes 1900–1914

- Limiting the size of the penalty area, which had previously stretched the width of the pitch
- Goalkeepers restricted to handling the ball only in their penalty area. Previously they could handle the ball anywhere on the pitch
- Opponents having to retreat ten yards before the taking of free kicks and corners

*Above: The team from Finland lines up for Olympic football at the Stockholm Games of 1912.*

refused to join the new organization, although they were persuaded to join the following year.

A further development was that the Olympic committee agreed to allow football as a competitive rather than a demonstration sport in time for the London Games of 1908. Five countries took part in the first football events of the Olympics – England, France (with two teams), Denmark, Holland and Sweden – and England beat Denmark 2–0 in the final. Later that same year, England travelled to Vienna to beat Austria 6–1, the country's first ever international match in continental Europe. In the 1912 Stockholm Olympic Games, with 11 countries competing, England took the gold medal for a second time after beating Denmark 4–2.

World War One was declared in Europe on 4 August 1914. In England, the League and Cup tournaments continued until the end of that season, and when Sheffield United beat Chelsea 3–0 in the 1915 FA Cup Final,

### Latin America

The South American Championship, the *Copa America*, was first contested in 1910 between Argentina and Uruguay, with Argentina winning 4–1. The first official championship was held in 1917 and it has been played irregularly ever since. Participation was limited initially to member nations of CONMEBOL, the South American Football Confederation, but in 1993 the tournament was expanded to include members of CONCACAF, representing countries from the Caribbean and North and Central America.

the match was tagged the "Khaki Cup Final" because of the thousands of spectators in the crowd dressed in military uniform. In England, Wales, Ireland, Germany, Belgium and Holland league games were suspended until the 1919–20 season, although in Scotland and Switzerland the league continued throughout the war years.

## The Home Championship

This fiercely patriotic contest between England, Scotland, Wales and Ireland began in the 1880s. England or Scotland won the trophy every year until 1902–03 when Ireland shared it and 1906–07 when Wales won outright. In 1928, Scotland achieved a memorable victory over England, earning themselves the nickname "Wembley Wizards" by taking the English apart 5–1. That Scottish team included some of the greatest players of the era – Arsenal's Alex James, Huddersfield's Alec Jackson, Rangers' Alan Morton and Newcastle's Hughie Gallacher – and the tallest forward was only 1.7m (5ft 7in). The next season, Scotland collected the Home Championship winning all their games, and Hughie Gallacher scored five times in Scotland's emphatic 7–3 victory over Northern Ireland.

## The Inter-war Years

England regarded themselves as unbeatable in Europe until they played Spain in Madrid, in 1929, and lost 4–3. In May 1931, an under-prepared England were, astonishingly, beaten 5–2 by France, although they regained their confidence after thrashing Spain 7–1 later that year. The standard of football in Europe was clearly rising.

In December 1933, Austria played England at Stamford Bridge, and the visitors were known as the "Wunderteam". They were managed by one of the fathers of European football, Hugo Meisl, and coached by the ex-Bolton player Jimmy Hogan. Although England were 2–0 ahead at half-time, Austria were technically better and England were flattered by their 4–3 win.

The World Champions Italy played England at Highbury in November 1934, in a match that was supposed to determine who was the best in the world. The game became infamous as "The Battle of Highbury", and was a bruising display, with the Italians exacting revenge after England's

*Above: Scotland's Alec Jackson makes it Scotland 5, England 1 in the Home Championship of 1928.*

Ted Drake broke the foot of Italian star-player Luisito Monti early on. England, with seven Arsenal players, won 3–2, and Italy were universally condemned for their conduct.

*Below: England's Ted Drake tangles with Italy's keeper at Highbury in 1934.*

### The Offside Law

At the beginning of the 1925–26 season, a momentous change occurred in the offside law. The existing law stated that three opponents had to be between a player and the goal when the ball was played. The game became too defensive and several clubs perfected an offside trap, leading to dreary encounters punctuated by numerous free kicks. The new rule reduced the number of players from three to two, and the goals started pouring in.

### The Mitropa Cup

The influential Austrian manager Hugo Meisl was behind the launch of this tournament for the countries of central Europe. The Mitropa Cup, which takes its name from the abbreviation of *Mittel Europa*, or central Europe, became a major competition in the inter-war years, and it was the forerunner for today's European Cup tournament.

The Mitropa Cup was an annual two-leg knockout competition between the league leaders of Austria, Czechoslovakia, Hungary, Yugoslavia, Italy, Switzerland and Romania. With visits from leading British clubs such as Arsenal, Huddersfield Town and Rangers also a possibility, Meisl envisaged the expansion of the tournament across Europe. The first competition, held in 1927, was won by Sparta Prague. The Mitropa Cup was suspended in 1939 but it resumed in 1950.

### Political Unrest in Europe

At the end of the 1937–38 season, England travelled to Berlin for an exhibition match against Germany. The rapidly worsening political situation in Europe had overtaken events but the game went ahead and it took place on the eve of World War

*Below: England's players give the Nazi salute to Berlin's Olimpiastadion in 1938, on the eve of World War Two.*

Two. At the request of the British ambassador, the English team gave the Nazi salute while the German national anthem was played. The English went on to beat the Germans 6–3 in front of a partisan crowd that included leading Nazis, one of whom was Josef Goebbels.

### The Televised Game

The first football game ever to be shown on television was an Arsenal practice match at the Highbury ground in 1937.

# The World Cup Before 1939

In 1920, the FIFA and French federation president Jules Rimet and the secretary Henri Delauney persuaded FIFA that it should hold its own international competition to co-exist with the Olympic Games. However, it was not until 1930 that the first competition was played, and only three World Cup tournaments were held before the outbreak of World War Two.

## 1930 World Cup

Uruguay, celebrating the centenary of its independence, won the right to stage the first ever tournament. As part of its bid, Uruguay had offered to pay the travel expenses of all competing nations in order to guarantee interest, but for teams from Europe the three-week boat trip to South America was a high price to pay and many did not enter. England, Scotland, Ireland and Wales had all withdrawn from FIFA in 1928 following a dispute over broken time payments for their amateur players. This meant that they missed the 1928 Olympic Games and, more importantly, the 1930 World Cup. In fact, only France, Romania, Belgium and Yugoslavia took part from Europe, and they joined Argentina, Bolivia, Brazil, Chile, Mexico, Paraguay and Peru, along with the hosts Uruguay and a team from the United States that was largely composed of British ex-professionals.

Uruguay had built a new stadium, the Centenario, in Montevideo to host the final. Both winning semi-finalists, Uruguay and Argentina, notched up 6–1 wins. In attack for Argentina was the tournament's top scorer, Guillermo Stabile. The final that year was a thrilling match of fluctuating fortunes but Uruguay, with the home advantage, won 4–2, their fourth goal coming in the very last minute.

## 1934 World Cup

The World Cup tournament of 1934 was held in Italy. Uruguay, insulted by the modest European presence at their 1930 event, did not attend (they are the only World Cup winners in history not to defend their title). Twenty-two teams from Europe, eight from the Americas, and one each from Asia and Africa took part in the qualifying rounds that year, including the hosts, Italy. The competition was entirely knock-out and by the second round, four American representatives – Argentina, Brazil, Mexico and the United States – had been eliminated. They had crossed the Atlantic for just one game. Italian manager Vittorio Pozzo's use of Argentinian-born Italian internationals, the *orundi*, paid dividends when Italy knocked out pre-tournament favourites Austria, Hugo Meisl's "Wunderteam", in the semi-final. In the other semi-final, Czechoslovakia beat Germany 3–1. Italy and Czechoslovakia met for the final in Rome. The Czechs were a goal ahead until the seventieth minute, when Raimundo Orsi scored the equalizer. Angelo Schiavo scored the winner seven minutes into extra time, and Italy won their first World Cup title.

### Vittorio Pozzo

For the early decades of the 20th century, Vittorio Pozzo (1886–1968) was the driving force of Italian football. He had coached the Italian team at the 1912 Olympic Games, and it was there that he met the influential Austrian manager Hugo Meisl. Back in Italy Pozzo was given the task of reshaping the national side. With a regimented training programme, tactical innovation (the creation of an attacking centre-half) and the inclusion of Agentinian-born Italians in the squad, Pozzo turned Italy into an awesome force and credible rivals for their central European neighbours, Austria, Czechoslovakia and Hungary. In just one decade, Italy won consecutive World Cups, in 1934 and 1938, and the 1936 Olympic gold medal.

*Left: Italy's triumphant players carry coach Vittorio Pozzo around the stadium in Rome in celebration of their 1934 victory.*

*Above: A Swiss defender heads clear against Hungary in the 1938 quarter-final.*

*Above: The captains of Italy (left) and Hungary meet before the 1938 final.*

## 1938 World Cup

World champions Italy triumphed a second time at the tournament hosted by France in 1938. Six South American countries, led by Argentina, boycotted the competition in protest at it being held in Europe for a second, consecutive time. The threat of war added to the bad feeling. Japan had pulled out of the qualifying rounds because of war with China, while Austria had qualified but had to forfeit its place after being subsumed into Greater Germany by the *Anschluss* in March that year. The tournament's knockout format proved a further deterrent and only three non-European nations – Cuba, Dutch East Indies and Brazil – attended. The four countries of the United Kingdom were again notable by their absence (the English FA had refused an invitation from FIFA for England to take Austria's place).

Brazil fought a thrilling 6–5 first-round tie with Poland, with four goals coming from Leonidas, but they lost 2–1 to Italy in the semi-final. In the final, the holders and 1936 Olympic Champions faced Hungary, at that time the best team in Europe, who had eliminated Sweden 5–1 in their semi-final. Italy went ahead in the fifth minute and, although Hungary equalized within two minutes, the midfield direction of Italian captain Giuseppe Meazza, who had also played in the 1934 final, inspired two more goals before half time. In the seventieth minute, Hungary pulled one back through Gyorgy Sarosi, but Piola made the final score 4–2 in the last few minutes. There now followed a 12 year gap before the next World Cup tournament.

*Right: Italy celebrate with the Jules Rimet trophy after their 1938 triumph.*

# Arsenal in the 1930s

Every club has its era, but very few can look back to a time when they revolutionized the game with a new style of play.

Arsenal dominated English football in the 1930s. Their manager Herbert Chapman had already transformed English club Huddersfield Town from an average, mid-table side into three-time league winners in the mid-1920s. He joined Arsenal as manager in 1925 and immediately set about rebuilding the fading side. The club had been relegated just before World War One and were promoted just after it, and their history until then had been one of underachievement. Chapman changed all that when he repeated his magic at Highbury.

By 1927, he had bought the great inside-forward Charlie Buchan from Sunderland, and had added right-back Tom Parker and centre-forward Jack Lambert. Other new faces included the stopper Herbert Roberts from Oswestry, Kettering's left-back Eddie

*Above: Herbert Chapman, the inspired leader behind the 1930s Arsenal side.*

Hapgood, who became captain of Arsenal and England, and Bolton's England international, inside-forward David Jack. Chapman's most important acquisitions were the brilliant Scot Alex James from Preston North End,

and the 16-year-old winger Cliff "Boy" Bastin from Exeter City.

The change in the offside law in 1925–26, requiring two rather than three opposition players between the forward and the goal, had led Chapman and Buchan to adopt a revolutionary new system, the "WM formation", to cope with the sudden flood of goals. Chapman introduced a defensive centre-half, with the full-backs playing wide and the inside-forwards dropping back and acting as suppliers to the forwards. The wingers were encouraged to cut inside the opposing full-backs and create chances for themselves and the centre-forward, rather than race outside and cross. James had been a striker at Bolton and was now asked to drop into midfield and become a playmaker. After initial hesitation he settled into the role and became one of the finest players in the

*Below: Highbury, home ground of the Gunners, photographed in 1927.*

Above: The team parades Alex James and the FA Cup around Wembley after beating Sheffield United in 1936.

history of the club. Chapman had picked the men to optimize his system, and Arsenal moved into top gear.

In 1930, they won their first FA Cup against Huddersfield Town at the "Graf Zeppelin Final" (so-called because of the giant airship that hovered overhead during the game), with James engineering the 2–0 win.

The following year they gained the club's first league title with a record number of points (66), and 127 goals, and they became the first southern club to win the trophy. They were league and FA Cup runners-up the following season, but won the league title again the next two seasons.

Left-winger Bastin demonstrated the wisdom of Chapman's tactical change by scoring 33 league goals in 1932–33. In fact, he scored 178 goals in 396 appearances for the club, a record

that stood until 1998, when it was broken by Ian Wright. Lambert and Jack were also in prolific goalscoring form, and were flourishing from the support provided by the little genius James. However, the FA Cup was more elusive. They only won one Cup Final under Chapman, and the team, which boasted seven England internationals, were beaten 2–0 in the third round in 1933 by Third Division Walsall.

In early 1934, Chapman died suddenly from pneumonia at the age of 55. Arsenal director George Allison took over team affairs, ably assisted by trainer Tom Whittaker, who later became the club's manager. Allison continued Chapman's winning ways, buying striker Ted Drake from Southampton three months after Chapman's death. The following season, in 1934–35, Arsenal achieved their third league title in succession, and new signing Drake scored a club record of 42 league goals. The next season, Drake scored seven against Aston Villa, and Arsenal won their second FA Cup Final, beating Sheffield United 1–0, with Drake scoring the winner. By the time the war ended Drake's career in 1939, he had scored 124 league goals in 168 appearances.

Arsenal won the league in 1937–38, but the inspirational Alex James had retired the previous year, leaving a big hole in the team. The invincible side was disintegrating, with England goalkeeper Frank Moss also retiring and Joe Hulme departing. Arsenal were at the end of a glorious decade of achievement and, although they won a further six league titles that century, the 1930s was their greatest era.

> **Arsenal's League and Cup Successes in the 1930s**
> English league titles: *1930–31, 1932–33, 1933–34, 1934–35, 1937–38*
> FA Cup winners: *1930, 1936*

# Club Football, 1945–59

League football resumed in the 1946–47 season. With a bitter winter in Europe and bomb damage to football grounds and infrastructure, league matches in every country suffered postponements. However, the world had been starved of football for five long years and the games drew in record crowds. Passions for football ran as high as ever, and the period between the end of World War Two and the 1960s saw the inauguration of some of the world's leading football tournaments at club level.

## European Cup

Real Madrid were the undisputed giants of European club football in the latter half of the 1950s and they dominated the early years of the new European Cup. In the final of the first tournament, held in Paris in 1956, Real beat French club Stade de Reims 4–3. The following year it was Fiorentina's turn to face Real in the final, losing 2–0 after goals from Paco Gento and Alfredo Di Stefano. In the final of 1958, Real took on AC Milan. This time, Hector Rial added his name to the score sheet, along with Gento and Di Stefano, and Real Madrid took the title for the third consecutive year. Reims were back to face the Spanish masters in the Stuttgart final of 1959, but goals from Di Stefano and Mateous ended any hope they might have had of taking the title that decade, and Real became the unbeaten Champions with a 2–0 win. However, Benfica and Inter Milan were waiting in the wings, and between them, they would take control of the tournament in the early 1960s.

## Moscow Dynamo On Tour

The warm, post-war relationship with Russia encouraged Moscow Dynamo to visit Britain in late 1945 for a series of friendlies. They drew 3–3 with Chelsea (below) and crushed Cardiff 10–1. They beat Arsenal 4–3, but the fog was so dense that they had 12 men on the pitch at one point and the referee did not notice. After a scrappy 2–2 draw with Scottish side Rangers, the Soviet side suddenly went home.

## Fairs Cup Finals

Originally named the Inter-Cities Fairs Cup when it first began in 1955, the Fairs Cup, as it was more commonly known, was the forerunner of the UEFA Cup, which began in 1972. The idea for the tournament came from the Swiss vice-president of FIFA, Ernst Thommen. Friendly matches were commonly held between teams from cities holding trade fairs, as part of a move to encourage pan-European business links. Injecting a more competitive spirit into the friendly matches would boost the

*Left: Harry Johnston (left) and Stanley Matthews are chaired after the "Matthews Final" in 1953, when Matthews-inspired Blackpool won the FA Cup.*

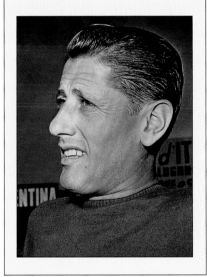

interest in trade fairs, which in turn
would help business and strengthen the
bond between countries.

The competition was to be held
over two seasons to avoid clashes
with domestic matches. The original
entrants were representative teams from
cities attending the trade fairs, and
because the matches were designed to
coincide with the fairs,
the first tournament, which began in
1955, ran over into a third year and
didn't end till 1958.

Twelve cities entered teams for
the first Fairs Cup. The teams were a
mixture of representative selections and
straight club sides, and it quickly
became clear that the club sides would
dominate. The finalists of the first
tournament were London and
Barcelona. London's team was
composed of players from the city's
11 professional teams, whereas
Barcelona was FC Barcelona with

*Right: London beat Lausanne 2–0 at
home to take their aggregate score
to 3–2 in the semi-final to reach the
European Fairs Cup Final of 1958.*

one token player from Espanyol. After
a scrappy 2–2 draw at Stamford Bridge,
Barcelona won with a confident 6–0.
It was the first of Barcelona's two
consecutive Fairs Cup titles, the second
one coming in 1960, and the first of
six in a row for Europe's Latin clubs,
which were enjoying supremacy in
European football.

## Mitropa Cup

The Mitropa Cup had been suspended
after 1939 because of the outbreak of
war. In was restarted in 1950, and the
1951 final was won by Rapid Vienna.
Hungarian clubs dominated the
competition for the rest of the decade.
Voros Lobogo took the tophy in
1955, with Vasas Budapest taking
consecutive titles in 1956 and 1957, and
Honved winning in 1959.

## Latin Cup

The top club event in Europe in the
immediate post-war period was the
Latin Cup. It was played between the
league champions of France, Spain, Italy
and Portugal, and despite the
involvement of only four countries,
the tournament produced some
breathtaking games. The competition
was first held in 1949 and it ended only
eight years later, in 1957, yet the years
of the Latin Cup produced some of the
most exciting club football Europe
had seen. With the continent's leading
southern European clubs pitted against
each other, the matches were always
well supported. The Latin Cup was won
by Barcelona in 1949 and 1952, Benfica
in 1950, AC Milan in 1951
and 1956, Stade de Reims in 1953,
Real Madrid in 1955 and 1957.

# World Football, 1945–59

International football was expanding, both in terms of the number of clubs formed and the international matches being played. The broadening reach of the game, and the ever-rising standard of play, was beginning to alter the balance of footballing power.

## Exhibition Friendlies

The four Football Associations from the United Kingdom had withdrawn their membership from FIFA in 1928 following a dispute over amateurism. England, Scotland, Northern Ireland and Wales all rejoined FIFA in May 1946, and their return was celebrated at Wembley with a game between a Great Britain XI and the Rest of the World. Inside-forward Wilf Mannion and centre-forward Tommy Lawton both scored twice in Britain's 6–1 win.

In May 1947, Switzerland dealt a blow to England's international prestige when they beat them 1–0 in a friendly match in Zürich. Walter Winterbottom was appointed the new England manager and, in their next game, England beat Portugal 10–0 in Lisbon, with four of the goals coming from debutant Stan Mortensen.

## Olympic Games

The London Games of 1948 was the first world tournament to take place after the end of World War Two. That year, the football gold medal was won by Sweden, who faced Yugoslavia in the final at Wembley and won 3–1. The Swedes paraded the "Gre-No-Li" attacking trio of Gunnar Gren, Gunnar Nordahl and Nils Liedholm for the first time, and the threesome were to prove equally devastating when they played together at club level for AC Milan throughout the 1950s.

Yugoslavia reached the final again in the 1952 Olympics in Norway. This time they faced Hungary's "Mighty Magyars" of Ferenc Puskas, Zoltan Czibor and Sandor Kocsis, who took the gold medal with a score of 2–0. Yugoslavia made their third Olympic Final in succession, in Melbourne in 1956, but they lost once again, this time to a team from the Soviet Union inspired by keeper Lev Yashin.

*Below: Yugoslavia score in the Olympic Final of 1948. The goal was ruled offside, and Sweden went on to win 3–1.*

## European Championship

The world's youngest continental tournament is the European Championship. The idea for the tournament first came from Henri Delaunay, secretary of the French football federation, and was designed to bring together the many regional tournaments of Europe – such as the British Home International Championship, the Nordic Cup of Scandinavia and the Mitropa Cup in central Europe. The European Championship is now the world's second biggest international tournament after the World Cup.

The first tournament was held in 1959–60, with all matches being played on a home-and-away knockout basis. Among the absentees from the first meeting were Italy, West Germany, the four nations of the United Kingdom, Holland, Switzerland and Sweden. The Soviet Union beat Yugoslavia 2–1 in the first final, held in Paris in 1960.

## South American Championship

Until 1959 the tournament to decide the champion nation of South America took place every two years. While six of the first 11 tournaments had been won by Uruguay, the period between 1945

*Above: England's Alf Ramsey watches as the USA's goal beats keeper Bert Williams.*

and 1960 was dominated by Argentina, who took the title six times, three times from 1945 to 1947, and again in 1955, 1957 and 1959.

## 1950 World Cup

Brazil hosted the 1950 World Cup and had built the 180,000 capacity Maracana Stadium in Rio for the event. However, the disorganization (the stadium was not finished for the opening game) and the long distances

### Scotland Stay Away From 1950 World Cup

FIFA had generously offered two World Cup finals places to the winner and runner-up in the 1949–50 Home International tournament. Scotland insisted they would only travel to Brazil if they won the championship outright. A 1–0 defeat by England at Hampden Park condemned them to second place and, true to their word, they stayed at home and missed the World Cup.

between the games deterred many countries from entering, and only 13 teams took part.

England had qualified for its first-ever place in the World Cup finals, but after a 2–0 win against Chile, an astonishing 1–0 defeat by the USA and then another 1–0 defeat by Spain saw England take an early plane home. The administrative chaos of the competition was such that Italy played all its group matches in one city, while other teams had to travel hundreds of miles around Brazil for their games. Even more unfairly, one of the groups

featured just two teams – Uruguay and Bolivia – while the other three groups had four teams each. Uruguay and Brazil made it to the final.

Bizarrely, the organizers had completely forgotten to include the final in the itinerary. However, the pool system fortuitously concluded with the last game between the two top sides, Uruguay and Brazil. Brazil were favourites and, in front of 199,854 partisan spectators in the new stadium, they piled on the pressure and went ahead through Friaca early in the second half. Centre-forward Juan Schiaffino equalized in the sixty-fifth minute and, with just 11 minutes to go, Uruguayan winger Alcide Ghiggia scored the winner. The result was a shock for the creative and talented Brazilians, but they would be back in style eight years later.

## Changes at the Top

England's belief in their dominance in international football was finally undermined in November 1953 at Wembley, when the 1952 Olympic champions, Hungary, destroyed the English 6–3 in a marvellous display

*Below: FIFA's Jules Rimet presents the World Cup trophy to Uruguay in 1950.*

Hungary were the clear favourites and they eliminated Brazil 4–2 in the quarter-final, infamously known as the "Battle of Berne", with three players sent off and punch-ups taking place on the pitch. In a semi-final regarded as one of the best games of football ever played, Hungary went through 4–2 against Uruguay after extra time, their last two goals coming from Sandor Kocsis. Also making it through to the final were West Germany, who had outplayed Yugoslavia in the quarter-final and smashed a defensively poor and disappointing Austria 6–1 in the semi-final.

Hungary played West Germany in the final. Eight minutes into the game, Hungary was leading 2–0, with goals from Ferenc Puskas and Zoltan Czibor, but first Max Morlock and then inside-right Helmut Rahn had levelled the score by the eighteenth minute. With under five minutes to go, Rahn capitalized on a Boszik error to score the German winner. The best team in the world, and undefeated for four years, Hungary had provided another shock result in the World Cup.

*Below: Brazil's Didi jumps for the ball against Hungary in the 1954 World Cup.*

*Above: The Hungary keeper Grosics foils England's Mortensen in 1953.*

of attacking football. It was the first time that England had been beaten at home by continental opposition and it was a sign that the old order was changing. Ferenc Puskas, Nandor Hidegkuti and the "Mighty Magyars" emphasized their superiority with a 7–1 crushing of England in a return in Budapest the following year.

## Asian Games

In 1951, six Asian nations came together, in India, in the football tournament of the Asian Games. As with the Olympic Games, the Asian Games was originally open to amateur athletes only, and for this reason the games were only 80 minutes long. The hosts India beat Iran 1–0 in the final in the first year. Three years later, Taiwan beat South Korea 5–2, and they repeated the feat in 1958 with a 3–2 win over South Korea.

## 1954 World Cup

England, having rejoined FIFA, were back in the competition and reached the quarter-final, where they lost to Uruguay. Scotland, who were making their first World Cup appearance, finished at the bottom of their qualifying group with no points and a 7–0 defeat by Uruguay.

*Above: Pelé celebrates Brazil's fourth goal in the 1958 final against Sweden.*

## Asian Cup

The Asian Cup was launched in 1956 as a regional contest between national teams from Asia. Qualifying rounds were held across the continent and the ten-nation finals were first hosted by Hong Kong in 1956. The event was not without political tension: Afghanistan and Pakistan refused to play their qualifying matches against Israel, and this gave Israel an easy passage to the finals. The format for the finals was a league system, and South Korea topped the league that first year, with Israel the runners-up, just one point behind.

## African Nations Cup

The tournament to decide the champion nation of Africa was first held in 1957, the inaugural year of the *Confédération de Football Africain* (CAF). The first finals were held in Khartoum, Sudan, and the competing teams were the hosts, along with Egypt and Ethiopia. South Africa had been scheduled to take part but they withdrew their entry when CAF insisted they send a multi-racial team. Egypt won the tournament with a 4–0 win in the final against Ethiopia. The same three countries took part in the second tournament in 1959. This time a league system was in operation. Egypt took the title again after topping the group, with Sudan as runners-up.

## 1958 World Cup

The 1958 tournament was held in Sweden. The brilliant Brazilian team with Vava, Didi, Garrincha and the 17-year-old Pelé played their new 4–2–4 formation, and beat Austria and the USSR in the group stage. In the quarter-finals, a Pelé goal in the second half eliminated Wales, while centre-forward Just Fontaine scored two in France's 4–0 defeat of Northern Ireland, who had earlier knocked out Italy. Fontaine ended the tournament with 13 goals, still a record for the World Cup. West Germany's 1954 hero Rahn scored the goal against Yugoslavia that put West Germany through to the semi-finals, and the hosts Sweden progressed at the expense of the USSR.

In the France v Brazil semi-final, Vava scored in the first minute for Brazil and Fontaine equalized. However, a Didi strike and a hat trick from Pelé in the second half ensured Brazil's presence in the final. They were to meet Sweden who had knocked out West Germany 3–1. Although star striker Nils Liedholm put Sweden in front within four minutes, Brazilian winger Garrincha sped down the touchline five minutes later, crossed to Vava and the game was level. After 33 minutes, Vava scored another. A sensational piece of skill and a volley from Pelé made it three. Zagalo added another with 20 minutes to go and, although Sweden pulled one back, a brilliant Pelé header gave Brazil a 5–2 victory. It was Brazil's first World Cup Final victory, and the young Pelé left the pitch in tears.

# The Busby Babes, 1955–58

The "Busby Babes" were one of the great unfulfilled teams in footballing history. Robbed of true greatness by tragedy, their three years together nonetheless marked them out as an exceptional side who had so much to offer the game.

The brief era of the Babes began in 1955. The Manchester United manager Matt Busby knew he had to replace his ageing 1952 English League-winning side, and he embarked on an intensive youth policy. Powerful, multi-talented left-half Duncan Edwards and forward Bobby Charlton were spotted and

*Below: The young Bobby Charlton, a great footballer in the making.*

signed as juniors, and centre-forward Tommy Taylor came from Barnsley for a record transfer fee. They joined home-grown young players including right-half Eddie "Snakehips" Colman, forward Dennis Viollet, captain and left-back Roger Byrne and the big centre-half Bill Foulkes. By the end of the 1955 season, the Busby Babes were in place.

The following season, they vindicated Busby's emphasis on youth, winning the English League by a massive 11 points over Blackpool. Although Chelsea had been invited to play in the inaugural European Cup in 1955–56, they had pulled out under pressure from the Football League. Busby persuaded the

*Above: The powerful Duncan Edwards represents his country.*

League to allow United to enter the following season. They began the new tournament with a resounding 12–0 aggregate win over Belgium's Anderlecht, with Viollet scoring four in the 10–0 demolition in Manchester. Borussia Dortmund were their next victims, and in the quarter-final, a 6–5 win over Athletic Bilbao, with a last-minute winning goal at Old Trafford from right-winger Johnny Berry, meant a semi-final against Real Madrid. Real took a 3–1 lead to Manchester where they drew 2–2, United's goals coming from Taylor and Charlton. The Babes were out, but everyone could see their potential.

That season, they easily won the English League and scored 103 goals. Although they unluckily lost the 1957 FA Cup Final to Aston Villa, by the time they had played what proved to be their last game on English soil –

*Above: Matt Busby leads his team out on to the Wembley pitch in 1957.*

a memorable, see-saw 5–4 win over Arsenal at Highbury in February, 1958 – they were well placed for their third successive League title. They had already eliminated Shamrock Rovers 9–2 and Josef Masopust's Dukla Prague 3–1 in the European Cup, and had to defend a 2–1 home advantage over Red Star in Belgrade in the return leg. They were 3–0 up at half-time (with one from Viollet and two from Charlton) and, although Red Star equalized on the night, Manchester United were through to the semi-final against AC Milan.

On 6 February the flight from Belgrade to Manchester stopped at Munich airport to refuel. In snowy weather the twin-engined plane carrying the team, staff and press had to abort two take-offs. On the third attempt, the plane failed to lift up from the ground: it came off the runway, crashed into a fuel store and exploded. Twenty-three passengers died. Colman, Byrne, Taylor, Geoff Bent, Mark Jones, David Pegg and Liam Whelan were killed instantly. Duncan Edwards died from his injuries two weeks later, and Busby was in a critical condition, although he survived. Potentially one of the greatest sides in world football had perished.

Red Star suggested that the European Cup be awarded to United as a mark of respect but UEFA insisted that the competition go on. United faced AC Milan at Old Trafford and goals from Viollet and Ernie Taylor gave them a 2–1 lead. However, at the San Siro a depleted and traumatized United caved in 4–0. In a gesture of sympathy, UEFA invited United to enter the 1958–59 European Cup along with League champions Wolverhampton, but the English League refused to grant them permission.

Manchester United now had to rebuild, and the team did not play in the European Cup again until the 1960s, when Busby impressed Europe again with his third great side.

> **An Emotional Triumph**
> Crash survivors Bobby Charlton and Bill Foulkes both played in Busby's European Cup-winning side of 1968, with Charlton scoring twice in the final.

# Real Madrid, 1956–60

The history of Real Madrid's greatest era is essentially the history of two men, Santiago Bernabeu and Alfredo Di Stefano. The ex-Real player Bernabeu became President of the then unsuccessful club in 1943 and set about the construction of the magnificent Bernabeu Stadium, capable of holding 125,000 spectators. Di Stefano helped to fill it.

The multi-talented Argentinian forward arrived from Millionaros of Bogotà in 1953 and announced his

*Below: Striker Raymond Kopa helped Real take the European Cup of 1957.*

intentions by scoring four goals in his first game, against Barcelona. Around Di Stefano were some high-quality players. Fellow Argentinian Hector Rial played inside-forward, on the left wing was the speedy provider-in-chief Paco Gento, while defenders Marcos Marquitos and Juan Zarraga supplied the steel at the back. As Spanish champions, Real were invited to the newly instituted European Cup in 1955–56, and they made the trophy their own over the next five years.

Real Madrid disposed of Servette, Partizan Belgrade and AC Milan in the competition to reach the inaugural

*Above: Santiago Bernabeu, ex-player, President and patron of Real Madrid.*

final against French club Stade de Reims, with their star forward Raymond Kopa. Two-nil down after 12 minutes, Real replied with a Di Stefano strike and a Rial header. Reims went ahead again but Marquitos levelled the score at 3–3. Finally, a Gento cross was finished off and Real had won the first European Cup.

With the addition of Kopa, who had joined from Reims after the 1956 final, Real knocked out Manchester United in the semi-final to meet Fiorentina at the Bernabeu. Di Stefano scored a penalty and Gento claimed another goal in their 2–0 win, and Real Madrid had retained the European Cup.

In the close season, Real recruited the Uruguayan centre-half José Santamaria to bolster the defence, and they made it to the final again in 1957–58, against Italian champions AC Milan. Milan's Uruguayan forward Juan Schiaffino scored first and, inevitably, Di Stefano equalized. Ernesto Grillo made it 2–1 but Rial levelled the score a minute later. Gento scored from a rebound in extra time, and Real were three-time winners of the competition.

*Above: Alfredo Di Stefano prepares to challenge against Inter Milan.*

In the summer of 1958, Real acquired the Hungarian inside-forward Ferenc Puskas. Puskas had captained the "Mighty Magyar" side of the early 1950s but he was now in exile after the Hungarian Revolution. In the 1958–59 European campaign, Real survived a play-off through a Puskas penalty against Atlético Madrid to play Reims again in the final. In spite of Puskas being injured, Real won 2–0 with goals coming from Mateos and Di Stefano.

After the final, Kopa returned to Reims and the Brazilian winger Canario took his place. Luis Del Sol took over from Rial, and the ex-captain Miguel Munoz became coach. Real progressed easily through the 1959–60 European Cup and met Helenio Herrera's Barcelona in the semi-final. In the first game, with Barcelona missing their star Hungarian forwards Ladislav Kubala and Zoltan Czibor, Di Stefano scored twice in a 3–1 win. In thereturn they again won 3–1, with two of the goals coming from Puskas.

In the final, Real played Eintracht Frankfurt, who had beaten Rangers 12–4 in their semi-final, at Glasgow's Hampden Park. In front of nearly 130,000 spectators, Real produced a dazzling display in what many people still regard as the finest game of football ever played. Di Stefano, Gento and Puskas were unstoppable and, although Frankfurt opened the scoring, Di Stefano got a hat trick (making him the only player to score in five consecutive finals) and Puskas grabbed four in a memorable 7–3 victory. Real received a standing ovation from the awe-struck crowd as they collected their fifth European Cup in succession.

The game was to be the swansong of this remarkable Real Madrid side. They lost the 1962 final 5–3 to Eusebio's Benfica, despite a first-half hat trick from Puskas, and in 1964 they lost 3–1 to Inter Milan; the balance of footballing power had swung away from Spain. Real won the trophy again in 1966, but only Gento was left from the original line-up. Puskas and Di Stefano had retired and with them had passed the legend of the invincible Real Madrid. Real did not win the European Cup again for another 32 years.

> **Real Madrid's Successes in the 1950s**
> European Cup winners: *1956, 1957, 1958, 1959, 1960*
> Spanish League titles: *1956–57, 1957–58*
> World Club Cup: *1960*

# Club Football in the 1960s

*Above: Real Madrid receive the 1960 European Cup from the UEFA President.*

Latin clubs from Spain, Portugal and Italy dominated European football for the first half of the decade, but by the late 1960s, northern European teams were beginning to hit back. Meanwhile, in South America the top teams were Uruguay's Penarol and Independiente Estudiantes from Argentina.

## European Cup

Having dominated the European Cup since 1956, Real Madrid won their fifth title in succession in 1960, at Glasgow's Hampden Park. Often cited as the best game of football ever played, Real beat Eintracht Frankfurt 7–3, with four goals from Ferenc Puskas and a hat trick from Alfredo Di Stefano. The trophy remained in Latin hands for the next six years.

In 1961, Benfica, under manager Bela Guttman, staved off the attacking flair of Barcelona, with its Hungarian forward line, to win the cup 3–2. The Portuguese club won again in 1962 against Real Madrid, in spite of Puskas' first-half hat trick, courtesy of two late goals from the 19-year-old Eusebio. In 1963, two goals from José Altafini put AC Milan ahead against

*Right: Manchester's George Best is riled by a cynical foul from Benfica in 1968.*

Benfica in the final at Wembley. The cup stayed in the Italian city for the next two years, although it was Milan's rivals Inter who won after beating Real Madrid in 1964, and Benfica in 1965. In 1966, Real Madrid saw off Partizan Belgrade in the final.

In 1967, the two goals from Tommy Gemmell and Steve Chalmers cancelled out Sandro Mazzola's early penalty to give Celtic a 2–1 triumph over Inter Milan. In 1968, Manchester United secured Europe's ultimate prize when George Best, Brian Kidd and Bobby Charlton all scored in extra time in the final against Benfica to take the European Cup to England. The Latin stranglehold on the Cup was broken, and although AC Milan won in 1969, the trophy was to remain in northern Europe until Juventus' victory in 1985.

## Fairs Cup Finals

Barcelona's attempt to win a hat trick of Fairs Cup titles ended with a shock result in the 1960–61 quarter-finals, when they lost to Scotland's Hibernian. After no fewer than three matches in their semi-final against Roma, Hibs were finally beaten. Birmingham City

---

### Rule Changes

At the start of the 1965–66 season, the English League agreed to the use of a substitute if a player was injured. It soon became apparent that players would feign injury so the injury requirement was dropped. In 1967–68, goalkeepers were only allowed four steps with the ball before they had to release it.

reached their second final in two years but it was also their second defeat. After a 2–2 draw at home against Roma, they lost 2–0 on the return.

The following season, the rules were changed to allow three teams per country to enter, and Spanish clubs started to dominate. Barcelona faced Valéncia in the 1962 final, and Valéncia took the title with a 7–3 win on aggregate. In 1963, Valéncia met Dinamo Zagreb in the final and won again with a 4–1 aggregate score.

*Left: Billy McNeill lifts Europe's greatest club prize for Celtic in 1967.*

Spanish teams continued their run the following year, although Valéncia couldn't make the hat trick. In a one-off match, the holders lost 2–1 to compatriots Real Zaragoza.

In 1965, a record number of entries (48) was proof of the rising status of the Fairs Cup. That year, Latin teams were unable to match the success of previous years and the title went to Hungary's Ferencvaros after a single goal beat Juventus in the final in Turin.

In 1966, the two-game format was resumed for the final. However, ugly scenes of violence, on and off the pitch, meant that the tournament attracted attention for all the wrong reasons. Chelsea were pelted with rubbish in Rome, and Leeds United's players fought a battle with Valéncia, which ended with three dismissals. An unrepentant Leeds also had Johnny Giles sent off in the semi-final against Real Zaragoza. Zaragoza won a place in the final but lost 4–3 to Barcelona, who took the trophy for the third time.

The tournament of 1967 showed the growing strength of English clubs in Europe. Leeds United went through to the final that year, and although

*Above: The Fairs Cup-winning Leeds squad of 1968. Manager Don Revie stands at the right of the centre row.*

they lost 2–0 to Dinamo Zagreb, they collected the Fairs Cup in 1968, beating Ferencvaros 1–0. In 1969, Newcastle United beat Ujpest Dozsa 6–2 for the title. English clubs went on to win the Fairs Cup three times in succession, with Arsenal taking the title in 1970.

### Mitropa Cup

In the first year of the decade, the Cup was won by Vasas Budapest of Hungary, when a revised rule based the result on a clubs' representation system. In 1961, the title was won by Bologna but they couldn't make it two in a row, and in 1962 the Cup went back to Vasas; although Vasas reached the final again in 1963, they lost to MTK Budapest. Eastern European teams were already dominating the tournament by 1964, with Sparta Prague beating Slovan Bratislava in the final. In 1965, Vasas beat Fiorentina. Fiorentina came back to win against Trencin in 1966, but they lost in the semi-finals a year later, and the 1967 Cup went to Spartak Trnava. Red Star Belgrade beat Trnava in 1968, and Inter Bratislava won in 1969.

## European Cup Winners Cup

The European Cup Winners Cup was launched in Vienna on 13 February 1960, and involved the federations of Austria, Belgium, West Germany, France, Italy, Yugoslavia, Switzerland, Spain, Czechoslovakia and Hungary.

By the time the first competition was held, England and Scotland had both joined as competitors. Fiorentina beat Dinamo Zagreb in the semi-final that year, while in an all-British event, Scotland's Rangers beat England's Wolverhampton Wanderers. It was the only Cup-winners Final to be played over two legs. Fiorentina won both and became the first Italian club to take a major European trophy.

The 1960–61 tournament had been organized by a clubs' committee but the success of the first event prompted a takeover by UEFA. This, in turn, raised the Cup's profile and 23 club

*Above: West Ham's Bobby Moore exchanges pendants with the captain of Munich 1860 in 1965.*

sides entered the 1961–62 competition. Atlético Madrid faced Fiorentina in the final at Hampden Park, Glasgow. A draw meant that a replay match was needed, the first of three in the first decade of the contest. Atlético won the rematch 3–0.

Tottenham Hotspur made football history the following season by becoming the first British side to win a European trophy. They took the Cup with a 5–1 score against title-holders Atlético Madrid.

British teams were starting to make a name for themselves in the tournament. Spurs were beaten by Manchester United in the second round in 1963–64. That win took United through to the quarter-finals,

but they were beaten convincingly by Sporting Lisbon. The Portuguese side won their semi-final match against Olympique Lyon, while in the other semi-final Celtic lost to MTK Budapest. The Hungarians went on to win the cup.

The surprise of 1964–65 came when little-known Welsh side Cardiff City knocked out the previous season's runners-up, Sporting Lisbon. In the final that year, England's West Ham beat Munich 1860 in an outstanding match at Wembley stadium.

In 1965–66 the trophy looked like it was heading back to the United Kingdom. Only one non-British team, Borussia Dortmund, made it as far as the semi-finals, and Liverpool were the favourites to win. After Liverpool's defeat of Celtic and Dortmund's win over West Ham, Liverpool faced the Germans in the final at Hampden Park. Dortmund took the title 2–1 after an extra-time goal, becoming the first German side to win a European trophy.

The following year brought a rule change and the play-off was scrapped. Goals scored in away matches would now count double in the event of clubs drawing level on aggregate. Germany and the United Kingdom faced each other again in the 1967 final in Nuremberg, and the trophy stayed in Germany after Bayern Munich beat Rangers 1–0.

The 1967–68 season almost saw a third successive win for German clubs. The title holders Bayern went out to AC Milan (who were making their debut in the tournament) in the semi-final. Instead, Germany pinned its hopes on Hamburg after their semi-final second-leg win against Cardiff City took them through to the final in Rotterdam. However, the game ended 2–0 to Milan and the Italians took home the trophy.

Political events overshadowed the tournament in the 1968–69 season, following the Soviet Union's brutal invasion of Czechoslovakia. The original draw was abandoned by UEFA in favour of a new draw, in order to keep apart the teams from East and West. Most Eastern-bloc countries withdrew their teams in protest, but the Czechs stayed in, and Slovan Bratislava went on to win the title, beating the favourites Barcelona 3–2 in the final in Basle.

## Copa Libertadores

Following the success of the European Cup, the South American football confederation, CONMEBOL, started its own annual competition to decide the top club of the continent.

The first *Copa Libertadores* was held in 1960. Seven league winners competed in home and away matches on a knock-out basis, with the winners being decided not by the number of goals scored but by the number of games won. In the first competition, Penarol of Uruguay beat Olimpia of Paraguay 1–0. The scorer that day was Alberto Spencer, and he still holds the record for tournament top scorer with a total of 50 goals. Penarol won again in 1961, and Santos of Brazil took the title in 1962 and 1963. With the exception of a Penarol win in 1966, for the rest of the decade the trophy stayed in Argentina as Independiente won in 1964 and 1965 and Estudiantes in the three years from 1968–1970.

## African Champions Cup

Membership of the Confederation of African Football (CAF) increased rapidly during the mid-1960s as more countries gained their independence. After the success of the African Nations Cup, a club-level tournament similar to UEFA'S European Cup was the natural step forward, and the African Champions Cup was launched in 1964. The 14 club sides competing for the first contest were the champions and defending champions from countries with CAF membership, and they played on a knockout basis for a place in the

final in the Ghanaian capital of Accra. The first competition was won by Cameroon's Oryx Douala, who beat Stade Malien of Mali 2–1.

Attendence figures for the final had been disappointingly low, however, and the competition was not held in 1965 to allow time for the planning of a better tournament. The revised structure meant that games were now played on a knock-out basis until the semi-finals, with the final being staged as a two-leg home and away event.

Clubs from the sub-Sahara regions of Africa dominated the competition throughout the 1960s. Kumasi Asante Kotoko of Ghana, probably the most famous team in Africa at that time, had won the league in 1959, 1963, 1964 and 1965, but they lost to Stade Abidjan of Ivory Coast in the second final, in 1966. Asante were back in the final a year later, this time against Tout Puissant (TP) Engelbert of Zaire. The two sides drew in both legs of the final. Away goals did not count for double at that time, and the African federation ordered a play-off to decide the winner. However, Asante objected to the dates chosen by CAF and the

*Below: Manchester United score against Estudiantes in Argentina in the World Club Cup Final of 1968.*

cup went to TP Engelbert. The Zaire side took their second successive title in 1968, beating 5 Etoile Filante of Togo 6–4 on aggregate. Their run ended in 1969, when they lost 3–5 on aggregate to Al Ismaili of Egypt.

## World Club Cup

The World Club title was started in 1960, based on a set of rules that have since seen much revision. Real Madrid, who had just won the European Cup for the fifth successive year, played Uruguay's Penarol, winners of the first *Copa Libertadores*. The Spanish side, which featured Alfredo Di Stefano, Ferenc Puskas and Paco Gento, drew 0–0 in the first leg in Chile. However, they were unstoppable in the return, and they won the title 5–1.

Penarol defeated Benfica in 1961. The title stayed with Pelé's Santos for the next two years, but Inter Milan achieved a win over over Independiente of Argentina in 1964. The same clubs met in 1965 and Inter retained the title. Penarol beat Real Madrid in 1966, and for the next two years the title stayed in Argentina, with Racing Club winning in 1967 and Estudiantes de la Plata in 1968. The contest was troubled with violence in the last years of the 60s and this lasted well into the 70s. AC Milan beat Estudiantes in 1969.

# World Football in the 1960s

More countries than ever were now playing football at international level, and the list of FIFA-affiliated teams was still growing. Football mostly superseded the political pressures of the decade, but occasionally it did become apparent how much diversity the game now encompassed.

## Olympic Games

Throughout the 1960s, the Olympics were dominated by "state amateurs" from the Communist countries. Marxist-Leninist theory considered sport a leisure activity, and this makes sportsmen of all levels amateurs, even when they are paid a salary. In practice, the amateurs from the Eastern-bloc were professionals, holding down jobs or armed service ranks on a purely nominal basis, and this gave them an enormous advantage over the rest of the competition.

At the 1960 Olympic Games, Yugoslavia, appearing in their fourth consecutive Olympic Final, took the gold after a 3–1 victory over Denmark. Four years later, it was Hungary's turn, and they beat Czechoslovakia 2–1 in

*Above: Soviet goalkeeper Lev Yashin in the Rest of the World colours, 1963.*

the final. In 1968, Hungary became Olympic Champions again, after beating Bulgaria 4–1 in the final in Mexico City.

## European Championships

The 1960 finals were hosted by France. Once again, the Eastern-bloc countries dominated, taking three out of the four places in the semi-finals. Yugoslavia and

*Below: Mexico's defence crowds out a West German attacker in the '64 Olympics.*

the Soviet Union met in the final in Paris: the Balkan team looked threatening but Lev Yashin's side could not be beaten and they won 2–1 in extra time. Four years later, the Soviets were back in the final, but this time the home crowd in Madrid lifted the Spanish to a 2–1 win. In 1968, an expansion to the qualifying groups meant more games to be played. Yugoslavia beat England in the semi-final and faced the hosts Italy in the final in Rome. After a 1–1 draw, Italy won the replay (also in Rome) 2–0.

## South American Championship

Only two tournaments of the South American Championship took place in the 1960s. In 1963, the hosts Bolivia surprised everyone by beating Paraguay, proving beyond doubt the benefits of a home advantage. In 1967, in Chile, it was the old favourites Uruguay and Argentina who fought it out, with Uruguay taking the title.

## Asian Games

The first two decades of the Asian Games were dominated by India and the countries of South-east Asia – South Korea, Malaysia, Burma and Singapore. In 1962, the Games were held in Jakarta, Indonesia. India came through their semi-final against South Vietnam with a 3–2 score. In the other semi-final, South Korea beat Malaysia 3–1. For the third time in a row, South Korea went home with the silver medal after India won the final 2–1. Malaysia played South Vietnam in the third-place play-off and won 4–1 to take the bronze medal.

The Games of 1966 were staged in Bangkok, Thailand. Iran, making its first appearance in the tournament, met Burma in the final and lost 1–0. The match is remembered in Burma as one of the greatest in the country's football history. Japan and Singapore drew 2–2 in the third-place play-off and shared the bronze medal.

## Asian Cup

The league system used in the 1956 tournament was used again in the 1960 finals held in Seoul. The hosts South Korea finished at the top of the four-team league of the finals, with Israel their runners-up, Taiwan in third place and South Vietnam at the bottom. The 1964 event was hosted by Israel, who finished as league-leaders with India as runners-up. The host advantage made the difference for Iran in 1968, and they topped the league of five teams, with Burma as runners-up.

## African Nations Cup

Ethiopia hosted the third African Nations tournament at the Haile Selassie stadium in Addis Ababa in 1962. Tunisia and Uganda had joined the competition since the three-teamed event of 1959. The holders Egypt were the favourites, and they beat Uganda 2–1 in the semi-final. Ethiopia defeated Tunisia 4–2 in the other semi-final, and they prevented Egypt from a third consecutive title by beating them 4–2 after extra time. Emperor Haile Selassie presented the Ethiopian captain Luciano Vassallo with the trophy.

## 1962 World Cup

Surprisingly, Chile, recovering from a recent major earthquake, won the right to host the World Cup finals, in which 16 nations took part. England reached the quarter-finals and played Brazil, for whom Pelé was injured and did not play. Garrincha headed one for Brazil and, although Gerry Hitchens equalized, Garrincha made one for Vava and scored another himself. In the other quarter-finals, Yugoslavia beat West Germany, Chile finished off the Soviet Union and Czechoslovakia beat Hungary. Czechoslovakia and Brazil won their semi-finals and went through to the final.

In the final, the Czechs went ahead with a goal from left-half Josef Masopust, soon to be named European

Footballer of the Year. Amarildo, equalized with a brilliant shot two minutes later, and then, in the eighty-seventh minute, Amarildo crossed for Zito to put Brazil ahead. Vava scored the final goal, when Schroiff dropped Djalma Santos' cross at his feet. An impressive Brazil had retained the Cup, and mightily deserved their victory.

## 1966 World Cup

England hosted the competition four years later and were the only country from the United Kingdom to take part. In the qualifying groups, two of the favourites, Italy and Brazil, were surprisingly eliminated. Italy went out 1–0 to the crowd favourites, the lively underdogs North Korea, while Brazil were defeated 3–1 by Eusebio's Portugal. Pelé was viciously kicked and limped off the pitch after the game, vowing never to play again in the World Cup competition.

In the quarter-finals, England's "Wingless Wonders" beat Argentina through a Geoff Hurst header and Argentina's captain Antonio Rattin was sent off. England manager Alf Ramsey described the Argentinians as "animals" after the game. North Korea played inventive, attacking football against

*Above: Captain Bobby Moore lifts the World Cup trophy after England's 4–2 defeat of West Germany in 1966.*

Portugal, but four goals from Eusebio and a fifth from Augusto put Portugal into the semi-final. Two Uruguayan players were sent off in the game between Uruguay and West Germany, and Germany eased into the last four, while the USSR beat Hungary 2–1. West Germany reached the final, knocking out the USSR, and two goals from Bobby Charlton saw England through against Portugal, although Eusebio scored his ninth goal of the tournament and became top scorer.

In the final, West Germany went ahead with a goal from Helmut Haller, but a header from Geoff Hurst levelled the score. With 12 minutes to go, Martin Peters shot England ahead but West Germany equalized in injury time. Ten minutes into extra time, a shot from Hurst hit the underside of the bar and the referee, consulting with the linesman, gave a goal. The debate about that "goal" still continues, but Hurst's 25-yard stunning shot in the last seconds wrapped it up. England had become the first host nation since Italy in 1934 to win the World Cup.

# Club Football in the 1970s

In Europe, the powerful Latin clubs of the 1960s were now replaced by a group of sides from northern Europe. In South America, Argentinian clubs continued to dominate, while in Africa clubs from Zaire and Cameroon held on to their top-slot positions.

## European Cup

The European Cup in the 1970s was the story of four clubs, Ajax, Bayern Munich, Liverpool and Nottingham Forest. Ajax, inspired by the creative genius of Johan Cruyff and the talents of Johan Neeskens and Johnny Rep, won the European Cup for three consecutive seasons from 1971–73, the first team to do so since Real Madrid. Ajax manager Rinus Michels developed the concept of "total football", in which players constantly changed positions as the game demanded. Ajax beat Ferenc Puskas' Panathinaikos at Wembley in 1971. Inter Milan lost to them in 1972, as did Juventus in 1973.

Bayern Munich, under the command of "Der Kaiser" Franz Beckenbauer and featuring Gerd Müller and Sepp Maier, took over Ajax's European mantle. They repeated the European triple, taking the title in 1974, 1975 and 1976, and also won the *Bundesliga* three times between 1972 and 1974.

Their 1974 final against Atlético Madrid is the only final ever to have gone to a replay, when two goals from Uli Hoeness and two from Müller gave Bayern a 4–0 victory. Bayern's 2–0 defeat of Leeds United in the final of 1975 sparked off rioting by Leeds fans and led to a European ban for the Yorkshire side. Bayern's Franz Roth scored the second-half goal that beat the spirited French side Saint Etienne 1–0 at Hampden Park in 1976.

Liverpool, with Kevin Keegan playing his last season for the club, opened the scoring in the 1977 final against Borussia Mönchengladbach, and they went on to take their first European Cup. Liverpool won again

*Above: Johan Cruyff, an irreplacable member of the Ajax team in the 70s.*

against Club Brugge the next season, courtesy of a Kenny Dalglish lob. Brian Clough's Nottingham Forest were the next winners, beating Malmo 1–0 in the 1979 final.

## Fairs Cup Finals/UEFA Cup

Arsenal won the Fair's Cup in 1970 with a 3–0 victory at Highbury, overturning a 3–1 defeat by Anderlecht. The following season, English clubs scored their fourth successive triumph. Leeds United drew both legs of the final against Juventus, and were awarded the Cup on away goals.

However, the days of the Fair's Cup were numbered. UEFA, having decided it wanted complete control of European competitons, asserted its power over the Fairs Cup committee. By replacing the trophy, renaming the competition and revising the entry regulations, UEFA effectively ended the old contest. In September 1971, a one-off match between the first and last Fairs Cup winners decided which club should retain the trophy. Barcelona, given home advantage as the first winner, played Leeds. The three-times champions won the match and took home the Cup.

The UEFA Cup was launched in 1972 and, despite changes to the system, English clubs continued to dominate. The first UEFA final was an all-English affair between Tottenham Hotspur and Wolverhampton Wanderers, which Spurs won. A year later, it was Liverpool's turn to take the honours to England when they beat Borussia Mönchengladbach in the final. In 1974, Tottenham returned to the final but lost to Feyenoord amid scenes of appalling violence from the Spurs fans. West Germany won the World Cup in 1974, and in the 1975 season, Borussia Mönchengladbach took the UEFA Cup, beating the Dutch side Twente Enschede. In 1976, Liverpool beat Club Brugge, and in 1977, it went to Juventus on away goals after a draw on aggregate against Athletic Bilbao. In 1978, PSV Eindhoven beat Bastia of Corsica with a 3–0 aggregate score. It was the first appearance in a European cup final for both clubs. The next year, with a new seeding system in place, Red Star Belgrade lost in the final to Borussia Mönchengladbach.

*Below: Franz Beckenbauer showing leadership qualities for Bayern.*

*Above: Mönchengladbach's Berti Vogts with the UEFA Cup trophy in 1975.*

## European Cup Winners Cup

Chelsea won the first trophy of the decade, beating Real Madrid in the final. In 1972, Rangers won their first, and Scotland's second, European trophy against Lev Yashin's Moscow Dynamo in Spain. A pitch battle raged after the final between Rangers supporters and Spanish police, and the Glasgow club were banned by UEFA for a season. British teams were back in the final a year later, but this time they were on the losing side, with Leeds finishing runners-up to AC Milan. Milan reached the final again, in 1974, but they lost to FC Magdeburg, who became the only East German side to take the Cup. Kiev Dynamo beat Ferencvaros in 1975. The following season, Anderlecht began their run of three appearances in the final. After beating West Ham United in 1976, they lost to Hamburg the year after, but were back in 1978 with a 4–0 win over FK Austria. In 1979, no fewer than seven goals were scored in the final, when Barcelona beat Fortuna Düsseldorf 4–3.

## Copa Libertadores

The competition was streamlined at the beginning of the decade, following the 1969 boycott by Brazil and Argentina in protest of the disruption caused to domestic championships. Argentinian clubs appeared in all ten finals of the decade, winning six of them. Estudiantes won the 1970 competition, and reached the final in 1971 but lost out to Nacional. In 1972, Independiente embarked on a winning run that brought them the trophy four times in succession until 1975. The Brazilian side Cruzeiro won in 1976, and Boca Juniors won in 1977 and 1978. In 1979, Olimpia of Paraguay beat Boca Juniors. It was Boca's third consecutive final but the Argentina-Uruguay-Brazil domination was over, and it marked the start of a new era for the South American tournament.

## African Champions Cup

The first final of the decade featured Asante Kotoko of Ghana and Tout Puissant Englebert of Zaire. A bad penalty decision threatened to disrupt the game, but when play resumed the penalty, which could have given TP the equalizer, was missed, and Asante won. Asante repeated the win in 1971. Hafia Conakry of Guinea won in 1972 against Simba FC of Uganda. Hafia took the title again in 1975 and 1977; they appeared in the final of 1976 but lost to the Algerian side Mouloudia Chalia. Asante were back in the final in 1973 but failed to regain their title and were beaten by AS Vita of Zaire. CARA Brazzaville of Congo won in 1974, and the decade ended with a Cameroon double, Canon in 1978 and Union Duoala in 1979.

## World Club Cup

The early 1970s saw the World Club Cup risk becoming a non-event because of repeated scenes of extreme violence on the pitch from South American players against their European opponents. Rather than risk their players, the champion teams from Europe refused to take part. They were replaced by the beaten European Cup finalists but this situation was clearly less than ideal.

*Below: Glasgow Rangers celebrate victory over Moscow Dynamo, 1972.*

# World Football in the 1970s

International football now benefitted from improved organization and an increasingly open level of competition.

## Olympic Games

The top honours continued to be won by the Eastern-bloc countries. At the 1972 event in Munich, Poland ended Hungary's run from the previous decade, beating them 2–1 in the final to take the gold. East Germany defeated Poland at the final of the Montreal Games in 1976.

## European Championship

The finals of the 1972 event were hosted by Belgium, and the European Nations Cup was renamed with its present title. The most outstanding side that year were Helmut Schön's West Germany. With a line-up that incorporated the best of Borussia Mönchengladbach and Bayern Munich, including Franz Beckenbauer, Günter Netzer, Paul Breitner and Gerd Müller, the Germans stormed through to the final and hammered the Soviet Union 3–0 to take the trophy.

Germany were back in the final in 1976, after beating the hosts Yugoslavia in the semi-final in extra time. In the

*Below: Czechoslovakia take the 1976 European title after a penalty shoot-out.*

other semi-final Holland, with two men sent off, took the game against Czechoslovakia to extra time before losing 3–1. In the final against the title holders, the better-prepared Czech side won the Championship after a penalty shoot-out, while Holland beat Yugoslavia in a play-off for third place.

## South American Championship

Only two tournaments were staged in the 1970s, and the competition was reorganized, as the South American football federation tried to appease the protests of competing countries, who complained that their star players could not be released from their league commitments for the month-long finals. In 1975, the event was retitled the *Copa America* and Peru beat Colombia to take the title. Paraguay beat Chile on goal difference in 1979.

## Asian Games

The 1970 Games were staged in Bangkok as they had been in 1966. Burma reached the final again, where they drew 0–0 with South Korea; both teams shared the honours. The expansion of membership to the Asian Football Confederation (AFC) meant that it now spanned wide margins, geographically and politically, and this was apparent at the 1974 Games in

Tehran. The Gulf states had refused to compete that year because of the presence of Israel, who went on to lose to the hosts Iran 1–0 in the final. However, that year was the last time Israel was to appear in the Games. The AFC voted to expel Israel and the Chinese nationalist state of Taipei in 1975. The FIFA president Joao Havelange stepped in and managed to get the Chinese reinstated, but he could do nothing about Israel, who were later invited to join UEFA. The 1978 event was held in Bangkok for the third time in four contests. Mainland China, making its debut in the tournament, beat Iraq in the play-off for the bronze medal. South Korea played North Korea in the final, and the two sides shared the gold after a 0–0 draw.

## Asian Cup

Iran followed up its 1968 success and made it a hat trick by winning the Cup again in 1972, beating South Korea 2–1 in extra time, and in 1976, with a 1–0 defeat of Kuwait.

## African Nations Cup

In 1970, Ghana went to their fourth consecutive final, in Sudan, but the host's advantage proved beneficial and Sudan won the cup 1–0. The next time, in 1972, Ghana didn't make it even to the semi-finals; that year Congo beat Mali 3–2. In Egypt in 1974, Zaire faced Zambia in the final. After a 2–2 draw the game went to a replay, which Zaire won 2–0.

A group format was introduced for the tournament in 1976, in Ethiopia, replacing the semi-finals and finals. Guinea and Morocco were rivals for the Cup. In their last game of the table, Guinea took the lead halfway through the first half but Morocco equalized four minutes from the end; they had one point more than Guinea and they took the title. The original format was restored in 1978, where the hosts Ghana beat Uganda 2–0 in the final.

## 1970 World Cup

The 1970 matches in Mexico produced some of the most exciting matches to date in the competition. The multi-talented Brazil romped through the group stage, winning their three games. Two hat tricks from Gerd Müller, against Bulgaria and Peru, saw Germany through to the quarter-finals. England came second in Brazil's group and also qualified.

Hosts Mexico met Italy in the quarter-finals and lost 4–1, Gigi Riva scoring two, and Brazil played out a six-goal thriller with Peru, emerging 4–2 victors. In a repeat of the 1966 final, England took on West Germany and were 2–0 ahead early in the second half through Alan Mullery and Martin Peters. England made two unwise substitutes and suffered, with Beckenbauer scoring a 20-yard goal in the seventieth minute and Uwe Seeler backheading over keeper Peter Bonetti with eight minutes to go. An extra-time, close-range volley from Müller eliminated England. The other quarter-final saw Uruguay defeat the USSR 1–0.

A sensational semi-final produced a 4–3 victory for Italy over West Germany, and Brazil triumphed 3–1 over Uruguay. In the final, a goal from skipper Carlos Alberto sealed a magnificent 4–1 win over a dejected Italy, and the world celebrated the flamboyant footballers of Brazil.

## 1974 World Cup

At the tournament in West Germany, there were two group stages, the winners of the two second-round groups providing the finalists. England had failed to qualify for the finals. Scotland were in their first tournament in 16 years but they failed to get through the league stage, losing out to Brazil on goal difference, and Sweden qualified behind Holland after beating Uruguay 3–0. The other surprise omission in the last eight was Italy, beaten by Poland and drawing with Argentina.

Holland were the in-form country, boasting the talents of Cruyff, van Hanagem, Krol, Neeskens and Rep. The young Dutch side opened their second group with a 4–0 win over Argentina, Cruyff scoring two, and they beat East Germany 2–0. To reach the final, Holland would have to win their last game against Brazil. Cruyff and Neeskens each scored superb goals to overcome Brazil 2–0. Meanwhile, West Germany, under the on-field direction of Beckenbauer, had beaten Yugoslavia and Sweden, and finished with a 1–0 win over Poland, the goal coming from Müller. However, Poland's Grzegorz Lato was the tournament's top scorer.

In the first minute of the final in the *Olympiastadion* in Munich, an incisive Cruyff run was unfairly ended by Uli Hoeness in the penalty box, and Neeskens converted the penalty, the first penalty ever taken in a World Cup Final. Paul Breitner equalized from the spot, after Bernd Holzenbein had suspiciously tumbled in the penalty area. Two minutes before half-time, Gerd Müller met a cross from Rainer Bonhof, and smashed the ball past Dutch keeper Jan Jongbloed. A tough and physical West Germany, with Sepp Maier in goal, held out and the game ended 2–1. West Germany had won their second World Cup.

## 1978 World Cup

Argentina, hosts of the 1978 finals, were a hugely talented side, with midfielder Osvaldo Ardiles and striker Mario Kempes the stars, and they qualified from their first round group behind Italy. Holland, with Johan Cruyff absent, went through on goal difference from Scotland, although the Scots beat them 3–2. Scotland finally played well after disastrous performances against Peru and Iran.

In the second round, Holland beat Austria, drew 2–2 with West Germany and beat Italy 2–1, with Arie Haan's 35-yard goal proving the winner.

*Above: Mario Kempes, Player of the Tournament at the 1978 World Cup.*

The Dutch were in the final. In the last game of the other second round group, Brazil beat Poland 3–1 thanks to two goals from Roberto. Argentina had to beat Peru by four goals to finish ahead of Brazil. In fact, they won 6–0 and, as manager Cesar Menotti remarked, "We could have scored ten if we had wanted".

The Argentinians were greeted by a huge ticker-tape reception in the stadium in Buenos Aires when they faced Holland in the final. Kempes opened the scoring following a pass from Leopoldo Luque and a run through the Dutch defence. Holland pressed forward in the second half, with Neeskens outstanding, and eight minutes from time, substitute Dick Naninga headed Holland level. On the ninetieth minute, Rob Rensenbrink hit the post with a long-range shot and the ball rebounded clear. A splendid solo goal from Kempes in extra time, when he beat three players, including keeper Jongbloed, restored Argentina's lead and, with six minutes left, Kempes created the chance for Bertoni to score the winner. Argentina had won 3–1 and Kempes was named Player of the Tournament for his performance.

# Brazil 1970

For most football fans, the Brazilian national side that appeared in the 1970 World Cup finals in Mexico represents the epitome of "the beautiful game". The team's attacking flair, exuberant self-expression and obvious delight in its own dazzling abilities entranced everyone, and knocked aside all of the competition.

The team's inspiration was the incomparable Pelé, the creative, goalscoring genius. The star-studded side also featured the moustachioed Rivelino with the thunderous left foot; the speedy centre-forward Tostao; Jairzhino, the right-wing successor to the great Garrincha, who scored in every game including the final; the non-stop running of Clodoaldo and the chain-smoking Gerson in midfield; and in defence the stylish Carlos Alberto and centre-half Wilson Piazza. Brazil had won the 1958 and 1962 World Cup finals but had failed in England in 1966, with Pelé kicked off the pitch by a merciless Portugal in the group stage. Now, in Mexico, they had the players to sweep all before them.

They began their group matches against Czechoslovakia, going down 1–0 but recovering to win 4–1, with Jairzinho scoring twice and Pelé and Rivelino claiming the other two, Pelé, famously, nearly scoring from the halfway line. Their next game was against England in Guadalajara, in front of 75,000 spectators. After just ten minutes a Pelé header forced Gordon Banks to make a miraculous save, but Banks could do nothing about a second-half Jairzinho goal, crafted by Tostao, to give an absorbing game to Brazil 1–0. Romania were the next to suffer the Brazilian magic, losing 3–2, with two goals from Pelé and one from Jairzinho.

In the quarter-final against Peru, Rivelino scored after 11 minutes and Tostao added another just four minutes later. Although Peru rallied and scored twice, Tostao again and, inevitably, Jairzinho made the final score 4–2. Uruguay were Brazil's next opponents in the semi-final. Uruguay went ahead in the eighteenth minute through Cubilla but, just before half-time, Clodoaldo equalized from a perfect Tostao pass, and Jairzinho and Rivelino made the game safe for Brazil with goals in the last 15 minutes. The game is particularly memorable for Pelé's spectacular dummy of Uruguay keeper Mazurkiewicz, where he narrowly failed to score what would have been the goal of the century.

*Below: The multi-talented Brazilian side lines up for a photo-call at the 1970 finals in Mexico.*

Brazil's opponents in the final, in Mexico City's Aztec Stadium on 21 June, were Italy. In a thrilling semi-final encounter, the Italians had eliminated West Germany 4–3 in extra time with a Gianni Rivera goal. Both teams, as two-time winners of the Jules Rimet trophy, were playing to keep the trophy outright, but the playing styles of the two finalists were very different. Italy used defensive caution and counter-attacking tactics, while Brazil played an out-and-out attacking game; the match turned out to be a classic.

Italy began the game dropped back in defence with Brazil patiently trying to find a way through. After 18 minutes Pelé rose to meet a cross from Rivelino and his header beat Italian keeper Albertosi. Then in the thirty-seventh minute, a hash of a pass-back from Clodoaldo to his keeper Felix allowed Italy's Roberto Boninsegna to nip in and score; the score was 1–1 at half time.

Brazil went back on the attack in the second half, and in the sixty-fifth minute, an unstoppable left-foot shot from Gerson from outside the penalty area put Brazil ahead. Brazil were now in command of the game and were producing some sparkling inter-passing and movement. Five minutes later, a Gerson free kick was nodded down by Pelé to the onrushing Jairzinho, who made no mistake for Brazil's third. The fourth was a beauty. Pelé, in possession near the Italian penalty area, spotted Carlos Alberto thundering up the right. He flicked the ball nonchalantly into the path of his skipper, who unleashed a rocket past Albertosi. The Italians were too exhausted to come back, and the flair and excitement of Brazil had brought them their third World Cup victory.

As crowd favourites, Brazil were mobbed by the Mexican fans after the end of what was probably the finest-ever World Cup Final.

*Above: Pelé and Bobby Moore exchange shirts after Brazil's group-stage match against England.*

After their triumph, the Brazilian team gradually broke up, and by the time of the next tournament four years later, only Jairzinho and Rivelino were present in the squad. Brazil could only manage fourth place in 1974 and they lost their world crown to West Germany. Brazil did win the World Cup in 1994 and 2002, but they still have not found a side as spectacularly talented as the 1970 World Cup winners. Quite simply, they were the best.

# Club Football in the 1980s

The 1980s saw some new clubs get their names on the trophies, especially in Europe, where it was no longer a case of the giant clubs dominating.

## European Cup

In 1980, Brian Clough's Nottingham Forest repeated their success of the previous season, thanks to an early John Robertson goal against Hamburg. Liverpool picked up their third European Cup in 1981 in a 1–0 defeat of Real Madrid, thanks to a late goal from left-back Alan Kennedy. Aston Villa made it six in a row for English clubs when a Peter Withe goal beat Bayern Munich in Rotterdam. Unfancied Hamburg broke the English run in 1983, when a Franz Magath goal finished off Juventus in the final, playing with six members of Italy's World Cup-winning team.

Liverpool were back in 1984 against Roma, when Alan Kennedy was again the hero, scoring the decisive penalty in the shoot-out. The horror of the Heysel tragedy in 1985 overshadowed the game, which was won 1–0 by Juventus

*Below: Ian Bowyer of Nottingham Forest with the 1980 European Cup.*

with a Michel Platini penalty. UEFA, appalled by this latest outbreak of English hooliganism, voted to ban English clubs from Europe indefinitely.

Barcelona, who for all their proud history had never won the European Cup, faced Steaua Bucharest in the 1986 final and crashed out on penalties, with Barcelona failing to convert any. Porto won their only cup trophy against Bayern Munich in 1987, the skills of Paulo Futre and Rabah Madjer bringing the Portuguese club a 2–1 win in Vienna. PSV Eindhoven and Benfica ground out a tedious draw the following year, and PSV won after a penalty shoot-out. A brilliant display from AC Milan, with two goals apiece from Ruud Gullit and Marco Van Basten, brought victory over Steaua Bucharest in 1989. Milan won again in 1990, with a 1–0 win over Benfica, the goal coming from Frank Rijkaard.

## UEFA Cup

West Germany's success the previous season meant that it entered five clubs in 1980, four of which reached the semi-finals. Eintracht Frankfurt beat Bayern Munich, while Borussia Mönchengladbach beat Stuttgart. Eintracht took the title on away goals.

In 1981, English club Ipswich Town beat AZ '67 Alkmaar for their first and only European title. There was a further triumph for smaller clubs in 1982, when IFK Gothenburg beat Hamburg. Coach Sven-Göran Eriksson was the motivation for Gothenburg but within the year he had been lured away to Benfica, who he took to the 1983 final, where they lost to Anderlecht. Anderlecht were back in the final in 1984, this time against Tottenham Hotspur. Tottenham won on penalties but the tournament is remembered as much for the scandal concerning Anderlecht, which emerged years later.

In 1985 Tottenham's hopes for a third title ended with a quarter-final defeat by Real Madrid, who went on to win

their first European trophy since 1966. Real won again in 1986, against FC Köln, who were making their first appearance in a European final.

Real had won the Spanish league in 1986, which meant they did not defend the UEFA title in 1987. Barcelona replaced them from Spain but lost to Scotland's Dundee United in a shock quarter-final result. Dundee went on to beat Borussia Mönchengladbach in the semi-final but they ran out of steam and lost the final to IFK Gothenburg.

Germany's Bayer Leverkusen won the 1988 final against Espanyol, after a penalty shoot-out. The 1989 event saw the start of a run for Italian clubs. Napoli beat Stuttgart and gave Diego Maradona his only European title.

## European Cup Winners Cup

The 1979–80 season was Arsenal's debut in the tournament, and they made it through to the final against

*Above: River Plate take on Deportivo Espanyol in the 1989 Copa Libertadores.*

Valéncia. In a penalty shoot-out to decide the winners, the Argentine Mario Kempes, hero of the 1978 World Cup, missed his shot but Arsenal missed two, and the title went to the Spanish side. Valéncia were knocked out in the second round in 1981 by East German side Carl Zeiss Jena, who were beaten in the final by Soviet club Tbilisi Dinamo.

Tbilisi was beaten in the semi-final in 1982 by Standard Liège. As luck would have it UEFA had chosen the Camp Nou as the venue for the final, and Liège had to face Barcelona in their home stadium. The Belgians made a confident start but the score was equal at half time and Barcelona scored after sixty-one minutes to take the title.

Spain would have kept the trophy for a second year in 1983 were it not for Scotland's Aberdeen, who were enjoying an exceptional run under manager Alex Ferguson. Against a Real Madrid side coached by Alfredo Di Stefano, Aberdeen went ahead after seven minutes. Real equalized but Aberdeen scored the winner in extra time. Juventus beat Porto in the 1984 final with one of its strongest sides, which included Michel Platini, Paolo Rossi and Zbigniew Boniek, and was coached by Giovanni Trapattoni. Everton beat Rapid Vienna in 1985 but the celebrations were short-lived for English football. Two weeks later UEFA banned English clubs from Europe after the violent scenes at Liverpool's European Cup tie at the Heysel stadium.

Kiev Dynamo became the UEFA champions of 1986, repeating their 1975 success with another 3–0 win, this time over Atlético Madrid. Marco Van Basten scored against Lokomotiv Leipzig to give Ajax, coached by Johan Cruyff, the 1987 title. Ajax were back in the final in 1988, this time without Van Basten, now at Milan, or Cruyff, now coach of Barcelona; Ajax lost to the little-fancied Mechelen from Belgium. Cruyff's Barcelona beat the Italian side Sampdoria to take the Cup Winners Cup of 1989.

## Copa Libertadores

Uruguay's Nacional wrested the title away from Internacional PA of Brazil in 1980. Chilean league winners Cobreloa reached two consecutive finals in 1981 and 1982, but lost them both, the first to Flamengo of Brazil and the second to Penarol of Uruguay. The same thing happened to America Cali, who lost three successive finals between 1985 and 1987. The Brazilian club Gremio beat the holders Penarol in 1983, but they couldn't defend their title, which went to Independiente of Argentina in 1984. Argentinian clubs dominated for much of the decade: Argentinos Juniors won on penalties in 1985, River Plate won in 1986. Penarol won in 1987 and Nacional took their second title of the decade in 1988; no Uruguayan club has won the title since. Colombian side Atlético Nacional de Medellin won their first Cup title in 1989, beating Paraguay's Olimpia.

## African Champions Cup

The 1980s saw North African countries strengthen their position with increased financial support and better league organization. Canon of Cameroon won their second title in 1980. In 1981, the champions were the Algerian side Jeunesse Electronique Tizi-Ouzou. Al Ahly of Egypt beat Asante Kotoko of Ghana in 1982. The same clubs contested the 1983 final and this time the Egyptians lost, although Zamalek of Egypt triumphed over Nigeria's Shooting Stars in 1984. Moroccos' Forces Armées Rabat won in 1985. Zamalek were the 1986 champions and Al Ahly won again in 1987. The Algerian side Entente Plasticiens took the 1988 title, and in 1989 it went to Morocco's Raja Casablanca.

## World Club Cup

The competition was reorganized in 1980 and the two-leg format was changed to a single game to be held in Tokyo. The Japanese car manufacturer Toyota was now the official sponsor and it was a timely solution to the protests and violence of the 1970s. The clean up of the event persuaded Europe's champions to come back, but it was the South American clubs that dominated, winning every year from 1980 to 1984 and again in 1986 and 1988. Juventus won on penalties in 1985, FC Porto won in 1987, and AC Milan won in 1989.

# World Football in the 1980s

A greater number of teams than ever before were now competing in world tournaments, and some fine-tuning was needed for events to run smoothly.

## Olympic Games

In a move to limit East European rule-bending and open up the competition, FIFA banned any European or South American player who had previously played in a World Cup qualifier. Czechoslovakia beat East Germany in the Moscow Games of 1980 before the new rule was in place, but by the Los Angeles event in 1984 the aim was achieved and France took the gold. The Soviet Union beat Brazil to take the gold medal in 1988. That year saw one of the most surprising results in world football: Zambia 4 Italy 0.

## European Championship

In 1980 Italy hosted the finals for the second time, the first country ever to do so. The event that year had more countries competing in the finals than ever before (8) and a new format to accommodate them; two groups of four with the group winners meeting in the final. West Germany established themselves as the favourites early on,

*Below: The USSR defeat Brazil to take gold in the 1988 Olympic Final.*

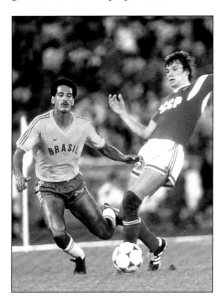

and they saw off Belgium 2–1 in the final in Rome. Italy lost the play-off to Czechoslovakia in a game notable only for the lack of enthusiasm from the players. UEFA decided to scrap the "losers' final" soon after.

France entered the finals of 1984 as hosts and with what was probably the best side in Europe in the early 1980s. For the first time, the entire UEFA membership entered the contest; there were 33 international sides in the days before the break up of the Soviet Union, Czechoslovakia and Yugoslavia. France met Spain in the final in the *Parc des Princes*. The Spanish were suffering the effects of earlier injuries and suspensions. France took an early lead with a goal from Michel Platini but they never looked threatened, and they scored one more to take the title.

At the 1988 tournament, hosted by West Germany, Holland achieved its long-awaited European Championship success. In the final, Holland faced the Soviet Union, who were missing their defensive anchorman Oleg Kuznetsov through suspension. But Marco Van Basten and Ruud Gullit were unstoppable in the Dutch attack. Gullit scored first and Van Basten followed it with the second, a spectacular volley off Arnold Muhren's cross. When the Dutch keeper conceded a penalty, it looked as if the Soviets might stage a comeback but Igor Belanov's spot-kick was saved and Holland had a safe 2–0 win and the championship title.

## Copa America

The event of 1983 followed the direct elimation format of 1975 and 1979, with competing countries divided into preliminary-round groups, playing on a home and away basis, followed by a knock-out semi-final and a two-leg final. However, the increased number of games meant that player release was now an even greater problem than before. In 1987, the old system was resumed, with all matches now

being played in one host country. To streamline the system teams were divided into first-round groups, followed by knock-out games to the final. The new design got the backing of television and the sponsors, and, after some fine-tuning, this is how the contest is played today. Uruguay won the tournaments of 1983 and 1987. Brazil hosted the 1989 event and took their first title in 40 years.

## Asian Games

In 1982, Kuwait qualified for the World Cup finals in Spain, and they came runners-up to Iraq in the final of the Asian Games. Four years later, in Seoul, the host team South Korea, also competitors in the World Cup finals that year, beat Saudi Arabia for the gold medal.

## Asian Cup

The financial investments made in football by the Gulf States began to pay dividends in the 1980s. Kuwait beat South Korea in the 1980 final, while Saudi Arabia won the next two tournaments, in 1984 and 1988.

## African Nations Cup

Nigeria hosted the Cup in 1980 and won, cheered on against Algeria in their home stadium in Lagos by 80,000 spectators. In 1982, the African football confederation lifted the restriction on the number of overseas players who could play in a team (with so many players now earning a living in Europe it had become impracticable, and meant that countries were not able to select their best players). Libya met Ghana in the final that year, with the more experienced Ghanaians winning on penalties. In 1984, Cameroon beat Nigeria to take their first cup victory. The 1986 event in Egypt narrowly missed cancellation when a curfew was imposed following a riot by security police conscripts the week before the opening. The curfew was lifted,

*Above: Nigeria score against Algeria in the 1980 African Nations Cup Final.*

although tanks surrounded the stadiums in case of trouble. Meanwhile, on the pitch, there were angry protests that year about the standard of refereeing. The defending champions Cameroon lost on penalties to Egypt in the final, amid strong support among the home fans for the Egyptian team. Cameroon came back to win the Cup in 1988, beating Nigeria 1–0 in the Moroccan capital Casablanca.

## 1982 World Cup

The tournament in Spain was expanded to include 24 countries, including three British teams – England, Scotland and Northern Ireland. Drawn with Brazil and the Soviet Union, Scotland again failed to qualify on goal difference. Northern Ireland surprisingly topped their group, heroically beating Spain 1–0, but failed to win a game in the second round. England went into round two with an unbeaten record, and in their final group game needed to beat Spain 2–0 to qualify for the

semi-final. A tactically inept 0–0 draw saw West Germany go through in their place. The Germans scrambled through in a penalty shoot-out against France to meet Italy in the final.

Italy had only qualified in second place to Poland in their group. Yet they rallied to beat Brazil in a magnificent second-round game, Paolo Rossi scoring a hat trick in their 3–2 win, and they also defeated Argentina. Rossi proved his worth again in the semi-final when he scored two more in their 2–0 win over Poland.

In the final in Madrid, Antonio Cabrini missed a twenty-fifth minute penalty, dragging the ball past the post. In the fifty-sixth minute, Rossi dived to head in a Claudio Gentile cross. This, his sixth goal, made him top scorer in the tournament. Marco Tardelli's left-foot shot in the seventy-second minute made the score 2–0, and substitute Alessandro Altobelli wrapped it up with a third in the eightieth minute. A German goal from Paul Breitner two minutes later was mere consolation, and Italy won 3–1, their first World Cup since 1938.

## 1986 World Cup

In Mexico, England progressed with a Gary Lineker hat trick against Poland and, in the revived knock-out second round they beat Paraguay 3–0, with Lineker scoring two. A wonder goal from Maradona, running virtually the length of the pitch, knocked out England in the quarter-final, although Lineker pulled one back to become tournament top scorer with six goals.

West Germany qualified in second place behind Denmark and beat Mexico on penalties in the quarter-final. A 2–0 semi-final win over France saw them in the final with Argentina, who had powered through their games.

In the final in Mexico City, Lothar Matthäus, Maradona's marker, fouled the Argentine captain early in the game. Jorge Burruchaga swung in the free kick and José-Luis Brown headed in past Harald Schumacher. Jorge Valdano scored the second. West Germany, however, came back into the game and Karl-Heinz Rummenigge scored from a Rudi Voller corner with 17 minutes to go. In the eighty-second minute Voller equalized, again from a corner. Two minutes later, a Maradona through-pass found Burruchaga, and he slid the ball past Schumacher for the winner and Argentina's second World Cup trophy.

### The Hand of God

Before Maradona scored his brilliant goal in the 1986 quarter-final against England, he had risen with English goalkeeper Peter Shilton for a high ball in the penalty area and had punched the ball into the net. Although the cheating was obvious, neither linesman nor referee spotted it and a goal was awarded. After the game, a rather smug Maradona referred to the incident as "the hand of God".

# Club Football 1990–2009

Finance now plays a huge role in football, and pressure for success has never been greater, particularly when it comes to the game's biggest money-spinner after the World Cup, The European Champions League Cup.

### European Champions League/Cup

In a bid to prevent Europe's big clubs from forming their own "super league", UEFA established the Champions League from the start of the 1992–93 season as a replacement for the European Cup. The format changed and became increasingly unwieldy throughout the 1990s, the emphasis being more on mini-leagues and less on knockout

### The English Premier League

The first English Premier League season was in 1992–93. The old First Division was changed to the Premier League, and the old Second, Third and Fourth Divisions were altered respectively. At the start of the 1995–96 season the Premiership was reduced from 22 clubs to 20 and in the mid 2000s, the first Division was retitled the Championship.

*Above: AC Milan's Roberto Donadoni breaks away from Barcelona in 1994.*

matches. This, with a seeding process that meant they need not play in qualifying rounds, guaranteed the successful big clubs a certain number of games in the competition and huge revenues. In the 1999–2000 season, the winners Real Madrid picked up over £25 million. By that season, Italy, Spain and Germany could enter four clubs each and the rationale behind the European Cup, that only league champions were eligible to enter, had disappeared.

After Marseille, "winners" in 1993, had been stripped of the title for bribing opponents, the highlights of the competition in the 1990s included the crushing 4–0 win inflicted on Johan Cruyff's Barcelona in 1994 by Arrigo Sacchi's AC Milan. Then came Manchester United's 1999 injury-time win against Bayern Munich, and a stunning display by Real Madrid against Valéncia in 2000. Real won again in 2002, beating Bayer Leverkusen 2–1 in the final, with Zinedine Zidane scoring a

memorable winner. It was Real's ninth win, and it came in their centenary year. In 2003, Real were knocked out in the semi-final by Juventus, who then met rivals AC Milan in the Final at Old Trafford. After a goalless draw, the match was decided on penalties, and Milan won their sixth European Cup title. In 2004

*Below: Manchester United after their Champions League victory in 2008.*

Porto easily beat Monaco 3–0 to add to their win in 1987. Liverpool staged a fantastic comeback in 2005 to beat AC Milan on penalties, and Samuel Eto'o and Belletti overturned Arsenal's 1–0 lead the following year for Barcelona to claim the title for a second time. In 2007 Milan gained revenge when two Filippo Inzaghi strikes gained them their seventh European Cup, beating Liverpool 2–1. An all-English final in 2008 was decided on penalties after a 1–1 draw, Manchester United edging rivals Chelsea 6–5.

## UEFA Cup

For most of the 1990s, the UEFA Cup belonged to Italian clubs, and the run that had been started by Napoli in 1989 was broken only three times that

*Below: Inter's Ivan Zamorano scores against Lazio in the 1998 UEFA Cup Final.*

decade. In the 1990 final, Juventus beat Fiorentina with a 3–1 aggregate score. It was another all-Italian battle in 1991, when Inter Milan beat Roma. Ajax beat Torino on away goals after drawing both legs of the 1992 final, but Juventus brought the title back to Italy a year later, beating Borussia Dortmund. Inter Milan took the title again in 1994, after two 1–0 victories over Salzburg, and in 1995 it went to Parma, who beat Juventus 2–1 on aggregate. In 1996, Bayern Munich and Bordeaux made it an Italian-free final, which Bayern won. In 1997, Schalke beat Inter Milan in a penalty shoot-out.

In 1998, the format was changed in favour of a single-leg final in order to raise the profile with one all-or-nothing match. Inter won their third title in eight seasons, beating Lazio 3–0 in yet another all-Italian final.

In 1998–99, the regulations were changed to allow in the 16 losers from the qualifying rounds of the Champions League, as well as the basic 84 clubs and those from the InterToto Cup. Parma maintained the Italian record with a win over Marseille in the final.

Leeds United and Arsenal stormed through to the semi-finals in 2000. Sadly, two Leeds fans were stabbed to death in Istanbul as Galatasaray became the first Turkish team to make a European final. They won, beating Arsenal on penalties after a 0–0 draw. Spanish clubs dominated in Europe around the turn of the century, and in 2000–01 four of them reached the quarter-finals. It was the unfashionable Alaves, never Spanish champions or Cup-winners, who reached the final, but they lost an amazing game against Liverpool on a sudden-death own-goal

in the 117th minute, after the score at 90 minutes had been 4–4. The following year Feyenoord beat Borussia Dortmund 3–2. Valencia, after two Champions League disappointments, deservedly won the UEFA Cup in 2004, easily beating Marseille. CSKA Moscow claimed the prize in 2005, beating Sporting Lisbon 3–1, and in 2006 Sevilla won their first major trophy for 58 years with an emphatic 4–0 defeat of Middlesbrough. The Spaniards retained the trophy the following year beating Espanyol on penalties in Glasgow, while in 2008, Dick Advocaat's Zenit St Peterburg's 2–0 victory over the Dutchman's former side Rangers brought the UEFA Cup back to Russia.

## Copa Libertadores

After their 1989 victory, Olimpia of Paraguay won again in 1990, beating Barcelona of Ecuador, 3–1 on aggregate. In 1991, the title went to Chile's Colo Colo with a 3–0 aggregate score against Olimpia.

In 1992, Sao Paulo beat Argentina's Newell's Old Boys on penalties, and became the first Brazilian side to win the *Copa Libertadores* in almost a decade. From then on, until the end

Above: *Vasco da Gama with the Copa Libertadores trophy in 1998.*

of the 1990s, the Brazilians dominated. Sao Paulo, triumphed again in 1993. This time they overcame Chile's Universidad Catolica 5–3 on aggregate and became the first club to retain the *Copa* trophy since Boca Juniors in 1978.

In 1994, Sao Paulo came close to a hat trick before losing on penalties to Argentina's Velez Sarsfield. A year later, Gremio reclaimed the title for Brazil, beating Nacional of Colombia 4–2 on aggregate. In 1996, River Plate beat America Cali in the final in a repeat of the 1986 result. Three victories for Brazilian teams finished off the decade; Cruzeiro in 1997, Vasco da Gama in 1998 and Palmeiras in 1999, but as the new millennium began Boca Juniors of Argentina won in 2000 and 2001. Olimpia of Paraguay won on penalties in 2002, beating Sao Caetano, before Boca Juniors won again, beating Santos in the 2003 Final. Surprise first-time winners in 2004 were Colombia's Once Caldas, with another first timer, Ecuador's LDU Quito, winning in 2008. In between, the title was predictably won by Sao Paulo, Internacional and, again, Boca Juniors.

## African Champions Cup

Clubs from the north continued their dominance at the top of African football for the first half of the decade.

Jeunesse Sportive Kabyle of Algeria beat the Nkana Red Devils of Zambia in 1990. In 1991, Tunisian side Club Africain beat Nakivubo Villa of Uganda with a 6–2 aggregate score. Wydad Casablanca of Morocco beat El Hilal of Sudan in 1992. The following year, Asante Kotoko of Ghana and Zamalek of Egypt met in the final, with the Egyptian side winning on penalties. Zamalek made it to the final the following year, but lost to Esperance Sportive of Tunisia. However, in 1996 they beat Nigeria's Shooting Stars.

South Africa made its return to the continental and international football scene in the mid-1990s, following the collapse of the apartheid regime. Orlando Pirates beat ASEC of Ivory Coast 3–2 on aggregate in 1995 to become the first champions from South Africa. In 1997 Raja Casablanca beat Goldfields of Ghana on penalties. The title returned to Ivory Coast in 1998, when ASEC Abdijan beat Dynamos Harare of Zimbabwe. After no score in either leg of the final in 1999, Raja Casablanca beat Tunisia's Esperance 4–3 on penalties. Ghana's Hearts of Oak won

*Above: Juventus with the World Club Cup and Toyota Cup trophies in 1996.*

in 2000, and Al Ahly of Egypt beat South Africa'a Mamelodi Sundowns in 2001. In 2002, Zamalek of Egypt won, but the first Nigerian team to win triumphed in 2003, with Enyimba beating Ismali of Egypt 2–1 on aggregate, and they won again in 2004. Five-time winners Al Ahly triumphed in 2005 and 2006, but the Egyptians were defeated 3–1 in 2007 by Tunisia's Etoile du Sahel, their first win in the competition.

## World Club Cup

The 1990s saw renewed optimism for European clubs in the competition. AC Milan beat Paraguay's Olimpia in the final in 1990. Then, in 1991, Red Star Belgrade beat Colo Colo of Chile 3–0 and became the first East European side to take the honours. The South Americans set about reclaiming their territory the following year. Sao Paulo proved too strong for European giants Barcelona in 1992 and AC Milan in 1993. Milan made it to a second final in 1994 but lost to Argentina's Velez Sarsfield.

It wasn't until Ajax beat Brazil's Gremio on penalties in 1995 that Europe took back the trophy. In 1996, a goal from Alessandro Del Piero secured a 1–0 win over River Plate and gave the title to Juventus. In 1997, Borussia Dortmund defeated Cruzeiro and claimed Germany's

*Below: Boca Juniors (in blue) and Real Madrid in the World Club Cup of 2000.*

first title since Bayern Munich defeated the same Brazilian side 21 years earlier. The following year Real Madrid took back the trophy it had first won in 1960 with a win over Vasco da Gama. In 1999 Manchester United beat Palmeiras. Boca Juniors beat Real Madrid 2–1 in 2000, but the following year they were beaten 1–0 by Bayern Munich in extra time. Real Madrid beat Olimpia in 2002, but Boca Juniors prevented Milan bringing Europe's wins equal to South America's with a penalty win after a 1–1 draw in 2003. In 2004 Porto saw off Once Caldas 8–7 on penalties, and Sao Paulo and Internacional won in 2005 and 2006. In 2007, AC Milan beat Boca Juniors 4–2 in the final in Yokohama.

## Major League Soccer

In April, 1996, San José Clash kicked off against Washington DC United in the inaugural game in the new, United States Major League Soccer (MLS) Championship. The league now comprises 14 clubs and is divided into the Eastern and Western Conferences. Each club plays 30 matches split equally between home and away games and the title is decided by a play-off. The MSL's biggest coup has been LA Galaxy securing superstar player David Beckham in 2006 on a five-year contract.

# World Football 1990–2009

Politics and civil war caused tinkering to the rules and regulations of some of the biggest international tournaments of the 1990s.

## Olympic Games

For the Barcelona games of 1992, FIFA amended the rules to make Olympic football an under-23 contest. Spain beat Poland in a memorable final to claim victory and take the gold.

At Atlanta in 1996, the Olympic committee redrew the entry regulations again, allowing three over-age players in each squad to help promote football in the United States. Nigeria, with a squad built around the experienced World Cup team of 1994, became Olympic Champions after a 3–2 win over Argentina in the final in Atlanta.

Another African nation took the title in Sydney in 2000, when Cameroon came from two down in the final to draw 2–2 with a Spanish team reduced eventually to nine men, and then won the penalty shoot-out. Argentina triumphed in both 2004 and 2008.

## European Championship

The 1992 Championship, hosted by Sweden, made headlines even before the finals began. With the unification of Germany just after the start of the qualifying rounds, the GDR withdrew its entry and the team was disbanded. The former Soviet Union was now known as the Commonwealth of Independent States. Meanwhile, the Balkans were on the verge of civil war. UEFA barred Yugoslavia from the tournament on security grounds, and Denmark, runners-up in the qualifying group, were invited to replace them.

They reached the final, and although Germany were the clear favourites goals from John Jensen and Kim Vilfort completed the fairytale and against all the odds Denmark won 2–0.

In 1996, the Championships were held in England, for the first time. Germany met the Czech Republic, in a

final that was to be decided by a "golden goal". Patrick Berger scored for the Czechs with a penalty but substitute Oliver Bierhoff equalized. In extra time, Bierhoff struck again, and Germany had won.

Euro 2000 took place in Holland and Belgium, and was remarkable for close finishes involving "golden goals" and penalty shoot-outs. Holland, Spain, Italy and Portugal topped their groups in the initial stage, with Holland beating world champions France 3–2. England and Germany were both eliminated at this stage, finishing below Portugal and Romania in group A. France, however, reached the semi-finals and beat Portugal 2–1 with a 117th-minute "golden goal", scored by Zinedine Zidane from a penalty awarded when Abel Xavier handled by a post.

Italy, their final opponents, scored first and very nearly held out to the end, but Wiltord scored an equalizer for France in the overtime minutes added on. Thirteen minutes into extra time David Trezeguet, who had been brought on as a substitute, scored the "golden goal" winner as France added the European crown to the world title.

The 2004 finals provided shocks, with England, Germany, Italy, Spain and holders France all eliminated early.

*Above: Captain Theodoras Zagorakis lifts the cup for Greece at Euro 2004.*

The 100–1 outsiders, Greece, beat hosts Portugal 2–1 in the opening game and beat them again in the final. They also beat France and the Czech Republic by 1–0, the latter by a "silver goal".

In the 2008 finals, hosted by Austria and Switzerland, holders Greece were absent, having gained no points in the group stage. In the semi-finals a rejuvenated Turkey were level 2–2 with Germany until German full-back

*Below: Didier Deschamps lifts the trophy as France celebrate their Euro 2000 win.*

Philipp Lahm scored in the last minute, and a profligate Russia lost 3–0 to Spain, the Spaniards' win assisted by the introduction of substitute Cesc Fabregas' playmaking genius in the second half. In the final, a splendid first-half goal from Fernando Torres was enough to bring Spain their first major international victory for 44 years against a formidable German side.

## Copa America

The 1991 event was held in Chile, and Argentina won. Ecuador played host the next time round, in 1993, and the tournament underwent more changes, with Mexico and the United States being invited to take part as guests. Mexico made it to the final but Argentina managed a 2–1 win to keep the title in South America.

Mexico and the United States were invited once again in 1995, and this time the United States made it to the semi-final, where they lost to Brazil. Brazil went on to lose to the hosts Uruguay in a penalty shoot-out after a 1–1 draw.

The guests from Mexico made it to the semi-final again in 1997, losing to the hosts Bolivia. Despite strong home support, Bolivia went down 3–1 to Brazil in the final.

Mexico again suffered a semi-final defeat by Brazil in 1999. With Rivaldo and Ronaldo now on board, Brazil were unstoppable and they encountered few problems in the final to beat Uruguay 3–0 for the title.

Colombia hosted the 2001 Copa America, and won it by winning all of their six games without conceding a single goal. Honduras had sprung a surprise by beating Brazil 2–0 in a quarter-final, but Colombia squarely beat them 2–0 in the semis. Honduras beat Uruguay on penalties for third place. The two best teams in the tournament, Colombia and Mexico, fought it out in the final, the hosts winning 1–0.

*Above: Saudi Arabia beat the UAE on penalties to take the 1996 Asian Cup.*

In 2004 and 2007 Brazil met Argentina in the final, winning the first game on penalties and the second 3–0, their fifth title in ten years.

## Asian Games

Iran won the event in 1990 but chose not to enter again for several years. Following the break-up of the Soviet Union, a number of newly independent states entered the 1994 event in Hiroshima. One of these, Uzbekistan, proved the surprise of the tournament, beating China 4–2 in the final to take the title. Iran returned to the Games in 1998 and won the final 2–0 against Kuwait, repeating their success in 2002 with a 2–1 win over Japan, and in 2006 Qatar won their first title, beating Iraq 1–0.

## Asian Cup

The holders Saudi Arabia lost the 1992 final 1–0 to the host nation Japan. However, the Saudis got their hat trick of titles four years later, in 1996, beating the hosts the United Arab Emirates 4–2 on penalties in the final after a 0–0 draw. Japan once again beat Saudi Arabia 1–0 in Beirut in 2000, and won again in 2004, defeating China 3–1. Iraq picked up their first title in 2007 when they defeated Saudi Arabia by a single goal.

## African Nations Cup

The 1990 tournament was hosted by Algeria. The three-times runners-up Nigeria made it to their fourth final, but were beaten 1–0 by Algeria, in front of a partisan crowd of 80,000.

The 1992 tournament featured 12 teams in the final round, with Ivory Coast and Ghana reaching the final. The game finished goalless and was decided by a gripping penalty shoot-out, which ended 11–10 to Ivory Coast.

In 1994, Nigeria made it to their fourth final in ten years, and this time they won, beating Zambia 2–1. Zambia, who had had to rebuild their team after losing 18 players in a catastrophic plane crash only a year earlier, were rightfully proud of their achievement.

Kenya was forced to withdraw as hosts of the 1996 event through lack of funds, and South Africa stepped in to provide the venue. South Africa surprised everyone by beating Tunisia 2–0 in the final.

South Africa had the chance to take a second title in 1998, but Egypt, who had given poor perfomances in the Cup for almost a decade, made it through to the final and won.

The 2000 event was co-hosted by Ghana and Nigeria. Ghana lost out to South Africa in the quarter-final, while Nigeria went through to the final but lost a penalty shoot-out to Cameroon.

The 2002 event was held in Mali, where Cameroon retained their title with another penalty shoot-out in the final. They did not concede a goal in their six matches, but could not score one either in 120 minutes against finalists Senegal. Cameroon fell behind in the shoot-out, but prevailed 3–2.

A North African final in 2004 saw Tunisia beat Morocco 2–1, and hosts Egypt became the most successful team in the tournament's history in 2006, eliminating Cote d'Ivoire on penalties. Egypt won for the sixth time in 2008 with a 1–0 win over Cameroon.

## 1990 World Cup

Italy were hosts for the fourteenth World Cup. The surprise team of the tournament was Cameroon, who went all the way to the quarter-finals, where they were beaten by England with an extra-time goal from Gary Lineker which saw his team into the semi-final against West

*Below: President Nelson Mandela with South Africa's African Nations Cup winning team in 1996.*

Germany. The Germans went ahead in the sixtieth minute, but Lineker was on hand again to equalize with ten minutes remaining. England, however, lost on penalties, and Paul Gascoigne's tears summed up England's frustration.

The tournament of 1990 was notable for the low goal tally and the cynical level of play, with a proliferation of dismissals and bookings. The final, between West Germany and Argentina, who had knocked out Italy on penalties in the other semi-final, was no different. In a boring, negative match, neither side seemed interested in playing attacking football. Monzon was sent off in the 68th minute for what appeared to be a fair tackle on Jürgen Klinsmann, giving Germany the advantage. In the 85th minute, it was Voller's turn to fall in the penalty area and Brehme converted. With three minutes to go, Dezotti was sent off and Maradona booked for dissent. West Germany won 1–0, but by this point few people outside Germany cared.

## 1994 World Cup

The 1994 tournament, held in the United States, was a massive success, helped by FIFA's ban on the tackle from behind, a relaxation of the offside law, and the introduction of three points for a win in the group stage.

No British teams qualified, but the Republic of Ireland, playing a defensive, long-ball game, reached the second round only to be knocked out 2–0 by Holland. The host nation reached the second round, as one of the third-placed qualifiers, for the first time in their history. They were then beaten 1–0 by a well-organized Brazil.

Bulgaria and Romania were the surprise teams. Bulgaria, inspired by the tournament's top scorer Hristo Stoichkov, reached the semi-finals beating Germany 2–1 in Chicago with a late goal from Iordan Lechkov. Italy scraped their way to the semi-final, where two goals from Roberto Baggio defeated Bulgaria. Ilie Dumitrescu scored twice for Romania to eliminate Argentina, but they lost on penalties to Sweden in the quarter-final. Brazil beat Sweden 1–0 to meet Italy in the Pasadena final.

Sweeper Franco Baresi was at the heart of Italy's defending and counter-attacking strategy, while Brazil probed for any weakness in Italy's defensive shell. Maurio Silva and Romario went close for Brazil, and Baggio nearly scored for Italy in extra time. After extra time it was still 0–0, and the game went to penalties for the first time in a World Cup Final. Baggio had to score with the last of Italy's five penalties but he skyed his shot over the bar and hung his head in despair, as Brazil won their fourth World Cup Final.

## 1998 World Cup

Thirty-two teams entered the 1998 tournament held in France. England got through to play Argentina, but a petulant kick from David Beckham meant a sending-off and Argentina won 4–3 on penalties.

Croatia, with the tournament's top marksman Davor Suker, were in the competition for the first time and eliminated Germany 3–0 in the quarter-finals. Two goals from defender Lilian Thuram gave France a 2–1 win over Croatia in the semi-final. Meanwhile an exquisite, last-minute strike from

Dennis Bergkamp gave Holland a 2–1 quarter-final win over Argentina, but the Dutch were beaten on penalties by Brazil in the semi-final.

Mystery still surrounds top striker Ronaldo's poor form in the final, and his sluggishness seemed to affect his Brazilian team-mates. France seized the initiative. In the twenty-seventh minute midfielder Zinedine Zidane rose to meet an Emmanuel Petit corner and France were 1–0 ahead. Zidane met another corner with a second firm header into the net. French defender Marcel Desailly was sent off, but France kept their grip on the game against the under-achieving Brazilians. In the last minute, Emmanuel Petit stroked the ball past Brazilian keeper Taffarel for France's third. Images of France's World Cup-winning stars were flashed on to the *Arc De Triomphe* that evening, and France celebrated in style.

## 2002 World Cup

Jointly hosted by Japan and South Korea, the 2002 competition was notable for its shock results. France, pre-tournament favourites, lost to Senegal in the opening match and were also beaten by Denmark before being eliminated without scoring a goal. Rival favourites Argentina were beaten 1–0 by England and also went out at the group stage. Portugal, beaten 3–2 by USA and 1–0 by South Korea, and Russia, beaten 1–0 by Japan, also went home early. Japan and South Korea, who between them had not won a match in 17 attempts in six previous finals matches, both topped their groups unbeaten. Japan went out 1–0 to Turkey in the knock-out stage, but South Korea beat mighty Italy, three times winners, 2–1 on a "golden goal", and then went on to beat Spain, who had looked likely winners, on penalties in the quarter-finals. It was in these two matches that controversial refereeing decisions went against the Europeans, with Italy's Francesco Totti being sent off for "diving", and Spain having two apparently good goals disallowed.

The last eight were four established football nations, England, Brazil, Germany and Spain, and four in very unfamiliar territory, USA, Senegal, Turkey and South Korea. Brazil beat England 2–1, Germany, who escaped a penalty after a handling in the area, were lucky to beat USA 1–0, Turkey beat Senegal on a "golden goal" and South Korea beat Spain. The South Korean dream ended in the semis, when Germany beat them 1–0, the same score by which Brazil beat Turkey. Turkey beat South Korea 3–2 to take third place.

Brazil, who had played the best football throughout, won 2–0, with both goals coming from Ronaldo, who ended up with the Golden Boot as the tournament's top scorer (eight goals). It was Brazil's fifth win, and their captain, Cafu, set a record by appearing in his third World Cup Final.

## 2006 World Cup

Held in Germany during a heatwave, the tournament was a great success with the whole country in a party mood. As well as the usual suspects, smaller African nations – Angola, Togo,

*Below: Italy celebrate their first World Cup triumph in 24 years at Germany in 2006.*

Cote d'Ivoire – were attending their first World Cup finals. In the last sixteen Germany beat Sweden and then defeated Argentina on penalties, who had previously knocked out Mexico with an extra-time Maxi Rodriguez goal. A free kick from David Beckham put out Ecuador, but England were beaten on penalties by Portugal in the quarter-final, with Wayne Rooney sent off. Two goals from Luca Tonni helped Italy cruise past Ukraine 3–0, and holders Brazil were eliminated by France and a Thierry Henry goal.

In the most exciting game of the competition, two goals in the semi-final in the last two minutes of extra time from Fabio Grosso and Alessandro del Piero meant that Italy qualified for the final at Germany's expense, while a Zinedine Zidane penalty against Portugal saw France also reach the final, 1–0.

In the final at Berlin's Olympiastadion, watched by an estimated 700 million TV audience, Zidane scored for France with an early penalty but Marco Materazzi quickly equalized. The game remained 1–1 till the end of extra time, although Zidane had been sent off for inexplicably head-butting Materazzi. Italy won the trophy 5–3 on penalties, their first World Cup triumph for 24 years.

# International Competitions

After the universal World Cup and (to a much lesser extent) the Olympic Games, there are now regional international tournaments in all parts of the world.

## World Cup

The World Cup is the most popular sporting event in the world, eclipsing even the Olympic Games in its ability to grab headlines. It is now a truly global event, with most of the nations on earth attempting to qualify for the final rounds.

The idea for a worldwide football competition came from the FIFA and French federation president Jules Rimet and the secretary Henri Delauney in 1920. Following the enthusiasm of the European and South American nations for the football event at the Olympic Games, it was clear that a challenge Cup for the world title was needed, which would bring together the world's

*Below: The Holy Grail of football, the FIFA World Cup trophy.*

*Above: Shameful scenes as the police break up the game between the host nation Chile and Italy in 1962.*

professional players in a head-to-head contest. Football's governing body was persuaded to stage an international competition that would co-exist with the Olympic Games. After almost a decade of planning, the first World Cup finals were launched in 1930. The finals were suspended because of World War Two but they resumed in 1950, and the event has since been contested every four years.

The tournament is played out between the member nations of FIFA, and the finals are held in one nominated country (two in 2002); nations submit a bid to host the tournament, and the FIFA Congress of members then votes to make its choice. The World Cup invariably proves a lucrative boost to the national economy: the 1994 tournament in America pulled in more than £60 million in profits, and four years later in France that figure was multiplied by four. The 2002 finals were for the first time co-hosted by two nations, Japan and South Korea.

The qualifying rounds for a place in the finals begin two years before the tournament. The FIFA-affiliated nations who enter are divided into groups and the top-ranking nations of each group will go through to the

finals. At the first finals held in Uruguay in 1930 there were 13 competing sides in the finals but by 2006 that number had risen to 32.

This means there are a total of 64 matches played over less than five weeks. This kind of scheduling is a tall order by any standard. Teams are already under pressure to perform at their best, and television, now such an integral part of football, demands high levels of entertainment. One of the factors that can increase the pressure on the teams is

---

**Record World Cup Attendance**
Brazil v Uruguay,
199,854 Maracana Stadium,
Rio de Janeiro
World Cup final pool, 1950

**Most Goals in a World Cup Final**
Geoff Hurst, 3
England v West Germany, 1966

**Most Goals in World Cup Finals Tournaments**
Gerd Müller, 14
West Germany, 1970 and 1974

---

*Above: Luque, Kempes and Bertoni celebrate as Argentina wins in 1978.*

the size of the host nation. Roughly half the teams at the World Cup finals will have travelled across the world to be there. At the 1994 event in the United States the teams faced huge demands on their stamina because of long distances between venues, climatic changes and acclimatization to different time zones within the host country.

In spite of the high number of matches at the 1998 event the pressure on the teams was eased, at least in part, by shorter distances between venues and the more temperate climate of France. In 2002, there were again journeys to make between two countries, South Korea and Japan, and afternoon matches were played in heat and high humidity. In Germany in the 2006 competition, although the weather was hot, the stadiums were close together with excellent transport links between the cities.

Patience is needed by the teams, as well as by the supporters, if they are to survive the challenges imposed upon them. Sensitive situations can arise, with rival countries in football or in politics facing each other on the pitch. The referees who officiate the matches have a huge responsibility to get it right, especially in distinguishing between what is a genuine foul and what is a "dive". The World Cup finals is the greatest show on earth and the world's greatest players have to be able to perform at their best.

*Below: Michael Owen keeps his head under pressure from Argentina in 1998.*

| World Cup Top Scorers |
| --- |
| **1930** Stabile (Argentina) 8; Cea (Uruguay) 5 |
| **1934** Nejedly (Czechoslovakia) 5; Schiavio (Italy), Conen (Germany) 4 |
| **1938** Leonidas (Brazil) 8; Szellenger (Hungary) 7 |
| **1950** Ademir (Brazil) 9; Schiaffino (Uruguay), Basora (Spain) 5 |
| **1954** Kocsis (Hungary) 11; Morlock (West Germany), Hugi (Switzerland) 6 |
| **1958** Fontaine (France) 13; Pelé (Brazil), Rahn (West Germany) 6 |
| **1962** Ivanov (USSR), Sanchez (Chile), Garrincha (Brazil), Vava (Brazil), Albert (Hungary), Jerkovic (Yugoslavia) 4 |
| **1966** Eusebio (Portugal) 9; Haller (West Germany) 5 |
| **1970** Müller (West Germany) 10; Jairzhino (Brazil) 7 |
| **1974** Lato (Poland) 7; Szarmach (Poland), Neeskens (Holland) 5 |
| **1978** Kempes (Argentina) 6; Cubillas (Peru), Rensenbrink (Holland) 5 |
| **1982** Rossi (Italy) 6; Rummenigge (West Germany) 5 |
| **1986** Lineker (England) 6; Butragueno (Spain), Careca (Brazil), Maradona (Argentina) 5 |
| **1990** Schillaci (Italy) 6; Skuhravy (Czechoslovakia) 5 |
| **1994** Stoichkov (Bulgaria), Salenko (Russia) 6; Romario (Brazil), Baggio (Italy), Klinsmann (Germany) 5 |
| **1998** Suker (Croatia) 6; Vieri (Italy), Batistuta (Argentina) 5 |
| **2002** Ronaldo (Brazil) 8; Rivaldo (Brazil), Klose (Germany) 5 |
| **2006** Klose (Germany) 5; Crespo (Argentina), Rodriguez (Argentina), Ronaldo (Brazil), Henry (France), Zidane (France), Podolski (Germany), Torres (Spain), Villa (Spain) 3 |

## European Championship

Originally called the European Nations Cup, the European Championship was the brainchild of Henri Delauney, secretary of the French Football Federation, and was first staged in 1958–60. The tournament involves member nations of UEFA, and the finals are held every four years.

## Landmarks

**1958–60** The first tournament is held, with matches played on a home and away basis. France hosts the semi-finals and final, which is won by the USSR who beat Yugoslavia 2–1.

**1964–66** Spain hosts the semi-finals and final, and wins the trophy.

**1966–68** Now renamed the European Championship, the format changes from the knock-out system to eight group qualifying matches, with the semi-finals and final taking place in Italy. The Home International

*Below: France's Michel Platini with the European Championship trophy, 1984.*

## Memorable Matches of the European Championship

### 1972 West Germany v USSR

The genius of midfielder Günter Netzer and sweeper Franz Beckenbauer had helped West Germany reach the final against the Soviet Union in Belgium. West Germany dominated the first half, held out by Soviet keeper Rudakov, until Gerd Müller scored late in the first half. In the second half defender Herbert Wimmer slid in a second from a cross from Jupp Heynckes, and five mintutes later Müller sent the keeper the wrong way. The Soviets were finished and West Germany protected their 3–0 lead until the final whistle. The same side, minus Netzer, was to win the World Cup Final two years later.

### 1984 France v Spain

The superb Michel Platini, along with midfield teammates Alain Giresse and the elegant Jean Tigana, were at the centre of the team that reached the 1984 final in Paris to face Spain. France pounded away in the first half against the defensive Spaniards to no avail. They finally achieved a deserved breakthrough in the fifty-sixth minute when keeper Luis Arconada failed to hold a Platini free kick, his ninth goal in the tournament. French centre-back Yvon Le Roux was sent off with six minutes to go and Spain went on the offensive. With a minute remaining, and the French goal under pressure, Tigana intercepted a French pass and found Bruno Bellone, who ran to chip the advancing Arconada. France had won the match 2–0.

### 1988 Holland v Soviet Union

A famous 2–1 semi-final victory over West Germany put Holland into the final against the Soviet Union, who had beaten Italy 2–0 to get there. Holland started on the attack. In the thirty-second minute Marco Van Basten's header found Ruud Gullit who nodded the ball past keeper Renat Dasayef. Eight minutes into the second half, Holland were two ahead. Adri Van Tiggelen picked up a loose ball in the midfield and found Arnold Muhren who sent in a perfect cross to Van Basten on the edge of the penalty area. The striker unleashed a magnificent volley, which gave Dasayef no chance. Although the Soviets went on the attack, Holland nearly scored again through Frank Rijkaard. The score stayed at 2–0 and Holland had won their first ever Championship.

Championship is the qualifying group for countries from the UK. The record attendance for the competition is set in 1968 when a Scotland v England qualifier attracts 134,000. Italy beat Yugoslavia 2–0 in the final.

**1972** Günter Netzer's West Germany triumph in Belgium.

**1976** Czechoslovakia beat West Germany in the final in Yugoslavia in the first penalty shoot-out used to determine the outcome of an international competition.

**1980** Two rounds of groups produce two finalists. Italy, the host country received a bye directly into the final eight. West Germany won.

**1984** The top two teams from each group contest a semi-final. France beats Spain in the final, and Michel Platini's

*Above: Denmark triumphant in 1992.*
*Below: Germany's Dieter Eilts (centre) and*
*Croatia's Davor Suker (left) at Euro '96.*

nine goals in the competition sets a
record which still stands.

**1988** Holland, inspired by Gullit and Van
Basten, and twice runners-up in the
World Cup Final, win their first major
championship, beating the USSR 2–0 in
West Germany.

**1992** Yugoslavia are suspended from the
finals due to civil war; Denmark,
runners-up in their qualifying group, are
invited to take their place, and shock
Europe by beating Germany 2–0 in the
final in Gothenburg.

**1996** Germany win their third
championship, held in England, beating
the Czech Republic 2–1. Oliver
Bierhof's "golden goal" in extra time
decides the match.

**2000** World Cup holders France add the
European championship by beating
Portugal in the semi-final and Italy in the

final both by 2–1 and each time with a
"golden goal" in extra time. In the final,
France forced extra time with an
equalizer in stoppage time.

**2004** Sixteen teams took part in the
finals. In the knock-out stage, a team
won if ahead at the break in extra time –
the "silver goal". Greece beat the hosts
Portugal 1–0 in the final.

**2008** Hosted by Austria and Switzerland,
Germany and Spain defeated respectively
Turkey and Russia to meet each other in
the final, where Spain won 1–0. The goal
was scored by Fernando Torres.

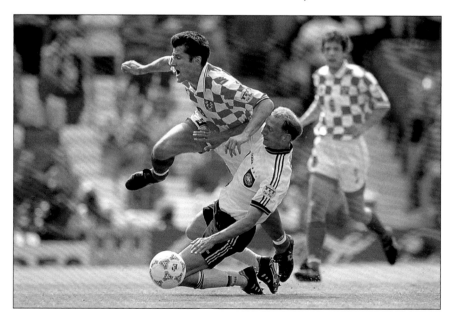

some of the country's top players, beat Denmark 2–0 in the final at the White City stadium.

The first South American team to compete in Olympic football was Uruguay in 1924. The European teams were no match for the dazzling skills of the South Americans, and Uruguay beat Switzerland 3–0 in the final. Uruguay retained the Olympic title in 1928, beating Argentina 2–1 after a replay. The win was proof that South America was equal to Europe in terms of footballing strength, and it added momentum to the idea of a World Cup championship, which came to fruition just two years later.

The regulations of Olympic football have seen much revision over the years. From the 1950s through to the late 1970s the event was dominated by Communist Eastern Europe. Marxist-Leninist theory considered sport a leisure activity, and this interpretation of the Olympic rule allowed Eastern-bloc countries to submit teams composed of full-time

*Below: Germany v Brazil in the women's Olympic Bronze Medal Match 2000.*

## Olympic Games

Football has been an official Olympic sport since the London Games of 1908, although matches were played in the three previous Olympics as a demonstration sport. The World Cup did not yet exist and in the absence of any other worldwide competition, the Olympics offered the only challenge for the world title. However, the Olympic policy on amateurism meant the absence of crowd-pulling star players and Olympic football could no longer compete with the World Cup

*Above: Spain's Raúl Tamudo gets to the ball before Cameroon's Serge Mimpo in the Olympic Final of 2000.*

for public attention. More recently, rule revisions have attempted to raise the profile of the Games once again.

In the first three modern Olympics, when football was a demonstration sport, the total entries numbered three, two and three. The London Games of 1908 saw football entered in the main programme for the first time. England, with an amateur team that included sportsmen who were registered as state employees for the sake of the Olympic regulations.

The Western world could not hope to compete against these "state amateurs", and in 1980 the world governing body responded with a change of rule to ban players who had competed in a World Cup qualifier. This meant that professionals could compete as long as they hadn't played in any World Cup event. The new rule was a compromise but it did break the Communist monopoly. By the time of the Barcelona Games of 1992, Olympic football was restricted to players under the age of 23, but at the Atlanta Games, in 1996, a further rule change allowed each nation to send three "over-age" players. The idea was to encourage interest for football in the United States by including star names from the leading footballing nations, who would give a more competitive edge to the event. The rule was kept for the 2000 Games in Sydney, and remained in force for 2004 and 2008, but there is much dissatisfaction with these arbitrary rule changes and some would like to see the competition open to all players.

## Copa America

The South American Championship was first played in 1910 and is the longest running international football tournament in the world, with the exception of the Olympic Games. In 1975 the Championship was renamed the *Copa America*, and it is now staged every two years between the countries of the South American football confederation, CONMEBOL. Since 1993 "guest" nations – usually Mexico and the United States – have been invited to take part in order to expand the competition and generate income from television and sponsorship deals.

The *Copa America* is a highly prestigious event but it has not always been so, even though rivalry between the continent's leading footballing nations is historically fierce. Argentina, Brazil and Uruguay have previously shown a relaxed attitude to the competition, entering their weaker B-teams and youth squads when European and domestic clubs showed reluctance, or even refused, to release players for the national team.

The format for the tournament has fluctuated over the years, first in favour of group matches with play-off games to decide the tournament winner. However, television demands the drama of a head-

*Below: Ivan Zamorano celebrates Chile's equalizer against Uruguay in 1999.*

to-head final, and the Championship now works as a league system, with quarter-finals, semi-finals and a final.

Uruguay took six of the first 11 *Copa America* titles before Argentina stormed ahead to take ten out of the next 16 from the 1920s through to the 1950s. Brazil's success record was limited against Uruguay and Argentina in the early years, but they have made their mark in more recent times; Brazil were twice Champions and twice runners-up in the 1990s. Colombia won the *Copa America* for the first time in 2001, with Brazil winning yet again in 2004 and 2007.

## African Nations Cup

The *Confédération Africain de Football* (CAF) had been set up in June 1957, and at the inaugural meeting it was decided to mark the event with a football tournament between the nations of the continent. Sudan, celebrating its recent independence and building its first national stadium, requested to stage the event, and the first African Cup of Nations, as it was then known, was played in Khartoum in September 1957. The African Nations Cup is now the most coveted award in African football and it takes place every two years in a nominated host country.

Egypt, Ethiopia, South Africa and Sudan entered the first tournament and semi-finals were scheduled to decide the finalists. South Africa was scheduled to play Ethiopia in the semi-final but was

*Above: The Nigerian captain lifts the African Nations Cup in 1980.*

forced to withdraw its entry after refusing to send a multi-racial team. Seven years later South Africa had its FIFA membership suspended and was not allowed the rejoin the African or international footballing circuit until the end of apartheid in 1992. Without South Africa, Ethiopia received a bye into the final. After beating Sudan, Egypt had few problems with Ethiopia and took the first Cup title with a 4–0 win. Egypt are the most successful team in the competition's history, picking up their sixth title in 2008.

Membership of CAF expanded rapidly in the second half of the 20th century, as more countries gained independence from colonialism and built the financial

*Below: Ghana beat Ivory Coast 11–10 on penalties in the 1992 Nations Cup.*

resources to fund and develop professional football. The popularity of the Nations Cup also grew: by 1965 it had doubled its participants with six competing countries, and by 1968 there were 15. Qualifying rounds were introduced that year to restrict the number of teams competing in the finals.

The format of the finals has also been revised to accommodate the new numbers, and it now operates as a league system, with semi-finals and a final. In 1965 CAF introduced a controversial rule to limit the number of overseas players in each team to two. The aim had been to help the development of the continental game by encouraging players to play their club football in Africa. However, for most players, a lucrative career move to Europe was a more attractive option than playing in the Cup; they continued to play overseas and as a result nations were unable to send their best teams. The rule was dropped in 1982.

## Asian Games

The football section of the Asian Games is the longest running international tournament in Asian football. The Games are held every four years in a nominated country, and are run along similar lines to the Olympic Games. Considerable kudos is associated with winning the event; unlike the Olympic event its status has not diminished over the years.

The first football tournament took place in 1951, in New Dheli, with six competing nations – India, Indonesia, Afghanistan, Japan, Iran and Burma. All players were amateurs and for this reason it was decided that the matches should last just 80 minutes. Iran, who won outright in 1990, 1998 and 2002, have proved the most successful at the Games to date, and Qatar won their first title in 2006.

## Asian Cup

The Asian Cup is held in every Olympic year for countries of the Asian Football Confederation, which

*Above: Li Ming of China battles with Qatar's Mubarak in the 2000 Asian Cup.*

now includes India, Indonesia, Japan, South Korea, Malaysia, Philippines, Singapore, South Vietnam, Taiwan, China and the Gulf states of the Middle East. Israel joined in the 1950s but its presence caused political tensions and the confederation was forced to withdraw Israel's membership in 1976.

The first four finals tournaments were played as a league format but this was changed in 1972 to the current system, which has mini-leagues in the first round, followed by a knock-out system and a one-off final.

Political tension has long been a feature of the Asian Cup, and this is due largely to the broad political spectrum spanned by the confederation. Towards the end of the 20th century the huge financial investments made in football by the Gulf states began to pay off, with Iran, Saudi Arabia and Kuwait making their names in the Cup. Saudi Arabia won three times in the 1980s and 1990s (1984, 1988 and 1996), and they share with Iran and Japan the record of three Asian Cup titles; the Saudis were also runners-up to Japan in 1992 and 2000. Japan won again in 2004 and Iraq claimed their first title in 2007, when the tournament was co-hosted by Indonesia, Malaysia, Vietnam and Thailand.

# World Club Competitions

The growing affluence of fans now allows them to follow their clubs abroad for the big matches.

## European Cup

The European Cup or, to be more formal, the European Champion Clubs Cup, came about as the result of the efforts of Gabriel Hanot, a journalist with the French sports newspaper *L'Equipe*. In 1955 he held a meeting in Paris to which he had invited 17 of Europe's leading clubs, all from different countries. He suggested an annual knock-out competition, with two legs (home and away), to find the best club in Europe. UEFA gave its approval the following month, and the first game in the tournament, Sporting Lisbon v Partizan Belgrade, kicked off in September 1955.

The first five years of the tournament were dominated by Real Madrid. They won the title from 1956–60, culminating in their unforgettable 7–3 crushing of Eintracht Frankfurt in 1960, after which Portugal's Benfica beat Barcelona and Real in successive finals. In 1963, two goals from AC Milan's José Altafini at Wembley,

*Below: The European Cup is the biggest prize in European football.*

*Above: Real Madrid's Paco Gento with the European Cup trophy in 1966.*

against Benfica, took the trophy to Italy for the first time.

It stayed in Italy when Helenio Herrera's defensive Inter Milan took two titles, and then Real Madrid recaptured the trophy in 1966. An exuberant Celtic became the first British side to win the tournament after their stirring defeat of Inter Milan in 1967. The trophy remained in Britain the following season when a three-goal burst, in ten minutes during extra time, gave Manchester United victory over Eusebio's Benfica.

AC Milan triumphed over an inexperienced Ajax in the 1969 final, while Feyenoord foiled Celtic's second final attempt the following year. For the next three years, Johan Cruyff's "total footballers" of Ajax reigned supreme until Franz Beckenbauer's Bayern Munich, with marksman Gerd Müller, assumed another three-year monopoly of the trophy.

It was now England's turn to assert their footballing authority over the

### European Cup Scorers With Over Ten Goals In A Season

1957–58 Alfredo Di Stefano (Real Madrid) 10
1958–59 Just Fontaine (Reims) 10
1959–60 Ferenc Puskas (Real Madrid) 12
1960–61 José Aguas (Benfica) 11
1962–63 José Altafini (AC Milan) 14
1970–71 Antonis Antoniadis (Panathinaikos) 10
1972–73 Gerd Müller (Bayern Munich) 12

continent and, for the next six years, the European Cup remained in English hands. Liverpool's memorable 3–2 defeat of Borussia Mönchengladbach in Rome in 1977 and their less entertaining 1–0 win over Bruges the next year, were followed by two successive victories by Brian Clough's unfashionable Nottingham Forest. Liverpool beat Real Madrid in 1981, and Aston Villa needed only one goal to defeat Bayern Munich in 1982.

Hamburg won the following year and Liverpool picked up their fourth

*Above: Manchester United lift the trophy after beating Benfica in 1968.*

victory, on penalties, against Roma in 1984. Juventus finally won in 1985, against the horrific backdrop of the Heysel disaster when 39 Italian spectators were killed at the final against Liverpool. English clubs were consequently banned from Europe for

six years. Steaua Bucharest surprised Europe the following year by beating star-studded Barcelona, and Porto outclassed Bayern Munich in 1987. A tedious victory for PSV Eindhoven over Benfica followed in 1988.

Silvio Berlusconi's millions had brought Ruud Gullit and Marco Van Basten to AC Milan, and the Dutchmen inspired an exhilarating 4–0 final win against Steaua Bucharest in 1989. Milan won again in 1990, Frank Rijkaard

scoring the only goal against Benfica. Another boring final took place in 1991, with Red Star Belgrade playing for penalties and winning, while the next year, Barcelona at last won the European Cup with a Ronald Koeman superstrike against Sampdoria. Scandal followed in 1993, with Marseille being stripped of their title due to allegations of matchfixing, after a Basile Boli header gave the French club victory over AC Milan.

The Champions League replaced the traditional knock-out competition in 1992–93, and the big European clubs were now assured lucrative financial gains from the tournament. AC Milan destroyed Johan Cruyff's Barcelona in 1994, with two goals from Daniele Massaro, but the Italians were beaten the following year by a late goal from

*Below: Predrag Mijatovic scores the winning goal for Real Madrid against Juventus in the 1997–98 final.*

Ajax's young forward, Patrick Kluivert. Juventus collected their second European Cup in 1996, beating Ajax on penalties, and two first-half goals from Karlheinz Riedle helped unfancied Borussia Dortmund collect their first European Cup in 1997.

An opportunist goal from Yugoslav Predrag Mijatovic gave Real Madrid their seventh Cup win in 1998, and two sensational injury-time goals from Manchester United defeated a disbelieving Bayern Munich in the 1999 final. The all-Spanish clash between Real Madrid and Valéncia in Paris in 2000 saw a superb performance from Real as they won 3–0 to pick up their eighth European Cup.

Valencia were losers again in 2001 to Bayern Munich on a penalty shoot-out. In their centenary year Real Madrid won for a ninth time when they beat Bayer Leverkusen 2–1 in Glasgow. They had won nearly a fifth of all the European Cups, an astonishing record. But in 2003 they only got as far as the semi-final, where they lost to Juventus and paved the way for an all-Italian final between Juve and AC Milan at Old Trafford. After a goalless match,

it went to a penalty shoot-out, and Milan took their sixth European Cup title. Porto took the cup back to Portugal after 17 years in 2004.

The romance and unpredictability is still evident in the competiton, as demonstrated by Liverpool's thrilling comeback and subsequent victory on penalties over AC Milan in the 2005 Final. Arsenal lost to Barcelona 2–1 in 2006, while Milan defeated Liverpool in 2007. Manchester United squeezed past Chelsea on penalties in 2008 to pick up their third trophy.

## European Cup Winners Cup

The Cup Winners Cup was initiated in 1960–61 as a knock-out competition between national Cup winners.

The first final saw Fiorentina beat Rangers 4–1 (agg). Tottenham became the first English club to win a European trophy when they beat Atlético Madrid 5–1 in 1963, and West Ham clinched the trophy two years later with a 2–0 win over Munich 1860.

*Below: John Wark scores for Ipswich Town in their UEFA Cup first-leg semi-final against Cologne, in 1981.*

British clubs were at the fore again from 1970–72 when Manchester City, Chelsea and Rangers won the trophy.

In the mid-1970s, Anderlecht made three successive appearances in the final, winning twice, and in 1983 Aberdeen overcame Real Madrid 2–1. In 1986, Kiev Dynamo won their second title in 11 years; the great Oleg Blokhin scored in both finals.

In 1991, when the ban on English clubs following the Heysel disaster was lifted, Manchester United defeated three-time winners Barcelona, Mark Hughes scoring both goals in United's 2–1 win. Parma won their first European trophy in 1993 with a 3–1 win over Antwerp, but lost it the following year, 1–0 to Arsenal. A 50-yard lob from Nayim gave Zaragoza victory over Arsenal in 1995, and Barcelona took their fourth victory in 1997, a Ronaldo penalty helping Barça to beat Paris Saint-Germain.

*Above: Chelsea's Gianfranco Zola celebrates his winner against Stuttgart in the Cup Winners Cup Final of 1998.*

Chelsea picked up another title in 1998, with a brilliant goal from Gianfranco Zola, and Lazio defeated Real Mallorca in 1999 at Villa Park to become the last holders of the European Cup Winners Cup. In 1998, UEFA had decided to end the tournament to allow the teams to concentrate on the expanded Champions League.

## Fairs Cup and UEFA Cup

Established in 1955, the UEFA Cup was originally the International Inter-Cities Fairs Cup, and was played between European cities hosting trade fairs. Twelve cities joined the first tournament which was played over three years so as not to disrupt domestic league games. In the first final, held over two legs, a London XI were beaten 6–0 by Barcelona, after drawing 2–2 at home.

Barcelona retained the trophy in 1960, followed by Roma, Valéncia (twice), Zaragoza and Ferencvaros of Hungary, the first Eastern European side to win. English clubs dominated from 1968–73, with Leeds United being the first English club to triumph, their winning goal coming from Mick Jones at their home ground, Elland Road.

The competition changed its name to the UEFA Cup in 1972. The 1972 winners Tottenham Hotspur were defeated 4–2 by Feyenoord in 1974, which provoked serious rioting in the Dutch city. Liverpool won for a second time two years later, and in 1981, the trophy returned to England, when Ipswich Town beat AZ 67 Alkmaar. Tottenham won again in 1984, in the first final to be settled on penalties, while Real Madrid won two years running, in 1985 and 1986. The next season, Dundee United failed to become the first Scottish club to win the Cup, losing 2–1 on aggregate in the final against Sweden's IFK Gothenburg.

Since 1989, Italian clubs have won

*Below: Ronaldo marks his arrival at Inter Milan, helping his new club to a UEFA Cup victory in 1998.*

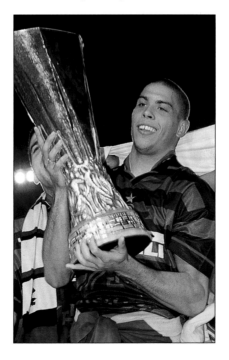

the trophy eight out of 16 times, four of the finals have been all-Italian matches and an Italian team has twice more reached the final, only to lose to foreign opposition. Diego Maradona's Napoli beat Stuttgart 5–4 in 1989, and both Juventus and Inter Milan won more than once in the 1990s; Juventus in 1990 and 1993, and Inter in 1991, 1994 and 1998. Ajax, Bayern Munich and Schalke were the only non-Italian teams to win in that decade, and Jürgen Klinsmann scored a record 15 goals in the 1996 tournament, when Bayern Munich beat Bordeaux 3–2 in the final.

In 1998, UEFA made all finals single-leg matches. In England, winners of the FA Cup and League Cup, and the fourth-placed Premiership club would qualify for the tournament, and the third-placed Premiership club could enter if it failed to qualify for the Champions League. Other countries' representatives are determined by their placings on the UEFA rankings.

## InterToto Cup

This much disparaged summer competition was launched in Europe for the benefit of pools companies and bookmakers, to provide football business in the summer months. It dates back to the 1960s but was reformulated in 1995. As an incentive to attract the bigger clubs, all four semi-finalists are granted entry to that season's UEFA Cup. In 1996, Bordeaux qualified by this method and reached the final of the UEFA Cup, only to be beaten by Bayern Munich. The tournament was finally abolished in 2009.

## Copa Libertadores

The South American Club Cup is the continent's key club football event, and in spite of its turbulent past, or perhaps because of it, it can rival the *Copa America* in terms of popularity.

An early continental champions cup had been held in South America in 1948, organized by the Chilean club Colo Colo. Brazil's Vasco da Gama won the title that year, but the event made huge financial losses and the idea was dropped as unworkable, though its European equivalent, the European Cup, became a massive success. Then, in 1958, UEFA proposed a world club title to be contested between the club champions of Europe and South America. The World Club Cup was an attractive option to CONMEBOL – not only would it help to unify the nations of the continent, it would also bring in valuable financial gains. In order to accept UEFA's proposal, CONMEBOL decided to relaunch the South American champions cup, and the first *Copa Libertadores* was staged in 1960.

League football had always been more popular than cup events in South America and at first the new

*Below: Players from Cruzeiro of Brazil and Boca Juniors of Argentina tangle in the* Copa Libertadores *final of 1997.*

*Copa* received little attention. Seven nations took part, with matches being played on a home and away knock-out basis. The final was also played over two legs, as it is today, with winners decided by the number of games won rather than goal difference; Uruguay's Penarol beat Paraguay's Olimpia and became the first champions.

The *Copa Libertadores* has seen high drama, excitement, passion and rivalry over the years, but it is now regarded as a repectable competition involving all of the continent's biggest clubs. In 1998 Mexico were invited to take part, and the event looks set to grow bigger still if more countries from Central and North America are allowed to join.

## African Champions Cup

The African Champions Cup was first staged in 1964 in response to a growing appetite in Africa for football tournaments that could provide entertainment to equal the highly successful African Nations Cup. Club football has long enjoyed strong support in Africa, with financial back-up traditionally coming from local business. The arrival of the Champions Cup brought in resources from television and sponsorship deals, which now provide the lion's share of financial support and will do much to further the development of African club football in the future.

The Champions Cup operates in a similar way to its European equivalent, the Champions League, and features the champions of each nation plus the defending champions. Games are played on a home and away knock-out basis, and the event is held every year, with the early rounds kicking off in February and March and the finals in late November and early December. The same pattern is used for the African Cup Winners Cup, which was launched in 1975, and for the CAF Cup, which is named after the African confederation and was started in 1992.

## CONCACAF Champions Cup

Football is hugely popular in parts of Central America, such as Mexico, but it faces stiff competition in the Caribbean, where cricket and basketball are the major sports, and in North America, where "soccer" is the poor relation to baseball and basketball. With such an imbalance of interest, development of international football within the region has been erratic.

CONCACAF was formed in 1961, on the instruction of FIFA, to replace the various authorities that had failed to bring a coherent strategy to football in the region. The CONCACAF Champions Cup was launched a year later, following as its model the European Cup and South America's *Copa Libertadores*.

Several difficulties have created problems for the competition over the years. The timing of the football season varies in parts of the region because of climatic differences. Many countries have trouble financing a squad, and long distances between countries makes for high travel costs. Clubs from Mexico have dominated the contest to date but, ultimately, winning has not carried the honours associated with its European or South American equivalents.

The champions and runners-up from each of the CONCACAF countries are eligible for entry. Only eight clubs took part in the first event in 1962, but the profile of the tournament, and of football in general, is rising steadily, and by the mid-1990s the number of participants had increased to 32. In 1992 CONCACAF went one step further with the launch of a Cup Winners Cup. In 2008 the competition was abolished and converted into a Champions League.

## World Club Cup

The Club World Championship launched by FIFA in 2000 is designed for club champions from Africa,

*Above: Boca Juniors celebrate their first goal in the World Club Cup, 2000.*

Asia, Central and North America and Oceania, as well as those from Europe and South America. It is essentially the World Cup of club football, and its progress will be monitored with interest as the emerging footballing nations strengthen their position on the world scene. In the meantime, the older World Club Cup offers the major challenge match for the "world" title, even though it is contested between the champions of just two continents. It is also known as the Intercontinental Cup or the Europe/South America Cup.

The idea for a competition between the club champions of Europe and South America came from UEFA general secretary Henri Delauney in the 1950s. Delauney was keen to see a head-to-head between the world's leading football continents, and he made the suggestion to CONMEBOL before a South American club championship existed. CONMEBOL agreed to the idea and the launch of the *South American Club Cup* in 1960 was followed the same year by the first World Club Cup, between Real Madrid, now five times Champions of

Europe, and Penarol, the first winners of the *Copa Libertadores*. After a 0–0 draw in Uruguay, two goals from Ferenc Puskas, and one each from Alfredo Di Stefano, Helenio Herrera and Paco Gento gave Real a 5–1 win to become club champions of the world.

The Cup is an annual event, which was originally played on a home and away basis; until 1968 winners were decided by points rather than on aggregate. For the first few years things went well but in the late 1960s the problems started.

There were violent clashes between players on the pitch, with injuries deliberately inflicted and missiles hurled from the crowd. In 1971, Ajax refused to play against Nacional of Uruguay and before long other European clubs were boycotting the event, so that the beaten European Cup finalists had to take their place in the competition. The World Club Cup was in danger of being suspended, but in 1980 Japan, keen to develop its own football through links at the top level of the game, came to the rescue. The car manufacturer Toyota became the new sponsor, the venue was moved to Tokyo, and the format was changed to a single-leg tie.

# The Women's Game

Football has been growing steadily in popularity with women around the world since the mid-1970s and it is now an established sport, regulated by FIFA in the same way as the men's game. Regular international matches are held, and a women's World Championship was launched in 1991.

Women's professional leagues have now been formed in several countries, mostly in Europe. The Woman's United Soccer Association was set up in the USA in the early 2000s but was not successful, and it was relaunched in 2009 as Women's Professional Soccer.

In fact, the United States has shown a tremendous enthusiasm for the women's game, and their commitment has been wholeheartedly supported by FIFA, who started the women's World Championship with the aim of promoting a widespread interest for football in the run-up to the men's World Cup of 1994. Amateur leagues have existed in the United States for some time; the system has been well organized and there is much competition for the top slot in the league. Most major cities have their own women's teams. Colleges and universities are also key breeding grounds for players, and they operate their own leagues and competitions through the National Collegiate Athletic Association (NCAA). Canada runs its own collegiate programme along similar lines.

The rules of women's football are the same as for the men, and the games are played over 90 minutes. Matches are officiated by female referees, and women referees have become accepted in areas of the men's game. In 1997, Canadian referee Sonia Denoncourt was invited to officiate at a professional

*Above: Brazilian striker Marta won the Golden Boot at the 2007 World Cup.*

*Below: Australia playing Sweden at the Sydney Olympic Games 2000.*

men's league match in Brazil – a further sign of the growing respect for the women's game.

Women's football became an Olympic event at the 1996 Games in Atlanta, with eight countries submitting teams for the first event. Qualification for Olympic football is reserved for the host nation, which is guaranteed a place in the competition, and the top seven teams from the women's World Cup, which is always held the previous year.

*Right: Norway's Olympic Champions of 2000 line up with their gold medals after beating China in the final.*

## Great Women Players

**Michelle Akers** was a powerful striker for the United States, and shares the record of ten goals in a World Cup with Germany's Heidi Mohr. Akers suffers from chronic fatigue syndrome, but she is a tireless worker and has a sharp organizational brain. She retired from the international team in 2000.

**Mercy Akide** is widely hailed as the top female goalscorer in Africa. The Nigerian striker has helped her country to success at the 1999 World Cup and the 2000 Olympic Games. Although she was dropped from the national team after the 2004 World Cup, she is a national hero, and is currently coaching football in the United States.

**Mia Hamm** is the youngest player to have played for the United States, at the age of 15. She was a skilful, tricky forward who could change the course of a game in a flash of inspiration. She is the United States' second most-capped

player, and is the top scorer in women's football with 158 goals. She retired in 2004.

**Kristine Lilly** is a small, left-sided forward, and the United States' most-capped player (340). She was just 16 when she began her international career. She played in the World Cup of 1991, and helped the United States to its first gold medal in the 1996 Olympics.

**Marta (Marta Vieira da Silva)** is a young striker, currently regarded as the world's finest female footballer, or 'Pele in skirts' as she is known in Brazil. She plays for Sweden's Umea IK. At the 2007 Women's World Cup she was not only voted best player but she also won the Golden Boot, although her country Brazil was beaten 2–0 in the final.

**Sissi** (Sisleide do Amor Lima) has played for ten different clubs in her 21-year football career. At the 1999 World Cup Sissi scored a hat-trick in Brazil's opening game against Mexico, and by the end

of the tournament she had won the Silver Ball for her performance; she was joint second-highest scorer with China's Sun Wen. She is now retired from the game.

**Pia Sundhage** is one of the most-capped players in women's soccer, having made 146 appearances for her country. The Swedish international gained her first cap in 1975, in a 0–0 tie against Finland, and she played her last game at the 1996 Olympic Games. Pia is Sweden's highest female goalscorer, with 71 international goals. She managed the US team in the 2008 Olympics.

**Sun Wen**, of China, scored the same number of goals (7) as Sissi of Brazil at the 1999 World Cup, and was awarded the Golden Ball for her all-round performance in the tournament. She played her club football in Shanghai and was a regular first-team choice for China's national team until her retirement in 2006.

# Women's World Cup

In front of over 90,000 spectators at the Pasadena Rose Bowl, and with over 40 million more watching live on television, the 1999 Women's World Cup Final, officially called the Women's World Championship Final, was conclusive proof that the women's game had arrived in North America.

## China, 1991

Twelve teams qualified for the group stage in 1991, divided into three groups of four. In Group A China, surprisingly, beat a strong Norwegian side, but Norway went through to beat Italy in the quarter-finals, and two goals from Linda Medalen ensured a 4–1 semi-final win against Sweden.

The United States reached the final with a 5–3 win over Germany. In the final in the Tianhe Stadium in Guangzhou, extra time seemed imminent at 1–1, when star forward Kathy Akers dribbled past the Norwegian goalkeeper and scored. The United States had won the first-ever Women's World Cup, with Akers top scorer with ten goals.

## Sweden, 1995

The 1995 tournament was dominated by Norway. They qualified from their group scoring 17 goals and conceding none,

*Above: Norway's veteran player Linda Medalen playing against China in 1999.*

and eliminated their neighbours Denmark 3–1 in the quarter-finals. Their opponents in the semi-final were the holders, the United States. Norway won 1–0. Germany beat China 1–0 in the other semi-final. A crowd of 17,000 watched a resilient performance from

*Below: The United States' Mia Hamm enjoys a moment with the trophy after her side win the World Cup of 1999.*

Norway in the final; goals from Hege Riise and Bettina Wiegamann gave them a 2–0 win over Germany to take the Women's World Cup.

## United States, 1999

The United States were the hosts for the 1999 tournament, which generated a huge amount of interest in the country. The four semi-finalists to emerge were China, Norway, Brazil and the United States. The much-improved "Samba Queens" of Brazil were knocked out by China, who thus made their debut in a World Cup Final – men's or women's.

The United States had powered through the group stage of the tournament, scoring 16 goals and conceding only three. They knocked out the holders Norway in the semi-final, and were now favourites to win the title. However, China were a fast, attacking side, with Sun Wen prominent in attack and the finest goalkeeper in women's football, Gao Hong.

The game was still goalless after 90 minutes and moved into extra time, with the Chinese on the attack. They came dangerously close to scoring three times, but the Americans held out for the penalty shoot-out. The US goalkeeper Briana Scurry saved China's third penalty attempt, while the first four American attempts found the target. Defender Brandi Chastain stepped up for the fifth, and sent her shot past Gao Hong. Chastain ripped off her shirt in celebration at the United States' second women's World Cup triumph.

## United States, 2003

The fourth Women's World Cup was switched from China to the United States because of the SARS virus, which broke out in China in the spring of 2003. The USA finished top of Group A, with Sweden second. In Group B, Brazil topped the group with Norway second. Germany won all their games in Group C, with Canada second. China won

Group D from Russia. Germany continued to score heavily in the quarter-finals, and met Sweden in the final. Sweden opened the scoring through Hanna Ljungberg and led 1–0 at half time, but Maren Weinert's equalizer took the match to extra time. After eight minutes, reserve Nia Keunzer headed in a "golden goal" for Germany.

## China, 2007

The tournament was automatically awarded to China, and it began in dramatic fashion with Germany trouncing Argentina 11–0, the biggest ever defeat in the history of the competition. Germany progressed to the final, having not conceded a goal, and they maintained this clean sheet by beating Brazil 2–0, becoming the first country in the women's World Cup to have won two consecutive finals. The tournament marked the emergence of Brazil's young striker Marta Vieira da Silva who picked up the awards for best player and also the Golden Boot.

*Above: A ticker-tape reception for the United States as they celebrate their win against China in 1999.*

*Below: Germany line up for a photograph prior to their opening defeat of Argentina in 2007.*

# Great Football Managers

For all a teams' dependence on the skills of its players, it is the manager or coach who directs the game, formulating the tactics that will inspire his men to perform at their best.

### Matt Busby (1909–1994)

Busby became Manchester United's manager just after World War Two. The Scots-born, ex-sergeant-major made good use of scarce resources available to him to win the FA Cup in 1948. His second fine team, the "Busby Babes", which centred around the commanding figure of Duncan Edwards, won two league titles in 1956 and 1957, but was virtually wiped out in the Munich Air Crash in 1958. Within a decade, however, Busby was back. His new side, starring Denis Law, Bobby Charlton and George Best, won two league titles, in 1965 and 1967, and in 1968, became the first English team to win the European Cup. Busby was honoured with a knighthood. Although he resigned in 1969, he remained a powerful force at the club, and by the time of his death in 1994, he was the club president.

*Above: Brian Clough took Notts Forest to two European Cup Finals.*

### Brian Clough (1935–2004)

"Cloughie", as he was known, was an eccentric, outspoken and extremely successful manager. As a player, he had been a prolific goalscorer for Middlesbrough and Sunderland, and he joined Hartlepool as manager in 1965. With his partner, Peter Taylor, he led Derby County to the league title in 1972

*Above: Sven-Göran Eriksson left Lazio to coach England's national team in 2001.*

and, after a brief stay at Brighton and a 44-day spell as manager at Leeds United, he joined Nottingham Forest in 1975. With Forest, his tactical grasp and powers of motivation took the club to two European Cup triumphs. In 1979 they beat Malmo, and in 1980 Hamburg, both by 1–0. Clough remained at Forest throughout the 1980s, winning the League Cup in 1989 and 1990. He retired from football in 1993.

### Sven-Göran Eriksson (b. 1948)

Eriksson made the headlines in 1982 when he inspired the small, provincial club IFK Gothenburg to victory in the UEFA Cup, making them the first Swedish club to win a trophy in Europe; Gothenburg also achieved the Swedish League and Cup double that year. Moving on to Benfica, Eriksson led the club to three Portuguese title wins, and they were the runners-up to AC Milan in the Champions Cup in 1990. In Italy, Eriksson coached Roma, Fiorentina and Sampdoria before moving to Lazio in 1997. In 1998, Lazio took the Italian Cup and were

*Left: Matt Busby (left) with Manchester United coach Jimmy Murphy.*

*Above: Ferguson led Manchester United to their third European Cup in 2008.*

runners-up in the UEFA Cup. He was appointed England manager in 2001. He took a mediocre England side to the World Cup finals and a quarter-final place, where they lost to eventual winners, Brazil. He left in 2006 and took over Manchester City for a brief term in 2007, followed by an unsuccessful stint as the Mexico national coach.

## Alex Ferguson (b. 1941)

Ferguson began his career as a centre-forward with Rangers, moving into a managerial role with East Stirling, St Mirren and, in 1978, Aberdeen. He brought the club three Scottish league titles, four Scottish Cups and the League Cup, as well as the Cup Winners' Cup, beating Real Madrid 2–1. He moved to Manchester United in 1986 and after a few barren years of preparation and development, his young team kicked into gear. With players of the quality of Eric Cantona, Ryan Giggs and David Beckham, and with Peter Schmeichel in goal, United were the English team of the 1990s. By the end of the 2001–02 season, "Fergie's Fledglings" had won seven English league titles, four FA Cups, the Cup Winners' Cup and, after a dramatic night in Barcelona in 1999, the European Cup, when they beat Bayern Munich with two injury-time goals. They won the European Cup again in 2008. Ferguson was knighted in 1999.

## Helenio Herrera (1917–1997)

Herrera began his managerial career in France before moving to Spain, where he coached Atlético Madrid, Valladolid and Sevilla. Argentinian by birth, Herrera was a disciplinarian who demanded total loyalty. He took over at Barcelona in the mid-1950s and developed a side featuring the Hungarian forwards Kocsis, Kubala and Czibor. He then moved to Inter Milan, where he developed the defensive *catenaccio* system, which won the club the European Cup in 1964 and 1965, and the Italian league three times. After Inter's 1967 European Cup Final defeat by Celtic, Herrera took over at Roma, where he won the Italian Cup in 1970. He led Spain to the 1962 World Cup finals, but they finished bottom of their first round group.

*Below: Rinus Michels, inventor of "total football" in the 1970s.*

## Marinus "Rinus" Michels (1928–2005)

The authoritarian Michels was the man responsible for "total football" and the magnificent Ajax and Holland teams of the 1970s. In his playing career Michels had been a Dutch international centre-forward in the 1950s, and he became coach at Ajax after retiring from the game in 1965. Michel's young team, featuring his discovery Johan Cruyff, won the Dutch league four times and the Dutch Cup three times between 1966 and 1971. He was tempted away to Barcelona, after Ajax's 1971 European Cup victory over Panathinaikos. He followed this with a spell as coach of the Dutch national team, leading them to the 1974 World Cup Final, which they lost 2–1 to West Germany. Michels was also in charge of Holland when they won the 1988 European Championship Final, beating the Soviet Union 2–0.

## Bob Paisley (1919–1996)

Paisley was a quiet, self-effacing man who, nonetheless, won more trophies than any other manager in the history of the English game. He joined Liverpool as a player in 1939 and retired in 1954 to

*Below: Bob Paisley proved a worthy replacement for Bill Shankly at Anfield.*

take over as club physiotherapist. He left the Anfield "boot room" in 1974, to take over from Bill Shankly, and he had managed Liverpool to six league titles, three League Cups and the UEFA Cup by the time he retired in 1983. His purchase of Kenny Dalglish, Graeme Souness and Alan Hansen provided the backbone of the all-conquering side, which also won three European Cup Finals under his stewardship. Paisley was elected to the Liverpool board in 1985. He died at age 77 in 1996.

### Alf Ramsey (1920–1999)

The dour and taciturn Ramsey is the only English manager to have lifted the World Cup. After a career as a full-back for Tottenham in the 1950s, he joined Third Division Ipswich Town as manager in 1955. Ipswich won the Second Division in 1961, and the following year they took the First Division title. Ramsey became England's manager in 1963 and the national team, playing a 4–4–2 formation, won the World Cup in 1966. Ramsey was knighted in 1967. He took England to the 1970 World Cup finals, where they were eliminated 3–2 by West Germany and, after England's

*Below: Alf Ramsey took his England side to World Cup success in 1966.*

*Above: Helmut Schön helped Germany to their first World Cup victory in 1974.*

elimination in the 1972 European Championships, his position became tenuous. After failing to qualify for the 1974 World Cup finals, Ramsey was sacked in 1975. He died in 1999 and every football ground in England held a one-minute silence in his honour.

### Helmut Schön (1915–1996)

German international inside-forward Schön began his managerial career as assistant to the West German national coach, Sepp Herberger, in 1955, and he succeeded him to the job in 1963. Schön took West Germany to the 1966 World Cup finals, losing 4–2 to England in the final, and he helped them achieve third place in the 1970 tournament. He finally claimed World Cup victory for his country in 1974, with a battling 2–1 win over Cruyff's Holland. Helped by the glittering skills of Günter Netzer, Schön's West Germany won the European Championship in 1972, by beating the USSR 3–0, but they were beaten themselves in the 1976 competition, on penalties, by Czechoslovakia.

*Above: Bill Shankly directed the rise of Liverpool with a canny eye for success.*

### Bill Shankly (1913–1981)

A blunt and often abrasive character, Scotsman Shankly was the mastermind behind Liverpool's re-emergence in the 1960s when, fielding such players as Ian St John and Ron Yeats, the club won the league in 1964 and 1966, and the FA Cup in 1965. His motivational powers and shrewd dealing in the transfer market brought in Steve Heighway, John Toshack and Kevin Keegan, and he led Liverpool to another league title in 1973. They took the UEFA Cup the same year, when they beat Borussia Mönchengladbach 3–2 in the final. To general surprise, Shankly resigned in 1974, immediately after Liverpool had won the FA Cup. He died in 1981, and the Shankly Gates at the Anfield stadium were erected in his memory.

### Jock Stein (1922–1985)

A single-minded and tactically astute manager, Stein started his coaching career with Dunfermline and Hibernian in the early 1960s, and in 1965 he moved to his old club Celtic, for whom he had been centre-half. Under his direction, Celtic became one of the top European teams, winning the European Cup against Inter Milan in 1967, the first British club to do so. Stein took the club to the final again in 1970, but they were beaten 2–1 by Feyenoord. In his time at Celtic he led them to ten Scottish League Championships, nine Scottish Cups and six Scottish League Cups. After a brief spell at Leeds United, he was back in Scotland, managing the national team, which he did for 61 games. Stein died from a heart attack immediately after the Scotland v Wales World Cup tie, when Scotland earned a place at the 1986 World Cup finals in Mexico.

### Giovanni Trapattoni (b. 1939)

Trapattoni was a midfielder in the AC Milan team that won the European Cup in 1963 and 1969. He joined Juventus as coach in 1976, and went on to produce the most successful Italian team of the next decade, winning six *Serie A* titles, two Italian Cups, the UEFA Cup and the Cup Winners Cup. Trapattoni's purchases, such as Michel Platini, Paolo Rossi and Zbigniew Boniek, helped the club to win their first European Cup, in 1985, against Liverpool at the Heysel Stadium in Belgium. He moved to Inter, Bayern Munich and Cagliari. He returned to Bayern in 1996, winning the *Bundesliga* title in his first season, the first foreign manager ever to do so. Trapattoni took over as Italian national manager in 2001, but the team failed in the 2002 World Cup. He resigned after another poor display at Euro 2004. He then moved to Benfica, Stuttgart and Salzburg, and was appointed Republic of Ireland manager in 2008.

### Arsène Wenger (b. 1949)

Frenchman Wenger began his career as a player for Strasbourg, and he became youth coach there in 1981. He moved on to Cannes and Nancy before winning the French title in 1988 with Monaco. He moved to Japan in 1995 and transformed

*Above: Mario Zagalo was national coach to Brazil for the 1970 World Cup.*

Grampus 8 from a relegation side to J-League runners-up, and in 1996 he moved to Highbury to take control of Arsenal. In less than two years Wenger had made history as the first non-British manager to lead his side to a championship win. He followed it

by leading Arsenal to two League and FA Cup doubles, in 1997–98 and 2001–02, another FA Cup win in 2003, and a wonderful League Championship in 2003–4, when Arsenal were unbeaten all season. He won the 2005 FA Cup but narrowly lost out to Barcelona in the 2006 European Cup final.

### Mario Zagalo (b. 1931)

Left-winger Zagalo won two World Cup medals with Brazil in 1958 and 1962, and became manager of Botafogo in 1967. Arriving with only three months to prepare the national team, he guided varying Brazil sides in the 1970 and 1974 World Cup, beating Italy 4–1 in the final in 1970. Zagalo took up a coaching position in the Middle East, but he returned to Brazil to partner Carlos Alberto as coach for the 1994 World Cup which won the competition in a final penalty shoot-out against Italy in Pasadena. Zagalo led Brazil to the World Cup finals once again in 1998 but, after a polished performance throughout the tournament, the Brazilians lost to France in the final.

*Below: Arsène Wenger celebrates his team's unbeaten league run in 2003–04.*

# A–Z GREAT PLAYERS

This chapter looks at the club and international careers of the world's greatest players, past and present. From Florian Albert to Cristiano Ronaldo, the roll call is a glittering one and, although one can argue about the criteria for inclusion (argument and disagreement are at the heart of football discussions), there is little doubt that these players deserve a place in the top echelon of footballing history. Transfer dates, number of caps and international goals have been given where possible.

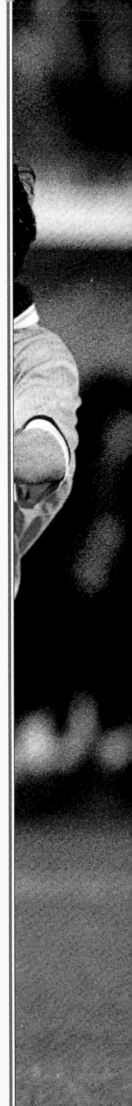

## Florian Albert
## (Hungary, b. 1941)

**Clubs:** *Ferencvaros (1956–74)*
**Caps:** *75 (27 goals)*

A naturally gifted and elegant centre-forward, Albert's ability was noticed by the youth coaches at Ferencvaros soon after his family's move to Budapest from the country, while Albert was still a young boy. He made his debut for Ferencvaros at the age of 16 and gained his first cap for Hungary, in 1958, in a 3–2 defeat of Sweden. His pace, dribbling ability and scoring prowess, with either foot, quickly established

*Left: The naturally talented goal scorer, Florian Albert, in action for Hungary in the 1960s.*

him as a Hungarian footballing hero with club and country. In his long career with Ferencvaros he won four league winner's medals, and he was three times Hungary's top goal scorer. He played in the 1962 World Cup finals, where he scored against England, and he claimed a hat trick in Hungary's 6–1 rout of Bulgaria, although Hungary were eliminated in the quarter-finals. In the 1966 World Cup finals, Albert produced an electrifying individual display when Hungary beat the mighty Brazil 3–1, though again they could not get beyond the quarter-finals. He decided to retire from international football in 1971, having been voted European Footballer of the Year in 1967. The Ferencvaros stadium was renamed Albert Florian stadium in his honour in 2007.

## José Altafini
## (Brazil, b. 1938)

**Clubs:** *Palmeiras (1956–58), AC Milan (1958–65), Napoli (1965–72), Juventus (1972–76), Chiasso (1976)*
**Caps:** *8 (4 goals) Brazil; 6 (5) Italy*

Altafini was a strong, opportunistic centre-forward, who first made his mark as a 19 year old in the 1958 World Cup finals. Known in Brazil as "Mazzola" for his resemblance to Valentino, the captain of Torino killed in the 1949 Superga air crash, he was bought by AC Milan. He then readopted his birth name and played for Italy in the 1962 World Cup finals, becoming one of only four players to have represented two countries in the tournament. He was a prolific scorer for AC Milan and was the top scorer in the 1963 European Cup with 14 goals, scoring two in the final against Benfica at Wembley. He moved on to Napoli shortly after, and then to Juventus, for whom he played at the age of 35 in the 1973 European Cup Final, which the Italian club lost 1–0 to Ajax. Altafini finished his career with Swiss league club Chiasso.

*Above: Two-time European Cup finalist José Altafini playing for his adopted country, Italy, where he played most of his club football.*

## Osvaldo Ardiles
## (Argentina, b. 1952)

**Clubs:** *Instituto de Cordoba (1969–74), Huracan (1974–78), Tottenham Hotspur (1978–82), Paris Saint-Germain (1982–83), Tottenham Hotspur (1983–88), Blackburn Rovers (1988), Queens Park Rangers (1988–89)*
**Caps:** *53 (8 goals)*

Ardiles, Argentina's star midfield player in the country's successful 1978 World Cup, stunned British football when, with fellow Argentinian Ricky Villa, he joined Spurs in the summer of that year. His sparkling ability, unselfish play and modest self-deprecation made "Ossie" a great crowd favourite at White Hart Lane, and he helped Spurs lift the 1981

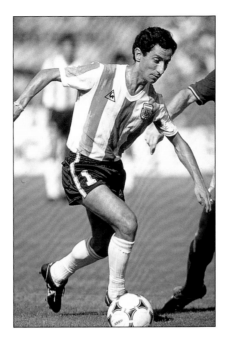

*Above: Ossie Ardiles, playing for his country in the 1978 World Cup Finals.*

FA Cup in a 3–2 replay win over Manchester City. He missed the final the following year due to the Falklands War, and went on loan to Paris Saint-Germain before rejoining Spurs in 1983, having played in the 1982 World Cup finals. He was part of Spurs' victorious 1984 UEFA Cup run when they beat Anderlecht on penalties, and left in 1988 to join Queens Park Rangers. He became manager of Swindon in 1989 and then took over at Newcastle United in 1991, but was sacked the following year. A spell at West Bromwich Albion followed before he rejoined Spurs in June 1993, but his defensive failings lost him the job 16 months later. He then coached Croatia Zagreb and Yokohama F. Marinos until 2001 when he returned to Argentina to coach Racing Club. He is currently coach of Paraguay's Cerro Porteno.

## Roberto Baggio
## (Italy, b. 1967)

**Clubs:** *Vicenza (1982–85), Fiorentina (1985–90), Juventus (1990–95), AC Milan (1995–97), Bologna (1997–98), Inter Milan (1998–2000), Brescia (2000–04)*
**Caps:** *55 (27 goals)*

Baggio, the "Divine Ponytail", is a forward of the highest class and was, at one time, the finest player in the world. Slight, skilful and a natural scorer, he became a star with Fiorentina and set a new world transfer record with his £8 million move to Juventus in 1990. His goals helped the Turin club to the *Serie A* title in 1995 and the UEFA Cup in 1993, the year he was voted World and European Footballer of the Year. He had a brilliant World Cup in 1990 and, with Brazil's Romario, was player of the tournament in the 1994 World Cup. His miss in the penalty shoot-out in the final gave the Brazilians the trophy. The arrival of Alessandro Del Piero hastened Baggio's departure to AC Milan in 1995, and his transfer to Bologna in 1997 was followed by a move to Inter Milan in 1998, and then to Brescia in 2000. He retired in 2004.

*Above: Italian forward Roberto Baggio, "little prince" of the Azzurri and World Footballer of the Year in 1993.*

## Gordon Banks
## (England, b. 1937)

**Clubs:** *Chesterfield (1955–59), Leicester City (1959–67), Stoke City (1967–75), Fort Lauderdale Strikers (1977–78)*
**Caps:** *73*

England's greatest-ever goalkeeper, Gordon Banks was a tall, dependable, agile stopper. He joined Leicester in 1959 and played on the losing side in the 1961 and 1963 FA Cup Finals, winning the League Cup in 1964, an achievement he repeated with Stoke City in 1972. He was in goal for England in their 1966 triumph in the World Cup Final, having made his international debut in 1963. Banks represented his country again in the 1970 World Cup in Mexico and is best remembered for his marvellous save from a disbelieving Pelé against Brazil, still called "the save of the century". He was awarded an OBE in 1970. Affectionately known as "Banks of England", he was voted Footballer of the Year in 1973. A car crash that year meant he lost the sight in his right eye, although he played one more season with Fort Lauderdale before retiring.

*Above: George Best closes in on England's Gordon Banks.*

## Franceschino Baresi
## (Italy, b. 1960)

**Club:** *AC Milan (1977–97)*
**Caps:** *81 (1 goal)*

Franco Baresi, the great sweeper and magisterial organizer of Arrigo Sacchi's marvellous AC Milan side, together with Costacurta and Paolo Maldini, provided the defensive platform for the scoring talents of, among others, Marco Van Basten, Ruud Gullit and Dejan Savicevic. A perceptive and intelligent centre-back, Baresi made his league debut in 1978 and remained with the club in its fallow period, until Silvio Berlusconi's millions made it one of the top clubs in Europe. He won six league titles and two European Cups with Milan, in 1989 and 1990, but was suspended for the 1994 final with Barcelona. He received his first cap in 1982 but, in his international career, he was overshadowed by the presence of Juventus' Gaetano Scirea as sweeper until the last years of that decade. He played in the 1990 World Cup finals hosted by Italy and, four years later, came close to lifting the World Cup trophy for his country as captain. Baresi's performance at USA '94 was all the more memorable (in spite of missing his first penalty in the shoot-out against Brazil in the final) because he had undergone surgery on his knee just two weeks before the tournament began. Franco Baresi retired in 1997.

*Right: Franco Baresi, the rock of the defence for AC Milan and Italy.*

*Above: Cliff "Boy" Bastin in the famous old Arsenal strip.*

## Cliff Bastin
## (England, 1912–91)

**Clubs:** *Exeter City (1927–29), Arsenal (1929–46)*
**Caps:** *21 (12 goals)*

Left-winger Cliff Bastin was only 16 years old when Arsenal manager Herbert Chapman spotted him playing for Third Division Exeter City. By the time he was 20, "Boy" Bastin, as he was nicknamed, had won every honour in the English game with Arsenal. He was the youngest player to play in a Cup Final in Arsenal's 1930 defeat of Huddersfield Town, and in his time with the London club he won another Cup medal in 1936 and five league medals. Playing up front with forwards Jack Lambert and David Jack, and supplied from midfield by the impishly skilful Alex James, Bastin's ball skills, pace and directness brought him a hatful of goals, including 28 in the 1930–31 season, and 33 in 1932–33. He held the record for the number of goals scored for Arsenal (178) until overtaken by Ian Wright in 1997–98. Cliff Bastin died in 1991.

## Gabriel Batistuta
## (Argentina, b. 1969)

**Clubs:** *Newells Old Boys (1988–89), River Plate (1989–90), Boca Juniors (1990–91), Fiorentina (1991–2000), Roma (2000–03), Inter Milan (2003), Al Arabi (2003–05)*
**Caps:** *78 (56 goals)*

Batistuta was a revered figure in his adopted city of Florence. With a statue in his honour at the club's Stadio Communale, Fiorentina was proud of his tremendous goal-scoring feats and fierce loyalty to the club. Before joining Fiorentina, Batistuta played in Argentina, and his six goals in the *Copa America* helped his country win the tournament. At Fiorentina, he quickly became the leading scorer, scoring 13 goals in his first season. He is also Argentina's highest-ever goal scorer with a tally of 56. Batistuta played for his country in the 1994, 1998 and 2002 World Cup finals but retired from the international game in 2002. He left Fiorentina for Roma in 2000, but was transferred on loan to Inter Milan in 2003. After a spell at Al Arabi in Qatar he retired in 2005.

*Above: Gabriel Batistuta on the attack.*

*Left: Scotland's "Slim Jim" Baxter.*

## Jim Baxter
## (Scotland, 1939–2001)

**Clubs:** *Raith Rovers (1957–60), Rangers (1960–65), Sunderland (1965–67), Nottingham Forest (1967–69), Rangers (1969–70)*
**Caps:** *34 (3 goals)*

"Slim Jim" Baxter was probably the most skilful left-sided footballer ever to have come out of Scotland. His immaculate passing, vision and ability to ghost through defences at will, marked him out as a player of genius. An idol to the Rangers fans of the 1960s, he was the playmaker in the all-conquering team that won three league championships, three Scottish Cups and four Scottish League Cups between 1960 and 1965, including the "treble" in 1964. Baxter left Rangers in 1965, just as Celtic were starting to challenge Rangers' dominance in the Scottish league. He moved across the border to England, but his brilliance only showed itself fitfully. Baxter never had the chance to demonstrate his class in the World Cup finals. However, Scottish football fans still remember his two goals past England's debutant keeper Gordon Banks in 1963 at Wembley, and his masterful performance against the "auld enemy" in 1967 when, along with Denis Law, he inspired a 3–2 win over England, the then World Champions. In 1969, Baxter returned to Rangers, and he made his retirement from football the following year. He died in 2001.

## Franz Beckenbauer
## (Germany, b. 1945)

**Clubs:** *Bayern Munich (1964–77),*
*New York Cosmos (1977–80),*
*Hamburg (1980–82), New York*
*Cosmos (1983)*
**Caps:** *103 (14 goals)*

Known by many of his fans as "*Der
Kaiser*" ("the emperor"), Franz
Beckenbauer was the attacking sweeper
for Bayern Munich and West Germany
through much of the 1960s and 1970s.
He had a profound influence on
German football and is generally
regarded as the greatest German
footballer of all time. An elegant player
with slide-rule distribution,
Beckenbauer made his debut for Bayern
in 1964 and played on the losing side
in the 1966 World Cup Final at
Wembley. However, he scored in West
Germany's 3–2 quarter-final victory
over England in the 1970 tournament
and, supported by the skills of Günter
Netzer, he led his country to their
European Championship triumph in
1972, when he was named European
Footballer of the Year. He captained his
country to further success in the 1974
World Cup Final, beating Johann
Cruyff's great Dutch team 2–1, and he
inspired Bayern to three European
Cups in succession from 1974–76. In
1976 he was voted European Footballer
of the Year for the second time, and the
following year he moved to the United
States to join the New York Cosmos.
He became West Germany's manager in
1984 and led the side to their 1986
World Cup Final defeat by Argentina.
He managed to successfully lead the
team to victory in the 1990 World Cup
Final, though, earning himself the
enviable accolade of being the first man
both to captain and manage a World
Cup-winning team. Beckenbauer is
currently club president at Bayern
Munich, and he pioneered Germany's
successful bid to host the FIFA 2006
World Cup finals.

*Right: Franz Beckenbauer initiates
another attack for West Germany.*

## David Beckham
## (England, b. 1975)

**Clubs:** *Manchester United (1993–2003), Real Madrid (2003–07), LA Galaxy (2007–)*
**Caps:** *106 (17 goals)*

London-born Beckham played his first league game for Manchester United in 1995. He quickly became a regular midfield provider to Alex Ferguson's attack, scoring some spectacular goals. He is particularly adept at lashing in pinpoint crosses and free kicks. He won his first cap in 1996, and achieved notoriety in the 1998 World Cup finals: he was sent off against Argentina for a petulant kick on Diego Simeone. His injury-time goal from a free-kick against Greece in the last qualifier for the 2002 World Cup famously won England a place in the finals.

Beckham has six League, two FA Cup and one European Cup winner's medal to his name. He was transferred to Real Madrid in 2003, remaining there for four years and winning the La Liga title once before joining Major League Soccer's LA Galaxy in 2007 on a highly lucrative contract. He returned to European football, however, at the start of 2009, joining AC Milan on loan.

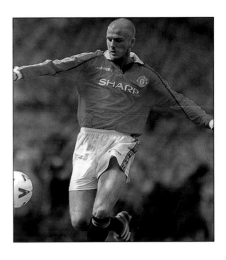

*Above: David Beckham about to curl in one of his trademark crosses.*

## Dennis Bergkamp
## (Holland, b. 1969)

**Clubs:** *Ajax (1981–93), Inter Milan (1993–95), Arsenal (1995–2006)*
**Caps:** *79 (36 goals)*

Bergkamp is a forward with guile, speed and a delicate touch, who is both an unselfish creator and a predatory finisher. Named after Denis Law, he made his Ajax debut under manager Cruyff at the age of 17. By the time he left Ajax to join Inter Milan in 1993, he had scored 103 league goals for the Amsterdam side and won a UEFA Cup medal in Ajax's 1992 defeat of Torino. His talents were utilized only rarely by the Italian club, and three years later he was brought to Arsenal for £7.5 million. He took a few games to settle in at Highbury but soon became a cult figure with the London club. In 1997–98, his 22 goals helped Arsenal to secure the "double", and he was named Footballer of the Year that season. He was also vital in Arsenal's "double" of 2001–02 and the unbeaten Premiership season of 2003–04. He played his last game for the club in 2006. He gained his first cap in 1990, and despite his much-publicized fear of flying, played for Holland until Euro 2000. His sensational, last-minute winning goal in the 1998 World Cup quarter-finals against Argentina will live long in football fans' memories.

*Above: Dennis Bergkamp, one of Holland's finest attackers of the 1990s and 2000s*

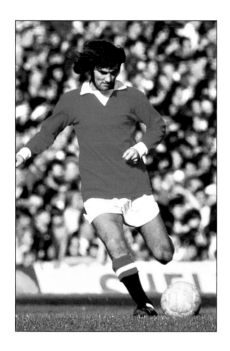

*Above: The multi-talented George Best in action for Manchester United.*

## George Best
## (N. Ireland, 1946-2005)

**Clubs:** *Manchester United (1963–74), Fulham (1976–78), Fort Lauderdale Strikers (1978–79), Hibernian (1979–81), Bournemouth (1982)*
**Caps:** *37 (9 goals)*

Best was a supremely gifted player whose talents were eventually squandered by his off-pitch problems. A fast, skilful forward, he could also tackle and defend when necessary, and he scored some audacious and important goals for Manchester United. He made his debut for the club at the age of 17 and soon became the first "pop star" footballer, his "swinging sixties" lifestyle regularly attracting the attention of the tabloid press. He scored twice in United's 5–1 thrashing of Benfica in the 1966 European Cup quarter-final, and he scored United's second with a marvellous extra-time goal when they again defeated Benfica in the 1968 European Cup Final. That year, he was European Footballer of the Year and was top English league scorer with 28 goals. United's influence over English football began to wane and Best left the club in 1974, having played over 350 games for United and won two English league winner's medals. He gained 37 caps for Northern Ireland but never played at the highest international level. He came back into the game briefly with Fulham in 1976, and finally retired in 1982. His alcohol addiction sadly led to his death in 2005.

## Danny Blanchflower
## (N. Ireland, 1926–93)

**Clubs:** *Glentoran (1945–49), Barnsley (1949–51), Aston Villa (1951–54), Tottenham Hotspur (1954–64)*
**Caps:** *56 (2 goals)*

Captain of Spurs and Northern Ireland, right-half Blanchflower radiated style and authority. He was at the heart of the successful Spurs side of the early 1960s, and his subtle but effective distribution, and ability to control the game, inspired Spurs to their greatest triumph. Under his visionary leadership, Spurs became the first side in the 20th century to achieve the "double" of League and FA Cup in 1961, and they won the Cup again the following year. In 1963 they were the first British team to win a European trophy when they beat Atlético Madrid 5–1 to win the Cup Winners Cup. Blanchflower made his international debut in 1949, and the highlight of his Northern Ireland career was captaining his country to the quarter-finals of the 1958 World Cup. He retired in 1964 to become a journalist; his foray into management was less productive.

*Above: Spurs' captain and inspiration Danny Blanchflower clears an attack.*

## Oleg Blokhin
## (Soviet Union, b. 1952)

**Clubs:** *Kiev Dynamo, Vorwärts Steyr*
**Caps:** *101 (39 goals)*

Blokhin was the former Soviet Union's most-capped player, and also the country's highest scorer. He began his career with Kiev Dynamo as a speedy left-winger (it is said he chose football over an athletics career as a sprinter), and gradually moved into the centre-forward position, where his pace and eye for goal helped Dynamo to seven Soviet league victories between 1974 and 1986. He scored in two Cup Winners' Cup Finals for Dynamo, beating Ferencvaros 3–0 in 1975, and beating Atlético Madrid by the same score in 1986. After being granted permission to move to Western Europe, he played out the last years of his career with the Austrian club Vorwärts Steyr. Blokhin made his international debut in 1972, and played in both the 1982 and 1986 World Cup finals. He was the first Soviet player to play more than 100 games for his country, scoring 39 goals in his 101 caps. Blokhin was voted European Footballer of the Year in 1975. After his playing career had ended, Blokhin became manager of the Greek club side Olympiakos in 1990 before managing two other Greek clubs: PAOK (1993–94) and Ionikos (1994–97). He was the manager of the Ukrainian national team in 2003 and became coach of FC Moscow in 2007.

*Right: Striker Oleg Blokhin, the Soviet Union's most-capped player.*

*Above: Zbigniew Boniek on the offensive for Juventus.*

## Zbigniew Boniek
## (Poland, b. 1956)

**Clubs:** *Zawisa Bydgoszcz (1971–75), Widzew Lodz (1975–82), Juventus (1982–85), Roma (1985–88)*
**Caps:** *80 (24 goals)*

Recognized as one of the finest Polish players ever, Boniek gained his first cap in 1976 and represented his country in the 1978 World Cup finals. He played again in 1982 and scored a hat trick in Poland's 3–0 defeat of Belgium in the second round, although he was injured for the semi-final elimination by the eventual winners, Italy. His prolific scoring abilities caught the attention of Juventus, who that year paid a then-record fee of £1.1 million to Widzew Lodz. Boniek played in the 1983 European Cup Final, when Juventus were beaten 1–0 by Hamburg, and he scored the winner in their 2–1 win over Portuguese side Porto in the 1984 Cup Winners' Cup Final. He also played in Juventus' 1–0 defeat of Liverpool in the 1985 European Cup Final. Boniek was voted European Footballer of the Year in 1982. He scored 24 goals in 80 international matches for Poland.

## Liam Brady
## (Ireland, b. 1956)

**Clubs:** *Arsenal (1973–80),
Juventus (1980–82), Sampdoria
(1982–84), Inter Milan (1984–86),
Ascoli (1986–87), West Ham United
(1987–89)*
**Caps:** *72 (9 goals)*

An attacking, left-footed midfielder,
"Chippy" Brady was the creative
playmaker for Arsenal throughout most
of the 1970s. A relatively slight figure,
he had a accurate and powerful shot
and his passing was immaculate.
He made the winning goal in Arsenal's
1979 3–2 FA Cup Final win over
Manchester United, and he moved on
to Juventus in 1980, helping the club
to win two *Serie A* titles in succession.
He played for three other Italian clubs
before returning to English football in
1987 with West Ham United. He
represented Eire from 1975–90, after
which manager Jack Charlton's
long–ball style made his stylish
midfield play redundant, and he gained
72 Irish caps. After his retirement, he
had unsuccessful spells as a manager
with Celtic and Brighton. Brady is
currently in charge of youth
development at Arsenal.

*Right: Liam Brady dictating play
for Arsenal.*

## Billy Bremner
## (Scotland, 1942–97)

**Clubs:** *Leeds United (1959–76),
Hull City (1976–78) Doncaster
Rovers (1978–82)*
**Caps:** *54 (3 goals)*

The fiery little red-haired Bremner
was the midfield motor of Don Revie's
Leeds United team in the late 1960s
and early 1970s. Bremner's skilful
distribution and competitive spirit

*Left: Billy Bremner chases the ball
for his country in 1973, watched by
England's Colin Bell.*

helped to bring the club two league
titles in 1968–69 and 1973–74, two
Fairs Cups in 1968 and 1971, and the
1972 FA Cup, when they beat Arsenal
1–0. He played in the 1975 European
Cup Final, when Leeds unluckily lost
2–0 to Bayern Munich, and moved to
Hull City soon after. Bremner was first
capped in 1965, and he played in the
1974 World Cup, where he missed a
chance against Brazil, which would
have seen Scotland qualify for the
second round. After retiring from the
game as a player, he became manager
first of Doncaster Rovers and then of
Leeds United in the 1980s. Bremner
died of a heart attack in 1997.

## Emilio Butragueño
## (Spain, b. 1963)

**Clubs:** *Real Madrid (1983–95),*
*Atletico Celaya (1995–98)*
**Caps:** *69 (26 goals)*

Playing in attack alongside the Mexican
Hugo Sanchez, Emilio "The Vulture"
Butragueño was Real Madrid's main
striker throughout the 1980s. A quick,
talented centre-forward, he made his way
through the club's youth team, and Real's
"nursery" club, Castilla, and his goals
brought to the Bernabeu two UEFA
Cups, in 1985 and 1986; in both years
Butragueño won the *Prix Bravo* as

Europe's best young player. He also helped
his Madrid club to five league titles in
succession from 1986–90. He made his
international debut for Spain against Wales
in 1984, scoring in the 3–0 win, and he
went on to become Spain's highest-ever
goal scorer. His five goals in the 1986
World Cup finals made him joint top
scorer, and he is especially remembered for
the four goals he scored in Spain's
unexpected 5–0 demolition of Denmark
in the second round of the tournament.
In 2004 he became vice president at Real
Madrid but he left two years later.

*Right: Butragueño was a Real striker
throughout the 1980s.*

## Eric Cantona
## (France, b. 1966)

**Clubs:** *Auxerre (1981–88),*
*Marseille (1988–91), Nîmes*
*(1991–92), Leeds United (1992),*
*Manchester United (1992–97)*
**Caps:** *45 (19 goals)*

Cantona has a complex and volatile
personality but was an immensely
gifted talent, and his football career has
been a rollercoaster ride of
unpredictability. His disagreements
with clubs and the French international
selectors led him to leave France and
join Leeds United in early 1992.
He spent enough time there to help
guide them to the league title but, to
the dismay of the Leeds supporters,
he moved to Manchester United
that summer. With Cantona at the
playmaking helm, United won the
league four times by 1997, including
two "doubles", and Cantona was revered
by the Old Trafford fans. His angry
Kung Fu kick at a Crystal Palace fan in
1995 brought him notoriety but, after a
suspension and a community service
order from the courts, he was back at
his peak. He was voted Player of the Year
in 1996, but he shocked Manchester
United at the end of the 1996–97 season
by announcing his retirement from
football. Cantona then embarked on an
acting and media career.

*Above: Manchester United's maestro Eric Cantona takes control of the ball.*

## Roberto Carlos da Silva
## (Brazil, b. 1973)

**Clubs:** *Palmeiras (1993–95), Inter Milan (1995–96), Real Madrid (1996–2007), Fenerbache (2007–)*
**Caps:** *125 (11)*

A stocky, attacking left-back with explosive acceleration, Roberto Carlos left Palmeiras in 1995 to join Inter Milan, but only stayed one season with

*Left: Roberto Carlos, Brazilian international and speedy left-back for Real Madrid.*

the Italian club before joining Real. He won the Spanish *Liga*, and has three European Cup Winner's medals after Real's 1998, 2000 and 2002 triumphs. Carlos made his international debut for Brazil in 1992 against the USA, and he played in the 1994 and 1998 World Cup finals. He scored a remarkable 35-yard free-kick in the 1997 Tournoi in France, curving the ball wickedly around the French wall past an astonished goalkeeper. He helped Brazil to World Cup victory as part of the squad in 2002 and retired from international football in 2006. He joined Turkey's Fenerbache on a 2-year contract in 2007.

## Carlos Alberto
## (Brazil, b. 1944)

**Clubs:** *Fluminense, Santos, Botafogo, Fluminense, New York Cosmos*
**Caps:** *53 (8 goals)*

Carlos Alberto stamped his name in footballing history in the 1970 World Cup Final when, as captain and right-back of Brazil, he hammered home an unstoppable right-foot rocket to seal a 4–1 victory for Brazil. A classy and elegant player, he spent his career in Brazil, leaving for the United States in the 1970s to play for New York Cosmos alongside Franz Beckenbauer and Pelé.

*Above: Brazil's captain Carlos Alberto cradles the 1970 Jules Rimet trophy.*

## John Charles
## (Wales, 1931–2004)

**Clubs:** *Leeds United (1949–57), Juventus (1957–62), Leeds United (1962), Roma (1962–63), Cardiff City (1963–65)*
**Caps:** *38 (15 goals)*

Although Charles began his Leeds career in 1949 as a centre-half, by the 1956–57 season he had moved to centre-forward and was top scorer in the First Division, with 38 goals.

*Left: John Charles rises above the England defence.*

A strong, bustling but skilful player, he was bought for his goal-scoring prowess and heading ability by Juventus in 1957, and he became a firm favourite with the Turin crowds who called him the "Gentle Giant". Creating a partnership with the Argentinian Omar Sivori, he scored 93 goals in his five seasons with Juventus. He moved back to Leeds for one season in 1962, then moved to Roma. In his day, he was the youngest player to play for Wales, at the age of 18 years 71 days, and he led his country to the quarter-finals of the 1958 World Cup against Brazil. His death in 2004 was widely mourned in Britain and Italy.

## Bobby Charlton
## (England, b. 1937)

**Clubs:** *Manchester United (1954–73), Preston North End (1974–75)*
**Caps:** *106 (49 goals)*

Charlton is one of those rare sportsmen whose name is recognized immediately across the planet, and in his long playing career with Manchester United and England he won virtually all the honours available to a footballer. He made his club debut in 1956, scoring two goals, and was part of the "Busby Babes" side that was virtually destroyed by the Munich air crash in 1958. In the 1960s, with team-mates Denis Law, Pat Crerand and George Best, he helped the club win the FA Cup in 1963, the league in 1967 and the European Cup in 1968, when he scored twice against Benfica in United's 4–1 victory. Initially a left-winger, he moved into the centre of the pitch later in his career, and by the time he retired in 1973, had scored nearly 200 league goals for the club. Internationally, his finest moment came in 1966 when he was part of the England team that beat Germany to win the World Cup at

*Above: Bobby Charlton moves upfield for Manchester United.*

Wembley stadium, and he played his last game for England in the 1970 World Cup finals. He was named European Footballer of the Year in 1966, and further honours included the OBE in 1969, the CBE in 1974 and also a knighthood in 1994. Bobby Charlton is England's all-time top scorer with a record of 49 goals. He is currently on the board of directors at his old club Manchester United, and is an international ambassador for the FA.

## Ray Clemence
## (England, b. 1948)

**Clubs:** *Scunthorpe United (1965–67), Liverpool (1967–81), Tottenham Hotspur (1981–88)*
**Caps:** *61*

Clemence was an assured, dependable goalkeeper, and would have won many more English caps had it not been for the presence of rival Peter Shilton. Clemence had quick reflexes and sound positioning sense, and he pulled out many fine saves for Liverpool and England. He joined Liverpool from Scunthorpe in 1967, and was the last line of defence in the side that won three European Cups, two UEFA Cups, five league titles and the FA Cup. Seeking a new challenge, he moved to Spurs in 1981 for £300,000 and won an FA Cup medal again in 1982. He made over 250 appearances for the North London club and left in 1988 to become manager of Barnet. Clemence then joined the England national team coaching staff.

*Above: Goalkeeper Ray Clemence organizes the Liverpool defence against Manchester United.*

*Above: Benfica's Mario Coluña (right) shakes hands with Manchester United's Bobby Charlton before the 1968 European Cup final. Man United won the match.*

## Mario Coluña
## (Mozambique, b. 1935)

**Clubs:** *Desportivo de Mapotu (1952–54), Benfica (1954–70), Lyons*
**Caps:** *73 (57 goals)*

Like Eusebio, the other great Mozambique player, Coluña began his career with Desportivo in the capital Mapotu, before moving to Benfica in 1954. Originally a forward with a thunderous left-foot, he was moved to midfield by Benfica's manager Bela Guttmann, and as captain he inspired the great Benfica side of the early 1960s. He scored in Benfica's European Cup Final victories against Barcelona in 1961 and Real Madrid in 1962, and played in three other losing finals that decade. He was captain of Portugal and led his country to third place in the 1966 World Cup. He moved to Lyons before retiring to become Minister of Sport in Mozambique.

## Johan Cruyff
## (Holland, b. 1947)

**Clubs:** *Ajax (1964–73), Barcelona (1973–78), Los Angeles Aztecs (1979), Washington Diplomats (1980–81), Levante (1981), Ajax (1981–83), Feyenoord (1983–84)*
**Caps:** *48 (33 goals)*

Cruyff was the undisputed king of "total football" in the early 1970s. Playing in their free-flowing, fast and exciting style, Cruyff's Ajax won the European Cup three times in succession. He was a graceful, elusive forward with perfect balance and control and an unerring eye for goal, and he was the unselfish inspiration for his gifted team-mates Johan Neeskens and Johnny Rep. He was named European Footballer of the Year in 1971, and in 1972 he scored both goals in Ajax's 2–0 European Cup Final win over Inter Milan. His ex-Ajax manager Rinus Michels persuaded him to join Barcelona in 1973 for £922,000, and in his first season Barça won the Spanish league title. That year, Cruyff captained Holland to the 1974 World Cup Final against West Germany, and his second minute run into the heart of the German defence earned the Dutch a penalty, converted by Neeskens. Germany, however, won the match 2–1. In 1973 and 1974 Cruyff was again voted European Footballer of the Year. He went to the United States in 1978 but came back to Holland in 1981.

*Above: Johan Cruyff playing for Holland in the 1974 World Cup finals.*

Cruyff launched his coaching career with Ajax in the mid-80s. He led his old club to two further league titles, adding to the six he had won with them as a player. Cruyff returned to Barcelona as manager in 1988, and he led the club to 11 titles and their first European Cup Final victory over Sampdoria, in 1992. Known as "the saviour", he remains at Barcelona as an advisor.

## Teofilio Cubillas
## (Peru, b. 1949)

**Clubs:** *Alianza, Basle, FC Porto, Fort Lauderdale Strikers*
**Caps:** *88 (38 goals)*

A predatory striker, Cubillas is probably the finest player ever to have come out of Peru. Nicknamed "El nene" he was renowned for his technical ability and punchy shot. He made his first international appearance in 1968 against Brazil, and he played in the 1970 and 1978 World Cup finals, scoring five goals in each tournament, as well as appearing in the 1982 finals. He played for his home team Alianza of Lima before moving to Swiss team Basle in 1973, and then had a spell with FC Porto. He returned to Alianza in 1977, and ended his career in the United States with Fort Lauderdale Strikers.

*Right: Teofilio Cubillas, goal-scoring hero for his country, scored five goals for Peru in both the 1970 and 1978 World Cup finals.*

## Zoltan Czibor
### (Hungary, 1929–1997)

**Clubs:** *Ferencvaros, Csepel, Honved, Barcelona, Espanyol*
**Caps:** *43 (17 goals)*

One of the "Magnificent Magyars" of the 1950s, along with Ferenc Puskas, Sandor Kocsis and Ladislav Kubala, Zoltan Czibor was a left-winger with a powerful shot. He left Hungary after the 1956 revolution and moved to Spain, where he signed for Barcelona –

*Left: Zoltan Czibor (right) contests possession for Hungary.*

along with his Honved team-mate Kocsis. Czibor won the Spanish league title twice with Barcelona, and he scored two goals in their 1960 Fairs Cup defeat of Birmingham. He also scored in the 1961 European Cup Final when Barcelona, unluckily, lost 3–2 to Benfica. He ended his playing career with a short spell at neighbouring Spanish club Espanyol. Czibor's international career for Hungary was limited and he only played in the 1954 World Cup Final, where the East Europeans were defeated 3–2 by West Germany. After retiring from professional football, Czibor returned to Hungary. He died there in 1997.

## Kenny Dalglish
### (Scotland, b. 1951)

**Clubs:** *Celtic (1966–77), Liverpool (1977–89)*
**Caps:** *102 (30 goals)*

Dalglish was a young Rangers supporter who became the darling of Celtic Park. A tenacious inside-forward with a deadly shot, he had immaculate ball control and could pass the ball in the tightest of defensive situations. While at Celtic he won four league titles and four Scottish Cups, but in 1977 he moved to Liverpool, as a replacement for Kevin Keegan, in a record £440,000 deal. He scored the winner in the 1978 European Cup Final against Bruges with a delicate chip over the keeper, and soon became the creative heart of Bob Paisley's side. In his Anfield career he won two more European Cups and six league winner's medals. First capped in 1971, he went on to collect a record 102 Scottish caps, including the World Cups of 1974, 1978 and 1982. He shares with Denis Law the record for the most goals scored (30) for Scotland. He became player-manager of Liverpool the day after the Heysel disaster of 1985, and later left to become manager of Blackburn Rovers and Newcastle United. Dalglish was appointed Director of Football with Celtic in 1999 but resigned in 2000.

*Above: "King Kenny" Dalglish on the attack for Scotland against England.*

## Edgar Davids
## (Surinam, b. 1973)

**Clubs:** *Ajax (1991–96), AC Milan (1996–97), Juventus (1997–2004), Barcelona (2004), Inter Milan (2004–05), Tottenham Hotspur (2005–07), Ajax (2007–)*
**Caps:** *74 (6 goals)*

Davids is a tough competitor famed for his control of midfield. Called "pitbull" by his team-mates because of his lack of fear and aggression, he is a clever passer of the ball and can hit a ferocious shot. Easily identified by the eyeglasses he sometimes wears for glaucoma, Davids is one of the many top players who came up through the Ajax youth team, making his first team debut in 1991. He won the European Cup with Ajax in 1995 and acquired three league title medals before joining AC Milan in 1996, and subsequently moving to Juventus in 1997. He was sent home from Euro 96 after an argument with Dutch coach Gus Hiddink, but he returned to play well in the 1998 World Cup. He was transferred on loan to Barcelona in 2004, and went on to join Inter Milan in the same year. In 2005 he joined Tottenham Hotspur, then went back to Ajax in 2007.

*Right: Edgar Davids in full flight.*

## Alessandro Del Piero
## (Italy, b. 1974)

**Clubs:** *Padova (1990–93), Juventus (1993–)*
**Caps:** *91 (27 goals)*

Likened early in his career to the young Roberto Baggio, Del Piero is a forward of genius. A right-footed player who is particularly effective in the inside-left position, he is fast, difficult to dispossess and can shimmy his way through packed defences to score some excellent goals. Del Piero moved from Padova to Juventus in 1993, and he scored a hat-trick in his third game for the Turin club, against Parma. He is particularly dangerous from the dead ball, and his goals have helped Juventus to win three *Serie A* league titles. In the 1997–98 season he scored 21 league goals for Juve, as well as a hat trick against Monaco in the semi-final of the European Cup, which took the Italian side into the final. Del Piero is prone to injury and he badly damaged his knee in late 1998 but, when fit, there are few more skilful forwards in European football today. He played for Italy in the World Cup finals of 1998 and 2002, and scored in the penalty shoot-out against France in 2006 to help his country win the title.

*Left: Juve's forward Alessandro Del Piero representing Italy against Brazil.*

## Kazimierz Deyna
## (Poland, 1947–1989)

**Clubs:** *Starogard, Sportowy (KS) Lodz, Legia Warsaw, Manchester City, San Diego*
**Caps:** *102 (38 goals)*

Deyna was the midfield supremo of the Polish side that included Kasperczak, Lato and Gadocha, and it was his skill in the centre that resulted in Poland's success on the world footballing stage during the 1970s. A natural attacking player, Deyna helped the national side take the gold medal in the 1972 Munich Olympics (where he scored two goals in the final and a total of nine in the tournament), and to its best-ever result of third place in the World Cup finals of 1974. Deyna died in a car crash in the United States in 1989.

*Right: Kazimierz Deyna (left) sets up a Polish attacking move.*

## Didi, Waldir Pereira
## (Brazil, 1928–2001)

**Clubs:** *Rio Branco, Lencoes, Madureiro, Fluminense, Botafogo, Real Madrid, Valéncia, Botafogo*
**Caps:** *85 (31 goals)*

The midfield maestro of the Brazilian sides of the 1950s, and a master of the spot-kick, Didi played in the 1954 World Cup finals, where he scored two goals. He was at the heart of the 1958 Brazilian team that introduced the 4–2–4 formation and won that year's World Cup Final, playing with the young Pelé, Vava and Zagallo. He played again in the 1962 tournament. He left South America for Real Madrid in 1959, but his playing style did not fit in with Di Stefano, and he left Madrid for Valéncia, before moving back to Botafogo. On retiring, Didi became manager of the Peruvian national team. He died in 2001.

*Left: Didi, Brazil's celebrated playmaker during the 1950s.*

## Alfredo Di Stefano (Argentina, b. 1926)

**Clubs:** *River Plate (1943–49), Millionaros Bogotá (1949–53), Real Madrid (1953–64), Espanyol (1964–66)*
**Caps:** *7 (7 goals) (Argentina), 2 (Colombia), 31 (23 goals) (Spain)*

For many, the greatest all-round footballer in the history of the game, Di Stefano alternated between midfield and attack, plundering goals and creating chances for his illustrious Real Madrid team-mates. He was at the centre of the magnificent Real side that won the European Cup five times running from 1956–60, and his partnership with Ferenc Puskas devastated defences throughout Europe. In his first game for Real, in 1953, he put four goals past Barcelona, and his arrival sparked off a revival in the fortunes of the Spanish side. Di Stefano scored in every European Cup Final from 1956–60, culminating in a hat trick against Eintracht Frankfurt in 1960, and played on the losing side in two more finals, in 1962 and 1964.

He scored 49 goals in his 56 games in the tournament, which is a record that still stands today. He collected eight Spanish league winner's medals with the club and was named European Footballer of the Year in 1957 and 1959. After the 1964 European Cup Final he moved to Espanyol. He retired as a player in 1966, but went on to manage Boca Juniors, Sporting Lisbon, River Plate, Valéncia and Real Madrid, where he is now Honorary President.

*Below: The incomparable Alfredo Di Stefano on the attack for Real Madrid.*

# William "Dixie" Dean
## (England, 1907–1980)

**Clubs:** *Tranmere Rovers (1924–25), Everton (1925–38), Notts County (1938), Sligo Rovers (1939)*
**Caps:** *16 (18 goals)*

Dean was a goal scorer extraordinaire and in the 1927–28 season, at the age of 21, he set a record, which still stands today, of 60 league goals in just one season. Dean was of medium height and build but he had a prodigious

*Left: William "Dixie"" Dean, Everton's great pre-war striker.*

heading ability, and he was a strong, two-footed player. He moved to Everton from Tranmere Rovers in 1925, and scored seven hat tricks in his record-breaking season, which helped to win Everton the league title. In 1931–32 he scored 44 goals, and Everton again claimed the league title. He moved to Nottingham County in 1938, and then to Ireland's Sligo Rovers, and retired in 1939, having scored an outstanding 379 goals in 438 league games and 28 goals in 33 Cup ties. He scored 18 goals in his 16 international appearances for England. Dixie died in 1980 while watching an Everton game at Goodison Park.

# Dragan Dzajic
## (Yugoslavia, b. 1946)

**Clubs:** *Red Star Belgrade, Bastia, Red Star Belgrade*
**Caps:** *85 (23 goals)*

Dzajic, nicknamed the "Magic Dragan", was a fast, intelligent outside-left and the most-capped player in the former Yugoslavia. He won five league titles and four Yugoslavian cups with Red Star Belgrade, and he scored 23 goals in 85 games for his country. Dzajic is best remembered in England for the 1968

European Championships, when he scored the goal, with four minutes to go, which eliminated England in the semi-final. He scored again in the final, but hosts Italy equalized and went on to win in a replay. Dzajic retired as a player in 1978, and became manager then president of Red Star, before stepping down from the post in 2004 due to ill health. In 2003 he was selected by the Serbian FA as their most outstanding player of the previous fifty years.

*Right: Dragan Dzajic (right) playing for Yugoslavia.*

# Duncan Edwards
## (England, 1936–1958)

**Clubs:** *Manchester United (1952–58)*
**Caps:** *18 (5 goals)*

With the potential to have been one of England's greatest all-round footballers, the powerful and skilful Edwards was one the "Babes" of Matt Busby's Manchester United team of the 1950s, and, tragically, he was one of the victims of the Munich air crash of 1958. Although a big man, he had pace

*Left: Duncan Edwards in one of his all-too-few appearances for England.*

and subtlety, and his thunderous shot – for which he was given the nickname "Boom-Boom" – brought him several important goals for his club and country. He made his club debut for Manchester United at the age of 16, and he gained the first of his 18 international caps in a 7–2 victory against Scotland two years later, aged 18. He was England's youngest-ever full international, and rated by Matt Busby "the most complete footballer in Britain – if not the world". In his brief career he made 175 appearances for Manchester United, and he helped the club to two league titles, in 1956 and 1957. Edwards' untimely death in Munich robbed England and United of a massively gifted talent.

## Steffan Effenberg (Germany, b. 1968)

**Clubs:** *Borussia Mönchengladbach (1987–90), Bayern Munich (1990–92), Fiorentina (1992–94), Borussia Mönchengladbach (1994–98), Bayern Munich (1998–2002), Wolfsburg (2002–03)*
**Caps:** *35 (5 goals)*

Midfielder Steffan Effenberg began his career with Borussia Mönchengladbach, winning the *Bundesliga* title in 1990. He moved to Bayern Munich the following season, and then spent two years in Italy with Fiorentina. He returned to Mönchengladbach in 1994 and won a German Cup medal with them in 1995. He then returned to Bayern, with whom he won more league titles in 1999 and 2000, and the 2001 European Cup. He was first capped in 1991, and played in Germany's 1994 World Cup squad. He joined Wolfsburg in 2002 and spent his last season in Qatar.

*Right: The combative Steffan Effenberg.*

## Samuuel Eto'o (Cameroon, b. 1981)

**Clubs:** *Real Madrid (1997–2000), Real Mallorca (2000–04), Barcelona (2004–)*
**Caps:** *80 (37 goals)*

Cameroon-born Samuel Eto'o is a hard-working, deadly goal-scorer with quick pace and impressive ball control. He joined Real Madrid as a 16-year-old, and was sent on loan until he was transferred to Mallorca in 2000. By the time he left Mallorca to join Barcelona in 2004 he had helped his club to win the Spanish cup in 2003 and, with 54 goals, had become Mallorca's all-time top league scorer.

Barcelona paid £28 million for his services, and his speed and awareness made him top La Liga scorer, with 26 goals, in 2005-06. He also scored six in Barcelona's run in the 2005-06 Champions League. In the Final he was tackled by Arsenal's Jens Lehman outside the box early in the game, with Lehman being sent off, and Eto'o scored the equalizer in the 76th minute before Barca went on to beat Arsenal 2–1. He missed much of 2006-07 due to a knee injury.

He first played for Cameroon in 1996, and was in the World Cup squads of 1998 and 2002. He was also in the squad that won the African Cup of Nations in 2000 and 2002, and he was voted African Player of the Year in 2004, 2005 and 2006.

*Left: Cameroon's Samuel Eto'o playing for Barcelona.*

## Eusebio da Silva Ferreira (Mozambique, b. 1942)

**Clubs:** *Sporting Club of Lourenço Marques (1958–61), Benfica (1961–75)*
**Caps:** *64 (41 goals)*

Eusebio, the "Black Pearl", played his first game for Bela Guttmann's Benfica in 1961. By the end of that season he had won a European Cup winner's medal, with his two goals against Real Madrid helping Benfica to a 5–3 victory. He scored again in the 1963 final, but this time his team was beaten by two goals from AC Milan's José Altafini. He played in two more finals, in 1965 against Inter Milan and in 1968 against Manchester United, but was on the losing side both times. Eusebio's trademark right-footed shot brought him the Portuguese top scorer award in seven seasons and, by the time he moved to play in North America in 1975, he had collected ten Portuguese league winner's medals. He was named European Footballer of the Year in 1965. He made his debut for Portugal in 1961 (playing as a national of Mozambique, one of its colonies), and was top scorer in the 1966 World Cup with nine goals. In 1977, Eusebio returned to Benfica as coach and remains a talismanic figure in Portuguese football.

*Above: Eusebio remains a legendary figure in both Portugese and world football.*

## Cesc Fàbregas (Spain, b. 1987)

**Clubs:** *Arsenal (2003–)*
**Caps:** *37 (1 goal)*

Comparatively light-framed for a central midfielder, Fàbregas has more than compensated for this with his footballing intelligence, impressive confidence and visionary distribution of the ball.
An essential playmaker for Arsenal and Spain, it's difficult to believe that he is still only 22 years old. He moved to Highbury from his native Barcelona and became Arsenal's youngest ever first team player aged 16 years and 177 days. He made his Premier League debut in 2004-05 and won an FA Cup winner's medal against Manchester United that season. The following season he made 49 appearances in all competitions, including Arsenal's 2-1 defeat by Barcelona in the European Cup Final. In 2006-07, having added more bite and aggression to his formidable skills, he played in every Arsenal league game, winning Arsenal Player of the Season and PFA Young Player of the Year. Not renowned as a natural goal scorer, he blazed into season 2007-08 with 11 goals in his first 16 games, before finishing the campaign with an astounding 20 league assists. He was in the Spanish team which won Euro 2008, playing in the final against Germany, and became captain of Arsenal towards the end of 2008.

*Above: Arsenal captain Cesc Fàbregas threads a pass from midfield.*

## Giacinto Facchetti
## (Italy, 1942–2006)

**Clubs:** *Trevigliese (1956–60), Inter Milan (1960–78)*
**Caps:** *94 (3 goals)*

Facchetti was a tall, elegant, attacking left-back at the heart of Helenio Hererra's *catenaccio* system at Inter Milan in the 1960s. He joined Inter in 1960 and won four league titles with the Milanese side in his time at the San Siro. He collected two European Cup medals in 1964 and 1965, and scored the brilliant goal that eliminated Liverpool in the semi-final of the 1965 European Cup. He made his international debut in 1963 against Turkey, and was appointed captain in 1966, the year in which he scored ten goals in the *Serie A*. He captained Italy to the final against Brazil in the World Cup of 1970, and he played again in 1974. He remained at Inter in various capacities, including president in 2004, and died of cancer in 2006.

*Above: Italy's Giacinto Facchetti (right) in the 1970 World Cup Final against Brazil.*

## Giovanni Ferrari
## (Italy, 1907–1982)

**Clubs:** *Alessandria, Juventus, Ambrosiana (Inter Milan), Bologna*
**Caps:** *44 (14 goals)*

Ferrari was an inside-forward with Vittorio Pozzo's remarkable and successful Italian team of the 1930s. He played in the 1934 World Cup Final team that beat Czechoslovakia 2–1 in extra time. With Giuseppe Meazza, he played again in the 1938 World Cup Final, when Italy beat Hungary 4–2. Ferrari won the Italian league title five times with Juventus, and in 1940 he joined Inter Milan (at that time called Ambrosiana) and took the league medal again. He ended his playing career with Bologna. He managed Italy for the 1962 World Cup, and was in charge for the infamous "Battle of Santiago", when Italy and Chile punched and kicked their way through a first-round match.

*Above: Ferrari (in front of man with hat) and the 1938 Italian World Cup team.*

## Luis Figo
## (Portugal, b. 1972)

**Clubs:** *Sporting Lisbon (1989–95), Barcelona (1995–2000), Real Madrid (2000–05), Inter Milan (2005–)*
**Caps:** *127 (32 goals)*

A powerful winger, Figo became one of the finest forwards in European football. A goal provider and a scorer, and able to play on either wing, he was outstanding in the Barcelona and Real attack. He made his debut with Sporting Lisbon at 17 and left the club in 1995. He was pursued by Parma and Juventus, but a confusion over contracts saw him banned from Italian football for 2 years and he was snapped up by Barcelona for £1.5 million. After success at Euro 2000, Figo was bought by rivals Real Madrid for £37 million. He was crowned European and World Footballer of the Year in 2000 and 2001 respectively. In 2005 he moved to Inter Milan, and captained Portugal to the 2006 World Cup semi-final.

*Above: Luis Figo, star of Euro 2000 and 2001 World Footballer of the Year, but disappointing at the 2002 World Cup.*

## Tom Finney
## (England, b. 1922)

**Club:** *Preston North End (1936–60)*
**Caps:** *76 (30 goals)*

Tom Finney was one of England's most versatile players in the years after World War Two. Although a conventional winger, he was tough in the tackle, two-footed and could score goals. He spent his career with Preston North End and never won any major domestic honours, but internationally he gained 76 caps and played in every forward position for his country. Finney made his debut for Preston in 1936 and for England in 1946. He played in the World Cup finals of 1950, 1954 and 1958, and won his last England cap in 1959. Finney retired in 1960. He was twice voted Footballer of the Year, in 1954 and 1957, and was knighted in 1997. Finney was never booked or sent off in his entire career, though he played almost 500 games for Preston, where he remains club president.

*Above: The flying Tom Finney, one of England's finest-ever wingers.*

 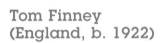

## Just Fontaine
## (Morocco, b. 1933)

**Clubs:** *AC Marrakesh, USM Casablanca (1950–53), Nice (1953–56), Reims (1956–62)*
**Caps:** *21 (30 goals)*

A small, strong striker with sharp acceleration and lightening reflexes, Fontaine led the French national attack in the second half of the 1950s. He joined Nice in 1953 and was bought by Reims in 1956 to replace Raymond Kopa, who was on his way to Real Madrid. In 1958 he helped Reims to the French "double". His entry on to the international scene, and his first

*Left: Just Fontaine made 21 caps for France between 1953 and 1960.*

cap for France, came in 1958, when he was called up to replace René Bliard, who had been injured on the eve of the World Cup finals. Fontaine scored a still-unbeaten record of 13 goals in the tournament that year (although much credit is owed to his team-mate Kopa, for creating the chances), in Sweden, and France reached third place in the tournament. Fontaine played in the 1959 European Cup Final, when Reims lost to Real Madrid but, in 1960, with Kopa now back at the club and the creative partnership between him and Fontaine again in evidence, Reims won the league. A double fracture of his leg ended his career prematurely in 1962. Later, Fontaine was president of the French player's union, and for a short time, in 1967, he took over the role of director of the French national team.

## Paulo Futre
## (Portugal, b. 1966)

**Clubs:** *Sporting Lisbon (1978–84), FC Porto (1984–87), Atlético Madrid (1987–92), Benfica (1992–93), Marseille (1993), Reggiana (1993–95), AC Milan (1995–96), West Ham United (1996), Atlético Madrid (1997–2002)*
**Caps:** *41 (6 goals)*

The much-travelled winger Futre was a teenage prodigy with Sporting Lisbon and Portugal, and he made his international debut at the age of 17. He moved to Porto, and his attacking link with the Algerian forward Madjer helped bring Porto their only European Cup, when they beat Bayern Munich 2–1 in 1987. Futre left soon afterwards to join first Atlético Madrid and then Benfica, in 1993. Marseille bought him but sold him within a few months to *Serie A* side Reggiana for £8 million. He moved to AC Milan, and had a season with West Ham United, before returning to Atlético in the late 1990s.

*Right: Paulo Futre playing for Porto in the club's triumphant European Cup Final of 1987.*

## Garrincha, Manuel Francisco dos Santos (Brazil, 1933–1983)

**Clubs:** *Pau Grande (1947–53), Botafogo (1953–66), Corinthians, Barranquilla Flamengo, Red Star Paris, Portugesa, Olaria*
**Caps:** *50 (13 goals)*

A small man with legs deformed by childhood polio, Garrincha, meaning "songbird", was nonetheless one of the greatest wingers of all time. He had electric pace, and was a dazzlingly effective dribbler with a powerful shot.

He created the first two goals in the 1958 World Cup Final, won 5–2 by Brazil, and he played again in the 1962 tournament. With Pelé unfit, Garrincha took over as centre-forward and scored two goals in the quarter-final against England, and another two in the semi-final against Chile. He collected his second World Cup winner's medal that year when Brazil beat Czechoslovakia 3–1. In the 1966 World Cup, an unfit Garrincha could not prevent his side's elimination in the first round. He died from the effects of alcoholism in 1983.

*Right: Garrincha (left) takes on Sweden.*

## Paul Gascoigne (England, b. 1967)

**Clubs:** *Newcastle United (1985–88), Tottenham Hotspur (1988–92), Lazio (1992–95), Rangers (1995–98), Middlesbrough (1998–2000), Everton (2000–2), Burnley (2002), Gansu Tianma (2003)*
**Caps:** *57 (10 goals)*

Paul Gascoigne is overweight, prone to childish antics and unpredictable, but at his best he was one of England's greatest ever midfielders. Strong, with a delicate touch, his passing and dribbling abilities were peerless, and he packed a powerful shot. Bought by Terry Venables from Newcastle in 1988, he helped Spurs to reach the 1991 FA Cup Final, where he badly injured his leg in a rash tackle. He moved to Lazio the following year but could not settle, and Glasgow Rangers bought him in 1995. His 14 goals helped Rangers win the Scottish league in 1995–6, when "Gazza" was voted Scottish Footballer of the Year. He got his first cap in 1988 and had a memorable World Cup in 1990, ending with the famous tears when England lost to West Germany in the semi-final. He scored the goal of the tournament in Euro '96 against Scotland, but his international career was terminated in 1998 by Glenn Hoddle. His subsequent managerial career was unsuccessful and he has recently suffered serious personal problems.

*Above: Paul Gascoigne in England's win over Scotland in Euro '96.*

## Claudio Gentile
## (Libya, b. 1953)

**Clubs:** *Arona, Varese, Juventus, Fiorentina*
**Caps:** *71 (1 goal)*

A tough, notoriously hard-tackling right-back, Gentile was the perfect foil for skilful sweeper Gaetano Scirea at Juventus and in the Italian national team. He helped Juventus to win six *Serie A* titles and two Italian Cups between 1977 and 1986, and he also played in the club's 1977 UEFA Cup and 1984 Cup Winners' Cup triumphs. He played in the 1978 World Cup finals, and was one of the six Juventus players who represented Italy in 1982 to win the World Cup trophy.

*Left: Italy's Claudio Gentile (left) takes on Argentina's Diego Maradona.*

## Francisco Paco Gento
## (Spain, b. 1933)

**Clubs:** *Santander (1950–53), Real Madrid (1953–70)*
**Caps:** *43 (5 goals)*

Gento was a fast, skilful outside-left for Real Madrid when the Spanish club ruled European football. He was arch-supplier to the deadly Alfredo Di Stefano and Ferenc Puskas in the side that won the European Cup for five successive years, from 1956–60. Gento played in eight European Cup finals, helping to win six of them, and he scored the extra-time winner in 1958, when Real Madrid beat AC Milan 3–2. He was Real's captain in their 1964 3–1 defeat by Inter Milan, and again in their 1966 2–1 win over Partizan Belgrade. In total, this great club servant made nearly 800 appearances for Real, and he helped the club to 12 Spanish league titles between 1954 and 1969. He retired from the game in 1971.

*Right: Winger Paco Gento in the all-white strip of Real Madrid.*

# Ryan Giggs
## (Wales, b. 1973)

**Clubs:** *Manchester United (1991–)*
**Caps:** *64 (12 goals)*

Cardiff-born Giggs signed for Manchester United in 1990 and made his league debut for the club in 1991. A strong and speedy left-winger with an eye for goal, he quickly became a first-team regular and he has since gained a host of honours with the club, including European Cup winner's medals in 1999 and 2008. Giggs has scored many important goals for United, but probably none as impressive as the goal against Arsenal in the 1999 FA Cup semi-final, when he ran almost half the length of the pitch to score the winner with a rasping shot in extra time. Gaining his first cap at the age of 17 years and 332 days, Giggs beat John Charles' record to be the youngest player to represent Wales, although he lost that title to the young Welsh international Ryan Green. In 2008, he overtook Bobby Charlton to become United's leader in club appearances.

*Right: Ryan Giggs speeds towards goal for Wales against Turkey.*

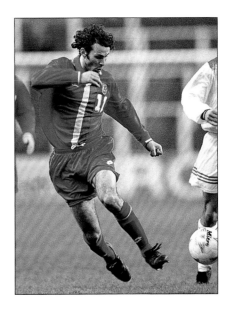

# Johnny Giles
## (Ireland, b. 1940)

**Clubs:** *Manchester United (1957–63), Leeds United (1963–75), West Bromwich Albion (1975–77), Shamrock Rovers (1977–80)*
**Caps:** *59 (5 goals)*

A gifted midfield player, with a strong shot and a precise ability to find a team-mate with a short or long ball, Giles began his career on the right wing with Manchester United. He won an FA Cup winner's medal with the club in 1962 and transferred to Leeds United in 1963. He moved to midfield and, with his partner Billy Bremner, formed the creative engine of Don Revie's team. His skill was matched by an uncompromising determination, and he drove on Leeds to win two Fairs Cups, in 1966 and 1968, and two league titles, as well as playing in the 1975 European Cup Final, when the club were beaten 2–0 by Bayern Munich. This disappointment was Giles' last appearance for Leeds. He moved first to West Bromwich Albion as player-manager, and then to Shamrock Rovers in the same role. He was the youngest-ever player to represent Ireland, and he played his last international game in 1979.

*Left: Johnny Giles (right) rises to the occasion for Leeds United.*

## Jimmy Greaves
## (England, b. 1940)

**Clubs:** *Chelsea (1957–61), AC Milan (1961), Tottenham Hotspur (1961–70), West Ham United (1970–71)*
**Caps:** *57 (44 goals)*

A cool, devastatingly effective striker with close control and mesmerizing dribbling skills, Greaves was the finest goal scorer of his generation. By the age of 20 he had scored 100 goals for Chelsea. He moved to AC Milan in 1961, but after only ten league games for the Italian club he joined Spurs for £99,999 (to avoid being Britain's first £100,000 player). In his nine years at White Hart Lane he was top scorer in the First Division six times. Greaves gained his first international cap in 1959, scoring against Peru, and in 1961 he scored 11 times in five internationals, including a hat trick in England's 9–3 hammering of Scotland. He played in the 1962 World Cup finals and in three of England's matches in the 1966 finals, but he was not selected for the final itself. A deeply disappointed Greaves never played for England again. His total of 44 international goals places him just behind Bobby Charlton and Gary Lineker in the scoring stakes. On his retirement, he endured a period of alcoholism but came back as a popular newspaper and TV pundit.

*Above: Greaves, Spurs' prolific goal scorer, playing for the club against Everton.*

## Gunnar Gren
## (Sweden, 1920–1991)

**Clubs:** *IFK Gothenburg, AC Milan (1949–53), Fiorentina (1953–55), Genoa (1955–56), GAIS Gothenburg (1956–59)*
**Caps:** *57 (32 goals)*

Known as "The Professor" because of both his premature baldness and his intelligent play, Gren was an astute inside-forward who began his career with IFK Gothenburg. He played for Sweden in the 1948 Olympic Games, helping the team to win a gold medal in the final against Yugoslavia, and he moved to AC Milan in 1949, where he teamed up with fellow Swedes Gunnar Nordahl and Nils Liedholm to form the famed "Gre-no-li" attack. Gren helped Milan to the *Serie A* title in 1951 before returning to Sweden in 1956. He played again for his country, in what was to be the last of his international games, in the 1958 World Cup Final. Although Sweden were the first to score, they were deservedly beaten 5–2 by Pelé and Brazil. Gunnar Gren died in 1991.

*Above: "The Professor", Gunnar Gren.*

## Ruud Gullit
### (Holland, b. 1962)

**Clubs:** *Haarlem (1979–82), Feyenoord (1982–85), PSV Eindhoven (1985–87), AC Milan (1987–93), AC Milan (1994), Sampdoria (1994–95), Chelsea (1995–98)*
**Caps:** *65 (16 goals)*

A tall, athletic player with delicate touch and control, Gullit was the inspiration behind the success of AC Milan and Holland in the late 1980s and early 1990s. Bought by Milan in 1987 from PSV Eindhoven for a record £6 million, Gullit led the Italian side to successive European Cup victories in 1989 and 1990. He played in the 1994 final, in Milan's 4–0 humbling of Barcelona, but soon moved to Sampdoria then Chelsea, taking over as player-manager in 1997. He left in 1998 to manage Newcastle United for a year. Internationally, he was capped in 1981 and won the European Championships in 1988. He played in the 1990 World Cup but did not appear in 1994, an argument with Dutch coach Advocaat prompting his walkout. He became coach of Feyenoord in 2004 and is now a TV pundit.

*Right: Ruud Gullit leaves Denmark's John Jensen on the ground in the 1992 European Championship.*

## Gheorghe Hagi
### (Romania, b. 1965)

**Clubs:** *Sportul Studentesc (1982–86), Steaua Bucharest (1986–90), Real Madrid (1990–92), Brescia (1992–94), Barcelona (1994–96), Galatasaray (1996–2002)*
**Caps:** *125 (34 goals)*

Romania's most-capped player, Hagi is a single-minded striker who gained his first cap at 18. In 1986 he joined Steaua Bucharest, and his scoring prowess propelled them to three league titles in

*Left: Romania's greatest footballer, Hagi.*

succession, and to the 1989 European Cup Final, where an unusually quiescent Steaua lost 4–0 to AC Milan. Known as the "Maradona of the Carpathians", Hagi moved to Real Madrid in 1990, and to Brescia in 1992. He joined Cruyff's Barcelona in 1994 but did not play to his potential. Hagi's last club was Galatasaray, with whom he won the UEFA Cup Final in 2000. He has played in three World Cup finals. In 1990 his Romanian side were eliminated on penalties by Ireland in the second round; in 1994 they made the quarter-final stage before being knocked out by Sweden; and in 1998 they lost to Croatia in the second round.

## Kurt Hamrin
### (Sweden, b. 1934)

**Clubs:** *AIK (1952–56), Juventus (1956–57), Padova (1957–58), Fiorentina (1958–67), AC Milan (1967–69), Napoli (1969–71)*
**Caps:** *32 (16 goals)*

A fast goal-scoring right-winger, Hamrin's goals helped Fiorentina to the 1961 European Cup Winners Cup: his goal, four minutes from time in the second leg killed off Rangers' hopes of taking the trophy. He had played for Juventus before joining Fiorentina, but he quickly adjusted to Italian football. Later, at AC Milan, he played in the side that beat Ajax in the 1969 European Cup Final. He ended his career with Napoli and then Caserta. He played for Sweden in the 1958 World Cup.

*Above: Sweden's Kurt Hamrin played most of his club football in Italy.*

*Above: Liverpool's cultured defender Alan Hansen.*

## Alan Hansen
### (Scotland, b. 1955)

**Clubs:** *Partick Thistle (1973–77), Liverpool (1977–90)*
**Caps:** *22*

A tall, cultured and elegant central defender, Hansen was a member of the team that brought Liverpool so much silverware in the 1970s and 1980s. He joined from Partick Thistle in 1977 for £100,000, and by the time he retired in 1990, he had won eight league titles, two FA Cups and three European Cups. He played over 600 games for Liverpool, captained the club to the "double" in 1986, and his calm authority and vision were crucial to the Reds' success. He played 22 times for Scotland, and appeared in the 1982 World Cup finals but was dropped for the 1986 tournament. He became a television commentator firstly for Sky TV and then the BBC, and made the famous proclamation, when discussing the prospects of the young Manchester United side, that "you can't win anything with kids." Alex Ferguson's team promptly went on to win the English "double".

## Ernest Happel
## (Austria, 1925–1992)

**Clubs:** *Rapid Vienna, First Vienna, Racing Club de Paris*
**Caps:** *51 (5 goals)*

Happel was a tough, skilful centre-half with Rapid Vienna in the 1950s. He was renowned for the ferocity of his shot from a dead ball, and he scored a hat trick against Real Madrid in a European Cup match in 1957. He played for the celebrated Austrian national side in both the 1954 and 1958 World Cup finals, and became a successful manager after retirement in 1959. He managed Feyenoord to their only European Cup triumph in 1970, beating Celtic 2–1 by playing an early brand of "total football". He also guided Hamburg to their European Cup Final 1–0 victory over Juventus in 1983, and led Bruges to their 1–0 1978 final defeat by Liverpool. He succeeded Rinus Michels as coach to the Dutch national team, and led them all the way to the 1978 World Cup Final. Happel died of cancer in 1992, aged only 66, and the Prater stadium in Vienna (the biggest stadium in Austria) was renamed the Ernest Happel-Stadion in his honour.

*Right: Ernest Happel lines up with the FIFA World X1 squad in 1953.*

## Johnny Haynes
## (England, 1934–2005)

**Clubs:** *Fulham (1952–69)*
**Caps:** *56 (18 goals)*

Although Haynes was one of the sweetest passers of a ball that England has ever seen, he never won a trophy with his only club, Fulham. He made his debut in 1952, and by the end of the decade had become a massive influence on the game. As well as his uncanny distribution skills, he was a frequent goal scorer, and he effortlessly dictated the pace and direction of play. Haynes was the first £100-a-week footballer, on the abolition of the maximum wage in 1961, and he captained the England international team from 1959–62, until a bad car accident led to his retirement from international football. In that period, he led England to their 1961 9–3 defeat of Scotland, scoring twice, and to the country's ill-fated 1962 World Cup finals in Chile. He left Fulham in 1969 to become player-manager with South Africa's Durban City, eventually returning to live in retirement in Edinburgh. He died in a car crash on his 71st birthday in 2005.

*Left: Fulham and England captain, Johnny Haynes.*

## Thierry Henry, (France, b. 1977)

**Clubs:** *Monaco (1994–99), Juventus (1999), Arsenal (1999–2007), Barcelona (2007–)*
**Caps:** *111 (48 goals)*

In 2003–04 Henry advanced claims to be the world's leading player. He spearheaded the Arsenal team, which went through the entire League season unbeaten. By scoring 30 goals he won the ESM Golden Shoe, as Europe's top goalscorer, and was voted the Player of the Year. Henry made his French debut in October 1997, and was a member of France's team that won the World Cup in 1998 and the European Championship in 2000. He won the French League in 1997 with Monaco, and, with Arsenal, won the English League and FA Cup "double" in both 2002-03 and 2003-04, and the FA Cup in 2005. Originally a winger, he was converted to a central striker and his speed on the break, control and accuracy make him the striker *par excellence*. He moved to Barcelona in 2007.

*Left: Henry's shows his speed and ball control for Arsenal in 2004.*

## Glenn Hoddle (England, b. 1957)

**Clubs:** *Tottenham Hotspur (1975–87), Monaco (1987–91), Swindon Town (1991–93), Chelsea (1993–95)*
**Caps:** *53 (8 goals)*

A creative midfield player with exceptional touch, control and a powerful shot, Hoddle was the hero of White Hart Lane in the early 1980s. He won two FA Cup medals, in 1981 and 1982, scoring in the latter and in the replay against Queen's Park Rangers. He also claimed his UEFA Cup medal in 1984, when Spurs defeated Anderlecht on penalties. After Spurs lost the 1987 FA Cup Final, Hoddle moved to Arsène Wenger's Monaco. He first represented his country in 1979, scoring against Bulgaria on his debut, and he played in the 1982 and 1986 World Cup finals. He moved back to England, in 1991, to become player-manager of Swindon Town, and he later performed the same role at Chelsea. He coached England from 1996 to 1999, but was quickly dismissed after making some ill-considered remarks about disabled people. He subsequently managed Southampton, Spurs and Wolves, to no great success.

*Right: Spurs' hero Glen Hoddle sets up another sweet pass.*

## Zlatan Ibrahimovic (Sweden, b. 1981)

**Clubs:** *Clubs: Malmo (1999–2001), Ajax (2001–04), Juventus (2004–06), Inter Milan (2006–08)*
**Caps:** *56 (20 goals)*

A toweringly lethal and speedy striker, Ibrahimovic was born in Malmo, Sweden. He began his career with Malmo and joined Ajax in 2001 for over £5 million. He netted four goals in Ajax's 2002 Champions League run, and he scored a marvellously brazen goal in 2004, when he dribbled past at least six NAC Breda defenders. He moved to Juventus for £15 million in 2004 but the 2006 match-fixing scandal saw him leave Turin to join Inter where he helped the Milanese side win the Serie A title in 2007 and 2008. He played for Sweden in Euro 2004 and the 2006 World Cup finals, and briefly came out of retirement for an ultimately unsuccessful Euro 2008 campaign.

*Left: Ibrahimovic joined Inter in 2006.*

## Jairzinho, Jair Ventura Filho (Brazil, b. 1944)

**Clubs:** *Botafogo (1959–71), Marseille (1971–73), Cruzeiro (1973–76), Portuguesa (1976–78)*
**Caps:** *82 (34 goals)*

The natural heir to Garrincha in the Brazilian national team, Jairzinho was a speedy, goal-scoring right-winger. He was capped in 1963. Despite a serious injury in 1967, he played in the 1970 World Cup finals, where he set a record by scoring in every round, including Brazil's third goal when he converted a header from Pelé in the 4–1 final win over Italy. He moved to Marseille for a brief, unsettled spell, and returned to Brazil with Cruzeiro, helping the club to win the *Copa Libertadores* championship in 1976. He ended his career with Venezuela's Portuguesa. Jairzinho is credited with discovering the young Ronaldo in the early 1990s.

*Above: Jairzinho, Brazil's goal-scoring star of the 1970 World Cup finals in Mexico.*

## Alex James
## (Scotland, 1901–53)

**Clubs:** *Raith Rovers (1922–25), Preston North End (1925–29), Arsenal (1929–37)*
**Caps:** *8 (4 goals)*

James was a short, aggressive inside-forward with marvellous ball skills and passing ability. He was Preston's leading goal scorer before he was bought by Herbert Chapman, in 1929; he added the final creative touch to the Arsenal team that dominated the 1930s playing their new "WM" formation. He was chief schemer and supplier to the Arsenal attack featuring Lambert, Jack and Bastin, which brought the club four league titles from 1930 to 1935, as well as two FA Cups in 1930 and 1936. He played for Scotland on only a few occasions, but he was a member of the "Wembley Wizards" side, which convincingly beat England 5–1 in 1928. James retired from football in 1937 and died from cancer 16 years later in 1953. He is remembered as a Highbury great and celebrated for his creative, attacking football.

*Left: Alex James, the creative hub of Arsenal's 1930s side.*

## Pat Jennings
## (N. Ireland, b. 1945)

**Clubs:** *Newry Town (1961–63), Watford (1963–64), Tottenham Hotspur (1964–77), Arsenal (1977–85)*
**Caps:** *119*

A gentle giant of a goalkeeper, the dependable Jennings joined Spurs from Watford for £27,000 in 1964, when he also made his international debut. In his time at Spurs, he made nearly 450 league appearances for the club, breaking the club's existing appearance record, and collected an FA Cup and a UEFA Cup winner's medal. Jennings also became Northern Ireland's most capped player. When Spurs were relegated in 1977, Jennings moved down the road to join Arsenal, for whom he played until 1985 (making way for John Lukic when he left). He won another FA Cup winner's medal in Arsenal's 3–2 defeat of Manchester United in 1979. He played for Northern Ireland in the 1982 and 1986 World Cup finals, retiring after their defeat by Brazil. Jennings once scored direct from a goal-kick, in a Charity Shield match against Manchester United in 1967. Jennings retired in 1985 and has since returned to Tottenham Hotspur as a goalkeeping coach.

*Right: Pat Jennings clutches the ball in his massive hands.*

## Jimmy Johnstone
## (Scotland, 1944–2006)

**Clubs:** *Celtic (1961–75), San José Earthquakes (1975), Sheffield United (1975), Dundee (1977)*
**Caps:** *23 (4 goals)*

"Jinky" Johnstone rose from being a ballboy at Parkhead in the 1950s to become one of Celtic's and Scotland's greatest-ever players, making his international debut in 1964. A small, ginger-haired right-winger, Johnstone was master of the dribble, a great crosser of the ball and an expert finisher. He was central to Jock Stein's memorable side of the 1960s and 1970s, when

Celtic won the Scottish League title nine times in a row, collected seven Scottish Cups and famously became the first British winners of the European Cup in 1967. Johnstone was often at his best in European competitions, and he relished the opportunity to demonstrate his skills on the international stage. However, he was marked out of the game in Celtic's 2–1 defeat by Feyenoord in the 1970 European Cup Final. He left Celtic in 1975. Fans voted him Celtic's greatest ever player in 2002. He died from motor neurone disease in 2006.

*Right: Jimmy Johnstone sets off on another dribble for Celtic.*

## Kaka
## (Brazil, b. 1982)

**Clubs:** *Sao Paulo (2001–03), AC Milan (2003–)*
**Caps:** *62 (23)*

Christened Ricardo Izecson dos Santos Leite, Kaka is a gifted playmaker and forward with a remarkable goal-scoring record. He joined Sao Paulo at the age of 8 and, after his outstanding performances as a teenager in the first team, he was picked up by AC Milan in 2003 for £7.3 million. He rapidly established himself as indispensable to the Italian side, and his trickery, ball-play and vision have been instrumental in Milan's success, particularly when he scored 10 goals in the 2007 Champions League tournament, culminating in a 2-1 final win over Liverpool. That year he was awarded the Ballon d'Or and voted FIFA World Player of the Year. He began his international career with Brazil in 2002 and scored his country's only goal in their opening 1-0 win over Croatia at the 2006 World Cup finals in Germany. A devout Christian, he celebrates his goals by pointing to his God above. He joined Real Madrid in June 2009 for a record £56 million.

*Left: Kaka is one of the most valuable players in world football.*

# Nwankwo Kanu
## (Nigeria, b. 1976)

**Clubs:** *Federated Works (1991–92), Iwanyanu (1992–93), Ajax (1993–96), Inter Milan (1996–98), Arsenal (1998–2004), West Bromwich Albion (2004–06), Portsmouth (2006–)*
**Caps:** *77 (13 goals)*

Nigerian striker Kanu joined Ajax in 1993. The lanky player immediately settled in and helped Ajax win three Dutch league titles from 1994 to 1996. He also came on as a substitute in Ajax's European Cup Final win over AC Milan in 1995, and played in the 1996 defeat by Juventus. A serious heart valve condition threatened to end his career, but following corrective surgery, Kanu joined Arsenal in 1998. He scored some memorable goals for Arsenal, including a winning hat trick in ten minutes against Chelsea, and a superb long-range back-heel against Middlesbrough. He represented Nigeria in the 1996 Olympic Games when they beat first Brazil in the semi-final and then Argentina to take the gold medal. Kanu was voted African Footballer of the Year in 1996 and again in 1999. He played in the 1998 and 2002 World Cups and is currently plying his trade at Portsmouth.

*Right: Kanu celebrates an Arsenal goal.*

# Roy Keane
## (Ireland, b. 1971)

**Clubs:** *Nottingham Forest (1990–93), Manchester United (1993–2006)*
**Caps:** *66 (9 goals)*

A strong, aggressive, ball-winning midfielder, with a fiery temper and a commanding on-pitch manner, Keane is also a skilful passer and he has a knack for scoring important goals. He left his native Cork for Nottingham Forest in 1990, and he moved to Manchester United three years later, becoming captain in 1997. He amassed seven League titles and three FA Cups, as well as a European Cup winner's medal, although he missed the 1999 final against Bayern Munich due to suspension. As captain of the Republic of Ireland squad for the 2002 World Cup finals, he was sent home before the start after disagreements with management. Keane left Manchester United for Celtic in 2006. He retired the same year and subsequently embarked on a managerial career at Sunderland, gaining promotion to the Premier League in 2007 before leaving midway through the season 2008-09. He is currently manager of Ipswich Town.

*Left: Roy Keane, Manchester United's hard-tackling midfielder.*

*Above: Kevin Keegan: "Mighty Mouse" of Liverpool, Hamburg and England.*

## Kevin Keegan
## (England, b. 1951)

**Clubs:** *Scunthorpe United (1968–71), Liverpool (1971–77), Hamburg (1977–80), Southampton (1980–82), Newcastle United (1982–84)*
**Caps:** *63 (21 goals)*

A small, dynamic creator and finisher, Keegan starred for Liverpool and England in the 1970s. Bought by Bill Shankly in 1971, he soon established himself in attack alongside John Toshack. Liverpool won the league twice and the 1976 UEFA Cup, with Keegan scoring in both legs of the final, and he was voted Footballer of the Year. He produced a fine performance the following year in the European Cup Final against Borussia Mönchengladbach, before moving to Hamburg in the summer of 1977. At Hamburg he was twice voted European Footballer of the Year, and he played in Hamburg's losing team in the 1980 European Cup Final against Nottingham Forest. Keegan returned to English football in 1980 to join Southampton, and then Newcastle in 1982, where his goals helped United gain promotion to the First Division. Keegan gained the first of his 63 international caps in 1972. After retiring, Keegan became manager of Newcastle United, Fulham and in 1999 England. He resigned in 2000 after losing a World Cup qualifying match against Germany and guided Manchester City to the Premiership in 2002. He again resigned from football, leaving the club in 2005, but went back to Newcastle as coach in 2008. He lasted only a few months, leaving the club in acrimonious circumstances in September that year.

## Mario Kempes
## (Argentina, b. 1954)

**Clubs:** *Instituto de Cordoba (1967–70), Rosario Central (1970–76), Valéncia (1976–81), River Plate (1981–82)*
**Caps:** *43 (20 goals)*

A long-haired, muscular centre-forward, Kempes was transferred from Rosario to Valéncia in 1976, having played for Argentina in the 1974 World Cup finals. The high point of his career came in the 1978 World Cup where, playing in front of his home crowd, he was voted Player of the Tournament. He scored six goals, including two in the final against Holland. The first was a touch-in from a Luque pass and the second, in extra time, was a superb solo goal past three Dutch defenders. He then supplied Bertoni with the pass that set up the third goal in Argentina's 3–1 triumph. He was voted South American Player of the Year in 1978. In 1980 he won a Cup Winners Cup medal with Valéncia, but in 1981 he returned to Argentina. He played in the 1982 World Cup, but he and Argentina were ineffectual in the tournament.

*Above: Mario Kempes celebrates as Argentina wins its first World Cup in 1978.*

## Jürgen Klinsmann (Germany, b. 1964)

**Clubs:** *Stuttgart Kickers (1980–84), VfB Stuttgart (1984–89), Inter Milan (1989–92), Monaco (1992–94), Tottenham Hotspur (1994–95), Bayern Munich (1995–97), Sampdoria (1997), Tottenham Hotspur (1997–98)*
**Caps:** *108 (47 goals)*

*Below: Jürgen Klinsman takes a tumble during his first spell with Spurs in 1994–95.*

Klinsmann is Germany's second-highest goal scorer (the highest is Gerd Müller). A top-class striker, with sharp anticipation and acceleration, Klinsmann moved from VfB Stuttgart in 1989 to join Inter Milan, where he won a UEFA Cup winner's medal in 1991. His three goals in the tournament helped Germany to win the 1990 World Cup Final, and he moved to Monaco that summer. He scored five goals for Germany in the 1994 World Cup finals, but the team was eliminated by Bulgaria in the quarter-finals. That autumn, Klinsmann made a surprising £2-million move to Tottenham Hotspur. By the end of the season he had scored 20 goals for the north London side, and been voted Footballer of the Year. He then moved to Bayern Munich, and he scored a record 15 goals in their progress through the 1995–96 UEFA Cup, which Bayern won 5–1 on aggregate against Bordeaux in the final. Klinsmann captained his country to victory in Euro '96, and he led Germany to the 1998 World Cup finals. He took over as coach of the German national team in 2004 but resigned after the 2006 World Cup finals. He then managed Bayern Munich.

## Patrick Kluivert
## (Holland, b. 1976)

**Clubs:** *Ajax (1994–97), AC Milan (1997–98), Barcelona (1998–2004), Newcastle United (2004–05), Valencia (2005–06), PSV (2006–07), Lille (2008–)*
**Caps:** *79 (40 goals)*

A fast and powerful striker, Kluivert is yet another successful product of the Ajax youth system. Playing in attack with Marc Overmars and Jari Litmanen, Kluivert's goals helped Ajax win the Dutch league title in 1995 and 1996. He also scored the winning goal in the 1995 European Cup Final against AC Milan, and came on as a substitute in the final in 1996 against Juventus. He joined AC Milan in 1997 but had a frustrating time due to injury, and was bought by mentor and former Ajax manager Louis Van Gaal for Barcelona the following year. He forced Brazil's Sonny Anderson out of the first team, and his understanding with Luis Figo and Rivaldo took Barcelona to the semi-final of the 2000 European Cup. He played for Holland in Euro 96, and his two goals against Yugoslavia and Argentina helped Holland secure fourth place in the 1998 World Cup finals. Kluivert was joint top scorer at Euro 2000, and his five goals eased Holland's passage to the semi-finals.

*Right: Kluivert with the European Cup.*

## Sandor Kocsis
## (Hungary, 1928–1979)

**Clubs:** *Ferencvaros (1944–49), Honved (1949–55), Young Boys Berne (1955–56), Barcelona (1956–63)*
**Caps:** *68 (75 goals)*

Another of the "Magnificent Magyars", inside-right Kocsis played alongside Ferenc Puskas in the Honved and

*Left: Sandor Kocsis (centre), lining up with the Hungarian team to play England at Wembley in 1953.*

Hungary teams of the early 1950s. He was top scorer in the 1954 World Cup finals with 11 goals, including two in the semi-final against Uruguay. He joined Barcelona after the 1956 Hungarian revolution. He helped the Spanish club to a Fairs Cup victory over Birmingham in 1960, and scored in their 3–2 defeat by Benfica in the 1961 European Cup Final. Kocsis scored all three of Barcelona's goals in the 7–3 aggregate defeat by Valéncia in the 1962 Fairs Cup Final. He won three Hungarian league titles with Honved, and one Spanish league title with Barcelona. Kocsis died in 1979.

## Ronald Koeman
## (Holland, b. 1963)

**Clubs:** *Groningen (1980–83),
Ajax (1983–86), PSV Eindhoven
(1986–89), Barcelona (1989–95),
Feyenoord (1995–98)*
**Caps:** *77 (14 goals)*

The blond-haired Koeman was a stocky,
attacking sweeper with a thunderbolt
shot, particularly from free kicks. He
moved from Ajax to PSV Eindhoven in
1986, where he scored 21 goals in his
first season. In 1988 he won a European
Cup winner's medal when PSV beat
Benfica, and he signed for Barcelona the
following year. Koeman scored in
Barcelona's 2–1 European Cup Winners
Cup defeat by Manchester United in
1991, and he scored again in the 1992
final to win the European Cup against
Sampdoria. He was a member of
Holland's victorious team in the 1988
European Championships, and he played
in the 1990 and 1994 World Cup finals.
Koeman left Barcelona in 1995 to
return to club football in Holland.
He retired in 1998 and subsequently
managed a handful of clubs, including
Ajax and Valencia.

*Right: The muscular, blond figure of
Holland's Ronald Koeman.*

## Raymond Kopa
## (Kopaszewski)
## (France, b. 1931)

**Clubs:** *Angiers (1949–51), Reims
(1951–56), Real Madrid (1956–59),
Reims (1959–67)*
**Caps:** *45 (18 goals)*

The son of an immigrant Polish miner,
Kopa was a centre-forward of skill,
poise and balance. He began his career
on the right wing at Angiers, in
Algeria, and joined the French club
Reims in 1951, moving into the centre
position. After playing against Real
Madrid in the 1956 European Cup
Final, Kopa joined the Spanish club but
he returned to his former position on
the wing to accommodate the great
Alfredo Di Stefano. He played in Real's
next three European Cup victories and
returned to Reims in 1959, where he
won the French league in his first
season back with the club. Kopa gained
45 caps for France, playing alongside
Just Fontaine for the 1954 and 1958
World Cup finals; the pair enjoyed
a highly successful partnership at the
front. Kopa scored three goals in the
World Cup of 1958, where France
reached third place, with a total of 18
goals in his international career.

*Left: Raymond Kopa in action
for Real Madrid.*

## Ruud Krol
## (Holland, b. 1949)

**Clubs:** *Ajax (1964–80),
Vancouver Whitecaps (1980),
Napoli (1980–82)*
**Caps:** *83 (2 goals)*

A big, attacking centre-back, Krol is
the most-capped player in Dutch
football history. Playing for Ajax, along
with Johann Cruyff, Günter Neeskens
and Johnny Rep, he was a vital cog in
Rinus Michels' "total football" system.
He collected two European Cup
winner's medals in 1972 and 1973,
beating Inter Milan and Juventus
respectively in the finals. He made
his international debut in 1969 and
played in two World Cup Finals –
against West Germany in 1974 and,
as sweeper, against Argentina in 1978 –
losing them both. He was one of the
last of the great team to leave Ajax,
and by the time he moved to his last
club Napoli in 1980, he had won six
Dutch league titles. He currently manages
South African team the Orlando Pirates.

*Right: Ruud Krol (right) playing for
Holland against West Germany in the
1974 World Cup Final.*

## Ladislav Kubala
## (Hungary, 1927–2002)

**Clubs:** *Ferencvaros, Bratislava, Vasas, Barcelona, Espanyol, FC Zürich*
**Caps:** *3 (Hungary), 7 (4 goals) (Czechoslovkia), 19 (10 goals) (Spain)*

Hungarian inside-forward Kubala escaped from Eastern Europe in the immediate post-war climate of the late 1940s. He signed for Barcelona, and was later joined there by his

*Left: Hungarian exile Kubala gained most of his club honours in Spain.*

compatriots and fellow exiles, Zoltan Czibor and Sandor Kocsis. Between them, the Hungarians created a much-feared forward line, which helped Barcelona to the European Cup Final and to two Fairs Cup victories. Kubala also achieved six Spanish league and six Spanish Cup titles with Barcelona for whom he scored 243 goals in 329 games, before moving to Espanyol and then FC Zürich. He played for Zürich in 1967, at the age of 39, in a European Cup tie against Celtic. He finished his playing career in Canada. Kubala was capped by three different countries, and he was also selected for the FIFA "Rest of the World" side that played against England in 1963.

## Grzegorz Lato
## (Poland, b. 1950)

**Clubs:** *Stal Mielec, Lokeren, Atlante*
**Caps:** *104 (45 goals)*

Poland's most-capped player, the predatory Grzegorz Lato, began his career as a right-winger with Polish club Stal Mielec, and he moved into midfield later in his career. He won two Polish league titles with Stal, before signing for the Belgian club Lokeren. He finished

his club football with Atlante in Mexico. Playing alongside Deyna and Gadocha in the strong Polish international side, Lato was top goal scorer, with seven goals, in the 1974 World Cup finals – the last goal was scored against Brazil with only 15 minutes to go, securing Poland's third place. Lato also played in the 1978 finals, but this time the team had less success. He became President of the Polish Football Association in 2008.

*Right: Grzegorz Lato, leading scorer in the 1974 World Cup finals.*

## Michael Laudrup
## (Denmark, b. 1964)

**Clubs:** *Brondby (1978–83), Lazio (1983–85), Juventus (1985–89), Barcelona (1989–94), Real Madrid (1994–96), Vissel Kobe (1996–97), Ajax (1997–98)*
**Caps:** *104 (37 goals)*

Laudrup was an elegant midfielder and Denmark's most-capped outfield player with 104 international appearances. He began his playing career with Brondby, before moving to Italy, first to Lazio, and

*Left: Michael Laudrup playing for Denmark. Laudrup made three World Cup appearances for his country.*

then to Juventus in 1985. In 1989 he moved to Barcelona, where his perceptive passing and attacking skills helped them to their first European Cup title in 1992, and to four consecutive Spanish league titles. He then transferred to Real Madrid, where he inspired the Spanish club to win the league. In 1996 Laudrup moved to the Japanese side Vissel Kobe. He made his international debut at the age of 18, and has played in the 1986, 1990 and 1998 World Cup finals. However, he missed out on Denmark's surprise 1992 European Championship victory after a dispute with coach Richard Moller Nielsen. Laudrup was coach of Brondby from 2002 to 2006 and then Getafe, followed by a period at Spartak Moscow.

Above: Denis Law adds to his goal tally for Manchester United in the 1971–2 season.

## Denis Law
## (Scotland, b. 1940)

**Clubs:** *Huddersfield Town (1957–60), Manchester City (1960–61), Torino (1961), Manchester United (1961–73), Manchester City (1973–74)*
**Caps:** *55 (30 goals)*

"The Lawman" was a slim, fair-haired striker of medium build, but he was lethal in the penalty box and in the air for Manchester United and Scotland. He joined Manchester City from Huddersfield for a record £55,000 fee in 1960, spent a few unhappy months with Torino, and joined Manchester United for £116,000 in 1961. Over the next few years his goal scoring, and his partnership with Best and Charlton brought two league titles to Matt Busby's side, in 1965 and 1967, and he was prolific in European games, scoring four hat tricks. However, he missed the club's 1968 European Cup Final victory due to injury. Law was first capped at the age of 18 and, though he only played in one World Cup finals, in 1974, he scored 30 goals for his country. He was selected for the FIFA "Rest of the World" side that played against England, in 1963, and he scored in the match. He moved to Manchester City in 1973, and his goal helped to send United into the Second Division in 1974, the year he retired.

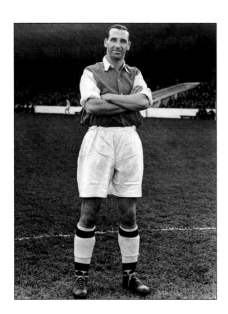

## Tommy Lawton
## (England, 1919–1996)

**Clubs:** *Burnley (1936–37), Everton (1937–45), Chelsea (1945–47), Notts County (1947–52), Brentford (1952–53), Arsenal (1953–56)*
**Caps:** *23 (22 goals)*

A direct, exciting centre-forward, Lawton joined Burnley in 1936 and became, at the age of 17, the youngest player to score a hat trick in the

*Left: Lawton, in his Arsenal strip, towards the end of his playing career.*

Football League. He moved to Everton the following year, as a replacement for "Dixie" Dean, and was top scorer in both 1938 and 1939, the year Everton won the English league title. In 1939 he made his international debut against Wales and scored. He joined Chelsea after World War Two and then moved to Notts County in 1947, for a record £20,000 fee. His 31 goals secured promotion for County in 1950, and Lawton moved on again to become player-manager of Brentford. He spent a couple of seasons with Arsenal before becoming manager of Kettering Town. Tommy Lawton died in 1996.

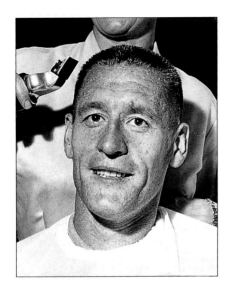

## Nils Liedholm
### (Sweden, 1922–2000)

**Clubs:** *Norköpping (1948–49), AC Milan (1949–61)*
**Caps:** *23 (11 goals)*

Liedholm was one-third of the "Gre-no-li" Swedish attack that brought AC Milan the *Serie A* title in 1951, for the first time in 44 years. He was an inside-forward with great skill and an exceptional shot, who had

*Left: The skilful Swede Nils Liedholm.*

joined Milan shortly after picking up an Olympic gold medal, when Sweden beat Yugoslavia in the final of the 1948 games. Liedholm played in the 1958 European Cup Final against Real Madrid, making the first goal for Schiaffino, but Milan lost 3–2 in extra time. He captained Sweden to the 1958 World Cup Final and scored the opening goal in the first four minutes, only to lose 5–2 to an exuberant Brazil. After retirement, Liedholm became Milan's coach, and also managed Fiorentina and Roma, whom he took to the 1984 European Cup Final.

## Gary Lineker
### (England, b. 1960)

**Clubs:** *Leicester City (1978–85), Everton (1985–86), Barcelona (1986–89), Tottenham Hotspur (1989–92), Grampus Eight (1992–94)*
**Caps:** *80 (48 goals)*

Lineker is England's second-highest goal scorer with 48 goals, one behind Bobby Charlton. A deadly finisher in the penalty area, he moved from Leicester to Everton in 1985; that season he scored 30 goals for the club and was voted Player of the Year. In 1986, he scored six goals for England in the World Cup finals, including a hat trick against Poland, and he finished as the tournament's top scorer. The same year Lineker moved to Barcelona, and his goals helped the club win the European Cup Winners Cup in 1989. He moved to Spurs in 1989 and the scoring continued, with Lineker netting a total of 28 league goals in 1991–92. In the 1990 World Cup, Lineker's two late goals saved England from embarrassment against Cameroon in the quarter-finals, although his late equalizer against Germany could not prevent England's elimination from the tournament on penalties in the semi-final. He moved to Japan to play with Grampus Eight, and, in the mid-1990s, came back to England to start a highly successful broadcasting career.

*Above: Gary Lineker, Spurs' and England's high-scoring centre-forward.*

## Sepp Maier
## (Germany, b. 1944)

**Clubs:** *Bayern Munich
(1960–1979)*
**Caps:** *95*

Maier was West Germany's best and most consistent keeper in the 1970s. He spent the bulk of his career with Bayern Munich, making a total of 422 consecutive appearances for the

*Left: Sepp Maier grabs the ball for West Germany against Italy.*

Bavarians. He was in goal for Bayern's 1967 extra-time 1–0 European Cup Winners Cup victory over Rangers and for their three European Cup victories. In particular, Maier's athletic and acrobatic performances in the 1975 final against Leeds United, and the 1976 final against Saint Etienne, helped Bayern lift the trophies. He also won four *Bundesliga* titles with Bayern. At international level Maier had an exceptional match in West Germany's 2–1 win over Holland in the 1974 World Cup Final. A road accident in 1979 ended his footballing career.

## Paolo Maldini
## (Italy, b. 1968)

**Clubs:** *AC Milan (1985–)*
**Caps:** *126 (7 goals)*

Son of ex-AC Milan captain and ex-Italian manager Cesare Maldini, Paolo has carved out his own name in football as probaby the best defender in the world. His cool and efficient tackling and sudden surges into attack mark him out as a special player, and the left-back position at Milan has been his since 1985. He has won six *Serie A* titles and five European Cup winner's medals, and has made over 600 appearances for the club. Maldini made his international debut in 1988, against Yugoslavia, at the age of 19. He played in the 1990, 1994, 1998 and 2002 World Cup finals, the last two as captain. He was also captain of Italy in Euro '96 and 2000. Voted World Player of the Year in 1994, he is the most-capped player in Italian footballing history. His final international coincided with Italy's exit from the 2002 World Cup, defeated by South Korea. He won his fourth European Cup winner's medal in 2003, when AC Milan beat rivals Juventus. He missed out on a fifth medal when Liverpool beat his team in the 2005 final. He missed out on a fifth medal when Liverpool beat his team in the 2005 final but claimed it in Milan's 2-1 win over the same club in 2007.

*Right: Paolo Maldini, captain of Italy.*

### Diego Maradona (Argentina, b. 1960)

**Clubs:** *Argentinos Juniors (1976–80), Boca Juniors (1980–82), Barcelona (1982–84), Napoli (1984–92), Seville (1992–93), Newell's Old Boys (1993–95), Boca Juniors (1995–97)*
**Caps:** *91 (34 goals)*

Maradona was at one time the best footballer in the world, immensely skilled, with exquisite touch and control, a lethal left foot and electric pace. His talents saw him leave Argentina for a world-record fee of £4.2 million, in 1982, to join Barcelona, where he suffered a bruising couple of seasons. He moved to Napoli in 1984 for a new world-record fee of £5 million, and by the end of the decade he had brought the club the Italian "double", in 1987, and the UEFA Cup, in 1989. He appeared for Argentina in the 1982 World Cup finals, being sent off against Brazil, and in 1986 he captained his country to World Cup triumph. He scored brilliant solo goals against England and Belgium, and was named Player of the Tournament. He was again captain in the 1990 competition but

*Above: Diego Maradona, voted the greatest player of the 20th century.*

Argentina lost a poor final to West Germany. A 15-months drugs ban followed, and he returned to Argentina in 1993. He played in the 1994 World Cup finals, but was sent home after failing another drugs test. Maradona retired in 1997, an exceptional talent destroyed by drugs and self-indulgence. In a FIFA poll, he was voted, with Pelé, joint Player of the Twentieth Century. He has since recovered from his personal problems and is now managing the Argentine national team.

## Josef Masopust (Czechoslovakia, 1931–2000)

**Clubs:** *Teplice (1948–51), Dukla Prague (1951–68), Molenbeek (1968–70)*
**Caps:** *63 (10 goals)*

A clever, elegant left-half, Masopust was the creative force behind the Czech and Dukla Prague teams of the 1950s and 1960s. He led his country to third place in the 1960 European Championships, and he scored the first goal in the 1962 World Cup Final – only for Brazil to score three and retain the trophy. That year Masopust was voted European Footballer of the Year. He won eight Czech league titles with Dukla Prague between 1953 and 1966.

*Right: Masopust, playmaker of Czechoslovakia in the early 1960s.*

## Lothar Matthäus (Germany, b. 1961)

**Clubs:** *Borussia Mönchengladbach (1978–84), Bayern Munich (1984–88), Inter Milan (1988–92), Bayern Munich (1992–2000), New Jersey Metrostars (2000)*
**Caps:** *150 (22 goals)*

Matthäus is the most-capped player in German football history, and has gained more caps than any other player in the world. A determined, ball-winning midfielder, his presence has pervaded German football over the last two decades. His spiky attitude and outspoken manner has often alienated team-mates and fans alike, but no one can question his talent. He joined Bayern Munich in 1984 and won three *Bundesliga* titles from 1985–87. He moved to Inter Milan in 1988, and won a *Serie A* title in his first season and a UEFA Cup winner's medal in 1991. He played in the 1986 World Cup Final, marking Maradona, and in 1990, as captain, he led Germany to victory over Argentina and was voted World Footballer of the Year. He played again in 1994 and, to the surprise of many, was selected for the 1998 finals. He moved back to Bayern in 1992 and helped the club to two further *Bundesliga* titles in 1994 and 1997, and to a UEFA Cup victory in 1996. Bayern lost to Manchester United in the dying seconds of the 1999 European Cup Final, after which Matthäus retired. He became coach of Hungary in 2004 before moving to Israel to coach Maccabi Netanya in 2008.

*Above: Matthäus, the irascible captain of Germany at Italia '90.*

## Stanley Matthews (England, 1915–2000)

**Clubs:** *Stoke City (1930–47), Blackpool (1947–61), Stoke City (1961–65)*
**Caps:** *54 (11 goals)*

Matthews, the "Wizard of Dribble", was a dazzling winger with sublime feinting and dribbling skills. His ability to take on and beat defenders was breathtaking, he could cross the ball with deadly accuracy, and he was a regular on the England right wing for over 20 years. A hero at Stoke City for 17 years, he left the club in 1947 to join Blackpool. In the 1953 FA Cup Final he inspired Blackpool, 3–1 down to Bolton in the second half, to a 4–3 victory, and the game is still remembered as "the Matthews Final". He was first capped in 1934 and played in the 1950 and 1954 World Cup finals, and he won the first European Footballer of the Year award in 1956; that year he also received a CBE. He rejoined Stoke at the age of 46, and continued playing until the age of 50, the oldest player ever to appear in the First Division. To mark his retirement he was awarded a knighthood. He died, to universal mourning, in 2000.

*Left: Stanley Matthews, about to launch another cross to his waiting forwards.*

## Alessandro "Sandro" Mazzola (Italy, b. 1942)

**Clubs:** *Inter Milan (1960–74)*
**Caps:** *70 (22 goals)*

Son of Valentino, the Torino captain who was killed in the 1949 Superga air crash, Mazzola was a tall, cultured inside-forward who spent his entire career with Inter Milan. He won his first *Serie A* league medal in 1963, and three more in 1965, 1966 and 1971, and played in three European Cup finals that decade. In the 1964 final, his two goals helped to finish off Real Madrid in Inter's 3–1 victory, and the following year Inter beat Benfica 1–0 in the final. In the 1967 European Cup Final Mazzola scored first against Celtic, but Jock Stein's men ran out the eventual 2–1 winners. He also played in the 1972 final, but this time it was Ajax that beat the Italian side 2–0. Mazzola was first capped in 1963, in a game against Brazil, scoring on his debut. He played in the Italian side that won both the 1968 European Championship and finished runners-up in the 1970 World Cup Final. He is now a football analyst and commentator for Italian television.

*Right: Mazzola at the 1970 World Cup.*

## Billy McNeill
## (Scotland, b. 1940)

**Clubs:** *Celtic (1957–75)*
**Caps:** *29 (3 goals)*

McNeill, known as "Caesar" for his imperious leadership and coolness under pressure, was centre-half and captain of Jock Stein's great Celtic side in the 1960s and early 1970s. A one-club man, McNeill steered Celtic to the European Cup Final in 1967, scoring a rare goal and the winner against Vojvodina Novi Sad in the quarter-final at Parkhead, and became the first British footballer ever to lift the trophy after Celtic's 2–1 victory over Inter Milan in the final in Lisbon. He also collected nine league winner's medals and seven Scottish Cups in his 832 appearances for Celtic. He made his first appearance for Scotland in 1961, when the Scots were hammered 9–3 by England at Wembley, and gained 29 caps. When his playing career ended McNeill managed Celtic, Aston Villa and Manchester City, and he returned to manage Celtic between 1987 and 1991.

*Above: Celtic's captain and centre-half Billy McNeill.*

*Above: Meazza collects the Jules Rimet trophy as Italy win the World Cup of 1938.*

## Giuseppe Meazza
## (Italy, 1910–1979)

**Clubs:** *Ambrosiana (Inter Milan) (1927–40), AC Milan (1940–42), Juventus (1942–43), Atalanta (1945–46), Inter Milan (1946–48)*
**Caps:** *53 (33 goals)*

Italy's second-highest goal scorer after Gigi Rivi, Meazza is only one of two players to have appeared in Italy's two World Cup Final triumphs in 1934 and 1938, the other being Giovanni Ferrari. Meazza was captain of the 1938 team, and he scored the winning goal, from the penalty spot, in the semi-final against Brazil. He played his first game for Inter Milan in 1927, and collected two *Serie A* winner's medals before moving to AC Milan in 1938. He ended his career at Inter, and when he died in 1979 the San Siro stadium was named after him as a tribute from the city of Milan.

## Lionel Messi
## (Argentina, b. 1984)

**Clubs:** *Newell's Old Boys (1995-2000), Barcelona (2000-)*
**Caps:** *36 (12 goals)*

You have to be a very special player when, still in your teens, you are annointed by Maradona as "my successor" but Messi, now in his mid-twenties, simply gets better and better. A playmaking, prolific goal-scoring forward, with scorching pace and an uncanny passing talent, he is the dazzling creator behind both Barcelona's and Argentina's star-studded teams. He began his career as a kid at Newell's Old Boys, but was lured to Barca as the

Argentine club found it difficult to pay for his growth hormone deficiency treatment. Now a Spanish citizen, he played his first senior game for Barcelona in 2005, and that season, at the age of 17, he became the youngest player to score for the club. Although he was injured for much of season 2005-06, he scored 11 of his 14 league goals in his last 13 games, including a memorable hat-trick against Real Madrid. His equalizing goal in the 3–3 game came in the 90th minute, and he became the first Barca player to score three in this fixture since Romario in 1994. The following season, his goal against Getafe, when he beat six players before scoring, drew comparisons with Maradona's "goal of the century" against

England in 1986. That season he was voted into second place, behind Kaka, as both FIFA and France World Player of the Year, and in 2008 he was an essential member of the Argentine side which won gold medal in the Olympics Final against Nigeria in China.

Inheriting the number 10 jersey after Ronaldinho's departure from Barcelona at the start of the 2008–09 season, Messi scored the club's 5,000th league goal after coming on as substitute in a 2–1 win against Racing Santander. He still remains one of the most exciting players in world football and is highly coveted by clubs across the continent.

*Above: Lionel Messi brings the ball under control for Barcelona.*

*Above: Roger Milla at Italia '90.*

# Roger Milla
## (Cameroon, b. 1952)

**Clubs:** *Tannerre Yaounde (1967–76), Valenciennes (1976–78), Monaco (1978–80), Bastia (1981–87), Saint Etienne (1987–2000)*
**Caps:** *81 (42 goals)*

Milla was the unlikely star of the 1990 World Cup finals. In the opening game, his unfancied Cameroon team beat defending champions Argentina 1–0, and they reached the quarter-finals, where only an extra-time penalty from Gary Lineker denied them further progress. Milla ended the tournament with four goals, and he delighted the crowds and the massive television audience with his flamboyant celebrations around the corner flag. He played again for Cameroon in the 1994 World Cup tournament in the United States – but this time with rather less success – and at the age of 42 he became the oldest player ever to play in a World Cup finals. He joined Valenciennes from Cameroon in 1976, and he spent his career with a variety of French clubs. Milla has been twice voted African Player of the Year, in 1976 and 1990. He retired in 2000.

# Bobby Moore
## (England, 1941–1993)

**Clubs:** *West Ham United (1958–74), Fulham (1974–76), Seattle Sounders (1976), San Antonio Thunder (1978)*
**Caps:** *108 (3 goals)*

A graceful, intelligent player, Moore was the defensive pivot of England and West Ham in the 1960s. His ability to read a game, his sharpness in the tackle and his passing skills brought him a total of 108 caps, an achievement that has been eclipsed only by Peter Shilton. Moore played his first game for West Ham at the age of 17, and he captained the Hammers to the FA Cup in 1964 and the Cup Winners Cup in 1965, beating 1860 Munich 2–0. Moore was first capped in 1962, and was made captain the following year. He was captain when England won the World Cup in 1966, and it was his pass that set up Hurst's third goal. He was named Player of the Tournament, and was awarded an OBE in 1967. In the 1970 World Cup finals he produced a magnificent performance against Pelé's Brazil in the group stage, but England were eliminated by West Germany in the quarter-final. He joined Fulham in 1974, later leaving to play in the United States. Moore retired in 1978 to pursue an unsuccessful management career. He died from cancer in 1993, aged 51.

*Above: Bobby Moore, captain of West Ham and England.*

## Stan Mortensen
## (England, 1921–1991)

**Clubs:** *Blackpool (1939–55),*
*Hull City (1955–57),*
*Southport (1957–60)*
**Caps:** *25 (23 goals)*

Mortenson was a speedy, goal-scoring centre-forward, with one of the strongest shots in English football. Nicknamed the "Electric Eel" for his ability to slither past defenders, he spent most of his career with Blackpool, playing alongside Stanley Matthews. In 1948 he scored in every round of the FA Cup, including the final where Blackpool lost to Manchester United, and he scored a hat trick in the 1953 final, bringing Blackpool their only major honour. He made his international debut in 1947, and scored four goals in England's 10–0 crushing win over Portugal. He scored another three goals against Sweden later that year. He played in England's disastrous 1950 World Cup finals, and he won his last cap in England's 6–3 defeat by Puskas' Hungary in 1953. He was manager of Blackpool for a brief period in the late 1960s. Stan Mortensen died in 1991.

*Above: Mortensen heads goalwards for Blackpool against Wolves in 1953.*

## Gerd Müller
## (Germany, b. 1945)

**Clubs:** *TSV Nordlingen (1962–64),*
*Bayern Munich (1964–79), Fort*
*Lauderdale Strikers (1979–81)*
**Caps:** *62 (68 goals)*

A stocky figure, Müller did not give the appearance of being a top footballer. However, he won three European Cup and a World Cup winner's medals, and he is the highest scorer in German international history. Müller was a natural striker, with fast reflexes and keen awareness, and he rarely squandered an opportunity inside the penalty box. Affectionately known as "*Der Bomber*", he spent nearly 16 years at Bayern Munich, where he scored a total of 365 goals in 427 league matches, and helped to win the European Cup in 1974, 1975 and 1976, as well as the *Bundesliga* four times. The international heir to the great Uwe Seeler, Müller scored ten goals in the 1970 World Cup finals and a further two in the 1972 European Championship Final against the Soviet Union. He claimed another four in 1974, when West Germany won the tournament, thanks to his goal in the final. Müller was named European Footballer of the Year in 1970.

*Left: "Der Bomber" Gerd Müller heads a goal for West Germany.*

## Johan Neeskens
## (Holland, b. 1951)

**Clubs:** *Ajax (1967–74), Barcelona (1974–80), New York Cosmos (1980–85), Groningen (1985–86)*
**Caps:** *49 (17 goals)*

An intelligent midfielder with a strong right-foot shot and a tough tackle, the 19-year-old Neeskens broke into the Ajax first team in 1970. He played in all three of Ajax's consecutive European Cup victories from 1971–73, supplying the ball to Cruyff and Swart in attack.

*Left: Ajax and Holland midfielder Johan Neeskens connects with the ball.*

Neeskens scored Holland's second-minute goal from the penalty spot in the 1974 World Cup Final, when Cruyff was fouled in the box, and he was the second top scorer of the tournament that year, with five goals. Neeskens played again in the final four years later, in 1978, with Holland losing 3–1 to Argentina. At club level he followed his Ajax and Holland team-mate Cruyff to Barcelona, in 1974, and helped the club win the European Cup Winner's Cup in 1979. He played his football in the United States the following season, returning to Holland five years later to take his place with Groningen, where he played out his career until his retirement.

## Günter Netzer
## (Germany, b. 1944)

**Clubs:** *Borussia Mönchengladbach (1961–73), Real Madrid (1973–76), Grasshoppers Zurich (1976–78)*
**Caps:** *37 (6 goals)*

Netzer's extravagant skills were the inspiration behind West Germany's 1972 European Championship triumph, with the long-haired midfield supremo linking play between Franz Beckenbauer and Gerd Müller. Netzer began his career with Borussia Mönchengladbach and led the club to two *Bundesliga* titles in 1970 and 1971. He left to join Real Madrid in 1973, and was dropped by German manager Helmut Schön for the 1974 World Cup Final. He helped Real to win two Spanish league titles in 1975 and 1976. He then spent two seasons in Switzerland with Grasshoppers before retiring from professional football in 1978. Netzer's first assignment as a manager was with Hamburg, and he helped the club to victory with their first *Bundesliga* title in 19 years, as well as making it through to the final of the 1979–80 European Cup.

*Right: Netzer (right) in the 1972 European Championship Final against the USSR.*

## Gunnar Nordahl
## (Sweden, 1921–1995)

**Clubs:** *Degerfors (1940–44),
IFK Nörrkoping (1944–49),
AC Milan (1949–56),
Roma (1956–59)*
**Caps:** *33 (43 goals)*

*Left: The strong, dependable Gunnar
Nordhal. Along with Gunnar Gren
and Nils Liedholm, he was one of the
Swedish trio in attack for AC Milan
during the early 1950s.*

A strong, consistent goal scorer, Nordahl helped Nörrkoping to four Swedish league titles before joining AC Milan to become part of the so-called "Gre-no-li" trio. That season he scored ten goals in *Serie A*. He was top scorer in 1949–50 with 35 goals, and top scorer again with 34 goals in 1950–51, when Milan took their first title in 44 years; he repeated the feat three years in succession from 1953–55. He won an Olympic gold medal with Sweden in 1948; it was to be his last cap for his country.

## Wolfgang Overath
## (Germany, b. 1943)

**Clubs:** *Cologne (1962–77)*
**Caps:** *81 (17 goals)*

Inside-left Overath joined his home club Cologne's FC Köln in 1962, and stayed there right through until his retirement in 1977. He was capped in 1963, and in 1964 helped his team to victory with the newly instituted *Bundesliga* title. He played in the German side which lost 4–2 to England in the 1966 World Cup Final, and he played again in the 1970 finals, scoring the only goal in the match against Uruguay and winning West Germany the third-place spot in the rankings. Günter Netzer was preferred to Overath in the 1972 European Championships, but Overath turned the tables and ousted Netzer for the 1974 World Cup finals, where he won a winner's medal when Germany beat Holland 2–1 in the final. This World Cup victory was the pinnacle of his impressive career and he retired from international football after that tournament. He was elected president of FC Köln in 2004.

*Right: One-club man Wolfgang
Overath playing for West Germany
in the 1974 World Cup, which they
hosted. Overath had played in two
previous World Cup finals, in 1966
and 1970, but it was in 1974 that his
country took the World Champions title.*

## Ariel Ortega
## (Argentina, b. 1974)

**Clubs:** *River Plate (1991–97), Valéncia (1997–98), Sampdoria (1998–99), Parma (1999–2000), River Plate (2000–02), Fenerbahce (2002–03), Newell's Old Boys (2004–06), River Plate (2006–08)*
**Caps:** *97 (19 goals)*

Small, tricky midfielder Ortega made his debut for Argentina's River Plate in 1991 and helped the club win the *Copa*

*Left: Argentinian midfielder Ariel Ortega.*

*Libertadores* and the Argentinian league in 1994 before moving to Valéncia in 1997. His first international was in 1993, and he replaced a disgraced Maradona in the middle of the 1994 World Cup finals. He won a silver medal in the Atlanta Olympics in 1996, and scored five goals in the qualifiers for the 1998 World Cup finals. In that tournament, Argentina were knocked out in the quarter-final by Holland, and Ortega was sent off for head-butting the Dutch keeper. He moved to River Plate on loan in 2000 and in 2004 he joined Newell's Old Boys from Fenerbahce. He returned to River Plate in 2006.

## Michael Owen
## (England, b. 1979)

**Clubs:** *Liverpool (1996–2004), Real Madrid (2004–05), Newcastle United (2005–)*
**Caps:** *89 (40 goals)*

Owen is one of the brightest striking talents to have emerged from the English game. A trainee at Liverpool, he made his debut in 1997 against Wimbledon and scored in his first game. By the end of his first season he had scored 18 league goals, and he bettered it with 23 the next year. At 18 years and 2 months, he was the youngest player to have played for England in the 20th century, and passed 50 caps before he was 25. He played in the 1998 World Cup finals and scored a memorable goal against Argentina. He was injured for much of the 1999–2000 season, but he was back in 2000–1, when he scored the two goals against Arsenal that won Liverpool the FA Cup. He got a hat-trick in England's 5–1 defeat of Germany in Munich on route to the 2002 World Cup finals. He was European Footballer of the Year in 2001. He moved from Liverpool to Real Madrid in 2004, and managed to impress despite rarely playing. A prolonged transfer saga saw him return to England in 2005, when he surprised many by choosing to join Newcastle over his old club Liverpool.

*Right: Owen in action for England.*

## Jean-Pierre Papin
## (France, b. 1963)

**Clubs:** *Valenciennes (1984–85), Bruges (1985–86), Marseille (1986–92), AC Milan (1992–94), Bayern Munich (1994–96), Bordeaux (1996–98)*
**Caps:** *54 (30 goals)*

A deadly accurate striker, Papin was the French league's top goal scorer four times in the late 1980s, and is still regarded one of the leading strikers of the modern game. Papin began his career with French club Valenciennes, before moving to the Belgian side Bruges in 1985. He returned to France a year later, and quickly became the captain and inspiration for the Bernard Tapie-funded Marseille. His goals helped Marseille to victory and they won the league title for four years in succession. He played in the 1991 European Cup Final in Bari, when Marseille were beaten on penalties by Red Star Belgrade. That year he was voted European Footballer of the Year. He also played in the 1993 final, this time for AC Milan, and was again on the losing side (ironically, the 1–0 winners were Marseille). Papin was transferred to Bayern Munich in 1994, and he received his last French cap in 1995. His two years at Bordeaux – the last years of his playing career – were marred by injury.

*Right: Jean-Pierre Papin, a much-travelled striker, in his national strip.*

## Daniel Passarella
## (Argentina, b. 1953)

**Clubs:** *Sarmiento (1971–73), River Plate (1974–82), Fiorentina (1982–86), Inter Milan (1986–88), River Plate (1988–89)*
**Caps:** *70 (22 goals)*

A commanding centre-half with an eye for goal, Passarella was captain of the River Plate team that won four Argentinian league titles in the 1970s. In 1978 his defensive play powered Argentina to victory in the World Cup Final, with Passarella collecting the trophy as captain. His playing career in Europe included first Fiorentina and then Inter Milan, but he returned to Argentina as the manager of River Plate. He was manager of Argentina for the 1998 World Cup finals, and his side reached the quarter-finals, where they were eliminated by Holland and a last-minute wondergoal from Dennis Bergkamp. Passarella managed the Uruguay national team for a short spell from 1999. He was appointed coach of Brazilian team Corinthians in early 2005 and then returned to River Plate.

*Right: Passarella (right) rises to prevent an Italian attack.*

## Pelé, Edison Arantes do Nascimento (Brazil, b. 1940)

**Clubs:** *Santos (1956–74), New York Cosmos (1975–77)*
**Caps:** *91 (77 goals)*

Pelé is generally regarded as the finest player ever to have graced the game of football. His passing and dribbling skills were breathtaking, his finishing ability was lethally accurate, and he had abundant pace and strength. He was, in short, the perfect footballer. He played all his club football with Brazilian side Santos and, latterly New York Cosmos, but he will be most remembered for his World Cup performances. In 1958, the 17-year-old Pelé scored twice in the 5–2 win over Sweden in the final, to add to the hat trick he collected against France in the semi-final. He was injured for the 1962 tournament and, as a marked man in the finals of 1966, he was brutally kicked off the pitch by Portugal. However, in the Mexico finals of 1970, Pelé was the undoubted star of the show. In the final he scored a remarkable header, and made two more goals to help Brazil beat Italy 4–1 and become the World Champions. When Pelé left Santos, his number ten shirt was permanently removed from the line-up as a lasting tribute to him. He retired in 1977 and became Minister for Sport in Brazil. In 1999 FIFA conducted a poll to find the player of the century, a title they awarded jointly to Pelé and Maradona.

*Below: Pelé in action.*

## Michel Platini
### (France, b. 1955)

**Clubs:** *Nancy (1972–79), Saint Etienne (1979–82), Juventus (1982–87)*
**Caps:** *72 (41 goals)*

An accomplished, stylish midfielder with a forward's instinct for goals, Platini captained France to the top of European international football in the 1980s. After spending his early years with Nancy and Saint Etienne (his 20 goals had won the French league for Saint Etienne in 1982) Platini moved to Juventus. He scored 16 league goals in his first season and helped Juventus reach the European Cup Final, losing 1–0 to Hamburg. In 1984 his goals helped Juventus win the league and the Cup Winners Cup. That year, playing with Tigana and Giresse, he scored nine goals for France in the European Championships, and his free kick in the final helped France beat Spain 2–0. Platini played in the Heysel European Cup Final in 1985, and his penalty gave Juventus a 1–0 win over Liverpool. He steered France to the semi-final of the 1986 World Cup, where they were beaten by West Germany, and he retired in 1987 to become manager of France. Platini was named European Footballer of the Year three times, in 1983, 1984 and 1985 and he became president of UEFA in 2007.

Above: Michel Platini, French captain in the 1984 European Championships, where he inspired his team-mates to victory in the tournament.

## Andrea Pirlo
### (Italy, b. 1979)

**Clubs:** *Brescia (1994–98), Inter Milan (1998–2001), AC Milan (2001–)*
**Caps:** *54 (8 goals)*

A strong, commanding central midfielder, Pirlo has been Milan's outstanding playmaker since 2001, backed up by Gennaro Gattuso and Massimo Ambrosini. He has won a league title (2004) and two European Cup medals (2003 and 2007), and his play has been critical to the club's domestic and European successes.

He has played over 200 senior games for Milan and is a firm favourite with the fans and, indeed, with anyone who enjoys watching skilful, penetrating and attractive football. He played for Italy in Euro 2004 and again in 2006, where his performances were peerless. He scored and was named Man of the Match in the group game against Ghana, and was Man of the Match again in Italy's exciting 2–0 semi-final win over Germany, when he laid on the opening goal for Fabio Grosso. In the Final against France his corner produced Marco Materazzi's equalizing header and he scored in the penalty shoot-out which Italy won to become world champions.

Above: Pirlo has over 50 caps for Italy

 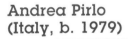

## Robert Prosinecki
## (West Germany, b. 1969)

**Clubs:** *Red Star Belgrade
(1987–91), Real Madrid (1992–94),
Real Oviedo (1994–95), Barcelona
(1995–96), Seville (1996–97),
Croatia Zagreb (1997–2000),
Standard Liege (2000–01),
Portsmouth (2001–02)*
**Caps:** *15 (4 goals) Yugoslavia;
49 (10) Croatia*

Born in West Germany to Yugoslavian
parents, Prosinecki was a playmaking
midfielder with flair and subtlety.
He won three league titles with Red
Star, and was a member of the Red
Star Belgrade side that won the 1991
European Cup Final against Marseille.
His performance prompted Real Madrid
to buy him, and he went on to play for
Real Oviedo, Barcelona and Seville,
although his time in Spain was marred
by injury problems.

  He had 15 caps with Yugoslavia and
then, after the Balkan wars of the early
1990s, 49 with the newly independent
Croatia, with whom he reached the
quarter-finals of Euro '96 and third place
in the 1998 World Cup finals. He also
played in the 2002 finals, and was the
first player to score in World Cup finals
for two different countries - Yugoslavia at
Italia '90 and for Croatia in 2002.

*Above: Robert Prosinecki breaks forward from midfield for Red Star.*

## Ferenc Puskas
## (Hungary, 1927–2006)

**Clubs:** *Honved (1943–56),
Real Madrid (1958–66)*
**Caps:** *84 (83 goals) (Hungary),
4 (Spain)*

The stocky Ferenc Puskas was a
legendary footballing wizard with a
rocket of a left-foot shot. Known as the
"Galloping Major", after his time spent
with the Hungarian army side Honved,
Puskas played in Hungary's 6–3 and 7–1
humiliations of England in 1953 and
1954, and he joined Real Madrid
in 1958. Puskas formed an immediate
partnership with the equally legendary

Alfredo Di Stefano and, fed by winger
Paco Gento, the pair terrorized European
defences over the next few years. Puskas
scored four goals in Real's demolition of
Eintracht Frankfurt in the outstanding
1960 European Cup Final, and he had a
hat trick in the first 35 minutes of the
1962 final, although Benfica finally came
through to win 5–3. Puskas scored 35
goals in his 38 European Cup
appearances. He retired in 1966, shortly
after Real's sixth European Cup
triumph. In his time with the club he
had won a total of five Spanish league
titles. Puskas took up management after
retirement, and he led Panathinaikos to
the 1971 European Cup Final, but they
lost 1–0 to an emergent Ajax.

*Above: Ferenc Puskas lines up for
Hungary against England in 1953.*

## Thomas Ravelli
### (Sweden, b. 1959)

**Clubs:** *Oster Vaxjo,
IFK Gothenburg (1989–97),
Tampa Bay Rowdies (1997–99)*
**Caps:** *143*

Goalkeeper Thomas Ravelli is the
most-capped player in Swedish history,
with a tally of 143 caps. He was first
capped in 1981, and was still pacing the
goal 11 years later when Sweden
reached the semi-final of the 1992

European Championships, which they
lost to Germany. He also played in the
1994 World Cup finals, with Sweden
claiming third place after their victory
over Bulgaria. In his time with IFK
Gothenburg, he won an impressive six
Swedish league titles. He ended his
career by moving play with the Tampa
Bay Rowdies, in the United States, in
1997. Ravelli retired from professional
football in 1999.

*Right: Sweden's long-serving
goalkeeper, Thomas Ravelli.*

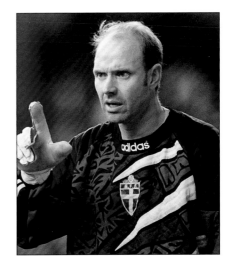

## Frank Rijkaard
### (Surinam, b. 1962)

**Clubs:** *Ajax (1980–88), Zaragoza
(1988), AC Milan (1988–93),
Ajax (1993–95)*
**Caps:** *73 (10 goals)*

One of three Dutchmen in Arrigo
Sacchi's AC Milan side, Rijkaard was
equally adept in midfield and defence.
He began his career with Ajax in 1980,
and won a European Cup Winners
Cup medal with the team in 1987.
After disagreements with manager Johan
Cruyff, he had a spell with Zaragoza
before joining Milan, with whom he
won European Cup winner's medals

in 1989 and 1990. On the morning of
Milan's European Cup Final against
Marseille, he announced his decision
to leave. Milan were beaten 1–0 and
Rijkaard moved back to Ajax. He won
another European Cup winner's medal
in 1995, when his pass to Kluivert
produced the winning goal in Ajax's 1–0
defeat of AC Milan. He played in
Holland's 1988 triumph in the European
Championships, but was sent off after an
altercation with West Germany's Rudi
Voller in the 1990 World Cup. Rijkaard
retired in 1995 to manage a relatively
unsuccessful Holland side, before taking
over as coach of Barcelona, leading the
Catalans to glory in 2006. He left in
2008 to be replaced by Pep Guardiola.

*Above: Rijkaard at Euro '88.*

## Luigi Riva
### (Italy, b. 1944)

**Clubs:** *Legnano (1962–63),
Cagliari (1963–76)*
**Caps:** *42 (35 goals)*

Left-winger Luigi "Gigi" Riva is the
highest goal scorer in Italian football.
He started his career as a teenager with
Legnano. He joined the second division
Cagliari in 1963 and played out his
entire career with the Sardinian side.
It was Riva's goals that helped the club
to their only *Serie A* championship, in
1969–70, and that season he scored 21
goals in 28 games. Riva's international
debut was against Hungary in 1965, and
he played alongside Mazzola and

Boninsegna in the 1970 World Cup
finals, where his extra-time goal
knocked out West Germany in the
semi-final. Riva had been key to Italy's
success in the quarter- and semi-finals
of that tournament, but he could
do little to counter Pelé's Brazilian
side, and Italy lost 4–1 to the South
Americans in the final. In spite of
breaking both his legs on the football
pitch (fortunately for him, in separate
incidents), Riva continued to play
professionally until the mid-1970s,
although in the end it was as a result
of these injuries that he was forced
into premature retirement.

*Right: Riva lines up with the Azzurri
at the World Cup finals of 1970.*

Above: Victor Rivaldo puts his left foot to good use for Barcelona.

## Rivaldo, Victor Barbosa Ferreira (Brazil, b. 1972)

**Clubs:** *Mogi–Mirim (1992–93), Corinthians (1993–94), Palmeiras (1994–96), Deportivo La Coruña, (1996–97), Barcelona (1997–2002), AC Milan (2002–2004),Olympiakos (2004–07), AEK Athens (2007–08), Bunyodkor (2008–)*
**Caps:** *95 (37 goals)*

Rivaldo's sublime talents earned him the World Footballer of the Year title in 1999. Starting his career as a 14-year-old with Paulista Santa Cruz, Rivaldo played for several Brazilian clubs before joining Spanish side Deportivo in 1996. A left-sided, attacking midfielder, he notched up 21 goals in 41 games with Deportivo. In his first two seasons with Barcelona, from 1997, he scored 43 goals, helping them to two Spanish league titles and a Copa Del Ray. In 1999 he was top scorer in the *Copa America* and he also appeared in the 1998 and 2002 World Cup Finals, winning the gold medal in the latter. With AC Milan in 2003 he won a European Cup Winner's Medal, but in 2004 he went to Cruzeiro on loan before returning for European stints with Olympiakos and AEK Athens. In 2008, Rivaldo joined Uzbek side Bunyodkor on a highly lucrative contract.

## Gianni Rivera (Italy, b. 1943)

**Clubs:** *Alessandria (1958–60), AC Milan (1960–79)*
**Caps:** *60 (14 goals)*

A slight, skilful inside-forward, Rivera had poise, exceptional passing ability and a powerful shot. A teenage prodigy, he joined AC Milan from his home-town club Alessandria in 1960, at the age of 16.

Known as "*Il Bambino d'Oro*" ("The Golden Boy"), he helped Milan to two European Cup Final wins in 1963 and 1969, two Cup Winners' Cups in 1968 and 1973, and two Italian league and Cup trophies. Winner of the European Footballer of the Year award in 1969, Rivera was capped for his country 60 times, although he only came on for the last few minutes of the 1970 World Cup Final, as a substitute for Roberto Boninsegna. He won his last *Scudetto* with AC Milan in 1979, helping the club claim their tenth league title. Rivera is one of the club's greatest servants, having spent close to 20 years playing for the team and notching up over 500 appearances. On retirement, he became president of Milan and moved into politics by becoming a member of Italian parliament.

*Right: Gianni Rivera, the "Golden Boy" for Italy and AC Milan, during the 1970 World Cup finals.*

## Robinho
## (Brazil, b. 1984)

**Clubs:** *Santos (2002–05), Real Madrid (2005–08), Manchester City (2008–)*
**Caps:** *60 (23 goals)*

Born into a poor family in Sao Paulo, Robson de Souza was coached by Pele at Santos and joined his mentor's old club. He soon joined Real Madrid for almost £20 million in 2005 and made 37 appearances for the Castilian club in 2005-06. After a difficult second season at Real, his 11 goals in season 2007-08 helped win La Liga. He gained his first national cap in 2003, his reputation soaring at the 2007 *Copa America* where he scored all four of Brazil's group-stage goals – including a hat-trick against Chile – and two more in the 6-1 quarter final rout of Chile. Brazil won the trophy and Robinho was voted best player of the tournament. Robinho transferred to Manchester City for £32.5 million in the summer of 2008, following huge investment in the Premier League club.

*Right: Robinho charges through midfield.*

## Paolo Rossi
## (Italy, b. 1956)

**Clubs:** *Juventus (1972–75), Como (1975–76), Lanerossi Vicenza (1976–79), Perugia (1979–80), Juventus (1981–85), AC Milan (1986–86), Verona (1986–87)*
**Caps:** *48 (20 goals)*

The young forward Rossi was bought by Juventus in 1972 and loaned out to various Italian clubs because of a knee injury that prevented him playing regular games for the *Serie A* side. After a fine display for his national side in the 1978 World Cup finals, where he scored three goals, Rossi was bought by Perugia – the provincial club had outbid the mighty Juventus, who were now keen to reclaim their

*Left: Rossi in the 1982 World Cup finals.*

former player. However, because of his involvement in a betting and bribes scandal, Rossi was banned from playing professional football for three years. The financial implications of this threatened to damage Perugia and, eventually, Juventus suceeded in buying him back. Rossi played for Italy in the 1982 World Cup finals, and was an unexpected sensation in the tournament, scoring a hat trick against Brazil in Italy's 3–2 quarter-final win, as well as both goals in the 2–0 semi-final defeat of Poland, and the first goal in the 3–1 final victory against West Germany. He came away with teh coveted accolade of top scorer in the tournment, and that year he was named European Footballer of the Year. Later in his career Rossi played briefly for AC Milan and Verona, but injuries forced his early retirement from the game, at the young age of 29.

## Bryan Robson
## (England, b. 1957)

**Clubs:** *West Bromwich Albion (1974–81), Manchester United (1981–94), Middlesbrough (1994–98)*
**Caps:** *90 (26 goals)*

Robson was England's most influential midfielder of the 1980s. He was a strong, aggressive player, and an inspirational captain for Manchester United and England. He joined United from West Bromwich Albion in 1981 for £1.5 million, and by the end of the decade he had led the club to three FA Cup Final victories. He gained his first cap in 1980 and scored the fastest goal ever, in 27 seconds, in the World Cup finals in 1982. Injury prevented him from playing in all of the 1986 finals games, and he received his last cap in 1991, the same year his United team collected the European Cup Winners Cup, beating Barcelona in the final. United won their first Premier League title in 1993, but Robson left for Middlesbrough in 1994 as player-manager, remaining manager till 2001. He returned to West Bromwich Albion as manager in 2004 and then to Sheffield United in 2007.

*Above: "Captain Marvel" Bryan Robson takes aim for Manchester United.*

*Above: Ronaldinho's brilliant attacking style makes him a key figure for Brazil.*

## Ronaldinho
## (Brazil, b. 1980)

**Clubs:** *Gremio (1998–2001), Paris Saint-Germain (2001–03), Barcelona (2003–07), AC Milan (2008–)*
**Caps:** *42 (15 goals)*

Romario, Rivaldo, Ronaldo... Ronaldinho is the latest in a long line of outstanding attacking Brazilian footballers. Born in 1980, he joined Paris Saint-Germain from his home-town club, Gremio, and was quickly mesmerising crowds with his genius. He was a Brazilian international at 19, and was one of the stars of the 2002 World Cup-winning team, most remembered for his 30-yard free-kick, which beat David Seaman and won the quarter-final against England 2–1. But Ronaldinho was later sent off, and his brilliant forward style was often mixed with reckless play on the field and playboy behaviour off it – so much so that in 2003 PSG put him up for sale. Ronaldinho chose Barcelona over Manchester United, and produced such dazzling form that he hoisted Barça to second in the table in 2003–04, and was voted Player of the Year by the Spanish media. However, he had a lacklustre and seemingly disinterested final season with Barcelona in 2007, and moved to AC Milan for almost £20 million the following year.

## Ronaldo Luiz Nazario da Lima (Brazil, b. 1976)

**Clubs:** *Cruzeiro (1993–94), PSV Eindhoven (1994–96), Barcelona (1996–97), Inter Milan (1997–2002), Real Madrid (2002–2007), AC Milan (2007–09), Corinthians (2009–)*
**Caps:** *96 (62 goals)*

Possibly the best-known player in the world, the lightning-fast, ultra-dynamic Ronaldo is a striker of the highest quality with an immense goal-scoring tally.

Beginning his career at Brazilian side Cruzeiro Esporte Clube, he moved to PSV Eindhoven in 1994, where he scored 35 goals in his first season. He was voted World Footballer of the Year in 1996, and joined Barcelona that year, scoring the goal that won Barcelona the European Cup Winners Cup. He joined Inter in 1998 for £18 million, scoring the third goal in the final of the UEFA Cup against Lazio. He also scored four goals in the 1998 World Cup finals, but suffered a fit on the day of the final and played poorly. His bad luck followed him domestically and a serious knee injury sustained in a match in *Serie A* consigned him to nearly two years' rehabilitation.

He returned four years later, however, securing the Golden Boot with eight goals at the 2002 World Cup Finals held in Japan and South Korea, including the only two of the final against Germany. His brace in the final put him on a par with the legendary Pele, matching his tally of 12 World Cup goals. He was transferred to Real Madrid for £30 million in 2002 and was again voted World Footballer of the Year. His time in the Spanish capital was mixed and he joined AC Milan in 2007 after winning one league title with the Spanish giants, before a horrible injury resulted in a move to Corinthians and possible retirement.

*Right: Ronaldo is considered one of the greatest strikers of all time.*

## Cristiano Ronaldo (Portugal, b. 1985)

**Clubs:** *Sporting Lisbon (2001–03), Manchester United (2003–)*
**Caps:** *64 (22 goals)*

Described by no less an authority than Johan Cruyff as "better than George Best and Denis Law", the young winger from Madeira is regarded as one of the world's most exciting players. After Ronaldo starred in a European Cup win for Sporting Lisbon against Manchester United in 2003, Alex Ferguson paid over £12 million for the prodigy. He was an immediate success at Old Trafford, with his speed and acceleration, electrifying dribbling skills and eye for goal installing him as a firm favourite with the Manchester United fans. Playing in the legendary number 7 shirt (its predecessors include Beckham, Cantona and Best), he lived up to his manager's expectations and rewarded such faith with an astonshing goal-scoring record.

Indeed, in season 2007–08 he scored 42 goals, helping Manchester United to yet another European and domestic double and comfortably securing that season's Golden Shoe and Ballon d'Or awards.

Although he has been criticized for allegedly unsporting behaviour, including accusations of helping to have his team-mate Wayne Rooney sent off in the quarter-final of England's 2006 World Cup game against Portugal, immediately after which he was spotted winking at Rooney sitting on his bench, there is no denying his growing maturity and immense talent for playing the game. Despite Alex Ferguson's fierce denial, rumours that Ronaldo would be moving to Real Madrid were cemented in July 2009 when it was announced that a historic £80 million deal had been reached. There is little doubt that Ronaldo will remain at the highest levels for many years to come.

*Left: Christiano Ronaldo won the coveted Ballon d'Or in 2008.*

## Wayne Rooney
## (England, b. 1985)

**Clubs:** *Everton (2002–04),*
*Manchester United (2004–)*
**Caps:** *51 (22 goals)*

When 16-year-old Wayne Rooney came off the Everton bench in October 2002 at Highbury and unleashed a stunning 30-yard curling goal, it not only ended Arsenal's 30-game unbeaten run but signalled the arrival of a major force in world football.

A product of the Everton youth ranks, Rooney made his first Premier League appearance in 2002. At the end of the 2003-04 season, however, he decided his club could not match his ambitions, and was duly snapped up by Manchester United for £26 million, the most expensive ever transfer fee for a teenage player. His creativity and dynamism helped the club win the Premiership in 2007 and 2008, and he was voted PFA Young Player of the Year in 2005 and 2006.

He gained his first cap in February 2003 against Austria and he scored twice against Switzerland at Euro 2004. He also played in the 2006 World Cup, but his quick temper resulted in his dismissal in the quarter-final against Portugal. If he can learn to control this unpleasant aspect of his personality, he will surely become one of the greats of the game.

*Above: Wayne Rooney goes for goal in front of the Old Trafford faithful.*

## Karl-Heinz Rummenigge
## (Germany, b. 1955)

**Clubs:** *Bayern Munich (1974–84),*
*Inter Milan (1984–87),*
*Servette (1987–88)*
**Caps:** *95 (45 goals)*

The young bank clerk Rummenigge joined Bayern Munich from Lippstadt in 1974. Within two years at the club the right-winger had won a European Cup winner's medal, when Bayern beat Saint Etienne in 1976. He made his international debut that year and played

*Left: Stylish winger Rummenigge playing for West Germany.*

in the 1978 World Cup finals, scoring three goals. He also starred in West Germany's 1980 European Championship victory. In 1980 and 1981 Rummenigge was voted European Footballer of the Year. He led West Germany to the World Cup Final in 1982, losing to Italy, and to the final of 1986, where they lost again, this time 3–2 to Argentina. In the 1982 tournament he scored five goals and finished as second top scorer in the competition. Inter Milan paid Bayern Munich £2.5 million for Rummenigge in 1984. He left the Italian club in 1987 for one final season with Switzerland's Servette. He is currently chairman of Bayern Munich.

## Ian Rush (Wales, b. 1961)

**Clubs:** *Chester (1978–80), Liverpool (1980–87), Juventus (1987–88), Liverpool (1988–96), Leeds United (1996–97), Sheffield United (1997–98), Newcastle United (1998–2000)*
**Caps:** *73 (28 goals)*

One of the most prolific strikers in modern English footballing history, Ian Rush spent the bulk of his career with Liverpool, whom he first joined in 1980, at the age of 18. Liverpool paid only £300,000 to secure the purchase of Rush from Chester, and their far-sightedness proved to be one of the great investments of the decade. Rush's goals and his selfless contribution to the team helped Liverpool win four league titles, four

League Cups and two European Cups over the next six years. He moved briefly to Juventus, for £3.2 million in 1986, but could not settle with the Italian club, and he returned to Liverpool the following year. He scored twice in the FA Cup Final against Everton in 1989, and picked up a fifth league winner's medal in 1990. He was the all-time top scorer at Anfield, with 336 goals, and he is the highest-ever scorer in the FA Cup with 42 goals. Leeds United wasted no time in signing Rush when Liverpool released him on a free transfer in 1996, but he stayed for only one season before moving across Yorkshire to Sheffield United. He then moved to Newcastle. He is currently involved in media work for the game.

*Right: Liverpool's Ian Rush strides forward towards goal.*

*Above: The tough, determined German sweeper Matthias Sammer.*

## Matthias Sammer (Germany, b. 1967)

**Clubs:** *Dynamo Dresden, VfB Stuttgart, Inter Milan, Borussia Dortmund*
**Caps:** *23 (6 goals) East Germany, 51 (8 goals) Germany*

A strong, attacking sweeper, Sammer, along with Andreas Thom, was the first East German to play for the newly unified German team in 1990. Apart from a brief spell with Inter Milan, he played in Germany, finally with Borussia Dortmund, whom he captained to a 3–1 European Cup victory over Juventus in 1997. He was in the German side that lost in the final of the European Championship in 1992, but was in the victorious 1996 side, scoring the winner against Croatia in the quarter-final. Sammer was voted European Footballer of the Year in 1996. An injury prevented him from appearing in the 1998 World Cup finals. He took over as coach at Dortmund and in 2002 became the youngest coach in history to win the *Bundesliga*. In 2004 he became manager of Stuttgart.

Above: Mexico's goal-scoring legend Hugo Sanchez in the 1986 World Cup finals.

# Hugo Sanchez
## (Mexico, b. 1958)

**Clubs:** *UNAM (1976–81), Atlectico Madrid (1981–85), Real Madrid (1985–88), North America (1988–93), Rayo Vallecano (1993)*
**Caps:** *60 (29 goals)*

Mexico's star player, Hugo Sanchez was an expert goal scorer, and he celebrated his goals with exuberant somersaults. He was leading scorer with Mexico City's UNAM, and then moved to Real Madrid where he was top scorer in the Spanish league for four consecutive seasons between 1985 and 1988. His goals, with contributions from fellow striker Butragueno, made Real the top Spanish side of the late 1980s, winning the Spanish league for five years in succession. Sanchez played for Mexico in the 1978 World Cup finals and he captained his country as far as the quarter-finals in the 1986 tournament.

# Gyorgy Sarosi
## (Hungary, 1912–1993)

**Clubs:** *Ferencvaros (1931–43)*
**Caps:** *61 (42 goals)*

A complete athlete, Sarosi was also a versatile footballer, and he played in several positions for Ferencvaros and Hungary. Essentially a striker, he could also operate in central defence, and he helped Ferencvaros win five Hungarian league titles between 1932 and 1941. He captained Hungary to the 1938 World Cup finals, where he scored four goals in the tournament, including one in the final to reduce Italy's lead to 3–2, although a Piola goal eventually finished off the Hungarians. After his retirement he moved to Italy, where he managed a number of clubs, including Juventus, Bari and Roma.

*Right: Hungarian captain Gyorgy Sarosi (right) before the World Cup Final of 1938.*

## Dejan Savicevic
## (Yugoslavia, b. 1966)

**Clubs:** *Boducnost Titograd
(1982–88), Red Star Belgrade
(1988–92), AC Milan (1992–98),
Red Star Belgrade (1998–99),
Rapid Vienna (1999–2001)*
**Caps:** *56 (20 goals)*

The talented Yugoslavian midfielder
Savicevic played in the Red Star
Belgrade side that won the European
Cup in 1991, beating Marseille on
penalties. He transferred to AC Milan in
1992, where his dribbling prowess and
flair for goals earned him the nickname
of "the genius". He was outstanding in
Milan's 4–0 defeat of Barcelona in the
1994 European Cup Final, where he
scored a memorable goal and collected
his second winner's medal. He left Milan
to return to Red Star in 1998, and
was appointed club captain, but he
surprisingly left to join Rapid Vienna
in 1999. In 2007 he was appointed
President of the Montenegro FA.

*Above: Dejan Savicevic (right), for AC Milan, glides through the Barcelona defence
in the European Cup Final of 1994.*

## Juan Schiaffino
## (Uruguay, 1925–2002)

**Clubs:** *Penarol (1945–54),
AC Milan (1954–60),
Roma (1960–62)*
**Caps:** *45 (Uruguay),
4 (Italy)*

A small but lethal inside-forward,
Schiaffino was transferred from Penarol
to AC Milan in 1954 for a
then world-record fee of £72,000.
He scored the opening goal in the
1958 European Cup Final against Real
Madrid, although Milan lost 3–2 in
extra time. He played for Uruguay in
the 1950 World Cup Final, and scored
the equalizer against Brazil to help
Uruguay win 2–1; Schiaffino provided
five goals that tournament. He played
again in the 1954 finals, and Uruguay
took fourth place. After retirement he
returned home to manage Penarol and,
in 1975, he was appointed manager of
the Uruguay national team.

*Above: Juan Schiaffino, Uruguay's greatest-ever football export.*

## Peter Schmeichel (Denmark, b. 1963)

**Clubs:** *Hvidvore (1984–87), Brondby (1987–91), Manchester United (1991–99), Sporting Lisbon (1999–2001), Aston Villa (2001–2), Manchester City (2002–3)*
**Caps:** *129 (1)*

A massive presence between the goalposts, Schmeichel was an athletic and acrobatic keeper. He won four Danish league titles with Brondby and moved to Manchester United, for £550,000, in 1991. By the time he transferred to Sporting Lisbon in 1999, Schmeichel's stopping ability had helped United to five league titles and a European Cup victory over Bayern Munich in 1999. His talent helped Sporting Lisbon to the Portuguese title in 2000, their first championship victory since 1982. He was first capped

*Above: The intimidating, athletic figure of Peter Schmeichel.*

in 1987 and his goalkeeping skill, particularly his save from Van Basten's penalty in the semi-final shoot-out against Holland, was instrumental in Denmark's shock success in the 1992 European Championships. He played in Euro '96, and captained Denmark to a quarter-final in the 1998 World Cup. On retirement, he became a TV pundit.

## Vicenzo "Enzo" Scifo (Belgium, b. 1966)

**Clubs:** *Anderlecht (1982–87), Inter Milan (1987–88), Bordeaux (1988–89), Auxerre (1989–91), Torino (1991–93), Monaco (1993–97), Anderlecht (1997–2000)*
**Caps:** *84 (18)*

One of Belgium's finest-ever players, Scifo made his debut for Anderlecht at the age of 17. His guile and his goals

*Left: Enzo Scifo, star of four World Cup tournaments for Belgium.*

were behind Anderlecht's three league titles in succession between 1985 and 1987, and he moved to Inter Milan in 1987. He was loaned to French clubs Bordeaux and Auxerre before joining Torino in 1990. Scifo was first capped in 1984, and he played in the 1986 World Cup finals where he guided Belgium to fourth place, losing 2–0 to Argentina in the semi-finals. In the 1990 finals in Italy, he played in the Belgium side that reached the second round but was knocked out by a late David Platt goal for England. Scifo played in the 1998 World Cup finals in France, making his fourth appearance in the tournament. He retired in 2000.

## Uwe Seeler
## (Germany, b. 1936)

**Club:** *Hamburg (1953–71)*
**Caps:** *72 (43 goals)*

Seeler was West Germany's top striker throughout the 1960s, eventually giving way to the young Gerd Müller. The son of a former Hamburg player, Seeler showed a loyalty to Hamburg throughout his professional career – playing his club football only for the north German side and turning down some tempting offers from Italian and Spanish clubs. He was captain when the club were beaten 2–0 by AC Milan in the 1968 Cup Winners' Cup Final. A small but powerful centre-forward,

he captained West Germany to the 1966 World Cup Final, losing 4–2 to England. He also scored a remarkable back-header in the 1970 World Cup finals to equalize against England in the quarter-final, when England threw away a 2–0 lead to lose 3–2. So central was Seeler to German football of the 1960s and early 1970s that the German fans adopted his name for their chant ("Uwe! Uwe!") at international football matches. He shares with Pelé the distinction of having scored in four World Cup finals, in 1958, 1962, 1966 and 1970. Seeler retired in 1971 and eventually became club president of Hamburg.

*Right: West German captain, Uwe Seeler.*

## Alan Shearer
## (England, b. 1970)

**Clubs:** *Southampton (1988–92), Blackburn Rovers (1992–96), Newcastle United (1996–2006)*
**Caps:** *63 (30 goals)*

A high-scoring striker, Shearer was a teenage sensation with Southampton. At 17, he became the youngest player to score a hat trick in Division One, in Southampton's 4–2 defeat of Arsenal in 1988. He moved to Blackburn in 1992 for £3.6 million. Blackburn won the league title in 1995, with Shearer scoring 34 goals, and in 1996 he became the first player to score more than 30 goals in three successive seasons in the top division. Shearer joined Newcastle for a record figure of £15 million in 1996, making him the world's most expensive player, and his form revived when Bobby Robson became manager, following the departure of Ruud Gullit. He made his international debut in 1992, and in Euro '96 he was top scorer with five goals. He captained England to the 1998 World Cup finals, scoring twice. Shearer retired in 2006 and is currently a football analyst with the BBC. He re-joined Newcastle United as manager in 2009 and presided over the club's relegation to the Championship.

*Above: Alan Shearer on the attack for Newcastle United.*

## Peter Shilton
## (England, b. 1949)

**Clubs:** *Leicester City (1966–74), Stoke City (1974–77), Nottingham Forest (1977–82), Southampton (1982–87), Derby County (1987–92), Plymouth Argyle (1992–95), Wimbledon (1995), Bolton (1995), Coventry (1995–96), West Ham (1996), Leyton Orient (1996–97)*
**Caps:** *125*

The successor to Gordon Banks as England's goalkeeper, Peter Shilton had a long and illustrious career between the goal posts. After Leicester and Stoke City, Shilton joined Nottingham Forest in 1977 and, under the inspirational Brian Clough, he won two European Cup winner's medals, playing in the side that beat Malmo in 1979 and Hamburg in 1980. He was first capped in 1970 and played in the 1982 World Cup finals, letting in only one goal in five games. He played again in 1986, losing to Argentina and Maradona's infamous "Hand of God" goal in the quarter-final. He played in his last World Cup finals in 1990, when England lost to West Germany in the semi-final. Shilton played his 1000th league match for Leyton Orient in 1996, at the age of 47.

*Left: Peter Shilton dives to make a save for Nottingham Forest.*

## Omar Sivori
## (Argentina, 1935–2005)

**Clubs:** *River Plate (1952–57), Juventus (1957–65), Napoli (1965–69), River Plate (1969)*
**Caps:** *18 (9 goals) (Argentina), 9 (8 goals) (Italy)*

Playing alongside the big Welshman John Charles in the Juventus attack, Omar Sivori was a fiery inside-left with abundant skills and a sharp eye for goal. He began his career with River Plate and won three Argentinian league titles in succession between 1955 and 1957. After starring in the 1957 *Copa America*, Sivori moved to Juventus for a record £91,000, and his two goals brought Juventus the Italian league three times in 1958, 1960 and 1961. He was voted European Footballer of the Year in 1961. He joined Napoli in 1965, having scored nearly 150 goals for Juventus, and he became manager of the Argentinian national team in 1973.

*Right: Juventus' Argentinian forward, Omar Sivori.*

## Socrates
### (Brazil, b. 1954)

**Clubs:** *Botafogo (1974–76), Corinthians (1977–84), Fiorentina (1984–85), Flamengo (1985–87), Santos (1988–90)*
**Caps:** *60 (22 goals)*

The bearded Socrates, a qualified doctor, was a stylish midfielder who captained Brazil in the 1982 and 1986 World Cup finals. He played first with Botafogo as an amateur and, after collecting his medical degree, joined Corinthians as a professional in 1977. In 1982 he took Brazil to the World Cup quarter-final, having scored a brilliant goal against the Soviet Union, but despite scoring, his team lost to the eventual champions, Italy. In 1986 Brazil reached the semi-final but lost on penalties to France, with Socrates missing his first attempt. He played his club football in Brazil, moving without success to Fiorentina for one season in 1984, before rounding off his career with Santos.

*Right: Brazilian captain Socrates during the 1982 World Cup quarter-final.*

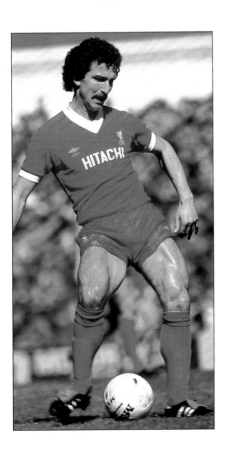

## Graeme Souness
### (Scotland, b. 1953)

**Clubs:** *Tottenham Hotspur (1968–73), Middlesbrough (1973–78), Liverpool (1978–84), Sampdoria (1984–86), Rangers (1986–91)*
**Caps:** *54 (3 goals)*

The tough-tackling, intimidating Souness was also a skilful and perceptive midfielder with Liverpool and Scotland. He joined Liverpool from Middlesbrough in 1978 and played in the 1978 European Cup Final, making Dalglish's winning goal. As captain of the side, he played in two further European Cup Finals with Liverpool, winning both, then moved on to the

*Left: Graeme Souness, Liverpool's midfield enforcer.*

Italian side Sampdoria in 1984, having played over 350 games for the Reds. Despite becoming a favourite with the fans at the Genovese club, Souness returned to British football in 1986, as player-manager of Rangers. He was the first Rangers manager ever to sign a Catholic (Mo Johnston), and under his stewardship the Glasgow side won their first league title for nine years. He represented Scotland in three World Cup finals, 1978, 1982 and 1986, and played his last international in 1986. Souness left Rangers in 1991 to become manager of Liverpool – taking over from his friend and former team-mate Kenny Dalglish. The appointment was less successful, however, and Souness stayed for less than three seasons.

His managerial career has included spells at Galatasaray, Southampton, Benfica, Blackburn Rovers and Newcastle United.

## Hristo Stoichkov
## (Bulgaria, b. 1966)

**Clubs:** *CSKA Sofia (1984–90), Barcelona (1990–95), Parma (1995–96), Barcelona (1996–98), CSKA Sofia (1998–99), Chicago Fire (2000–03)*
**Caps:** *83 (37 goals)*

Centre-forward Stoichkov is a Bulgarian national hero. He began his career with CSKA Sofia, and was bought by Barcelona for £2 million in 1990, after securing three Bulgarian league winner's medals. He scored 60 goals in his first three years with Barcelona, and played in two European Cup Finals, when they beat Sampdoria

in 1992 and lost to AC Milan two years later. He first played for Bulgaria in 1987, and his six goals in the 1994 World Cup finals made him the leading scorer and took Bulgaria to the semifinals, beating the holders Germany along the way. Stoichkov also played in Euro '96 and the 1998 World Cup finals, but this time Bulgaria did not impress. He left Barcelona for a season with Parma, but returned in 1996 and went back to CSKA in 1998. He retired from international football in 1999 and ended his club football in Japan, Saudi Arabia and the US. He was coach of the Bulgarian national team from 2004 to 2007.

*Right: The voluble Hristo Stoichkov.*

## Luis Suarez
## (Spain, b. 1935)

**Clubs:** *Deportivo La Coruña (1951–53), Barcelona (1953–61), Inter Milan (1961–70), Sampdoria (1970–73)*
**Caps:** *32 (14 goals)*

Midfield general Suarez was one of Spain's greatest players. The slim, tricky player left Deportivo La Coruña in 1954 for Barcelona, and played in Barcelona's 3–2 European Cup Final defeat by

*Left: Luis Suarez playing for Inter Milan.*

Benfica, in 1962. He was voted European Footballer of the Year in 1960, and he moved to Inter Milan for a then world record transfer fee of £150,000 in 1962. He led Inter Milan to two European Cup victories in 1963 and 1964 but missed playing in Inter's 2–1 defeat by Celtic in the 1967 European Cup Final due to injury. He helped Spain to their European Championship victory in 1964, and played in the 1966 World Cup finals in England. He took over the role of Spain's national manager in 1989 and led the team to the second round in the 1990 World Cup finals, having finished top of their group section.

## Davor Suker
## (Croatia, b. 1968)

**Clubs:** *FC Osijek (1985–89). Dynamo Zagreb (1989–91), Seville (1991–96), Real Madrid (1996–99), Arsenal (1999–2000), West Ham United (2000–01), 1860 Munich (2001–03)*
**Caps:** *69 (45 goals)*

Suker is Croatia's national team's leading goal scorer. He moved from Dynamo Zagreb to Seville in 1991, and then to Real Madrid in 1996. He helped Real Madrid win the Spanish league in 1997,

and came on as a substitute in their European Cup Final victory over Juventus in 1998. Suker made his international debut for the former Yugoslavia in 1990, and he scored a famous goal in Euro '96, chipping the ball over the retreating Peter Schmeichel. In the 1998 World Cup finals, Suker was the top scorer with six goals, and his goal against Holland helped Croatia claim third place. He has since played for Arsenal, West Ham and 1860 Munich and currently runs a soccer academy in Zagreb.

*Right: Croatia's Davor Suker playing up front for Arsenal.*

# Fernando Torres (Spain, b. 1984)

**Clubs:** *Atlético Madrid (2002–07), Liverpool: (2007–)*
**Caps:** *65 (22 goals)*

A strong, speedy and athletic forward, Madrid-born Torres (nicknamed "El Nino" – "The Kid") is recognized as one of the world's finest young strikers.

He began his career with Atlético Madrid, was made the team's captain at the age of 19 and scored 75 goals in *La Liga* in his five seasons with the club. Coveted by several English Premier clubs, he transferred to Liverpool in 2007 for a reported fee of £26.5 million and was given the famous number 9 shirt, previously worn by Anfield legends such as Ian Rush and Robbie Fowler. He scored on his debut against Chelsea and became the first player since Fowler in 1995–96 to score over 20 goals in a season, ending with an impressive 33 goals in all competitions.

He made his debut for Spain against neighbours Portugal in 2003 and he scored three goals for his country in the 2006 World Cup finals. Probably his finest moment was in the final of Euro 2008 against Germany when he raced on to a through ball from Xavi and sent a glorious shot over Jens Lehmann, securing his local hero status and his country's first major trophy for 44 years.

*Above: Torres leads the Spanish attack.*

# Marco Van Basten (Holland, b. 1964)

**Clubs:** *Ajax (1981–87), AC Milan (1987–95)*
**Caps:** *58 (24 goals)*

A tall, gifted striker, Van Basten was a prolific goal-scoring forward for Ajax, Milan and Holland in the 1980s and early 1990s. He made his debut for Ajax as a teenager, coming on as substitute for Johann Cruyff, and he lifted three Dutch league titles and scored 128 league goals in his five years at the club. Bought by AC Milan in 1987 for £1.5 million, his goals helped Silvio Berlusconi's team win two European Cups in succession, in 1989 and 1990. He played in Holland's triumphant team at Euro '88 and scored a brilliant 20-yard volley against the USSR in the final. He was named European Footballer of the Year in 1988, 1989 and 1992, and World Footballer of the Year in 1988 and 1992. He played in the 1993 European Cup Final, losing 1–0 to Marseille, but a series of injuries forced him to end his career at the age of 30. He had scored an outstanding tally of 90 goals in 147 games for Milan. He took over as coach of the Dutch team in 2004 and left to coach Ajax in 2008.

*Left: Van Basten, a truly world-class striker.*

## Carlos Valderrama
## (Colombia, b. 1961)

**Clubs:** *Atlético Nacional (1985–88), Montpellier (1988–91), Real Valladolid (1991–92), Atlético Nacional (1992–93), Atlético Junior (1993–96), Tampa Bay Mutiny (1996–97), Miami Fusion (1997–98), Tampa Bay Mutiny (1999)*
**Caps:** *111 (10 goals)*

Identified by his mane of frizzy, orange hair, midfielder Valderrama represented Colombia in six consecutive *Copa America* competitions, between 1987 and 1997, and in the World Cup finals of 1990, 1994 and 1998. He made his international debut in 1985 against Paraguay, and was voted South American Player of the Year in 1987 and 1994. In 1990 he helped take Colombia to the second round of the World Cup finals, but he could do nothing about Andres Escobar's own goal against the USA in 1994, and Colombia were knocked out. He played at France '98 at the age of 38.

*Right: Columbian hero Valderrama.*

*Above: Paul Van Himst (right) crosses the ball past the lunging Franz Beckenbauer.*

## Paul Van Himst
## (Belgium, b. 1943)

**Clubs:** *Anderlecht (1959–75), RWD Molenbeek, Enndracht Aalst*
**Caps:** *81 (31 goals)*

Centre-forward Van Himst was a young footballing prodigy and achieved eight Belgian league title winner's medals with Anderlecht, between 1962 and 1974. He represented Belgium at the 1970 World Cup finals and helped the team reach third place in front of a home crowd at Euro 72. After retirement, he managed former club Anderlecht, before leading Belgium to the 1982 and 1994 World Cup finals. He was recently voted Belgium's Footballer of the Century.

## Ruud Van Nistelrooy
## (Holland, b. 1976)

**Clubs:** *Den Bosch (1993–97), Heerenveen (1997–98), PSV Eindhoven (1998–2001), Manchester United (2001–2006), Real Madrid (2006–)*
**Caps:** *64 (33 goals)*

Van Nistelrooy is an outstanding goalscoring centre-forward who, despite two Premiership-winning medals and two *La Liga* titles, has not yet won as many honours or caps as his play merits. Joining PSV Eindhoven in 1998, and he scored a massive 60 goals in 57 games. Manchester United signed him in April 2001 for a record fee of £19 million. Van Nistelrooy made his international debut in 1998, but an injury kept him out of Euro 2000, and Holland failed to qualify for the 2002 World Cup. Dutch coach Dick Advocaat usually preferred Patrick Kluivert to lead Holland's attack, but Van Nistelrooy replaced Kluivert in the vital Euro 2004 qualifying play-off match against Scotland and scored a hat-trick in a 6–0 win to establish himself as a first choice for his country. He moved to Real Madrid in 2006.

*Right: Van Nistelrooy is currently the second highest ever goalscorer in European football.*

## Gianluca Vialli
### (Italy, b. 1964)

**Clubs:** *Cremonese (1980–84), Sampdoria (1984–92), Juventus (1992–96), Chelsea (1996–1999)*
**Caps:** *59 (16 goals)*

Born into a wealthy family in Cremona, northern Italy, striker Vialli joined his local club Cremonese in 1980 and moved to Sampdoria in 1984. Striking up a partnership with fellow forward Roberto Mancini, he helped his club to the 1990 Cup Winners' Cup Final, scoring both goals in their 2–0 win against Anderlecht. His last game for Sampdoria was the 1992 European Cup Final, when they lost 1–0 to Barcelona. He won the UEFA Cup again in 1993 with Juventus, and won the European Cup, as captain, in 1996, defeating Ajax on penalties. He joined Chelsea in 1996 and was appointed player-manager in 1998, following the departure of Ruud Gullit. He led the club to the Cup Winners' Cup Final, when they beat Stuttgart 1–0, and won the 2000 FA Cup Final. He became manager of Watford for a season in 2001 and now works as a commentator for Sky Italia.

*Left: Luca Vialli represents his country.*

## Christian Vieri
### (Italy, b. 1973)

**Clubs:** *Prato (1989–90), Torino (1990–92), Ravena (1993–94), Venezia (1994–95), Atalanta (1995–96), Juventus (1996–97), Atlético Madrid (1997–98), Lazio (1998–99), Inter Milan (1999–), Milan (2005–06), Atalanta (2006–07), Fiorentina (2007–08), Atlanta (2008–09)*
**Caps:** *49 (23 goals)*

Vieri is a big, strong, classic centre-forward and an excellent header of the ball. He briefly set the record for the world's most expensive player when he

*Left: Christian Vieri, briefly the world's most expensive player in 1999.*

moved from Lazio to Inter Milan in the summer of 1999 for £32 million. He has had something of a peripatetic career to date. He made his *Serie A* debut in 1991 in a 2–0 Torino win against Fiorentina, and played for four other Italian clubs before being transferred from Juventus (whom he represented in the 1997 European Cup Final) to Atlético Madrid in the summer of that year. He scored 24 goals in his season with the Spanish side, but a fall out with coach Arrigo Sacchi saw him join Lazio in 1998, and he was top scorer in the year he spent with them. He scored a hat trick on his debut for Inter, but missed much of the season due to injury. Vieri made his international debut in 1997 against Moldova, and he was second top scorer in the 1998 World Cup finals. He also played in the 2002 finals and Euro 2004.

## George Weah
### (Liberia, b. 1966)

**Clubs:** *Tonerre Yaounde (1986–88), Monaco (1988–92), Paris Saint-Germain (1992–95), AC Milan (1995–2000), Chelsea (2000), Manchester City (2000)*
**Caps:** *61 (22)*

Weah is the most respected man in Liberia, not only for his football skills, but also for his financial help and commitment to that war-torn country. A tall centre-forward with exceptional ball control and the ability to score explosive goals, he left Liberia in 1988 to join Monaco, who won the French league in 1991. In the 1995 European Cup he was tournament top scorer, with eight goals for PSG, and was voted European Footballer of the Year. He was four times African Footballer of the Year in 1989 and 1994 to 1996; he crowned this with the World Footballer of the Year award in 1996. Weah moved to AC Milan in 1995 and picked up two *Serie A* winner's medals. After short spells in England and the United Arab Emirates, he announced his retirement in 2002. He was a losing candidate in the 2005 Liberian presidential election.

*Right: Liberian star George Weah.*

## Billy Wright
### (England, 1924–1994)

**Clubs:** *Wolverhampton Wanderers (1941–59)*
**Caps:** *105 (3 goals)*

Wright was a solid and dependable defender, and captain of Wolverhampton Wanderers and England throughout the 1950s. He was a quiet but inspirational captain, with a precise tackle and effective heading and passing skills. He was centre-half in the Wolves side that won three league titles in the 1950s, under manager Stan Cullis, playing their robust, long-ball game. He was first capped in 1946, and played in the 1950, 1954 and 1958 World Cup finals, captaining the team for 90 of those games. He received his record one hundredth cap in a game against Scotland in 1959. He retired in 1959 and was awarded the CBE that year. He became manager of Arsenal in 1962, but left Highbury in 1966 to pursue a media career. He came back to Wolves as a director of the club in 1990. Wright died in 1994.

*Left: Wolves captain Billy Wright clears the ball out of defence.*

## Lev Yashin
### (Soviet Union, 1929–1990)

**Clubs:** *Moscow Dynamo (1949–70)*
**Caps:** *78*

Known as the "Black Panther" in Europe because of his distinctive all-black strip, Lev Yashin is widely regarded as the best goalkeeper in the history of football. His whole career was spent with Moscow Dynamo; he made his debut in 1951 and won five Soviet league winner's medals. He gained his first cap in 1954, won an Olympic gold in 1956 and played in the 1958 World Cup finals. With Yashin in goal, the Soviet Union won the inaugural European Championships in 1960. Yashin played in the 1962 World Cup finals and was in goal for the international FIFA side, the "Rest of the World", against England in 1963. The same year he became the only goalkeeper ever to be made European Footballer of the Year. In 1966 another error by Yashin in the World Cup allowed Franz Beckenbauer to score the winning goal in the semi-final. Yashin was awarded the Order of Lenin in 1968, and when he retired in 1970, the event was marked with a testimonial match at the Lenin stadium in Moscow. He became manager of Dynamo in 1971. He died in 1990.

*Right: Goalkeeping legend Lev Yashin keeps his hands firmly on the ball.*

## Zico, Artur Antunes Coimbra (Brazil, b. 1953)

**Clubs:** *Flamengo (1970–83), Udinese (1983–85), Flamengo (1985–92), Kashima Antlers (1992)*
**Caps:** *66 (45 goals)*

Known as the "White Pelé", Zico is Brazil's second-highest goal scorer after the master. The wiry forward played in the 1978 World Cup finals and thought he had scored the winning goal against Sweden, but referee Clive Thomas blew his whistle for full time while the ball was in mid-air, between Zico and the back of the net. Zico played again in the 1982 and 1986 tournaments. It was his 11 goals in South America's *Copa Libertadores* that helped Flamengo to win the title in 1981. After the 1982 World Cup finals Zico moved to Italy's Udinese. He was voted World Footballer of the Year in 1983, and he returned to Flamengo in 1985. He retired in 1992 and became Brazil's Sports Minister before moving to Japan a year later, to the Kashima Antlers, to help establish the new J–League. Zico was Brazil's assistant coach at the 1998 World Cup finals. He later returned to Japan to manage the national team and Fenerbahce in 2006.

*Above: The "white Pelé" Zico (left) shoots.*

*Above: The talents of Zinedine Zidane brought him the awards of World Footballer of the Year in 1998, 2000 and 2003, and European Footballer of the Year in 1998.*

## Zinedine Zidane (France, b. 1972)

**Clubs:** *Cannes (1988–92), Bordeaux (1992–96), Juventus (1996–2001), Real Madrid (2001–)*
**Caps:** *93 (26 goals)*

A midfielder with tight ball control, perceptive passing talents and a thunderous shot, Zidane is the finest French footballer of his generation. The son of Algerian parents, he moved from Cannes to Bordeaux in 1992. In 1996 he moved to Juventus, and helped them to two consecutive European Cup Finals, although they lost both. Zidane made his first appearance for France in 1994, and was an inspiration as they won the 1998 World Cup. Against Brazil, Zidane headed in two of the goals that won the final 3–0 for the French. He was voted both European and World Footballer of the Year. His electrifying performances at Euro 2000 were a crucial contribution to France's triumph and he was again voted World Footballer of the Year. In 2001 he was transferred to Real Madrid for a world record £47.2 million, and scored a great winning goal in the 2002 Champions League Final against Bayer Leverkusen. Zidane was once more voted World Footballer of the Year in 2003. He retired from international football after being infamously sent off at the World Cup final in Germany in 2006.

## Dino Zoff
## (Italy, b. 1942)

**Clubs:** *Udinese, Mantova, Napoli (1967–72), Juventus (1972–83)*
**Caps:** *113*

Zoff was probably Italy's finest-ever goalkeeper. The most-capped Italian keeper of all time, with 113 appearances for his country, he had spells with Udinese, Mantova and Napoli before joining Juventus, in 1972, at the age of 30, where he became the automatic choice in goal.

*Left: Dino Zoff makes sure his defence is in order.*

Zoff helped Juventus win the UEFA Cup in 1977 (beating Athletic Bilbao on away goals) and the Italian league six times, and he captained Italy to their World Cup triumph in 1982. As the Juventus manager, he won the UEFA Cup again in 1990, and then moved to Lazio in an administrative role. Zoff replaced Cesare Maldini as the manager of the Italian national team, after some disappointing performances from Maldini's side in the 1998 World Cup finals. He took Italy all the way through to the final of the European Championships in 2000, but defeat by France, and some vociferous public criticism, led to his prompt resignation and his replacement by Giovanni Trapattoni.

## Andoni Zubizarreta
## (Spain, b. 1961)

**Clubs:** *Alaves (1979–81), Athletic Bilbao (1981–86), Barcelona (1986–94), Valéncia (1994–99)*
**Caps:** *126*

The Basque-born goalkeeper Zubizarreta holds the record for the highest number of Spanish international appearances, with 126 caps. He began his career with his home club, Alaves, and joined Athletic Bilbao in 1981, gaining his first cap in 1985. He joined Barcelona the following year and played in the World Cup finals, losing to Belgium in a quarter-final penalty shoot-out. He played again in the 1990 tournament, and was a member of the Barcelona side that won the 1992 European Cup. However, he let in four goals against AC Milan in the 1994 European Cup Final, and he left the club soon after, on a free transfer, to join Valéncia. He played in two more World Cup finals, in 1994, when Spain were eliminated by Italy in the quarter-final, and again, in 1998, when they failed to qualify from the group stage.

*Right: Spanish goalkeeper Andoni Zubizarreta dives to prevent a goal.*

# THE COUNTRIES

The international game is football at its highest level, and every footballer dreams of playing for his country. World competitions are played between the members of FIFA, the world governing body for football. There are currently more than 200 FIFA-affilliated countries, which are grouped geographically between six confederations – Europe (UEFA), South America (CONMEBOL), North and Central America (CONCACAF), Asia (ACF), Oceania and Africa (CAF). In this chapter we profile 36 of the most established FIFA sides.

# Belgium

**World Cup Appearances:** *11 (1930, 34, 38, 54, 70, 82, 86, 90, 94, 98, 2002)*

**World Cup Record:** *fourth place 1 (1986)*

**European Championships:** *runners-up 1 (1980); third place 1 (1972)*

**Olympic Games:** *winners 1 (1920)*

**Shirts:** *Red*

Belgium's greatest footballing achievements to date came in the 1980s. That decade saw the national team finish as runners-up in the 1980 European Championship, and in fourth place at the World Cup finals in 1986. Under the careful stewardship of coach Guy Thys, the Belgium team of this era was, for a brief time at least, one of Europe's leading lights; it was a huge achievement considering the country's tiny population of just ten million.

*Below: Belgium's Enzo Scifo is tackled by Germany's Guido Buchwald at USA '94.*

Prior to the high point of the Thys era, Belgium had taken part in five World Cup finals but had failed to make any significant impression. In the European Championships the Belgians had fared slightly better, progressing to the last four of the 1972 competition with a notable victory over reigning champions Italy. In the semi-final, however, West Germany proved too strong and won 2–1. Belgium did at least secure the consolation of third place with a 2–1 victory over Hungary.

Eight years later, and with Thys in charge, Belgium made good progress at the European Championships. This time the "Red and Blacks", whose team was based around the attacking talents of Francois Van der Elst and Jan Ceulemans, progressed to the final at the expense of England, Spain and Italy. However, just as they had in 1972, the West Germans proved the Belgium nemesis, winning the final with a goal from Horst Hrubesch in the last minute of the match.

*Above: Luc Nilis is one of the modern day heroes of Belgian football.*

In 1986 the Belgian national team enhanced their reputation with a series of entertaining performances which propelled them through to the semi-finals of the World Cup in Mexico. Their most memorable display came against the USSR, a match that saw the Soviets surrender a 2–0 lead before crashing out 4–3 on aggregate. It was a result that ensured Belgium were never again underestimated. The 1980s and 1990s brought new heroes, such as Enzo Scifo, Philippe Albert, Luc Nilis, Marc Wilmots and Luis Oliveira, but despite qualifying for six World Cup finals in succession, from 1982 to 2002, Belgium have failed to reattain the heights that they achieved during the reign of Thys. At the finals in 2002, they reached the second round, but lost 2–0 to the eventual winners of the tournament, Brazil. They failed to qualify for the finals of both Euro 2004 and 2008.

# Bulgaria

**World Cup Appearances:** *7 (1962, 66, 70, 74, 86, 94, 98)*

**World Cup Record:** *fourth place 1 (1994)*

**Olympic Games:** *runners-up 1 (1968)*

**Shirts:** *White and green*

In 1994 Bulgaria travelled to the World Cup finals in the United States with a less than impressive international pedigree. The Balkan nation had failed to win a single match during five previous tournament appearances, but this time things were different. First to suffer the Bulgarian backlash were Greece, who were thrashed 4–0, but it was the 2–0 win against 1990 runners-up Argentina that guaranteed progress to the second round.

Bulgaria's team of 1994 remains the most talented and successful in the country's history, and the undoubted star of the show was Barcelona's Hristo Stoichkov. A left-sided forward, he combined a rare blend of raw

*Below: Emil Kostadinov, part of the great Bulgarian team at USA '94.*

aggression and power with subtle skills and a high-velocity shot, and he was voted European Footballer of the Year in 1994. However, Stoichkov was not the only top-class player in the Bulgaria line-up, as first Mexico and then Germany discovered in the knockout phase of USA '94. The Mexicans were beaten on penalties but Germany, the reigning World Champions, were dealt with in 90 minutes with goals from Yordan Lechkov and Stoichkov in a 2–1 victory. Bulgaria became the neutrals' favourite, and although Italy narrowly beat them 2–1 in the semi-finals, they left with a greatly enhanced reputation.

Alas, by the time of the World Cup finals in France in 1998, Bulgaria were in decline. The old guard were now past their best and coach Hristo Bonev

*Above: Spain's Andoni Zubizarreta clashes with Bugaria's Hristo Stoichkov in the first round of Euro '96 in England, the match was a 1–1 draw.*

was unable to inspire his team to further glory. Bulgaria won just one point from their three games in France 1998, and their only goal came in the humiliating 6–1 defeat against Spain. Bulgaria's flirtation with success ended with a repeat of the scoreline inflicted on them by Hungary in their first World Cup finals in 1962. Stoichkov played in the unsuccessful Euro 2000 qualifying campaign, but retired in June 1999. Although Bulgaria qualified top of their group for Euro 2004, they came away from the final tournament with no points, and they failed to qualify in 2008.

# Croatia

**World Cup Appearances:** *3 (1998, 2002, 06)*

**World Cup Record:** *third place 1 (1998)*

**Shirts:** *Red and white checker-board*

On 17 October 1990, Croatia returned to international football after an absence of almost 50 years. They had previously played a number of matches against fellow Axis powers during World War Two, but at war's end Croatia was subsumed, both in politics and sport, by Yugoslavia. Its rebirth as a footballing nation began with a 2–1 victory over the United States, although it was not until 1992 that the new Croatia was allowed to join FIFA. Thereafter, progress was rapid, and by the end of the 20th century Croatia had established itself as the strongest team to emerge from the former Yugoslavia.

*Above: Zvonimir Boban captained Croatia to the World Cup finals of 1998.*

*Below: Croatia's highly rated young midfielder Luka Modric.*

The qualifying campaign for Euro '96 provided Croatia's first taste of competitive football, but the newcomers showed no nerves and topped their group, which included Italy and Ukraine, to book a place at the finals. The instant acclimatization to the international game put Miroslav Blazevic's squad in the spotlight. However, several of the players had played internationals with the pre-civil war Yugoslavia, and most played in Europe with their club sides. It soon became clear that Croatia would be no whipping boys. Blazevic established a settled line-up based around the abundantly talented midfield trio of Zvonimir Boban, Aljosa Asanovic and Robert Prosinecki, the unyielding defensive combination of Slaven Bilic and Igor Stimac, and the prolific strike partnership of Davor Suker and Alen Boksic. The line-up proved successful throughout the 1990s.

Croatia were one of the more entertaining teams at Euro '96, and won many admirers. However, a lack of discipline in their quarter-final clash with Germany cost Blazevic's team dear, and following Stimac's sending-off they were beaten 2–1. It was a defeat that Croatia avenged in fine style at the 1998 World Cup finals in France, where they exceeded all expectations, and breezed past Germany with a 3–0 victory in the quarter-finals. The dream, however, came to an end against eventual champions France in the semi-finals. Victory over Holland in the third place play-off provided some consolation, as did the fact that Davor Suker finished the tournament as top scorer with six goals.

Croatia reached the World Cup finals in 2002 and 2006 but could not progress beyond the initial group stages. In Euro 2008 they were knocked out by Turkey on penalties after battling their way through to the quarter-finals.

# Czech Republic

**World Cup Appearances:** *9 (1934, 38, 54, 58, 62, 70, 82, 90, 2006)*

**World Cup Record:** *runners-up 2 (1938, 62)*

**European Championships:** *winners 1 (1976); runners-up 1 (1996); third place 1 (1980); semi-finalists 1 (2004)*

**Olympic Games:** *runners-up 2 (1920, 64)*

**Shirts:** *Red*

*Note: Records up to 1994 are for Czechoslovakia*

The Czech Republic are a team whose relatively modest status belies their significant achievements. Formerly the western half of the old Czechoslovakia, the Czech Republic have developed into arguably the strongest of the many teams that have emerged from Eastern Europe, following the velvet revolutions of the early 1990s. The Czech Republic's short footballing history has already included a runners-up performance at Euro '96, and at the start of the new millennium the country rose to second place in FIFA's rankings.

*Below: Czechoslovakia reached their second World Cup Final in 1962.*

The Czechs, whose successes are seldom mentioned, were among Europe's leading nations prior to World War Two, finishing as runners-up to hosts Italy in the 1934 World Cup. They were back in the World Cup Final in 1962 but, despite the efforts of star defender Ladislav Novak and a goal from wing-half Josef Masopust, they lost 3–1 to Brazil. Czechoslovakia were also a significant force in the European Championships, finishing third in 1960 and 1980, and winning the competition through a penalty shoot-out against West Germany, in 1976.

The Czech Republic's debut in major tournament football came at Euro '96 and, despite qualifying by winning a group that included Holland and Norway, Dusan Uhrin's team travelled to England as rank outsiders. They were beaten 2–0 by the Germans in their opening game.

Against Italy at Anfield, however, Uhrin's men tore up the script and claimed a 2–1 victory, courtesy of goals from Radek Bejbl and promising young midfielder Pavel Nedved. A 4–4 draw against the Russians was enough to book a place in the quarter-finals

*Above: Captain Thomas Rosicky in a game against the United States.*

against highly fancied Portugal, but the game was a let-down. The match was eventually won by the Czech Republic, thanks to an incredible piece of skill from Karel Poborsky; from the edge of the box, he scooped the ball over Portugal's keeper Vitor Baia, while running at pace, to score the game's only goal. A 6–5 penalty shoot-out win against France followed in the semi-final, leaving the Czech Republic to face Germany at Wembley in the final.

The game started brightly for Uhrin's underdogs, with Patrik Berger scoring from the penalty spot after Poborsky had been up-ended, but German substitute Oliver Bierhoff equalized in the second half and struck the winner with a golden goal in extra time.

The Czechs made their way through to the 2006 World Cup finals, and they reached the semi-finals in Euro 2004, but were knocked out after an extra-time goal from eventual winners Greece. In Euro 2008, they were knocked out at the group stage.

# Denmark

**World Cup Appearances:** *3 (1986, 98, 2002)*

**European Championships:** *winners 1 (1992); fourth place 1 (1964)*

**Olympic Games:** *runners-up 2 (1912, 60)*

**Shirts:** *Red*

In 1992 Denmark gatecrashed the European Championships and won a competition for which they had failed to qualify, completing one of the most compelling tales in the history of international football. The Danes had finished as runners-up to Yugoslavia in their qualifying group for Euro '92 but, with the Balkans on the verge of a vicious conflict, Yugoslavia withdrew and Denmark received a late pass into the tournament.

The national team's manager, Richard Moller Nielsen, was in the midst of decorating his house when he heard the

*Below: John Jensen celebrates scoring against Germany in the final of Euro '92.*

news, while most of his players had to be recalled from holidays. Preparations were necessarily short.

Unsurprisingly, given the nature of their inclusion, Denmark started Euro '92 in less than spectacular fashion. A goalless draw with England was followed by a 1–0 defeat against Sweden, and left Moller Nielsen's team needing a victory over France to have any chance of qualifying for the semi-finals. Goals from Larsen and Elstrup were enough to overcome a highly fancied French team, and set up a match against the even more promising Dutch side. It seemed that Holland, with Bergkamp, Van Basten, Koeman, Rijkaard, Gullit and Van Tiggelen in their line-up, could not fail to win, but the Danes were on top of their game and they never fell behind in a match that ended 2–2 after extra time. Denmark won the penalty shoot-out following a miss from, of all people, Marco Van Basten. The footballing gods were clearly on Denmark's side, and the Danes were now

*Above: Schmeichel and team-mates enjoy their victory at Euro '92.*

the neutrals' favourite against Germany in the final. The fairytale came true with goals from John Jensen and Kim Vilfort in a 2–0 victory.

Ironically, Denmark's triumph at Euro '92 was achieved without the country's greatest player, Michael Laudrup, who was in dispute with Moller Nielson over tactics. Laudrup had been Denmark's star at the 1986 World Cup finals, playing a key role in the 2–0 victory over West Germany and in the 6–1 thrashing of Uruguay. he appointment of coach, Swede Bo Johansson, following a poor showing at Euro '96, meant Michael Laudrup returned to the fold.

With their star player back, alongside brother Brian, Denmark did well at the 1998 World Cup finals, losing in the quarter-finals 3–2 to tournament runners-up Brazil.

Without the Laudrups, now retired, Denmark still reached the knock-out stage in the World Cup finals in 2002, and the finals of Euro 2004, although they failed to reach the finals stages of World Cup 2006 and Euro 2008.

# England

**World Cup Appearances:** *12 (1950, 54, 58, 62, 66, 70, 82, 86, 90, 98, 2002, 06)*

**World Cup Record:** *winners 1 (1966); fourth place 1 (1990)*

**European Championships:** *semi-finals 1 (1996); third place 1 (1968)*

**Olympic Games:** *winners 2 (1908, 12)*

**Shirts:** *White*

England has a special place in football's history; it is the birthplace of the game, and the site of the world's most famous domestic competition, the FA Cup. England also played in the first recorded international match, drawing 0–0 with Scotland in 1872.

In the early years of international football, England competed exclusively against Wales, Scotland and Ireland, and it was not until 1908 that "foreign" opposition was encountered in the shape of Austria. England beat the Austrians 6–1, and later that year recorded victories against Hungary (7–0) and Bohemia (4–0). Confidence soon grew into arrogance, and by the inter-war period England were convinced that they were the greatest team in the world. They did not get the chance to prove it because of a dispute with FIFA over broken time payments for amateur players, which meant they did not participate in the early World Cup finals of the 1930s.

Under manager Walter Winterbottom, England made their World Cup debut in Brazil in 1950. It was a disastrous experience, with the team suffering the indignity of a defeat by the USA and elimination at the first hurdle. Worse followed when, in 1953, England were beaten 6–3 by Hungary at Wembley. England quickly learned that they were no longer, if indeed they ever had been, the best in the world. Another poor World Cup campaign in 1962 proved too much for Walter Winterbottom, who resigned and was replaced by Ipswich Town boss Alf Ramsey.

The pragmatic Ramsey made better use of the talented players available, and on home soil in 1966 the famous "Wingless Wonders" claimed the nation's only World Cup success to date. The 4–2 win over West Germany, in which striker Geoff Hurst scored a hat trick, remains the most celebrated game in England's footballing history.

Ramsey and his team, which was led by Bobby Moore and built around the abundantly talented Bobby Charlton, attempted to repeat the trick in Mexico four years later, but were beaten by West Germany in the quarter-finals. England entered a steady decline in the 1970s, and when the team failed to qualify for the 1974 World Cup finals, Ramsey retired. Only Bobby Robson, of seven successive managers to 2001, managed to approach Ramsey's achievement, with England going out on penalties to Germany in the 1990 World Cup semi-final and finishing in fourth place.

Sven-Göran Eriksson, took over when England looked unlikely to qualify for the 2002 World Cup finals, leading England to the last eight, where they lost to eventual winners Brazil. In 2006 in Germany, England again reached the last eight, but only Owen Hargreaves could score in the penalty shoot-out, and Portugal went through to the semis. England are currently managed by Fabio Capello, after a brief and unsuccessful tenure under Steve McClaren.

*Below: That goal! Michael Owen takes on Argentina at France '98.*

# France

**World Cup Appearances:** *12 (1930, 34, 38, 54, 58, 66, 78, 82, 86, 98, 2002, 06)*

**World Cup Record:** *winners 1 (1998); runners-up 1 (2006); third place 2 (1958, 86); fourth place 1 (1960)*

**European Championships:** *winners 2 (1984, 2000); fourth place 1 (1960)*

**Olympic Games:** *winners 1 (1984)*

**Shirts:** *Blue*

The evolution of world football owes a great debt to France - the game's greatest prize was, after all, the brainchild of Frenchman Jules Rimet - so it was fitting that the last World Cup finals of the 20th century was won by "*Les Bleus*" in Paris. France's only previous international trophy win came at the European Championships of 1984, a competition that had another Frenchman, Henri Delaunay, as its architect.

France's World Cup success of 1998 was memorable not only because it arrived on home soil, but also because it was achieved with a comprehensive 3–0 victory against Brazil, the reigning champions and the tournament's resounding favourites. The man behind this long-awaited triumph was coach Aimé Jacquet, who produced a

*Below: Zinedine Zidane, scorer of two goals in the 1998 World Cup Final.*

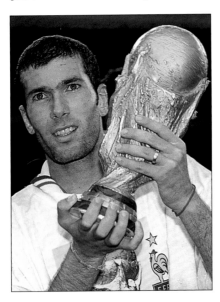

*Above: The incomparable Michel Platini scores against Italy in 1986.*

team that combined an impressive work ethic with a high degree of skill. The defensive unit of Fabien Barthez, Lilian Thuram, Laurent Blanc, Marcel Desailly and Bixente Lizarazu was the finest on display at France '98, and the team's outstanding talent, Zinedine Zidane, ruled the midfield.

*Les Bleus*' previous best World Cup performances had been their third place at the finals of 1958 and 1986. The team of 1986, which bowed out to West Germany in the semi-finals, still contained many of the players who won the 1984 European Championships under coach Michel Hidalgo. That 1984 side is widely regarded as France's greatest ever line-up, and its strength was the midfield quartet of Luis Fernandez, Jean Tigana, Alain Giresse and Michel Platini. However, just as in 1998, Hidalgo's team lacked an outstanding striker. It was a problem that was finally resolved at Euro 2000. Coach Roger Lemerre retained the 1998 defence and midfield and with the potent attacking

quartet of Anelka, Henry, Wiltord and Trezeguet, France justified their billing by cruising through to win the European Championship.

With much the same team as 1998 and 2000, France were favourites for the World Cup of 2002, but suffered a shock 1–0 defeat to Senegal in the tournament's curtain-raiser. They went on to finish bottom of the group, without scoring a single goal. Under new coach Jaques Santini, France qualified for the Euro 2004 finals in Portugal, but he resigned after France were beaten by Greece in the quarter-final. Under new coach Raymond Domenech France reached the 2006 World Cup Final but were defeated by Italy after penalties and the sending-off of Zidane for a bizarre head butt on Marco Materazzi. In Euro 2008, they failed to score a single point in their group, with a 2-0 defeat by Italy sealing their fate.

# Germany

**World Cup Appearances:** *16 (1934, 38, 54, 58, 62, 66, 70, 74, 78, 82, 86, 90, 94, 98, 2002, 06)*

**World Cup Record:** *winners 3 (1954, 74, 90); runners-up 5 (1966, 82, 86, 2002, 06); third place 2 (1934, 70); fourth place 1 (1958)*

**European Championships:** *winners 3 (1972, 80, 96); runners-up 2 (1976, 92)*

**Shirts:** *White with black trim*

*Note: Records for 1950–91 are for West Germany*

Despite the protestations of English and Italian fans, Germany are Europe's most successful international football team. Eight appearances in World Cup Finals, including three victories, and three successes in the European Championships, provide irrefutable evidence of their superiority.

Prior to World War Two, Germany's record was modest, with third place at the 1934 World Cup tournament being the pinnacle of their achievements. However, after the war, the country was divided and the western half quickly

*Below: Oliver Bierhoff proved Germany's match-winner at the final of Euro '96.*

developed into a football superpower. In 1950, West Germany joined FIFA, and four years later they won their first World Cup with a shock 3–2 victory against the tournament favourites, Hungary, who had beaten West Germany 8–3 in the group phase. In England, twelve years later, West Germany were back in the World Cup Final. The match against the hosts proved an epic and controversial encounter. Having clawed themselves back into the match with a last-minute equalizer from Wolfgang Weber, the Germans fell victim to Geoff Hurst's controversial goal and England went on to win the match 4–2.

For West Germany the defeat was tempered by the emergence of sweeper Franz Beckenbauer, who became the single most important figure in German football. In the 1970s, Beckenbauer became the kingpin in West Germany's greatest team, playing alongside fellow legends Sepp Maier, Paul Breitner and Gerd Müller. It was a line-up that swept all before them, clinching first the European Championship of 1972 and then the World Cup two years later.

In the 1980s, Beckenbauer returned to national team duty as coach, and led the side to the 1986 World Cup Final. Four

*Above: Beckenbauer acknowledges the crowd after World Cup victory in 1974.*

years later, "*der Kaiser*" went one better, guiding his team, which was built around key players Jürgen Kohler, Lothar Matthäus and Jürgen Klinsmann, to victory against Argentina in the final of Italia '90. In 1996, a united Germany, captained by Klinsmann, claimed its first major trophy with victory over the Czech Republic in the final of Euro '96 at Wembley. They went into decline and, after failing to make a significant impression upon the 1998 World Cup finals, they gave a poor account of themselves at Euro 2000.

Germany qualified for the 2002 World Cup finals only after a play-off, but surprisingly, with what was regarded as one of their poorest teams, they managed to get through to the final itself. Under coach Rudi Voller, they tested Brazil before losing 2–0. They exited Euro 2004 without winning a game, but under new coach Jürgen Klinsmann they reached the World Cup semi-finals in 2006, conceding two extra time goals to Italy. At Euro 2008, Germany reached the Final, but a fine first-half goal from Spain's Fernando Torres was the only goal of the game.

# Holland

**World Cup Appearances:** *8 (1934, 38, 74, 78, 90, 94, 98, 2006)*

**World Cup Record:** *runners-up 2 (1974, 78); fourth place 1 (1998)*

**European Championships:** *winners 1 (1988); third place 1 (1976); semi-finalists 1 (2004)*

**Shirts:** *Orange*

Few international teams have been more deserving of the adjective "great" than the Dutch team of the 1970s. Although they did not win the World Cup, the team of Johan Cruyff, Rudi Krol and Arie Haan illuminated the modern game in a way that perhaps only Brazil have managed before or since. Holland, coached by former Ajax boss and the godfather of "total football" Rinus Michels, played with a fluency that made his team a favourite with neutrals and football purists alike.

It was not until the 1950s, however, that the country had its own professional league. Thereafter, progress was rapid, and in 1970 Dutch football hinted at what was to come when Feyenoord won the

*Below: Marco Van Basten and Ruud Gullit, Holland's heroes of Euro '88.*

European Cup against Celtic. The following season, Amsterdam club Ajax began a three-year reign as European Champions with victory against Panathinaikos at Wembley. Football was beginning to take notice, and in 1974, Holland qualified for their first World Cup finals for 36 years, having competed without success at both the 1934 and 1938 finals. The Dutch were at their irresistible best, and breezed through the first qualifying group before producing an outstanding display to beat reigning champions Brazil in the second phase and go into the final against hosts West Germany.

Holland began the World Cup Final of 1974 in dramatic fashion; Neeskens scoring from the penalty spot after Cruyff had been brought down in the first minute. The Dutch dominated the opening phase of the game but failed to convert their possession into a second goal and, after 25 minutes, the Germans struck an equalizer with a penalty of their own. A second-half goal from Gerd Müller clinched the game for the hosts.

The Dutch, minus Cruyff who had retired from international football, were back in the World Cup Final four years

*Above: Rinus Michels, coaching guru and godfather of "total football".*

later, but once more they came unstuck against a host nation, this time Argentina. It proved the swansong for the "total football" team, and it was not until a new generation of stars emerged in the late 1980s that Holland again found themselves fighting for major honours. The European Championships of 1988 saw the second great Dutch team, including Marco Van Basten, Frank Rijkaard, Ronald Koeman and Ruud Gullit, win the competition with a 2–0 victory against the USSR in Munich. Several Dutch teams have subsequently flirted with success, most notably Guus Hiddink's side that finished fourth in France in 1998, but all too often internal disputes over tactics, money and managers undermine attempts to recapture the glory days of the 1970s.

Under coach Marco Van Basten, Holland fought their way through to reach the final stages of both the 2006 World Cup and the Euro 2008 tournaments, but in spite of consistently producing attractive, attacking football, could not win either competition.

# Hungary

**World Cup Appearances:** *9 (1934, 38, 54, 58, 62, 66, 78, 82, 86)*

**World Cup Record:** *runners-up 2 (1938, 54)*

**European Championships:** *third place 1 (1964); fourth place 1 (1972)*

**Olympic Games:** *winners 3 (1952, 64, 68)*

**Shirts:** *Red*

In the 1950s Hungary rose to the pinnacle of the world game with a team that was years ahead of its time. "The Magnificent Magyars", as Hungary's great team were nicknamed, were built around the successful Honved line-up that claimed four league titles during the 1950s. Inside-forward Ferenc Puskas was the undoubted star for both club and country, but was by no means

*Below: Hungary's great team of the 1950s, starring Hidegkuti (centre), line up at Wembley in 1953.*

Hungary's only player of note. In 1952 Hungary won Olympic gold and, a year later, became the first continental team to beat England on home soil with a 6–3 victory at Wembley. England were not the first team to struggle to contend with Hungary's fluent attacking football and, as if to prove that the result had been no fluke, the Magyars crushed the same opponents 7–1 just six months later.

The attacking trio of Puskas, Nandor Hidegkuti and Sandor Kocsis provided the key to Hungary's success. At their best they were unplayable, with Hidegkuti, who frequently played as a deep-lying striker, proving a particular problem for his burly, and often pedestrian, markers. Tactically, Hungary were simply too advanced for their opponents, and it was with great confidence and an unbeaten run stretching back to 1950 that the Magyars travelled to the 1954 World Cup finals in Switzerland. Seventeen goals in two group matches were

*Above: "The Galloping Major" Ferenc Puskas, star of Hungary's 1950s team.*

followed by a quarter-final victory over Brazil, and a 4–2 win against Uruguay guaranteed Kocsis and company a place in the Final. Hungary's opponents were West Germany, a team the Magyars had trounced 8–3 in a group match, but a half-fit Puskas and a profound case of overconfidence saw the favourites throw away a two-goal lead to lose the match 3–2.

Defeat in 1954 was the second time Hungary had lost a World Cup Final. The first was in 1938 when, with a team inspired by centre-forward Gyorgy Sarosi, the Hungarians had lost 4–2 to Italy in Paris. There has, however, been no third final for the Magyars, whose great team of the 1950s rapidly disappeared following the Hungarian Uprising of 1956. Key players, including Puskas and Zoltan Czibor, defected to the West, and a period of steady decline, which continued into the 21st century, ensued.

# Italy

**World Cup Appearances:** *16 (1934, 38, 50, 54, 62, 66, 70, 74, 78, 82, 86, 90, 94, 98, 2002, 06)*

**World Cup Record:** *winners 4 (1934, 38, 82, 2006); runners-up 2 (1970, 94); third place 1 (1990); fourth place 1 (1978)*

**European Championships:** *winners 1 (1968); runners-up 1 (2000); fourth place 1 (1980)*

**Olympic Games:** *winners 1 (1936)*

**Shirts:** *Blue*

Italy were the first European team to win the World Cup and, having won the trophy on two further occasions, regard themselves as the continent's pre-eminent footballing nation.

Italy enjoyed its first taste of glory at the 1934 World Cup, winning the Jules Rimet trophy on home soil, with a team coached by Vittorio Pozzo and which included three Argentines, Pozzo led Italy to a second World Cup success four years later in France but, this time, the South American exiles had been replaced by Italian-born talent.

Italy's domination of world football was brought to an abrupt end by the outbreak of war in 1939, and it was not until 1950 that the *Azzurri* were given

*Below: Paolo Rossi scores in a 3–2 victory over Brazil in the 1982 World Cup.*

the opportunity to defend their title. Sadly, the Superga aircrash of 1949, which had wiped out the successful Torino team of the 1940s, left the national team without many of its first-choice players, and the dream of a hat trick of World Cups ended with elimination at the group phase.

In 1968, an Italian team that included Dino Zoff, Sandro Mazzola, Giacinto Facchetti and Gigi Riva, won the European Championships, beating Yugoslavia 2–0 in Rome. With the exception of Zoff, these players would also help Italy to the World Cup Final in Mexico two years later. The Italians, however, met arguably the greatest team in the history of the game, in the shape of Brazil, and were beaten 4–1.

In 1982, Italy finally added to the two titles they had won in the 1930s. The Spanish finals in 1982 began quietly for Italy, and they drew their opening three matches before finding form with victories against Brazil and Argentina. In the semi-final, controversial striker Paolo Rossi proved the hero, scoring both goals in a 2–0 victory against Poland to book the Italians' place in the final. Rossi struck again in the final against West Germany, and further goals from Marco Tardelli and Alessandro Altobelli secured a 3–1 victory. A record fourth World Cup

*Above: Paolo Maldini, son of Cesare, led Italy to the 1994 World Cup Final.*

was almost added at USA '94, but Italy were defeated in a penalty shoot-out against Brazil.

After being within seconds of winning the European Championship in 2000 (France equalized and won with a "golden goal"), Italian hopes were high for the World Cup in 2002. But Italy lost again to a "golden goal", this time in the second round against co-hosts South Korea. Along with questionable refereeing decisions, it caused bitter accusations of cheating from the Italian press and public.

A resurgent Italy entered the 2006 World Cup finals, winning their fourth Final after a 1–1 draw after extra time against their old rivals France and, for the first final ever, scoring all five penalties to clinch victory and claim the coveted trophy.

# Northern Ireland

**World Cup Appearances:** *3 (1958, 82, 86)*

**Shirts:** *Green*

Considering its relative size and the modest standard of its domestic league, Northern Ireland's achievements have been respectable. The green-shirted team of the Six Counties have qualified for three World Cup finals and have included a number of Europe's finest players, the most famous being the mercurial George Best. However, too often the disparity between the team's star players and the rest has been marked, and even today Premiership regulars find themselves lining up alongside compatriots from the lower reaches of the Football League.

Northern and Southern Ireland have had separate national teams since the 1920s, but it was not until the 1950s that the North enjoyed its first period of success. The team of the 1950s featured the Aston Villa duo, Danny Blanchflower and Peter MacParland. Blanchflower, who joined Spurs in 1954, was the team's captain and its creative inspiration, while MacParland was the kind of single-minded goal scorer that every successful side needs.

*Below: Goalkeeper Pat Jennings won 119 caps between 1964 and 1986.*

In 1956 Northern Ireland had its name inscribed on the Home International trophy for the first time, and two years later the Irish, coached by Peter Doherty, qualified for the World Cup finals in Sweden. Doherty's team had beaten Italy during the qualifying rounds, and at the tournament proper beat Czechoslovakia and drew with West Germany to progress to the quarter-finals where France beat them.

After 1958, Northern Ireland failed to qualify for the next five finals, and it was only with the appointment of Billy Bingham as manager in 1980 that 28 years of waiting came to an end with a place at Spain '82. And, just as in 1958, the Irish once more exceeded all expectation, beating Spain with a famous goal from Gerry Armstrong and progressing to the second group stage. Bingham led his team back to the finals in 1986, but this time there were no heroics, although goalkeeper Pat

*Above: The uniquely talented George Best won 37 caps in a 14-year career with Northern Ireland.*

Jennings earned headlines by making his one hundred and nineteenth international appearance, a world record, during the finals.

The 1990s saw Northern Ireland enter the doldrums once more, a situation not made any easier by the achievements of Jack Charlton's successful team south of the border. Billy Bingham retired in 1993 and Sammy McIlroy, a hero from Bingham's team of the 1980s, took over as coach. He was soon replaced by Lawrie Sanchez whose team, despite beating England 1-0 in a World Cup qualifier, did not reach the finals. Also, David Healy's tournament record tally of 13 goals in the Euro 2008 qualifiers were not sufficient for Northern Ireland to reach the finals.

# Norway

Europe (UEFA)

**World Cup Appearances:** *3 (1938, 94, 98)*

**Shirts:** *Red*

In 1990 Norway's national team had failed to qualify for the 11 World Cup finals of the post-war years, and had never reached the finals of the European Championships. The appointment of the eccentric Norwegian coach Egil Olsen, however, changed their fortunes. Norway was transformed into an effective team that was hard to break down, and in 1994 they qualified for their first World Cup finals for 56 years.

Norway had joined FIFA in 1908, and qualified for their first World Cup finals in 1938. They played just one game at those finals, in France, losing to

*Below: Olé Gunnar Solskjaer, one of numerous Norwegians now playing in the English Premiership.*

eventual champions Italy. The same opponents had also eliminated the Norwegians from that year's Olympic games in Berlin, although the Scandinavians had already secured their place in history by beating hosts Germany, much to the chagrin of the watching Adolf Hitler. Olsen's team of the 1990s brought a similarly distressed reaction from opposition coaches. The new Norway played the game with what is politely described as "direct" tactics. Olsen instructed his team to keep men behind the ball, pressurize opponents and when the ball was won back to put it into "key areas" of the field. Not for purists, but it brought results.

Evidence of Norway's growing status was provided by their qualification for USA '94, which was achieved at the expense of England. Olsen was proclaimed a hero in Norway, although his team's performances at the finals

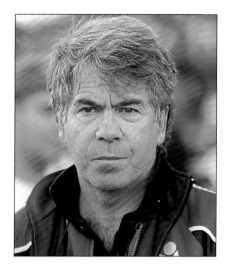

*Above: Coach Egil Olsen led Norway to the World Cup finals of 1994 and 1998.*

were, to say the least, disappointing. The Norwegians scored just one goal, and crashed out of the tournament with a display devoid of imagination and attacking intention against the Republic of Ireland. Many of Norway's players had, nevertheless, furthered their reputations during the finals; by the time they qualified for the World Cup four years later, 11 of Olsen's squad were playing for English clubs.

At France '98 Norway gave an improved display, defeating Brazil before falling to Italy in the second round. Shortly afterwards, Olsen moved on and was replaced by Nils Johan Semb. Any concerns that Norway would not survive the departure of their rubber-boot-wearing messiah proved unfounded. Under Semb, the Norwegians secured their first-ever place at the European Championships, topping their Euro 2000 qualifying group en route to the finals in Holland and Belgium, although they failed to reach the knockout stage of the tournament.

They also failed to qualify for the World Cup finals of 2002 and for the Euro 2004 finals and, under new coach Age Hareide, they failed to make it to the 2006 World Cup finals and Euro 2008.

# Portugal

**World Cup Appearances:** *4 (1966, 86, 2002, 06)*

**World Cup Record:** *third place 1 (1966)*

**European Championships:** *runners-up 1 (2004); semi-finals 2 (1996, 2000)*

**Shirts:** *Red with green trim*

Portugal made its international debut in 1921, but it was not until 1966 that they qualified for their first World Cup finals. The Portugal of 1966 was built around the successful Benfica team of the same era, and had the great Eusebio as its inspiration. Club-mates José Aguas and captain Mario Coluña joined Eusebio, who with nine goals was the tournament's top scorer, in a team that exceeded all expectation by finishing third. They defeated Brazil and Hungary before beating North Korea 5–3 in the quarter-finals. Hosts and eventual winners England beat Portugal in an epic semi-final that ended 2–1.

*Below: Eusebio, top scorer at the World Cup finals of 1966.*

*Above: The sublimely skilful Christiano Ronaldo, the latest in a long line of talented Portuguese playmakers.*

After the achievements of 1966, Portugal failed to qualify for the next four World Cup finals, and it was not until the 1980s that they re-emerged as a significant force. At the 1984 European Championships, Portugal fell to hosts France in a memorable semi-final that went to extra time. Two years later the Portuguese were back in the World Cup finals but, despite the addition of the prodigiously talented Paulo Futre, were eliminated at the group stage. The disappointing performances of the senior team, however, were tempered by the successes of Portugal's junior sides, which won the European Youth Championships in 1989 and the World Youth Championships two years later.

By the mid-1990s, members of Portugal's all-conquering youth team - "The Golden Generation" - were beginning to dominate the senior line-up, and at the 1996 European Championships players such as Rui Costa, Luis Figo and Joao Pinto made their mark. Portugal were, according to many pundits, the most entertaining team on show at Euro '96, although the lack of a convincing centre-forward ultimately proved costly in a run that ended with defeat by the Czech Republic in the semi-finals. Portugal failed to qualify for the 1998 World Cup finals, but lost just one of their games en route to Euro 2000, where they reached the semi-finals.

Portugal were amongst the favourites at the World Cup in 2002, but in one of the many big upsets of the tournament, they lost their opening game, a little unluckily, 3–2 to the USA. Portugal failed to recover their form, and a 1–0 defeat by South Korea meant elimination at the group stage. Hosting Euro 2004, they suffered a bitter disappointment in reaching the final but losing 1–0 to outsiders Greece. A Zinedine Zidane penalty in the semi-final of the 2006 World Cup finals prevented Portugal from reaching their first final, and they were knocked out by Germany in the quarter-final of Euro 2008.

# Republic of Ireland

**World Cup Appearances:** *3 (1990, 94, 2002)*
**Shirts:** *Green*

Soccer was, for many years, regarded with a certain amount of distrust in the Republic of Ireland. Gaelic football was the preferred sport of most schools and sports clubs, and soccer remained something of a minority interest, tainted by its strong links with England. Against this background the Irish national team was, unsurprisingly, slow to make its mark and the Republic remained in the shadows of the team from north of the border.

A change in Ireland's fortunes finally arrived, following the appointment of England World Cup winner Jack Charlton as team manager in 1986. Prior to Charlton's arrival, the pinnacle of Irish footballing achievements had come in 1965 when they lost in a World Cup play-off against Spain. However, the ruthlessly pragmatic Charlton quickly raised expectations, recruiting a host of new players to the Irish cause, many of whom had been

*Below: Robbie Keane, Ireland's talismanic captain.*

*Above: Midfield dynamo John Giles kept Ireland's engine room ticking during the 1960s and 1970s.*

born in England or Scotland but who qualified for the Republic by having Irish parents or grandparents. The most famous of these so-called "Anglos" were John Aldridge, Andy Townsend, Ray Houghton and Tony Cascarino. The effect was instantaneous and, in 1988, the Republic qualified for its first major tournament, the European Championships in Germany. The Irish were given no chance, but silenced the doubters by opening their campaign with a 1–0 victory over England, courtesy of a goal from Ray Houghton, and they were unlucky to be knocked out at the group stage after a 1–0 defeat against eventual champions Holland.

Charlton's team continued their incredible run by qualifying for the next two World Cup finals. At Italia '90 the Irish beat Romania in a second-round penalty shoot-out, before losing 1–0 to Italy in the quarter-finals. The adventure continued at USA '94 with a 1–0 victory against Italy at the Giants Stadium, and a run to the second round which ended in a 2–0 defeat by Holland.

However, the Republic failed to qualify for Euro '96 and Charlton stepped down as manager. The job passed to his former captain from Leeds United, Mick McCarthy.

The Republic qualified for the 2002 World Cup finals, but sensationally the captain, Roy Keane, was sent home before the first match after an argument with a coach and McCarthy. It did not hamper the team, who qualified from a tough group and lost in the second round only by penalties to Spain. Robbie Keane and Damien Duff proved to be excellent attackers in the sound all-round side in which veterans Steve Staunton and Niall Quinn ended international careers. Brian Kerr and Steve Staunton both replaced McCarthy as managers, but success and qualification to major tournaments proved elusive. Esteemed Italian coach Giovanni Trapattoni was appointed manager in 2008.

# Romania

**World Cup Appearances:** *7 (1930, 34, 38, 70, 90, 94, 98)*

**Shirts:** *Yellow*

For most of the 20th century Romania's record in international football was poor. However, a new look national team, based largely around the successful Steaua Bucharest line-up that won the European Cup in 1986, emerged in the 1980s and Romania quickly grew in status.

In 1990 Romania reached their fourth World Cup finals, ending a wait of 20 years since their appearance at the Mexico finals of 1970. Under former Steaua manager Emerich Jenei, the Romanians had topped their qualifying group, and they won their first match in the finals against the USSR. They then drew with Argentina to progress to a second-round clash

*Below: The incomparable Gheorghe Hagi, Romania's greatest player.*

with the Republic of Ireland where they were defeated in a penalty shoot-out. The tournament brought recognition to a number of players, many of whom would serve Romania with great skill throughout the coming decade. The team's undoubted star of Italia '90 was striker Marius Lacatus, although attacking midfielder Gheorghe Hagi and defender Gica Popescu were also notably impressive.

Romania were back in the World Cup finals in 1994, but this time Hagi took top billing on his own, and the player nicknamed the Maradona of the Carpathians inspired his team to a second-round meeting with Argentina. It was the match of the tournament, with the Romanian attacking trio of Hagi, Illie Dumitrescu and Florin Raducioiu playing with both skill and invention to mastermind a 3–2 win. Alas, it was not to be, and Romania were eliminated from the competition after losing a penalty shoot-out in

*Above: Illie Dumitrescu on the attack against Switzerland at USA '94.*

the quarter-finals against Sweden.

Romania did win a place at the European Championships in 1996, but a combination of controversial refereeing decisions and poor performances proved costly, and they were knocked out at the group stage. Euro '96 brought the curtain down on several international careers, and by the time qualification for the 1998 World Cup finals had been secured, Dumitrescu and Raducioiu had been replaced by the likes of Adrien Ilie and Viorel Moldovan. For the third World Cup finals running, the Romanians progressed through their group only to be beaten by a vital penalty in the knockout phase. This time their executioner was Croatia's Davor Suker who scored after 45 minutes. The run of tournament football continued for Romania with a place at Euro 2000, where the mercurial Hagi continued to add to his record tally of caps. Romania proved England's nemesis with a 3–2 victory, but crashed out to Italy in the quarter-finals.

However, Hagi and an era were now fading, and the team failed to qualify for the 2002 World Cup or Euro 2004, and, although they qualified for the Euro 2008 finals, they could not get past the opening group stage.

# Russia

**World Cup Appearances:** *9 (1958, 62, 70, 82, 86, 90, 94, 2002)*

**World Cup Record:** *fourth place 1 (1966)*

**European Championships:** *winners 1 (1960); runners-up 3 (1964, 72, 88); fourth place 2 (1968, 2008)*

**Olympic Games:** *winners 2 (1956, 88)*

**Shirts:** *White*

*Note: Records up to 1992 are for the Soviet Union*

Russian football has been affected as much by politicians in the Kremlin as by players, and it has struggled to fulfil its potential as a result. The Russian national team was born under the rule of the Tsar but, following the 1917 Revolution, Russians played alongside Ukrainians, Georgians and other nationalities in the red jersey of the Communist USSR. In the 1990s after a brief spell as the CIS, a Russian team re-emerged after the break up of the Soviet Union.

The team of the USSR did not compete in any of the pre-war World Cup competitions, but in 1956 success did come at the Australian Olympics. However, for much of its history the USSR struggled to match the achievements of club sides like Kiev Dynamo, Dynamo Tbilisi and Spartak Moscow. The disappointing form of the national team was often attributed to the fact that the players, from different states in the vast Republic, had marked differences in playing styles.

Nonetheless, the USSR qualified for the World Cup finals in 1958, in Sweden. They were eliminated at the group stage, but two years later, a team containing legendary keeper Lev Yashin and inspirational skipper Igor Netto won

*Above: Russia's post-Perestroika international football team made its World Cup debut at USA '94.*

the first European Nations Cup with a 2–1 victory against Yugoslavia

A second European final followed in 1964, although this time the competition's hosts, Spain, beat Yashin and company. The momentum continued and in 1966, the Soviets reached their World Cup zenith, progressing to the semi-finals in England. Thereafter, the USSR's success was restricted to the European Championships, in which they finished as runners-up in 1972 and 1988.

Disappointing early exits at the 1994 World Cup and 1996 European Championship gave the post-Perestroika Russians an inauspicious return to the international arena. However, with talented youngsters like Alexei Smertin and Alexander Panov, Russia improved. They qualified for the 2002 World Cup finals in Japan and for Euro 2004 in Portugal, but in each case, early defeats meant a quick return home.

In Euro 2008, they reached the semi-final having disposed of Holland through an Andrei Arshavin winner, but were beaten by eventual champions Spain 3–0.

*Left: Andrei Arshavin, talented playmaker of Russia's national team.*

# Scotland

**World Cup Appearances:** *8 (1954, 58, 74, 78, 82, 86, 90, 98)*

**Shirts:** *Blue*

In 1872 Scotland met England in the world's first international football match. Scotland's national team invariably often qualifies for major finals, but it has never progressed past the group phase at either the World Cup finals or the European Championships. However, the team usually manages to secure one heroic victory against the odds before its departure.

Scotland qualified for their first World Cup finals by finishing second in the 1950 Home International

*Below: The powerful figure of Joe Jordan in World Cup action.*

Championships. However, the Scots, not without some arrogance, had previously declared that they would only travel to the World Cup in Brazil if they won the Championships; but as they didn't, they stayed at home. Four years later they qualified again, and this time, in Switzerland, they lost both their games and conceded eight goals without reply.

During the 1960s, Scotland enjoyed mixed fortunes, twice failing to qualify for the World Cup finals. They also suffered a humiliating 9–3 defeat to England in 1961, before recovering their pride with a rousing 3–2 victory against the "Auld Enemy" in 1967. England, who were reigning World Champions at the time, had been unbeaten since their famous triumph against West Germany in 1966, but Alf Ramsey's team were unable to

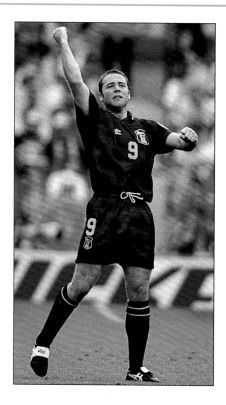

*Above: Ally McCoist, Scotland's regular centre-forward during the 1990s.*

overcome a Scotland line-up that included John Greig, Billy Bremner, Denis Law, Bobby Lennox and, the star of the show, Jim Baxter.

The unofficial World Champions of 1967 remain Scotland's most celebrated team, although the line-up that beat England 5–1 at Wembley in 1928 is no less deserving of praise. More recent highlights have included Archie Gemmill's solo goal in the 3–2 victory against Holland at the 1978 World Cup finals, the dramatic failure in the 1982 World Cup in Spain and the 2–1 victory over Sweden at Italia '90, which set up a memorable, though disappointing, finale against Brazil.

Bertie Vogts's reign as manager, from 2002 to 2004, saw Scotland take a tumble in the world rankings but the arrival of Walter Smith and then Alex McLeish in 2007 dramatically improved results, with Scotland beating France twice in the qualifiers for Euro 2008, although they failed to reach the final group stage.

# Spain

**World Cup Appearances:** *11 (1938, 50, 66, 78, 82, 86, 90, 94, 98, 2002, 06)*

**World Cup Record:** *fourth place 1 (1950)*

**European Championships:** *winners 2 (1964, 2008); runners-up 1 (1984)*

**Olympic Games:** *winners 1 (1992); runners-up 1 (2000)*

**Shirts:** *Red*

Despite having the world's strongest league and some of its finest players, Spain has nearly always disappointed in the final stages of the leading tournaments. Perhaps this is because Spaniards identify more with the regions in which they were born than with the collection of regions that calls itself Spain.

Spain made its World Cup debut in 1938, beating Brazil before losing to the hosts and eventual winners Italy, in a match that required extra time and a replay. The Spaniards' next World Cup appearance came in 1950, and they again reached the second round. Somewhat surprisingly, given Real Madrid's successes of the 1950s and 1960s, Spain missed the next three tournaments and

*Below: Spain celebrate their one major tournament success, the 1964 European Championship.*

*Above: Perez Munoz scores for Spain in the 1992 Olympic Final against Poland.*

were eliminated in 1966 at the first hurdle. It is often said that the many foreigners who play in Spain's *Primera Liga* undermine the progress of the national team, but in the 1960s this argument had little foundation, since a number of the league's imported stars declared for the Spanish red jersey, among them Alfredo Di Stefano, Ferenc Puskas and José Santamaria.

The players that claimed victory at the Bernabeu in the European Championships of 1964, however, were all Spanish-born. The USSR provided the opposition in the final but lost 2–1 to a team managed by José Villalonga, and inspired by midfielder Luis Suarez. Twenty years later Spain were back in the final of the European Championships, but this time they lost to France 2–0.

At USA '94 it took a late goal from Italy's Roberto Baggio to end Spanish hopes in the quarter-finals, while at Euro '96 England required a penalty shoot-out to get past Javier Clemente's team. Four years later, Spain lost to France in the quarter-finals of Euro 2000 in Bruges.

Bad luck again caused their exit from the World Cup in 2002, where they were among the favourites. Mistakes in their quarter-final against co-hosts South Korea caused two Spanish goals, including a "golden goal", to be ruled out, and Spain lost on a penalty shoot-out. For once the Spanish public was united with manager Jose Camacho in its indignation at the match officials.

In 2008 Spain's long wait for a second major trophy came to an end when a first-half goal from Fernando Torres brought them victory over Germany in Euro '08, and they rose to the top of the world rankings.

# Sweden

**World Cup Appearances:** *11 (1934, 38, 50, 58, 70, 74, 78, 90, 94, 2002, 06)*

**World Cup Record:** *runners-up 1 (1958); third place 2 (1950, 94); fourth place 1 (1938)*

**European Championships:** *semi-finals 1 (1992)*

**Olympic Games:** *winners 1 (1948)*

**Shirts:** *Yellow*

With a population of just 8.5 million the Swedes are not obvious candidates for success on the world stage. However, the great over-achievers have twice finished third in World Cup finals, and in 1958, they were the runners-up to the champions, Brazil.

Sweden's World Cup adventure began in 1934 with a 2–1 defeat by Germany. The Swedes were back in the finals four years later, receiving a bye to the quarter-finals, where they crashed eight goals past Cuba without reply. In the semi-final against Hungary, Sweden got off to the perfect start with a quick goal from Nyberg, but it sparked the Hungarians into life and they won 5–1.

After World War Two the team began the 1950 tournament with a 3–2 victory over reigning champions Italy. The Swedes eventually finished third, and eight years later they hosted the finals. Sweden mounted a significant challenge with a team built around stars players, such as the AC Milan trio of Gunnar Gren, Nils Liedholm and Gunnar Nordahl. Hungary, the Soviet Union and West Germany were all beaten en route to the competition's final. Even with the backing of the Stockholm crowd, however, the Scandinavians were powerless to resist a Brazil line-up that included Pelé, Vava, Didi and Garrincha. The match ended 5–2 to Brazil.

*Above: Sweden face Yugoslavia in the Olympic Final of 1948 in London. The Swedes won the match 3–1.*

Sweden's next period of significant achievement came during the 1990s, and started with a run to the semi-finals of the European Championships, which they hosted in 1992. Two years later, the team managed by Tommy Svensson exceeded all expectation by making it through to the semi-finals of the World Cup in the United States. Again they met Brazil, this time losing out by just one goal. There was consolation, however, with an emphatic 4–0 victory over Bulgaria in the third place play-off.

Sweden went out at the group stage in Euro 2000, but progressed to the second round in the World Cup of 2002, where they were beaten on a "golden goal" by Senegal. They progressed to the second round of the 2006 World Cup finals but were eliminated by hosts Germany, and could not get beyond the group stage in the finals of Euro 2008.

*Left: Tomas Brolin scored three times, and was Sweden's star of USA '94.*

# Wales

**World Cup Appearances:** *1 (1958)*
**Shirts:** *Red*

The red shirt of Wales has been graced by several of Britain's finest players (most notably John Charles and Ryan Giggs) but the Welsh national team has enjoyed little success since making its debut in 1876. The Welsh, in general, have a preference for the oval ball of rugby, and that certainly helps explain their football team's lowly status. A lack of support at club level, with the obvious exceptions of Cardiff City, Wrexham and Swansea, who all play in England's Football League, has affected the progress of the national side.

The Welsh national team enjoyed its most sustained period of success during the inter-war years, winning seven Home International Championships, including consecutive

*Below: Ryan Giggs was just 17 years old when he won his first Welsh cap.*

titles in 1932 and 1933. However, it was not until 1958 that Wales qualified for their first and only appearance at the World Cup finals. The Welsh team of the 1950s had been built around the considerable presence of John Charles, the country's greatest footballer and a player who had enjoyed successful spells with both Leeds United and Juventus. However, Charles, who could operate at either centre-half or centre-forward, was not the only star in the Wales team. Other key figures included the goalkeeper Jack Kelsey and Charles' brother Mel in defence, and the talented Ivor Allchurch and Cliff Jones in attack. Wales drew all three of their group matches at the 1958 World Cup finals in Sweden, and achieved a notable victory against Hungary in a "lucky losers" play-off to reach the last eight. The dream came to an end with a goal from a 17 year old called Pelé, in Wales' quarter-final tie against Brazil.

For the remainder of the 20th

*Above: The legendary John Charles played at both centre-half and centre-forward for Wales.*

century, Wales failed to qualify for the finals of the World Cup and the European Championships, narrowly missing out on several occasions. The 1980s was an era of particular disappointment because, with a team that included the formidable strike force of Mark Hughes and Ian Rush, expectations were unfairly raised. Success, however, never arrived and the wait for a second major tournament appearance continues, although they nearly qualified for Euro '04 under manager Mark Hughes but were beaten by Russia in a play-off. In recent years, the task has become even harder because, following the emergence of many new and ambitious footballing nations from Eastern Europe, qualification has become ever more competitive.

# Yugoslavia

**World Cup Appearances:** *10 (1930, 50, 54, 58, 62, 74, 82, 90, 98, 2006 as Serbia and Montenegro)*
**World Cup Record:** *fourth place 1 (1962)*
**European Championships:** *runners-up 2 (1960, 68); fourth place 1 (1976)*
**Olympic Games:** *winners 1 (1960); runners-up 3 (1948, 52, 56)*
**Shirts:** *Blue with white trim*

Yugoslavia was a name in world football until 2003, when the last side to use the name became known as Serbia and Montenegro and in 2006 simply as Serbia.

Many pundits believe that Yugoslavia would have won the World Cup or European Championships during the 1990s had it not been for the bloody civil war in the Balkans, which split the former Yugoslavia into several new countries. In 1992 the Yugoslavs qualified for the European Championships in Sweden with a team that reads like a Who's Who of Balkan football:

*Below: Predrag Mijatovic bursts past Norway's Erik Mykland at Euro 2000.*

Savicevic, Stojkovic, Jogovic, Mijatovic plus several emerging stars, who were lost to the new Croatia. But they were prevented from competing at Euro '92 due to United Nations sanctions against Yugoslavia, and their replacements, Denmark, went on to win the competition. A new Yugoslavia, whose territories encompassed little more than Serbia and Montenegro, made its return to international football at the 1998 World Cup finals.

The star-studded line-up of the 1990s, however, was not the first successful team from the former Yugoslavia. In 1930 a Yugoslav team travelled to the inaugural World Cup finals in Uruguay, where they brushed aside Brazil and Bolivia before losing to Argentina in the semi-finals. Yugoslavia missed the next two World Cup finals, but reached the quarter-finals in both 1954 and 1958 before enjoying their best run at the 1962 tournament in Chile. After progressing through their group they faced West Germany, who had beaten them in the quarter-finals of the two previous World Cups. It was third time lucky for the Yugoslavs, and a goal from Detar Radakovic secured a

*Above: Savo Milosevic was joint top scorer at Euro 2000 with five goals.*

1–0 victory. Heartache followed in the semi-final though, with Czechoslovakia scoring twice in the final ten minutes to win the game 3–1.

In the European Championships, the former Yugoslavia twice made it to the final, but on both occasions they were beaten. The first of these defeats came in extra time against the USSR at the inaugural Championships in 1960. Eight years later it was Italy's turn to celebrate victory against the Slavs, although this time the match needed a replay despite the Italians enjoying a home advantage. On both occasions Yugoslavia were unlucky to lose.

The national team of the post-civil war Yugoslavia clearly has much to live up to. A good start was made by qualifying for France '98 and Euro 2000. During the qualifying matches of Euro 2004, the team changed its name to Serbia and Montenegro, and just failed to gain a play-off place.

# Argentina

South America (CONMEBOL)

**World Cup Appearances:** *14 (1930, 34, 58, 62, 66, 74, 78, 82, 86, 90, 94, 98, 2002, 06)*

**World Cup Record:** *winners 2 (1978, 86); runners-up 2 (1930, 90)*

**Copa America Winners:** *11 (1921, 25, 27, 29, 37, 47, 55, 57, 59, 91, 93)*

**Olympic Games:** *runners-up 2 (1928, 96); winners 2 (2004, 08)*

**Shirts:** *Blue and white stripes*

If Brazil are the extravagant artists of South American football, then Argentina are the continent's great pragmatists. Twice world champions and 11-time winners of the *Copa America*, Argentina are one of the most successful teams in post-war international football. At their best, they combine South American flair with rigorous defending and a rare competitive spirit. At their worst, however, they can be cynical, at times with a brutal style of play. Fortunately, in recent years, Argentina's football has been more good than ugly.

In 1901 Argentina contested South America's first international football match, crossing the River Plate

*Below: Mario Kempes, star of Argentina's 1978 World Cup team.*

to defeat Uruguay 3–2 in Montevideo. Clashes with Uruguay dominated Argentina's fixture list during the early years of the 20th century, and the two teams also met in the first ever World Cup finals, held in Uruguay in 1930. Argentina reached the final, which was played before a crowd of 90,000 in Montevideo, after topping their group and beating the USA 6–1 in the semi-final. However, despite the services of the competition's most uncompromising player, Luisito Monti, and tournament top-scorer Guillermo Stabile, Argentina were beaten 4–2.

Forty-eight years after their first World Cup Final, Argentina progressed to a second, although this time they enjoyed the benefit of home advantage for the match against Holland at the Monumental Stadium in Buenos Aires. Manager Cesar Menotti had relied, with one exception, upon players based in Argentina throughout the 1978 tournament. The exception was Valéncia striker Mario Kempes who, having struck four times in earlier rounds, proved the hero of the final. Kempes scored twice in a dramatic match,

*Above: Diego Maradona, Argentina's inspirational skipper, in action at the World Cup finals in 1986.*

and Argentina eventually won 3–1 after extra time.

For their defence of the World crown in 1982, Argentina were buoyed by the addition of Diego Maradona to their squad. However, the talented 21 year old was subjected to crude man-marking against both Italy and Brazil, and Argentina crashed out of the competition. Four years later, Maradona, who was by now a match for any close marking, captained his country to victory in the World Cup Final against West Germany.

Argentina and West Germany again contested the final in 1990, but this time the Germans won 1–0. For the South Americans, the 1990 final was most memorable for the dismissals of Monzon and Dezotti, who became the first players ever to see a red card in a World Cup Final. In 2006 they were eliminated at the World Cup quarter-finals after a penalty shoot-out in a bad-tempered game against hosts Germany.

# Brazil

**World Cup Appearances:** *18 (1930, 34, 38, 50, 54, 58, 62, 66, 70, 74, 78, 82, 86, 90, 94, 98, 2002, 06)*

**World Cup Record:** *winners 5 (1958, 62, 70, 94, 2002); runners-up 2 (1950, 98); third place 2 (1938, 78); fourth place 1 (1974)*

**Copa America Winners:** *8 (1919, 22, 49, 89, 97, 99, 2004, 07)*

**Olympic Games:** *runners-up 2 (1984, 88)*

**Shirts:** *Yellow with green trim*

Brazil are quite simply the most successful and entertaining team in the world. The famous yellow jersey of Brazil is widely regarded as a symbol of footballing purity; in a country where football is everything, winning with style is essential.

Brazil's high reputation was established in the 1950s, when they reached two World Cup Finals. In 1950 the Brazilians crashed 2–1 to Uruguay on home soil. Eight years later Brazil were back in the Final with a team boosted by Didi, Garrincha and the 17-year-old Pelé.

*Below: Brazil dominated international football throughout the 1950s and 1960s. Vava, seen here, was one of the era's greatest players.*

Brazil's secret weapon was their revolutionary 4–2–4 system. A 5–2 semi-final victory against France, with goals from Vava and Didi, and a Pelé hat trick, ensured passage to the Final where hosts Sweden were beaten by the same score.

In 1962, Brazil successfully defended their world title, with a line-up that included seven members of the team that had beaten France four years earlier. Among the missing was Pelé, whose tournament was curtailed by an injury sustained in the group game against Czechoslovakia. Pelé again found himself on the treatment table after some brutal man-marking against Bulgaria and Portugal in the 1966 World Cup, but this time Brazil struggled to replace their ailing hero and crashed out of the competition at the first hurdle. Those who predicted the demise of Brazil were emphatically proved wrong at the 1970 World Cup tournament, in Mexico.

The Brazil line-up of 1970 is widely regarded as the finest attacking team the game has ever seen. From Carlos Alberto in defence to Rivelino and Pelé in attack, the football flowed in breathtaking fashion. After defeating Uruguay in the semi-final, Brazil made light work of overcoming Italy 4–1 in the final. The 1970s and 1980s saw a series of gifted players grace the yellow jersey, but

*Above: Left-winger Rivelino was a key member of the great Brazil team that won the 1970 World Cup.*

defensive frailties and a lack of cohesion prevented any further addition to their tally of World Cups. The waiting finally came to an end in 1994 when Mario Zagallo's much-maligned team beat Italy on penalties in the final of USA '94. Four years later, Brazil equalled the West German record by reaching a sixth World Cup Final but, despite the presence of star players Rivaldo and Ronaldo, who played after suffering a fit hours before, the reigning South American champions stumbled to a surprise 3–0 defeat.

Five of the players in that match redeemed themselves in 2002, when Brazil won the cup for the fifth time, beating Germany 2–0 in the Final. Cafu, the captain, became the first player to appear in three Finals, and Ronaldo scored both goals to win the Golden Boot with a total of eight. Without equalling the great side of 1970, Brazil were undoubtedly back on top of the world. They couldn't defend their title again, however, and in 2006 they lost 1–0 to France in the quarter-finals.

# Chile

**World Cup Appearances:** *7 (1930, 50, 62, 66, 74, 82, 98)*

**World Cup Record:** *third place 1 (1962)*

**Shirts:** *Red*

Chile's status within world football enjoyed something of a renaissance during the late 1990s, and they entered the 21st century as South America's fourth team. Chile, whose population of 14 million seems insignificant alongside rivals Brazil (154 million), Mexico (93 million) and Argentina (35 million), progressed to the semi-finals of the 1999 *Copa America*, and they were regarded as a significant threat to the continental dominance of Argentina and Brazil.

*Below: Marcelo Salas scores Chile's equalizer against Italy at the 1998 World Cup finals in France.*

Chile's recent progress has been in stark contrast to their early days in international football. The national team made its debut against Argentina in 1910, losing 3–1, to begin a run of defeats that extended for 13 games and nine years. Chile had to wait even longer for a first victory, success arriving in fine style with the 7–1 trouncing of Bolivia in 1926.

After their slow start, a slight upturn in fortune saw Chile become a regular feature of the World Cup after World War Two. However, it was not until 1962 that they progressed beyond the first round. Chile, then hosts, finished the tournament in third place after losing to eventual champions Brazil in the semi-finals. The shameful scenes during their violent group match with Italy, however, overshadowed the achievement. The so-called "Battle of Santiago" ended with two Italians being

*Above: Striker Ivan Zamorano, a key member of Nelson Acosta's Chilean line-up of the 1990s.*

sent off and, although Chile won the game 2–0, they emerged with little credit from the most brutal match in World Cup history.

During the 1970s and 1980s, Chile progressed to two *Copa America* Finals, but were defeated both times, and it was not until the late 1990s that they regained their status as serious contenders. The team of the 1990s, managed by Nelson Acosta, was built around the strike partnership of Ivan Zamorano and Marcelo Salas and, after a series of impressive results, rose to the heady heights of ninth place in FIFA's rankings prior to the 1998 World Cup finals in France. For the second time in their history, Chile progressed to the second round of the competition but, as in 1962, the Brazilian teamed proved their nemesis, inflicting a 4–1 defeat to eliminate one of the tournament's most hotly tipped outsiders.

# Colombia

**World Cup Appearances:** *4 (1962, 90, 94, 98)*

**Copa America Winners:** *1 (2001)*

**Shirts:** *Yellow with blue trim*

Colombia are one of South American football's great enigmas and, despite producing a number of talented teams, performances on the pitch have too often failed to live up to expectations. Off the pitch, there have been problems, with corruption scandals, financial worries and murders filling the sports pages.

International football came late to Colombia, with the country making its debut in the 3–1 defeat against Mexico in 1938. Eight more internationals were played that year but, thereafter, fixtures were separated by long periods of inactivity during the 1940s and 1950s. Consequently, results were poor and it came as something of a surprise that Colombia qualified for its first World Cup finals appearance in Chile, in 1962. Even though they failed to win a match, they did return home

*Below: Veteran midfielder Carlos Valderrama in action at France '98.*

*Above: Andres Escobar, whose tragic death rocked the football world.*

with some credit after an impressive 4–4 draw against the USSR.

Colombia had to wait until Italia '90, to make a second appearance at the World Cup finals, although in the 28 years in-between they did finish as runners-up to Peru in the 1975 *Copa America*. Colombia claimed their first World Cup finals win against the United Arab Emirates. The Colombians

also drew with eventual champions West Germany, but they were still eliminated at the group stage. Four years later, they were back in the finals in the United States, and this time they were tipped to do well. Colombia's squad, which still included wild-haired midfielder Carlos Valderrama, had been boosted by the emergence of star players Freddie Rincon and Tino Asprilla. However, the tournament ended in disappointment and tragedy. First came humiliating defeats against Romania and the USA. Then, defender Andres Escobar, who scored an own goal in the 2–1 defeat against the USA, was shot dead in Medellin shortly after returning home from the tournament.

The murder of Escobar shook Colombian football to its core, and although the team qualified for a third successive World Cup finals in 1998, its best chance of glory had passed. After defeats against England and Romania, the Colombians left France '98 on the first available flight.

Colombia enjoyed its first major success when hosting and winning the *Copa America* in 2001, beating Mexico 1–0 in the final.

# Peru

**World Cup Appearances:** *4 (1930, 70, 78, 82)*

**Copa America Winners:** *2 (1939, 75)*

**Shirts:** *White with a diagonal red stripe*

Peru may not be among the most successful of South America's footballing nations, but what they lack in silverware and consistency they make up for with entertaining and, at times, eccentric play. The team also have what many believe is international football's finest kit – white shirts with a diagonal red stripe.

The Peruvian Football Federation was founded in 1922, and five years later the national team made its debut with a 4–0 loss against Uruguay in the South American Championships. Defeat became an all too familiar experience for the early national sides, and they conceded 26 goals in their first seven games as they struggled against more experienced opponents. Despite this poor record, Peru were granted a place at the inaugural World Cup finals in Uruguay, though they lost both their games. However, by 1939

Peru were up to speed with the demands of international football and, on home soil, they won the South American Championships.

Peru's most successful team was assembled under the guidance of the former Brazil player Didi during the 1970s, and in 1970 the Peruvians served notice of their new strength by qualifying for the World Cup finals in Mexico. Here, Didi successfully led his team through the group phase, but not even he could mastermind victory against his old country in the quarter-finals. Five years later, and with midfielder Teofilo Cubillas as their inspiration, Peru claimed victory in the *Copa America*, by beating Colombia in Venezuela. Cubillas also starred at the 1978 World Cup finals, although his performances were overshadowed by the eccentrics of goalkeeper Ramon Quiroga.

Peru reached their fourth World Cup finals in 1982, but by then the stars of the previous decade had all but disappeared and, after a 5–1 defeat against Poland, they finished bottom of their group. A steady decline followed this disappointment, although under

*Above: Teofilo Cubillas, star of Peru's great team of the 1970s.*

coach Juan Carlos Oblitas there have been signs of a revival in recent years: he led his team, captained by midfielder Nolberto Solano, to the quarter-finals of the *Copa America* in 1999, a feat Peru repeated in 2001, 2004 and 2007.

*Below: Peru line-up for their national anthem at the Mexico World Cup, 1970.*

# Uruguay

**World Cup Appearances:** *10 (1930, 50, 54, 62, 66, 70, 74, 86, 90, 2002)*
**World Cup Record:** *winners 2 (1930, 50); fourth place 1 (1970)*
**Copa America Winners:** *10 (1917, 20, 23, 24, 26, 42, 67, 83, 87, 95)*
**Olympic Games:** *winners 2 (1924, 28)*
**Shirts:** *Light blue and white*

Uruguay are too often the forgotten World Cup winners, frequently overlooked and underestimated when the great teams of the past are reviewed and recalled. For the record, Uruguay were among the world's finest teams prior to World War Two, first winning the Jules Rimet trophy in 1930. They lifted the World Cup again in 1950 and, while they have ceased to be serious contenders for the game's top prize since the 1970s, their past achievements are worthy of greater recognition. Only West Germany, Italy and Brazil can better the Uruguayans' two World Cup successes.

*Below: The Uruguay team pose for the camera before their 1950 World Cup match against Brazil.*

As reigning Olympic champions, Uruguay were chosen to host the first World Cup finals in 1930, and after progressing with relative ease through their group matches against Romania and Peru, they trounced Yugoslavia 6–1 to reach the Final. Bitter rivals Argentina provided the opposition for a match in the new Centenario stadium in Montevideo, a clash of passion and controversy. Disagreements about match balls delayed the kick-off, but the waiting was worthwhile and, after trailing 2–1 at half-time, Uruguay came back with goals from Pedro Cea, Iriarte and Hector Castro to win 4–2.

Uruguay, who also claimed five pre-World War Two *Copa America* titles, did not defend their World crown in 1934. In 1950, they took what was arguably their greatest-ever team to the finals in Brazil. The side contained several big names, including Omar Miguez and Victor Andrade, but the great Juan Schiaffino was the real star. The finals of 1950 were organized as a league system, but in the deciding match, the hosts, Brazil, took on the Uruguayans, knowing that a draw would be enough to secure the World

*Above: Enzo Francescoli, Uruguay's prolific goalscorer of the 1990s.*

Cup. The Brazilians began the match in style and after 48 minutes took the lead, but a goal from the inspirational Schiaffino shook the favourites and, 13 minutes later, Uruguay struck a goal to secure their famous victory.

Uruguay reached the World Cup semi-finals again in 1954 and 1970, but on neither occasion were they able to recapture the success of the past. By the 1970, they found themselves struggling to keep pace with their rivals in both the World Cup and the *Copa America*.

An increasing trend for the country's best players, such as Daniel Fonseca, Gustavo Poyet and Enzo Francescoli, to move abroad has not helped national coaches foster any sense of team spirit, and undoubtedly led to a certain amount of underachievement during the 1980s and 1990s.

Nevertheless, victory in the 1995 *Copa America*, runners–up four years later and qualification, after a play-off with Australia, for the 2002 World Cup finals suggest a revival. They were unlucky in the World Cup: a refereeing error helped Senegal to a 3–0 lead, and Uruguay's second-half recovery to 3–3 was not enough to avoid elimination.

# Mexico

North and Central America (CONCACAF)

**World Cup Appearances:** *13 (1930, 50, 54, 58, 62, 66, 70, 78, 86, 94, 98, 2002, 06)*

**Shirts:** *Green*

Mexico are the outstanding team of CONCACAF (North and Central America and the Caribbean), where their regional dominance is so great that World Cup qualification has become almost a formality.

The Mexicans qualified for two of the three finals held during the 1990s, a decade during which they also won three out of four CONCACAF Gold Cups. In 1993 Mexico were invited to compete in the *Copa America*. It was a challenge that they rose to in fine style, reaching the final against Argentina who needed a late goal from Gabriel Batistuta to win 2–1. Mexico have continued to participate in the *Copa America*, achieving second place in 2001 and finishing third in 1997, 1999 and 2007.

Mexico have enjoyed their greatest World Cup successes, unsurprisingly, on the two occasions that they hosted the competition. In 1970 they progressed unbeaten through the group phase, but floundered against eventual runners-up Italy in the quarter-finals. Sixteen years later football's greatest competition returned to Mexico and the hosts again gave a good account of themselves.

The Mexicans, who conceded just one goal in their five matches at the World Cup finals of 1986, were one of the tournaments more entertaining sides, and in Hugo Sanchez they possessed its most flamboyant talent. Sanchez is still regarded as Mexico's finest-ever player, and on home soil he inspired his team to a quarter-final showdown with West Germany. The match proved tense and, in the overwhelming heat of Monterrey, the Germans triumphed in a penalty shoot-out.

In 1990, Mexico's World Cup campaign ended before it had started, with the team barred from competing

at the finals in Italy owing to a breach of rules at a previous youth competition. There have been other problems too, most notably at the *Copa America* in 1999, where the achievements of Manuel Lapuente's team were undermined by allegations of drug taking. Under coach Javier Aguirre, they also performed well in the 2002 World Cup finals in Japan and South Korea, winning their group unbeaten before losing to the USA in

*Above: The extravagantly-gifted Hugo Sanchez enjoyed a long and successful career in Spain, but his appearances for Mexico were somewhat restricted by commitments at club level.*

the second round knock-out stage. They again reached the second round in 2006, but a stunning extra-time volley from Argentina's Maxi Rodriguez saw them depart from the tournament, defeated 2-1.

# USA

**World Cup Appearances:** *8 (1930, 34, 50, 90, 94, 98, 2002, 06)*
**Shirts:** *White*

Association football has struggled to establish itself in the United States, where the gridiron game remains infinitely more popular. It would, however, be wrong to ignore the colourful history of the USA "soccer" team, which has achieved several impressive victories since 1990, enhanced, no doubt, by the establishment of the professional Major League Soccer in 1996.

The United States made its first significant impression upon the world game in 1930, when it was among the 13 nations to send a team to the inaugural World Cup finals in Uruguay. The USA team included six former British professionals and progressed to the last four of the competition, with victories over Belgium and Paraguay. But the fairytale came to an end in the

*Below: Kasey Keller, who competed with Brad Friedel for the goalkeeping post from the 1990s on.*

semi-finals where they were crushed 6–1 by eventual runners-up Argentina. Four years later they were back in the finals, but this time the crushing defeat came in the first round, with Italy dishing out a 7–1 beating.

Until 2002, the USA's greatest World Cup achievement came at the finals in 1950. A group match against a highly fancied England team that was unbeaten since World War Two seemed to offer little hope for a team of American part-timers. However, on a bumpy pitch in Belo Horizonte, Brazil, a lacklustre England conceded the game's only goal to Larry Gaetjens. *USA 1 England 0* remains one of the biggest shock results in footballing history.

In the 1970s United States football looked to be on the verge of a new era, with the expensively set-up North American Soccer League seeming to offer the sport a long-awaited lifeline. But the treatment proved ineffective and the league collapsed. Twenty years later the new era finally arrived when the USA qualified for Italia '90, their first World Cup finals for 40 years. Results were a disappointment in Italy,

*Above: There is rapidly growing support for "soccer" in the United States.*

with Bob Gansler's team losing all three of their games. The only consolation was that, since America had already been selected to host the next World Cup finals, there would be no need to qualify. In 1991 a new coach, Yugoslav Bora Milutinovic, was chosen to lead the USA into the 1994 finals. Milutinovic expertly blended youth, in the shape of Alexi Lalas and Cobi Jones, with experienced players such as Thomas Dooley and John Harkes, and the hosts gave an impressive account of themselves. The USA qualified through their group after a draw with Switzerland and a 2–1 win against Colombia, but went down 1–0 to eventual champions Brazil in the second round.

After losing all their games in the World Cup finals of 1998, the USA surprised the world in 2002. Under coach Bruce Arena, they qualified from the group stage, beating Portugal, then beat Mexico 2–0 before going out in the quarter-finals 1–0 to Germany. Although they exited the 2006 World Cup in the first round without winning a game, football is still very much on the upgrade in the USA.

# Japan

**World Cup Appearances:** *3 (1994, 2002, 06)*

**Asian Cup Winners:** *3 (1992, 2000, 04)*

**Shirts:** *Blue*

Although not yet a significant force in world football, Japan has made great strides in recent years and now has the fan base, not to mention the financial clout, to become Asia's dominant footballing nation. The co-hosts of the 2002 World Cup, Japan and South Korea, both exceeded expectations and went a long way towards joining the football "establishment".

The formation of the professional J-League in 1993 was a key factor in FIFA's decision to grant the Japanese and Koreans the first World Cup of the new millennium. The J-League proved an immediate success, attracting huge crowds and a host of foreign stars, among them England's Gary Lineker, Brazil's Dunga and Italy's Salvatore Schillaci. The formation of the J-League also coincided with an upturn in the fortunes of Japan's national team, although after winning the 1992 Asian Cup, they failed to qualify for the 1994 World Cup finals.

*Below: Philippe Troussier, Japan's coach for the 2002 World Cup finals.*

*Above: Midfielder Hidetoshi Nakata, Japan's most successful footballing export.*

Japan put the disappointment of 1994 behind them, and four years later, under the guidance of popular coach Takeshi Okada, they qualified for their first World Cup finals. However, France '98 proved a disappointment for the team, and defeats in their three games illustrated how much work still needed to be done. One positive aspect of the finals was the emergence of 21-year-old midfielder, Hidetoshi Nakata, who moved to Italian *Serie A*-side Perugia in 1998. Nakata was an instant hit in Italy and, after only one full season, the then-reigning Asian Footballer of the Year was transferred to AS Roma, then Parma, in multimillion dollar deals.

At the World Cup 2002 they surpassed themselves, topping their group with a notable win against Russia, before elimination 1–0 in the second round to Turkey. Players such as Nakata, Ryuzo, Morioka, Junichi Inamoto and Shinji Ono (in the 2002 UEFA Cup-winning Feyenoord side), made themselves known to a worldwide TV audience.

Japan qualified again for the 2006 World Cup, but first-round defeats by Brazil and Australia, and a goalless draw against Croatia, led to their early exit.

# Australia

**World Cup Appearances:** *2 (1974, 2006)*

**Shirts:** *Green and yellow*

Despite the lack of on-field success, soccer in Australia has been making steady progress since the 1960s. The decade began in controversy, when the Australian Soccer Football Association was found guilty of poaching Austrian players, and the ASFA was banned by FIFA for three years. Fortunately, the Australian Soccer Federation emerged to overthrow the ASFA in 1961. Two years later Australia was welcomed back by FIFA.

After missing out on qualification for the 1970 World Cup finals in Mexico, the "Socceroos" earned a place at the finals in Germany in 1974. The Australians won just one point from their three games, thanks to a goalless draw with Chile, but their achievements had been sufficient to stir interest back home. In 1977, a 14-team national league was formed, and with 350,000 registered junior players the future looked bright for Australian soccer.

*Below: Harry Kewell, the Socceroos' exciting playmaker.*

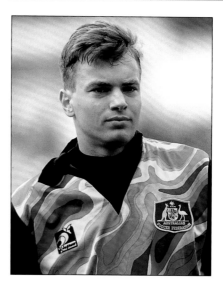

*Above: Goalkeeper Mark Bosnich is one of Australia's most experienced players.*

The mini-boom of the late 1970s, however, failed to develop into anything more significant, and it was not until the mid-1990s that the Socceroos again knocked rugby and cricket off the back pages of the national newspapers. In 1993, Australia narrowly missed qualifying for the World Cup finals in the United States when they lost 2–1 on aggregate in a play-off against Argentina. Four years later, a Socceroos team led by former England coach Terry Venables suffered similar heartache, surrendering a 2–0 lead in the second leg of the France '98 play-off against Iran.

The disappointment continued in 2002. Australia, featuring star players from the English Premiership, such as Harry Kewell, Marc Viduka and Mark Bosnich, won the home leg of their World Cup qualifying play-off with Uruguay, only to lose the away game in Uruguay 3–0.

Under new coach Guus Huddink, they surprised many by successfully negotiating their way into the second round of the 2006 World Cup from a group including Japan, Brazil and Croatia, only to lose in the knock-out stage to Italy's Francesco Totti's stoppage-time penalty and go out of the tournament 1-0.

# Cameroon

**World Cup Appearances:** *5 (1982, 90, 94, 98, 2002)*
**African Nations Cup:** *winners 4 (1984, 88, 2000, 2002); runners-up 2 (1986, 2008); third place 1 (1972); fourth place 1 (1992)*
**Olympic Games:** *winners 1 (2000)*
**Shirts:** *Green*

In the 1980s the "Indomitable Lions" of Cameroon became the leading lights of African football, reaching three consecutive African Nations Cup Finals, and qualifying for the 1982 World Cup finals in Spain. The Cameroon Football Federation only joined FIFA in 1962, but by the end of the 1990s the Lions had established themselves as a genuine force within the international game.

Centre-forward Roger Milla was the pivotal figure in Cameroon's ascendancy of the 1980s and 1990s.

*Below: Cameroon's indomitable striker Roger Milla at Italia '90.*

Milla, who was voted African Footballer of the Century, was a youthful 30 year old when he playedin his and Cameroon's first World Cup finals in Spain in 1982. The Lions were expected to be the whipping boys of their group, where they faced Italy, Peru and Poland. However, under Yugoslav coach Branko Zutic, the Africans played with great discipline and drew all three of their matches, conceding their only goal in the 1–1 draw with eventual champions, Italy.

Cameroon's reputation as an emerging footballing power was confirmed by victory in the 1984 African Nations Cup Final, and only a defeat on penalties against Egypt prevented them from retaining their African crown in 1986. A trilogy of consecutive finals was completed with victory over Nigeria in 1988, and the Lions travelled to the World Cup in Italy, in 1990, as the continental champions. Cameroon kicked-off the tournament against World

*Above: Rigobert Song beats Sweden's Tomas Brolin at USA '94.*

Cup holders Argentina and exceeded expectations by winning 1–0, despite having two players sent off. A 2–0 win against Romania in the next game had 38-year-old double-goal scorer Roger Milla dancing around the corner flag. Colombia were Cameroon's next opponents and Milla was again the hero, coming off the bench to score both goals in a 2–1 victory. England brought the fairytale to an end in the semi-finals, although Bobby Robson's team needed a last-minute penalty to avoid defeat, and a penalty in extra time to seal the victory.

Cameroon qualified for the World Cup finals of 1994, 1998 and 2002, but could not emulate their success of Italia '90. However they won the Olympic Games title in 2002, beating Spain in the final, and with players such as Rigobert Song, Etame-Mayer Lauren and Samuel Eto'o, they won the African Nations Cup in 2000 and 2002, but lost in the quarter-finals of the same tournament in 2004 and were runners-up in 2008.

# Morocco

**World Cup Appearances:** *5 (1970, 86, 90, 94, 98)*

**African Nations Cup:** *winners 1 (1976); runners-up 1 (2004); third place 1 (1980); fourth place 2 (1986, 88)*

**Shirts:** *Green*

Morocco were not admitted to FIFA until 1956, but they have made rapid progress since, and at France '98 they won many new fans with their open, attacking football. The North Africans beat Scotland, and in Mustapha Hadji they had one of the tournament's outstanding players. Hadji was voted African Player of the year in 1998 and has become the most famous Moroccan-born footballer since Just Fontaine.

Morocco qualified for their first World Cup finals in 1970, and kicked-off with a match against eventual runners-up West Germany. The newcomers were billed as whipping boys, but gave the Germans a fright before losing the match 2–1. Morocco had to wait 16 years to launch their next assault on the World Cup finals. In the interim they claimed their only victory in the African Nations Cup, topping the final table of the tournament held in Ethiopia in 1976.

*Below: Henri Michel joined Morocco in 1995 and had an instant effect.*

The 1986 World Cup finals saw a Morocco team, coached by José Faria, progress to a second-round meeting with West Germany, after finishing top of a qualifying pool that included Poland, England and Portugal. However, just as they had in 1970, the Germans proved too wily, winning a dour match with a last-minute free kick from Lothar Matthäus. At USA '94 Morocco lost all three of their games, but this was followed in 1995 by the appointment of Henri Michel as national coach. Under Michel, the team developed a fluent style of football.

*Above: Mustapha Hadji was voted African Player of the Year in 1998.*

Morocco were unbeaten in the qualifiers for France '98 and, after their impressive showing at the finals, were favourites to take the African Nations Cup of 2000, but did not progress beyond the group stage.

Morocco missed a place in the 2002 World Cup finals, squeezed out on goal difference by Senegal. With Mustapha Hadji's younger brother, Youssef, they were just beaten 2–1 in the 2004 African Nations Cup Final by Tunisia.

# Nigeria

**World Cup Appearances:** *3 (1994, 98, 2002)*
**African Nations Cup:** *winners 2 (1980, 94); runners-up 4 (1984, 88, 90, 2000); third place 5 (1976, 78, 2002, 04, 06)*
**Olympic Games:** *winners 1 (1996)*
**Shirts:** *Green and white*

In the 1990s, Nigeria were Africa's leading team, and the most significant threat to the European and South American stranglehold on the World Cup. For many years, African football had been patronized with endless comments about untapped potential, but such encouragement quickly dried up when Nigeria showed just what they could do in the early stages of the French World Cup finals in 1998.

Up until the 1990s, Nigeria's only major footballing success had been victory against Algeria in the final of the 1980 African Nations Cup.

*Below: Nigeria celebrate with their Olympic gold medals in 1996.*

The "Super Eagles" were also runners-up in the Nations Cups in 1984 and 1988, but it was their achievements at junior level that provided the real clues as to what would follow. In 1985 the junior Eagles became the first African team to win the World Under-17 Championships, beating Germany 2–0 in the final. In 1987 and 1989 Nigeria were runners-up in the World Under-17 and Under-19 Championships, and in 1993 they won the Under-17 title for a second time. Among the players who secured success in 1993 were several who became successes in the senior team, notably Nwankwo Kanu, Celestine Babayaro and Wilson Oruma.

In 1994 Nigeria's rapidly ascendant path swept them to a second African Nations Cup victory, and to their first World Cup finals. The Super Eagles made a dramatic start to USA '94, beating Bulgaria 3–0 and finishing top of their group, which included Argentina. In the second round, the Nigerians were eliminated in extra time by Italy, having led the three-time

*Above: Nwankwo Kanu was Nigeria's Olympic captain in 1996.*

winners with just a minute of normal time remaining. It proved no more than a minor setback and, although dictator Sani Abacha prevented Nigeria from defending their African Nations Cup in 1996, their momentum was maintained that year with victory against Argentina in the final of the Olympic Games in Atlanta.

Nigeria's progress has not gone unnoticed by scouts from Europe's big clubs, and by the time the Nigerians travelled to their second World Cup finals in France in 1998, Boro Milutinovic's 22-man squad contained just one African-based player. Two years later, and now under Dutch coach Jo Bonfrere, the Super Eagles contested the African Nations Cup Final on home soil with a team consisting entirely of players based in Europe. Nigeria were defeated by Cameroon on penalties in the 2000 Final and finished in third place in 2002, 2004 and 2006. They qualified for the 2002 World Cup finals, and played well but finished bottom of a tough group.

# South Africa

**World Cup Appearances:** *2 (1998, 2002)*

**African Nations Cup:** *winners 1 (1996); runners-up 1 (1998); third place 1 (2000)*

**Shirts:** *Yellow and green*

Football has a troubled history in South Africa but, despite its problems, it remains the country's most popular sport. For much of the 20th century the game was, like everything else in South Africa, blighted by apartheid, and for 28 years the South African FA was excluded from FIFA. A multi-racial national team, known as Bafana Bafana ("the boys"), finally emerged from the post-apartheid South Africa in 1992 and quickly made an impact.

The FA of South Africa was founded in 1893, but it was only during the 1940s that the country fell in love with the game. Professionalism was adopted in the 1950s, and a national league was formed shortly afterwards. The South African FA was also represented at the 1957 meeting that led to the first African Nations Cup, but the South Africans did not participate in the finals after the *Confédération Africain de Football* made it clear that it would only accept multi-racial teams. Seven years later, the SAFA was suspended by FIFA.

South Africa's return to international football in the early 1990s began inauspiciously, with the fledgling Bafana Bafana failing to qualify for either the 1994 World Cup finals or African Nations Cup finals. Two years later came better fortune when, following Kenya's decision to withdraw as hosts from the Nations Cup, South Africa filled the breach and made use of the opportunity to put on a memorable show. A 3–0 victory over Ghana booked the debutants a place in the final, which was played in front of Nelson Mandela in Johannesburg, and the trophy was clinched with two goals from Mark Williams in a 2–0 win against Tunisia.

In 1998, South Africa, coached by Frenchman Philippe Troussier, progressed to a second Nations Cup Final, but this time they lost to Egypt in Burkina Faso. Four months later, Troussier's team, which included European-based players Mark Fish, Lucas Radebe and Benni McCarthy, competed in their first World Cup finals at France '98. Confidence was high, but expectations were unrealistic and South Africa fell at the first hurdle. After reaching the Nations Cup semi-finals in 2000, they qualified for the World Cup finals of 2002, under Carlos Queiroz. They beat Slovenia, but Paraguay prevented them reaching the second round by scoring one goal more. South Africa will be hosting the 2010 World Cup Finals.

*Below: Lucas Radebe, South Africa captain and defensive stalwart.*

# THE CLUBS

Club football keeps the spirit of the game alive. While individual players and managers come and go, the clubs themselves live long in the hearts of their fans. It is here that the magic of football exists at grass-roots level. The drama and excitement of domestic League and Cup matches, Derby games and continental club competitions owes much to club rivalry and partisan support. While some clubs have proved themselves to be consistent champions over the years, others have achieved only sporadic glory; some have suffered tragedy, and some scandal and disgrace. This chapter looks at 42 of the biggest names in club football, charting the highs and lows and the personalities who have formed their history.

# Ajax

**Year formed:** *1900*
**Country:** *Holland*
**Stadium:** *Amsterdam Arena*
*(51,000)*
**Colours:** *White with red panel*
**Domestic Honours:**
*Championships: 29; Domestic*
*Cups: 17*
**International Honours:** *European*
*Champions Cup: 4 (1971, 72, 73,*
*95); European Cup Winners Cup:*
*1 (1987); UEFA Cup: 1 (1992);*
*European Super Cup: 3 (1972, 73,*
*95); World Club Cup: 2 (1972, 95)*

The name of Ajax will forever be associated with the production of talented young footballers, and in particular the development of the incomparable Johan Cruyff. It would, however, be wrong to regard the Amsterdam club as merely a nursery side where legends begin. Ajax has

*Below: Johnny Rep, a key player for Ajax and Holland in the 1970s.*

also seen much of its home-grown talent grow to maturity, and has assembled a collection of trophies that includes four European Cups.

Financially, Ajax cannot compete with the big teams from England, Spain and Italy, and to succeed it has had to rely on local talent and on young, unproven foreigners. No team has produced more top-class footballers; Johan Cruyff, Frank Rijkaard, Marco Van Basten, Dennis Bergkamp and Patrick Kluivert all began professional careers there.

Ajax is equally famous for its philosophy of free-flowing football. The Ajax style of play, often referred to as "total football" because of the importance it places on positional flexibility, requires a high degree of technical excellence and has its origins in the work of coaching guru Rinus Michels. Ajax were a struggling team when Michels, a former player at the club, returned as coach in 1964. Having previously won ten Dutch championships, Ajax were desperate for a return to

*Above: The combative Johan Neeskens patrols Ajax's midfield.*

former glories and Michels did not disappoint them. He built a team that has had few equals, and which claimed six championships in seven seasons between 1966 and 1973. This legendary line-up, which comprised such footballing luminaries as Cruyff, Johan Neeskens, Arie Haan and Johnny Rep, reached its zenith in 1972, winning the second of three consecutive European Cups to go with a domestic double and the World Club Cup. The Ajax team of the 1970s provided the backbone of the Dutch national team, which progressed to two successive World Cup finals.

After the successes of the 1970s, Ajax faded from their position as Europe's elite club during the 1980s. Domestic triumphs did continue though, and when Louis Van Gaal pieced together an impressive Ajax side in the early 1990s, the team won the European Cup, claimed against AC Milan in 1995. Under Ronald Koeman the club won a League and Cup double in 2002 and another League win in 2004. Koeman quit in 2005 and the club is now managed by legendary ex-player Marco Van Basten.

# Anderlecht

**Year formed:** *1908*

**Country:** *Belgium*

**Stadium:** *Constant Vanden Stock (28,000)*

**Colours:** *White with purple trim*

**Domestic Honours:**
*Championships: 29; Domestic Cups: 9*

**International Honours:** *European Cup Winners Cup: 2 (1976, 78); UEFA Cup: 1 (1983); European Super Cup: 2 (1976, 78)*

Naming a famous Belgian is a tricky business, or so the joke goes. However, in the case of Belgian football the task is a little easier. With nearly half the league championships from 1947 to the end of the 20th century, RSC Anderlecht is the most successful club in Belgian football by some distance. Fve European trophies in the 1970s and 1980s have ensured that Anderlecht can

*Below: Rensenbrink holds aloft the Cup Winners Cup, 1976.*

rival Jean-Claude Van Damme, beer and chocolates when it comes to the Belgian fame game.

Anderlecht did not take up their place at the pinnacle of Belgian football until after World War Two, only reaching the top division in 1935. Under the guidance of their English coach Bill Gormlie, Anderlecht soon made up for lost time and in 1947, they claimed the first of four League titles in five seasons. Anderlecht's domination of the domestic game continued through the 1940s and 1950s, but it wasn't until the appointment of coach Pierre Sinibaldi in the 1960s that the club first set its sights on European success.

In 1970 Anderlecht reached the Fairs Cup Final, losing 6–1 on aggregate to Arsenal. It was the first of six European finals that the Brussels club would reach during the 1970s. The final of the Cup Winners Cup in 1976 saw Anderlecht face English opposition again, in the shape of West Ham United. This time, however, the Belgians, inspired by the mercurial Dutchman Robbie Rensenbrink and

*Above: Anderlecht captain Paul Van Himst (left) and Arsenal's Frank McLintock exchange pennants ahead of the 1970 Fair's Cup Final.*

prolific goalscorer Francois Van der Elst, cruised to a 4–2 victory. Anderlecht reached the final of the Cup Winners Cup again in 1977, but lost to Hamburg 2–0 in Amsterdam. A third successive final followed a year later, setting a competition record. A comfortable 4–0 victory was secured, with two goals each from Rensenbrink and Van Binst.

In the 1980s, Anderlecht's European success came in the UEFA Cup. The Belgians reached successive finals in 1983 and 1984, winning the first against Benfica but losing the second on penalties against Tottenham Hotspur. The glories of these European successes, however, were tainted in 1997 when UEFA found the club guilty of having bribed the referee in the semi-final of the 1984 competition. Anderlecht were banned from European competition for one year and have won only domestic honours since.

# Arsenal

**Year formed:** *1886*

**Country:** *England*

**Stadium:** *Emirates Stadium, Ashburton Grove (63,000)*

**Colours:** *Red with white sleeves*

**Domestic Honours:**
*Championships: 13; Domestic (FA) Cups: 10*

**International Honours:** *European Cup Winners Cup: 1 (1994); Fairs Cup: 1 (1970)*

Arsenal is without question London's pre-eminent club. The Arsenal football club takes its name from the military factory at Woolwich, in south-east London, where it began life as a works' team in 1886. But the club was not shy in its ambitions, and within seven years it had gained election to the Football League. A controversial move across

*Below: Patrick Vieira celebrates Arsenal's 2004 League Championship success, crowning a season unbeaten.*

London followed in 1913, giving rise to an intense, instant rivalry with new neighbours Tottenham Hotspur.

Under the expert guidance of manager Herbert Chapman, Arsenal became the dominant force in English football during the 1930s, winning five league titles and two FA Cups. Arsenal were also tactical pioneers, and it was Chapman's team that first employed the "WM" formation. Arsenal's impressive run of success during the 1930s was brought to an abrupt end by the outbreak of World War Two and, despite league title successes in 1947–48 and 1952–53, it was not until 1970–71 that the Gunners resumed the lead role in English football. That season saw Arsenal complete the League and FA Cup "double", with Charlie George scoring a dramatic extra-time winner against Liverpool at Wembley.

Three more finals followed between 1978 and 1980, but it was only after George Graham was appointed manager in 1986 that the silverware began to flow as it had in the 1930s. The undoubted highlight of the Graham era, which brought six major trophies, was the 1988–89 championship. It was Arsenal's first League title for 18 years, and it was won in true style, when Michael Thomas flicked the ball over Liverpool goalkeeper

*Above: Arsenal's FA Cup-winning side of 1930, with manager Herbert Chapman seated centre row, far left. Chapman's team dominated English football throughout the 1930s.*

Bruce Grobelaar to score in the ninety-second minute of the final game of the season.

Graham's tenure ended following a scandal concerning the receipt of "unsolicited gifts" from an agent. He had been unable to provide Highbury with a style of play that met with critical approval, and it was not until Frenchman Arsène Wenger was appointed, in 1996, that the Gunners finally shook off their "boring" tag. Wenger led the Gunners to the League and FA Cup "double" in 1997–98, and repeated the feat in 2001–02. In 2002–03, they finished second in the League but kept the FA Cup, and the following season, with players like Henry, Vieira, Pires, Cole and Bergkamp, they won the Premiership title unbeaten, and went on to set a League record of 49 games without defeat. The current squad, featuring hugely talented young players such as Cesc Fabregas, Theo Walcott and Gael Clichy, will almost certainly reassert Arsenal's dominance in English football.

# Atlético Madrid

**Year formed:** *1903*
**Country:** *Spain*
**Stadium:** *Vicente Calderón
(57,000)*
**Colours:** *Red and white stripes*
**Domestic Honours:**
*Championships: 9; Domestic
Cups: 9*
**International Honours:** *European
Cup Winners Cup: 1 (1962); World
Club Cup: 1 (1974)*

Atlético Madrid is widely regarded
as Spain's third-biggest football club.
However, the bronze medal podium is
not one that Atlético's late president,
Jesús Gil, was willing to settle for. Gil
had a reputation as an idiosyncratic and
ruthless character, and his personality
dominated the club between 1987 and
his death in 2004.

*Below: Cacho Heredia (left) takes on
Bayern in the 1974 European Cup Final.*

Atlético were a successful club long
before the arrival of Jesús Gil. Formed in
1903, Club Atlético de Madrid won its
first silverware in 1940, claiming the first
of two successive league championships.
But by the late 1950s Atlético had been
cast in the shade by their city rivals,
Real, who beat them in the semi-final of
the European Cup in 1958, although it
took a replay to separate the two teams.
Four years later, Atlético fared rather
better in the Cup Winners Cup, winning
a replayed final 4–0 against Fiorentina.

In the 1970s, Atlético put their faith in
Argentinean employees, signing Ruben
Ayala, Panadero Diaz and Ramon
"Cacho" Heredia, as well as former
Argentina coach, Juan Carlos Lorenzo.
The results were impressive. The league
championship was won in 1973, and a
year later Atlético progressed to the
European Cup Final against a Franz
Beckenbauer-inspired Bayern Munich
side. However, the final proved a

*Above: The late Jesús Gil, millionaire
builder, politician and Atlético president.*

heartbreaking affair for Atlético, who
conceded an equalizer in the last minute
of extra time, and they lost the replay 4–0.

When Gil took charge, Atlético had
not won the league title for ten years
and was desperate for success. The new
president spent heavily, bringing in
a number of expensive signings, most
notably the Portuguese forward
Paulo Futre, but the championship
still proved elusive.

In 1996 Atlético, under the stewardship
of Yugoslavian coach Raddy Antic,
finally delivered the grail of the league
championship, adding the *Copa del Rey*
(Spanish Cup) for good measure. The
"double", however, brought no change
in the Gil strategy, and soon Antic
departed. The spending continued too,
with Italian Christian Vieri and Brazilian
Juninho arriving for large fees in the
late 1990s. Despite the signings and
managerial changes, or perhaps because
of them, Atlético were relegated in
1999–2000, and the predictable exodus
of star players followed. Atlético,
however, regained top division status
as Second Division Champions in 2002.
Although star striker Fernando Torres
was sold to Liverpool in 2007, he was
replaced by Diego Forlan, and winger
Jose Antonio Reyes also joined the club,
who finished 4th in the 2007-08
La Liga season. There appears to be
a revival in Atletico's fortunes.

# Barcelona

**Year formed:** *1899*

**Country:** *Spain*

**Stadium:** *Camp Nou (98,000)*

**Colours:** *Red and blue stripes*

**Domestic Honours:**

*Championships: 18; Domestic Cups: 24*

**International Honours:** *European Champions Cup: 2 (1992, 2006); European Cup Winners Cup: 4 (1979, 82, 89, 97); Fairs Cup: 3 (1958, 60, 66); European Super Cup: 2 (1992, 98)*

FC Barcelona is a Catalan institution, and not just a football club. It has provided the Catalans with a symbol of their culture about which they feel rightly proud, and which has survived wars, prejudice and the rule of fascist dictator General Franco. It is small wonder that the followers of this great club are so passionate and numerous (Barcelona currently has more than 100,000 members).

The club began life in 1899, and its foundation is attributed to Swiss

*Below: Dutchman Johan Cruyff, Barça's greatest foreign signing.*

*Above: Forward Lionel Messi signed for Barcelona at the age of 16 in 2003.*

businessman Joan Gamper, who placed an advert calling for players in the local press. Barça quickly grew in size and status and, in 1929, a professional FC Barcelona team claimed the first Spanish league championship. Difficult years followed, and the rise of Franco's fascists in the 1930s increased political tensions between Catalans and the government in Madrid. Matches between Barcelona and Real Madrid soon took on great significance, establishing a bitter rivalry that has lost none of its passion to this day.

Title success returned to Barcelona in 1945 when the club claimed the championship for the second time. There were further triumphs in the 1950s, with coach Helenio Herrera building a team of foreign stars including Zoltan Czibor and Sandor Kocsis. In 1957 Barça moved to the immense and impressive Camp Nou stadium, and a year later furnished their new trophy room with the club's first European trophy, the Fairs Cup.

The achievements of the 1950s, however, were soon forgotten as rivals Real Madrid set about dominating both

domestic and European football in the early 1960s. Barcelona attempted to keep pace by making a series of high profile purchases, most notably that of Johan Cruyff, who was bought from Ajax for a world record £922,000 in 1974. Alas, between 1961 and 1990 Barcelona claimed just two league titles and, despite signing still more superstars, including Diego Maradona, the European Cup success that the club craved continued to elude them.

The 1990s saw Barça at last return to the pinnacle of Spanish football and, with Cruyff as coach, Camp Nou celebrated four successive title-winning teams from 1991–94. The highlight of this era came when Barça claimed its first European Cup with a 1–0 victory over Sampdoria at Wembley in 1992. Under coach Frank Rijkaard they won their second European Cup in 2006, beating Arsenal 2-1 in the final in Paris. Rijkaard was replaced by former player and local hero Josep Guardiola in 2008.

# Bayern Munich

**Year formed:** *1900*
**Country:** *Germany*
**Stadium:** *Allianz Arena (70,000)*
**Colours:** *Red with white trim*
**Domestic Honours:**
*Championships: 21; Domestic Cups: 14*
**International Honours:** *European Champions Cup: 4 (1974, 75, 76, 2001); European Cup Winners Cup: 1 (1967); UEFA Cup: 1 (1996); World Club Cup: 1 (1976)*

In the mid-1970s Bayern Munich, led by the imperious Franz Beckenbauer, were the kings of European football. However, a decade earlier the club had languished in Germany's Second Division, having won just two major trophies in 65 years. Bayern's ascent was sensational, rising from obscurity to claim 14 league

*Below: The Munich maestros, Gerd Müller and Franz Beckenbauer (right).*

*Above: Lothar Matthäus, an inspiration for Bayern Munich in the late 1990s.*

championships between 1972 and 2000.

It was coach Tschik Cajovski who began Bayern's march to the summit of European football. Cajovski built his team around Beckenbauer, the brilliant goalkeeper Sepp Maier and the devastating striker Gerd Müller, and in 1965 Bayern won promotion to the *Bundesliga*. A year later, the Bavarians finished third in the top division and won the German Cup to secure a place in the Cup Winners Cup, which they won in 1967 with a 1–0 victory over Rangers. The 1968–69 season saw the ascent continue with the winning of the first League and Cup "double".

By the start of the 1970s, Bayern's previous mediocrity had been forgotten, and the Bavarian club was rightly regarded as a significant force in German football. Three consecutive championships followed from 1972 to 1974, confirming the club's improved status, but Bayern's European results were of greater significance. In 1974 Bayern became only the second German club to reach the final of the European Cup and, after beating Atlético Madrid 4–0 in a replay, the first German club to lift it. Bayern's players formed the backbone of Germany's World Cup-winning team that year. Six Bayern players took the field for the 1974 final against Holland, and two of them (Paul Breitner and Müller) scored in a 2–1 victory.

Bayern were European Champions again in 1975 and 1976, but by the early 1980s their great team had all but disappeared. New players arrived, including top-class performers such as Andreas Brehme, Lothar Matthäus and Karl-Heinz Rumenigge, but the heights of the 1970s could not be repeated. However, after European Cup Final disappointments against Aston Villa in 1982 and Porto in 1987, Giovanni Trapatoni led the club to UEFA Cup success in 1996, and Bayern ended a 25-year wait for the European Cup when, under new coach, Ottmar Hitzfeld, they beat Valéncia on penalties in the 2001 Final. Jürgen Klinsmann took over as coach in 2008.

# Benfica

**Year formed:** *1904*
**Country:** *Portugal*
**Stadium:** *Estádio da Luz (65,000)*
**Colours:** *Red and white*
**Domestic Honours:**
*Championships: 31; Domestic Cups: 27*
**International Honours:** *European Champions Cup: 2 (1961, 62)*

European football has a special place reserved for SL Benfica because it was Benfica, in 1961, that broke Real Madrid's five-year stranglehold on the European Cup. The club's stock has fallen in recent years, but with 31 League Championships and 27 domestic Cup wins, Benfica still remains the biggest name in Portuguese football.

Formed in 1904, Benfica won nine league titles prior to their golden era in the 1960s, and those early successes helped finance the move to the impressive *Estádio da Luz* (Stadium of Light) in 1954. The entrance to this

*Below: Eusebio joined a Benfica team that had already won the European Cup in 1961.*

*Above: The Benfica team line-up for the first leg of the 1962 European Cup against Tottenham Hotspur.*

enormous arena is adorned with a statue of the club's greatest player, Eusebio da Silva Ferreira. An all-action striker with a devastatingly powerful shot, Eusebio was one of a number of key players that Benfica gathered from Portuguese colonies such as Mozambique and Angola.

In 1961 Benfica played in their first European Cup Final, taking on a Barcelona team that had beaten Real Madrid in the semi-finals. After 20 minutes Benfica were one down, but two goals in a minute – the first through captain José Aguas, the second an own goal – established a lead that was added to in the second half by playmaker Mario Coluña. A close finish was ensured when Czibor scored for Barcelona with 15 minutes to go, but at the final whistle it was Aguas who collected European club football's greatest prize. A year later, Benfica's Hungarian coach Bela Guttmann added Eusebio to his already impressive squad. The new boy proved a key factor in Benfica's successful defence of their European crown, scoring twice in the final against Real Madrid to help turn a

3–2 deficit into a famous 5–3 victory.

Benfica were again in the final of the European Cup in 1963, but their 2–1 defeat by Milan at Wembley was the first of three final defeats in the 1960s. Domestic successes continued in the 1970s, with the club claiming six championships during that decade. However, in Europe, Portugal's leading club was losing ground. Eventually, Benfica decided to scrap their principle of only selecting players born in Portugal or its colonies, and in 1983 the club was back in contention for European honours, this time losing out to Anderlecht 2–1 in the final of the UEFA Cup. The heartache of final defeats continued in 1988 and 1990 with disappointments in the European Cup, first against PSV Eindhoven and later, AC Milan. In recent years Benfica have surrendered their domestic dominance to Porto, who won the league in consecutive seasons from 2005 to 2008.

# Boca Juniors

**Year formed:** *1905*
**Country:** *Argentina*
**Stadium:** *Estadio La Bombonera (58,000)*
**Colours:** *Blue with yellow band*
**Domestic Honours:**
*Championships: 24*
**International Honours:** *Copa Libertadores: 6 (1977, 78, 2000, 01, 03, 07); World Club Cup: 3 (1977, 2000, 03)*

Boca Juniors are one of Argentina's top club sides, and they brought Diego Maradona to prominence in the early 1980s.

Club Atlético Boca Juniors was formed in 1905, following the combined efforts of an Irishman and a group of Italians in Buenos Aires. Boca quickly developed into one of Argentina's leading teams, claiming its first championship in 1919. Eight more titles were added prior to World War Two, although there were two versions in the 1920s and 1930s.

After the war, Boca fell behind, and it was not until the early 1960s that they reaffirmed their status among Argentina's elite clubs. In 1963 Boca progressed to the final of the *Copa Libertadores* (South American Cup)

*Below: Boca, seen here on the attack, take on their great rival, River Plate.*

for the first time in their history, but they lost to Pelé's Santos.

It took Boca 14 years to make it back to the final of the *Copa Libertadores* when, under pragmatic coach Juan Carlos Lorenzo, they overcame Cruzeiro of Brazil 5–4 on penalties. It was the first of three successive South

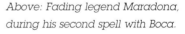

*Above: Fading legend Maradona, during his second spell with Boca.*

American Cup finals for Boca, who won the next against Deportivo Cali of Colombia before losing to Olimpia of Paraguay in 1979. Boca's greatest success also came in the 1970s, when they claimed the World Club Cup of 1977 with an emphatic away performance against Borussia Mönchengladbach, winning 3–0 for a 5–3 aggregate victory. There would, however, be a long wait for a repeat of the glories of the 1970s, despite the £1 million signing of Maradona in 1980. In 2000, the waiting came to an end with victory in the *Copa Libertadores*, to which they added the World Club Cup, beating Real Madrid 2–1, and the *Copa Libertadores* again in 2001. Another win in 2003 led to a third World Club Cup, when they beat AC Milan on penalties after a 1–1 draw.

# Borussia Dortmund

**Year formed:** *1909*

**Country:** *Germany*

**Stadium:** *Westfalenstadion (81,000)*

**Colours:** *Yellow and black*

**Domestic Honours:** *Championships: 6; Domestic Cups: 2*

**International Honours:** *European Champions Cup: 1 (1997); European Cup Winners Cup: 1 (1966); World Club Cup: 1 (1997)*

Prior to May 28, 1997, not even the most enthusiastic Borussia Dortmund supporter could have said that the club was among Europe's elite. However, on that memorable night in Munich the German champions forgot their lowly status to stun the spectators with a 3–1 victory over Italian aristocrats Juventus in the final of the Champions League. In truth, the real surprise was that so few had noticed the incredible progress that Dortmund had made during the 1990s. It was clear that the team in yellow and black could no longer be underestimated.

*Below: Andy Möller savours his moment with the European Cup trophy.*

*Above: Karlheinz Riedle heads goalward against Juventus in the 1997 Champions League Final.*

Borussia Dortmund was formed in 1909, but it was not until 1956 that the club began its collection of silverware, claiming the first of two successive league titles. A third title arrived in 1963 and was followed, in 1965, by Cup success that earned the club a place in the Cup Winners Cup. Dortmund progressed to their first European final, and a meeting with Liverpool, after an impressive 5–2 aggregate victory over holders West Ham United in the semi-finals. The Cup Winners Cup Final at Hampden Park proved a tense affair, but an extra-time goal from Reinhard Libuda ensured that Dortmund became the first German team ever to claim a major European trophy.

The success of 1966, however, proved something of an isolated incident, and it was not until the early 1990s that Dortmund returned to such heights. The signing of German international sweeper Matthias Sammer from Inter Milan in 1993, was undoubtedly a turning point. Sammer joined a team that progressed to the final of the UEFA Cup in his first season, and although Dortmund lost 3–1 to Juventus, the club was clearly moving in the right direction. New signings

continued to arrive, among them German internationals Karlheinz Riedle, Jürgen Kohler and Andy Möller. Riedle and Möller had played against Dortmund in the 1993 UEFA Cup Final.

Dortmund's heavy investment in experienced players brought its first reward in 1995, with success in the *Bundesliga*. A run to the quarter-finals of the Champions League followed in 1996 accompanied by another domestic championship, but in 1997 the club enjoyed its greatest moment. Champions League success was achieved in dramatic fashion when, in the space of five first-half minutes, Riedle scored two headed goals to stun Juventus and pave the way for a 3–1 win. It was the first European Cup for a German club since 1983.

Under Matthias Sammer and with more expensive signings, Dortmund won their sixth domestic championship in 2002. Sammer left in 2004 with the club suffering serious financial problems, consolidated by a disappointing finish of 13th in the Bundesliga in 2008.

# Borussia Mönchengladbach

**Year formed:** *1909*
**Country:** *Germany*
**Stadium:** *Bökelberg (34,500)*
**Colours:** *White with green trim*
**Domestic Honours:** *Championships: 5; Domestic Cups: 3*
**International Honours:** *UEFA Cup: 2 (1975, 79)*

The tale of Borussia Mönchengladbach provides an object lesson in the transience of success. In the 1970s, Borussia was a giant of the European game, winning five *Bundesliga* titles in eight seasons and reaching four European finals, but by the end of the century the Bökelberg stadium was hosting Second Division matches.

Prior to 1970, Borussia's only major success had come in the German Cup of 1960, but under the guidance of coach Hennes Weisweiler the club quickly grew in stature during the 1970s. Weisweiler, a

*Below: Jupp Heynckes, hat-trick scorer in the 1975 UEFA Cup Final.*

tactically astute coach who later served FC Barcelona, quickly assembled a team packed with talented players, among them Jupp Heynckes, Bertie Vogts and Danish striker Alan Simonsen.

Consecutive *Bundesliga* titles were claimed in 1970 and 1971, and two years later Borussia made their first significant impression in Europe when they reached the final of the UEFA Cup. However, in a two-leg encounter, Bill Shankly's Liverpool proved too strong for the German side, who lost 3–2 on aggregate. The following season saw Borussia's European adventure continue with a run to the semi-finals of the Cup Winners Cup. In 1975 the club returned to the more familiar waters of the UEFA Cup. This time they eclipsed all past achievements, thrashing Dutch side Twente Enschede 5–1 to lift their first European trophy.

By the late 1970s, Mönchengladbach were unquestionably Germany's pre-eminent team, but their efforts to claim Europe's greatest club prize were thwarted by Bob Paisley's Liverpool. In 1977, the two teams met in the final of the European Cup in Rome. It proved an epic and ultimately disappointing encounter, with Liverpool winning 3–1. A year later the two teams met again, in the semi-finals of the same competition; once more Paisley's team emerged victorious.

Successive UEFA Cup Finals followed in 1979 and 1980, with Borussia winning the first against Red Star Belgrade and losing the second, on away goals, to Eintracht Frankfurt. The match against Eintracht was notable for a goal scored by a young Borussia midfielder called Lothar Matthäus. However, the future captain of Germany could not prevent his club sliding into relative obscurity during the 1980s. The 1990s brought only further decline and, in 1999, relegation to the Second Division, where they stayed till 2002. They were relegated in 2007 but achieved promotion the following season.

# Celtic

**Year formed:** *1887*
**Country:** *Scotland*
**Stadium:** *Celtic Park (60,000)*
**Colours:** *Green and white hoops*
**Domestic Honours:**
*Championships: 42; Domestic
Cups: 34*
**International Honours:** *European
Champions Cup: 1 (1967)*

Celtic Football Club owes its creation
to Brother Walfrid, a Roman Catholic
priest who was working in Glasgow
towards the end of the 19th century.
Brother Walfrid had witnessed the
poverty and discrimination suffered by
the area's Irish immigrants and, having
observed the success of Hibernian
(Edinburgh's Irish-Catholic club),
he urged members of his parish to
start their own football team.

In 1893, five years after the club was
formed, the name Celtic Football Club
was inscribed on the Scottish League
Championship trophy. By the end of
the 20th century, Celtic had won the
League 36 times and had been

*Below: Henrik Larsson, hero of
Celtic's winning teams until 2004.*

runners-up 25 times. There were also
numerous cup successes for the club
nicknamed "The Bhoys".

Celtic's first game was against
Rangers, and the rivalry between
these two great clubs was quickly
established. By the start of World
War One, a footballing duopoly had
emerged that exists to this day: in short,

*Above: Danny McGrain (left), Celtic's
long-serving skipper.*

Celtic and Rangers win everything in
Scotland. Unfortunately, following the
1916 uprising in Ireland, an antagonism
developed between Protestants and
Catholics. Rangers has a Protestant
following, and matches against Celtic
now took on an ugly significance as
sectarian hatred became evident.

Celtic's golden era undoubtedly
arrived during Jock Stein's 13-year
managerial reign. Stein took charge in
1965, and produced a series of exciting,
attacking teams based around talented
players such as Jimmy Johnstone and
Billy McNeill. With Stein at the helm,
Celtic claimed an incredible nine
league titles in succession from
1965–74. The club's finest moment was
in 1967, when they became the first
British side to win the European Cup,
beating Inter Milan 2–1.

Under Martin O'Neill Celtic won
the Scottish championship in 2000–01,
2001–02 and 2003–04, when they
completed the "double". His successor,
Gordon Strachan, won the league three
times between 2006 and 2008.

# Chelsea

**Year formed:** *1905*
**Country:** *England*
**Stadium:** *Stamford Bridge (42,000)*
**Colours:** *Blue*
**Domestic Honours:**
*Championships: 3; Domestic (FA) Cups: 4*
**International Honours:** *European Cup Winners Cup: 2 (1971, 98); European Super Cup: 1 (1999)*

Up until the mid-1990s, glamour rather than silverware had for too long been the obsession with Chelsea. However, towards the end of the 20th century an unforeseen wave of ambition swept the club to the fore in both the domestic and European game.

Before 2005 Chelsea had won the English Championship only once, that success coming under the management of Ted Drake in 1954–55. The winning team, however, was quickly dismantled and the League Cup of 1965 was the only further addition to the Stamford Bridge trophy room during the 1950s and 1960s. In 1969–70, Chelsea at last

*Below: Chelsea celebrate their second League title 50 years after their first.*

produced a team that was as effective as it was skilful, and the Blues added an FA Cup to their 1954–55 championship. The following season saw Sexton's team claim a memorable victory over Real Madrid, in the final of the European Cup Winners Cup.

Chelsea's fortunes declined sharply following that victory and they were relegated to the Second Division. A series of high-profile managers tried to revive the club's fortunes with little success, and it was only following the arrival of Glenn Hoddle, in 1993, that Chelsea began to realize their potential. The combination of the ambitious young manager and committed, if controversial, chairman Ken Bates provided the catalyst for a more positive era in Chelsea's history.

Hoddle led the Blues to Wembley in 1994, where they were defeated by Manchester United in the FA Cup Final. The player-manager also brought a number of high-profile foreign players to Stamford Bridge, including Ruud Gullit, the man who succeeded Hoddle as Chelsea manager in 1996. The Dutchman continued the policy of buying foreign players, bringing in Italians Gianluca Vialli, Gianfranco Zola and Roberto di

*Above: Chelsea playmaker Frank Lampard in the heart of midfield.*

Matteo, and it was di Matteo who scored the winning goal in the 1997 FA Cup Final. A year later, Gullit was replaced by Vialli. The new boss won two trophies in what remained of 1997–98, with the team claiming the League Cup and the European Cup Winners Cup. Vialli, who led the Blues to FA Cup success in 2000, was then replaced by Claudio Ranieri.

In 2003, Russian Billionaire, Roman Abramovich bought Chelsea and ousted Bates. Chelsea immediately spent millions of pounds on new players. In 2003–04, they finished second in the Premiership and reached the semi-finals of the Champions League. Ranieri was replaced by José Mourinho of Porto. The charismatic Mourinho won the league twice in his first two seasons at the club. An apparent personality clash with Abramovitch, however, saw Mourinho leave in 2007. The following season, caretaker manager Avram Grant guided the team to their first European final, which they lost to Manchester United on penalties. Chelsea are currently managed by Guus Hiddink on a temporary basis.

# Feyenoord

**Year formed:** *1908*

**Country:** *Holland*

**Stadium:** *Feyenoord (51,000)*

**Colours:** *Red and white halves*

**Domestic Honours:**
*Championships: 14; Domestic Cups: 11*

**International Honours:** *European Champions Cup: 1 (1970); UEFA Cup: 2 (1974, 2002); World Club Cup: 1 (1970)*

Feyenoord's list of ex-players reads like a Who's Who of Dutch football, with Puck Van Heel, Coen Moulijn, Johan Cruyff, Ruud Gullit, Ronald Koeman and Wim Jansen all seeing service with the Rotterdam club. Feyenoord were also the first Dutch club to win the European Cup, claiming the continent's biggest prize a year before Ajax began their three-year reign as champions of Europe in 1971.

Feyenoord was formed in 1908, courtesy of money supplied by mining tycoon C. R. J. Kieboom. By 1924, the

*Above: Dutch legend Ruud Gullit made his name in the red and white shirt of Feyenoord.*

*Below: Wim Van Hanegem, star of Feyenoord's 1970 European Cup team.*

club had become sufficiently strong to win the Dutch championship. Sporadic success followed in the inter-war period, but it was during the 1960s that Feyenoord became a major force in Holland; four league titles and two Cups were won during that decade, then, in 1970, Ernst Happel's team brought the club its greatest success.

The 1970 European Cup Final saw Feyenoord face the 1967 champions, Celtic, in Milan. Dutch football, which had only had a professional league for 13 years, was still underestimated in Europe and Celtic began the match as firm favourites. The Scots, however, quickly realized that they were facing a team of skill and commitment. Swedish striker Ove Kindvall provided pace and energy in attack, which complemented the artistry of Wim Van Hanegem and the industry of Austrian Franz Hasil in midfield. Goals from Rinus Israel and Kindvall gave Feyenoord a deserved 2–1 victory.

Feyenoord's success in the European Cup was, however, soon eclipsed in Holland by the achievements of Ajax in the 1970s. A League and UEFA Cup "double" was won in 1974, but by the 1980s memories of the Celtic game in Milan in 1970 seemed all too distant. The signing of Johan Cruyff in 1983, and the emergence of a young Ruud Gullit, did provide a brief fillip to Feyenoord's fortunes, but the league title success of 1984 was the last for seven years. The Rotterdam club suffered financial problems during the 1980s, and also had to contend with its supporters' infamous taste for hooliganism. Fortunes improved after 1990, with six league championships up to 2000 and a 3–2 victory over Borussia Dortmund in the UEFA Cup Final of 2002.

# Flamengo

**Year formed:** *1895*

**Country:** *Brazil*

**Stadium:** *Gávea (8,000) and Maracana (95,000)*

**Colours:** *Broad red and black hoops*

**Domestic Honours:** *National Championships: 5*

**International Honours:** *Copa Libertadores: 1 (1981); World Club Cup: 1 (1981)*

Flamengo may now be among the most famous names in Brazilian football, but Clube de Regatas do Flamengo was formed as a sailing club in 1895. Flamengo's first association with the round ball came in 1911, courtesy of a number of "dissident" members of

*Below: Flamengo's Zico takes on Liverpool in the World Club Cup, 1981.*

Fluminense who joined the club and formed a football section. The following year, the newly founded team entered the Rio de Janeiro State Championship, claiming the title for the first time in 1914. Prior to World War Two, Flamengo claimed six more State Championships and vied with Fluminense, Botafogo and Vasco da Gama for dominance in Rio. The Flamengo team of the pre-war era was graced by a number of star players, most notably the national team's centre-forward, Leonidas da Silva.

Flamengo enjoyed continued success in the 1950s and 1960s, and by the time the National Championship was set up in 1971, the club had won 16 state titles. The new prize, however, eluded Flamengo throughout the 1970s, and it was not until 1980 that the team in the famous red and black

*Above: Romario left Spain to return to Brazil with Flamengo in 1995.*

hoops were crowned champions of Brazil. Success in 1980 had been largely due to the goals of Flamengo's centre-forward Zico. At 27 years old, in 1980, he was at the peak of his game. He finished the season as Brazil's top scorer with 21 of his team's 46 goals. He was top scorer again when Flamengo won the title in 1982.

Zico was also the key to Flamengo's greatest successes in international club football. In 1981 the Rio club claimed not only the *Copa Libertadores* but also the World Club Cup, and the goals and creativity of the team's star striker were behind both triumphs. In the *Libertadores*, Flamengo had beaten Cobreloa of Chile with four goals from Zico, while the World Club Cup had been claimed with a 3–0 victory over Liverpool.

Further National Championships were won in 1983, 1987 and 1992, but by the close of the 20th century, Flamengo were struggling against the country's leading clubs. There was, however, still much to excite Flamengo's fans, who were particularly animated by the signing of Romario for a second spell in 1999.

# Fluminense

**Year formed:** *1902*
**Country:** *Brazil*
**Stadium:** *Laranjeiras (8,000) and Maracana (95,000)*
**Colours:** *Maroon, green and white stripes*
**Domestic Honours:** *National Championships: 1*

In the early years of club football in Brazil, Fluminense were the biggest and best team in the land. Founded by Englishman Oscar Cox and a group of his compatriots in 1902, Fluminense were instrumental in the establishment of the Rio de Janeiro League and duly won the competition in each of its first four years from 1906–09. A striker named Welfare was the club's first real hero, scoring 163 goals in 168 games from 1913–24.

Flu's next sustained period of dominance in the State Championship began in the late 1930s, with the club claiming five out of six titles between 1936 and 1941. The success of coach Carlos Carlomagno's side was recognized when five Fluminense players, Hercules, Romeu, Tim, Batatais and Machado, were selected for the national team that travelled to France for the 1938 World Cup finals. Flu continued to provide a source of players for the national team right up until the 1990s, among the most successful of whom were goalkeeper Felix, a World Cup winner in 1970, and left-back Branco who played in Brazil's victory over Italy in the final of 1994.

The 1950s brought arguably Flu's greatest-ever player to the Maracana stadium. Didi, a midfield artist who could score and create goals for team-mates, spent seven years with Fluminense, scoring 95 goals but laying on many more for the prolific strike partnership of Valdo and Telê. Fluminense's talented team, however, somewhat underachieved in the 1950s, and were cast into the shade by the successes of their neighbours Flamengo. The intense rivalry between Rio's two biggest clubs is

*Above: Branco, a World Cup winner in 1994, made his name with Flu.*

illustrated by the fact that the 1963 "Flu" v "Fla" game attracted a world record club crowd of 177,000 to the Maracana.

In the 1970s, Flu and Fla dominated the Rio Championship, with Fluminense claiming five titles to Flamengo's four. However, the new Brazilian National Championship, which began in 1971, proved a trickier proposition, and it was

not until 1984 that Flu claimed their first and only victory in the competition. Success in 1984 had been achieved with the Paraguayan Romerito, who was voted South American Player of the Year in 1986. By the end of the century, however, they were in decline and, in 1997, Flu were relegated from the First Division of the National Championship and then to the Second Division the next year. They finished 2008 in 14th place in Division One.

# Galatasaray

**Year formed:** *1905*
**Country:** *Turkey*
**Stadium:** *Ali Sami Yen*
**Colours:** *Red and yellow shirts, black shorts*
**Domestic Honours:**
*Championships: 17; Cups: 14*
**European Honours:** *UEFA Cup: 1 (2000)*

Located in the heart of Istanbul on the European side of the Bosphorus sea, Galatasaray Spor Kulubu is the largest sporting club in Turkey, with thousands of members and even an island of its own in the Bosphorus. The club was formed in 1905 by a group of students who, on a visit to Switzerland, acquired the popular song "Jim, Bom, Bom" – the club's nickname is now *Cim Bom Bom*, although they are also known as "The Lions".

Galatasaray won the old Istanbul league ten times between 1928 and 1958, the year of the league's dissolution, and won their first Turkish league title in 1962. The club have won the league 13 times (the same number as Istanbul rivals Fenerbahce, based in

*Below: Galatasaray command intense loyalty from their fans.*

*Above: After disappointment in the 2000 Champions League, Gala went on to win the UEFA Cup that year.*

the Asian side of the city) aided in the 1970s by the goals of Metin Oktay and in the 1980s by Tanju Colak, who also played for Fenerbahce.

The club has played in several European Cup campaigns, their most successful season being in 1989, when they were beaten 5–1 on aggregate by Steaua Bucharest in the semi-final. In the 1994 tournament, they eliminated Manchester United by scoring three in

a stirring performance at Old Trafford to go through 3–3 on away goals, although they did not progress in the league stage. Knocked out of the 2000 Champions League, they played in that season's UEFA Cup and won their only European trophy when they beat Arsenal in the final. The intimidating atmosphere of the Ali Sami Yen Stadium and the fanatical support of the Gala fans allowed Galatasaray to remain unbeaten at home in European football from 1984 to 1994.

Coach Fatih Terim added Romanian superstar Gheorge Hagi to the midfield in 1997, and with local heroes Hakan Sukur and Arif Erdem in attack and Romanian Giga Popescu and Brazilian Claudio Taffarel in goal, the side dominated Turkish football. However Hakan went to Italy and only Popescu was left under new coach Mircea Lucescu in 2001. The league title was regained in 2002, 2006 and 2008, and nine Gala players were in Turkey's squad at Euro 2008.

# IFK Gothenburg

**Year formed:** *1904*
**Country:** *Sweden*
**Stadium:** *Gamla Ullevi (43,200)*
**Colours:** *Blue and white stripes*
**Domestic Honours:**
*Championships: 18; Domestic
Cups: 4*
**International Honours:** *UEFA Cup: 2
(1982, 87)*

IFK Gothenburg is the most successful
football club in Sweden, and the only
Scandinavian team to have won a major
European trophy. Based on the west
coast of Sweden in the provincial city
of Göteborg, IFK was formed
in 1904 and it won its first league

*Below: Thomas Ravelli, Gothenburg
stalwart and record-breaking Swede.*

championship four years later.
A record-breaking 17 further league
titles have been added in the interim,
making IFK Gothenburg Sweden's
pre-eminent team. IFK can also list a
host of internationals, from Gunnar
Gren in the 1940s to Jesper Blomqvist
and the country's most-capped player,
Thomas Ravelli, in the 1990s.

"The Angels", as they are known,
have a colourful history, as illustrated
by their relegation in 1970, just a year
after the club had won its seventh
league championship. IFK regained top-
flight status in 1975 and, four years
later, made its most astute signing,
appointing 31-year-old Sven-Göran
Eriksson as coach. Eriksson assembled
an intelligent team that played with
both energy and skill, and in 1979

*Above: Sven-Göran Eriksson was the
strength behind IFK's ascent in the 1980s.*

IFK won the Swedish Cup for the first
time in the club's long history.

In 1982 Eriksson's team reached its
peak, claiming a "treble" of league, Cup
and UEFA Cup. Success in Europe put
the spotlight on several IFK players,
notably Torbjorn Nilsson and Glenn
Hysen, but it was their coach who
received most adulation. Eriksson had
guided his team past Valéncia and
Kaiserlautern en route to the final, at
which the Swedes had beaten Hamburg
4–0 on aggregate. The second leg was
played in Germany, and IFK claimed a
3–0 win. Eriksson was in demand and
was snapped up by Benfica.

IFK, minus Eriksson, claimed a
second UEFA Cup success in 1987, this
time overcoming Dundee United 2–1
on aggregate in an anticlimactic final.
Since then, the Angels have won only
domestic silverware, although they
impressively won a record six league
championships in the 1990s. European
competition has provided occasional
highlights in recent years, most notably
in 1995 when IFK progressed to the
quarter-finals of the Champions
League, beating Manchester United
and Barcelona on the way.

# Independiente de Avellaneda

**Year formed:** *1905*

**Country:** *Argentina*

**Stadium:** *Estadio Libertadores de America (53,000)*

**Colours:** *Red with white trim*

**Domestic Honours:**
*Championships: 15*

**International Honours:** *Copa Libertadores: 7 (1964, 65, 72, 73, 74, 75, 84); World Club Cup: 2 (1973, 84)*

Above: In the 1970s the "Red Devils" won the Copa Libertadores an impressive four times.

Independiente's status as one of South America's great club sides comes more from their performances in international competition than for their domestic record. Based in Buenos Aires, the club has won 15 Argentine titles, a tally some way behind rivals River Plate (26 championships) and Boca Juniors (27). However, in both the South American Cup and the World Club Cup their supporters have had much to cheer about.

By the time Argentina's professional league was established, in 1931, Independiente had won two amateur titles. They had also enjoyed the services of Raimundo Orsi, one of the county's most accomplished players and the club's first superstar. Left-winger Orsi, who later won a World Cup winners' medal

*Below: Independiente's Albeiro Usuriaga, one of their more recent stars.*

with Italy in 1938, was a key member of the Independiente side that progressed to the Olympic final in 1928. Soon afterward Orsi moved to Juventus, and a new hero arrived, Paraguayan centre-forward Arsenio Enrico. Between 1937 and 1939, Enrico scored 130 goals and helped Independiente to two national championship titles.

Independiente were again champions in 1948, but 11 barren years followed. In the 1960s, however, the club enjoyed a resurgence, winning three domestic titles and two South American *Libertadores* Cups. Success in the *Libertadores* of 1964 was the first occasion that an Argentine team had won. Independiente retained

their title in 1965, and in the 1970s the club enjoyed continued success in that prestigious competition.

From 1972–75, Independiente recorded four successive victories in the *Libertadores*, as well as victory in the 1973 World Club Cup. This was achieved with a team full of international players, including Ricardo Bochini, Ricardo Pavoni and the 1978 World Cup Final scorer Daniel Bertoni, but Independiente still lacked an obvious star player.

In 1984, the club again celebrated victory in the *Libertadores*, and this time the team did possess a conspicuous talent. Jorge Burruchaga, an established international, scored the decisive goal in Argentina's World Cup Final victory over West Germany in 1986. He also helped Independiente win the World Club Cup in 1984, but he was soon lured away to play in Europe and, since then, the club has failed to maintain its place at the pinnacle of South American football, finishing bottom in the championship in 2002. Indpendiente has recently experienced debt problems and could only finish in 11th position in the 2007 league.

# Internazionale

**Year formed:** *1908*
**Country:** *Italy*
**Stadium:** *Giuseppe Meazza (San Siro) (85,000)*
**Colours:** *Blue and black stripes*
**Domestic Honours:**
*Championships: 16; Domestic Cups: 5*
**International Honours:** *European Champions Cup: 2 (1964, 65); UEFA Cup: 3 (1991, 94, 98); World Club Cup: 2 (1964, 65)*

Internazionale, with its packed trophy room and stadium, is one of the biggest names in Italian football. A sustained period of success in the 1960s, which brought three championship wins and two European Cups, raised Inter's expectations. Inter then watched as rivals AC Milan dominated European football during the 1990s. Undaunted, the club has spent heavily on transfers in recent years.

*Below: Brazilian striker Ronaldo in action for Inter Milan.*

*Above: Giacinto Facchetti, goalscoring defender for Inter in the 1960s and 70s.*

Inter was formed in 1908 by a group of former AC Milan members, and the club quickly grew in strength. Players of any nationality were free to join, (hence the name of the club), and two years after its formation, Inter celebrated its first championship win. A second title followed in 1920, but two years later Benito Mussolini's fascists rose to power and Inter were forced to change their name, which was considered far too liberal, to Ambrosiana. However, it was not all bad news for Inter in the 1930s: with Giuseppe Meazza, its most prolific goalscorer, they won the Italian league in 1938.

After World War Two, Ambrosiana-Inter was given permission to change its name back to Internazionale. In the 1950s, Inter, now coached by Alfredo Foni, developed an impregnable defence that, together with the goals of Hungarian Istvan Nyers, brought championship victories in 1953 and 1954. Inter's greatest successes, however, came under the guidance of Argentine coach Helenio Herrera during the 1960s. Herrera assembled one of Italy's great club sides, which included Giacinto Facchetti, Inter's most-capped player, and

the invaluable Sandro Mazzola. In 1965, Herrera's team reached the height of its powers, winning the league and recording victories in the European Cup and World Club Cup.

By the mid-1970s, however, Internazionale were in decline, a situation largely caused by the Italian football federation's ban on foreign players. The ban was lifted in 1980, the year that Inter won its first title for nine years, and the club quickly made up for lost time, signing a host of expensive imports during the 1980s and 1990s, including Lothar Mätthaus, Jürgen Klinsmann, Ronaldo and Christian Vieri, and claimed three victories in the UEFA Cup during the 1990s.

Under Roberto Mancini they won *Serie A* three times in succession between 2006 and 2008 - their first league title for 17 years - as well as the cup in 2005 and 2006. The club's president Massimo Moratti, however, craved a resurgence in European glory and replaced Mancini with Jose Mourinho at the start of season 2008-09.

# Juventus

**Year formed:** *1897*
**Country:** *Italy*
**Stadium:** *Stadio Olimpico (27,500)*
**Colours:** *Black and white stripes*
**Domestic Honours:**
*Championships: 28; Domestic
Cups: 9*
**International Honours:** *European
Champions Cup: 2 (1985, 96);
European Cup Winners Cup: 1
(1984); UEFA Cup: 3 (1977, 90, 93);
European Super Cup: 2 (1984, 96);
World Club Cup: 2 (1985, 96)*

The story of Juventus is one of
unreserved success. At some point
in their history, "The Zebras" have
claimed every major trophy they have
competed for, including the World Club
Cup, and have won the *Scudetto* (the
Italian championship) more times than
any other club.

*Below: Gianluca Vialli captained Juve
to European Cup success in 1996.*

Juventus began life in 1897, founded
by a group of students who set up the
club for their own recreation. The club
adopted its famous black and white strip
in 1903, after a club official was
impressed by Notts County's kit on a
trip to England, and in 1905 the Zebras
of Turin claimed their first Italian
Championship. But it was in the 1930s
that Juventus leapt to the pinnacle of
Italian football. The Turin side, led by
trainer Carlo Carcano, won five *Scudetti*
in succession between 1930 and 1935.
Juventus players, most notably goalkeeper
and captain Gianpiero Combi, defender
Luisito Monti and forwards Giovanni
Ferrari and Raimundo Orsi, also inspired
Italy's 1934 World Cup triumph.

In the 1950s and 1960s, Juventus
assembled a series of star-studded teams
based around imported talent. Danes Karl
and John Hansen were the first to arrive,
followed by Welshman John Charles and
Spaniard Luis Del Sol. However, Italian
forward Giampiero Boniperti was

*Above: Claudio Gentile helped Juve
to Cup Winners Cup success in 1984.*

Juventus' undoubted star of the era,
scoring a club record 177 goals. In 1961,
Juventus became the first club to adorn
their kit with a gold star, signifying
ten Championship victories.

Juventus' first European title arrived
with a victory over Athletic Bilbao in the
1977 UEFA Cup Final. In the 1980s
Juventus built a formidable team, with
France's Michel Platini and the stars of
Italy's 1982 World Cup winning team,
Marco Tardelli, Claudio Gentile and
Paolo Rossi. The Zebras completed their
collection of trophies by claiming the
Cup Winners Cup in 1984, and the
European Cup in 1985. Continued
success the following decade brought
further rewards, with Marcello Lippi
guiding Juventus to the *Scudetto* in 1995
and the European Cup in 1996. They
won the Championship again in 2002
and 2003, but lost the 2003 Champions
League final to AC Milan on penalties
after a 0–0 draw. Juventus were implicated
in a match-fixing scandal in 2006
and were relegated to *Serie B* the
following season. They immediately
gained promotion, however, and finished
3rd in *Serie A* in 2008.

# Kiev Dynamo

**Year formed:** *1927*
**Country:** *Ukraine*
**Stadium:** *National Sport Komplex Olimpiyskyi (83,000)*
**Colours:** *White with blue trim*
**Domestic Honours:** *(USSR and Ukraine) Championships: 25; Domestic Cups: 18*
**International Honours:** *European Cup Winners Cup: 2 (1975, 86); European Super Cup: 1 (1975)*

Kiev Dynamo was the dominant team in the USSR from the mid-1960s onward. Formed in 1927, Dynamo was the football club of the Kiev secret police. The club was among the original members of the inaugural national Soviet Championship in 1936, but it was not until 1961 that the Kievites became the first non-Moscow

*Below: Kiev's Igor Belanov was voted European Footballer of the Year in 1986.*

side to win the league. Twelve more Soviet titles were added, before a separate Ukrainian championship was formed in 1991–92.

Dynamo was also the first Soviet club to win a European trophy, claiming the Cup Winners Cup with a 3–0 victory against Ferencváros of Hungary in 1975. This success was followed with an impressive 3–1 win over a Bayern Munich side that included Franz Beckenbauer in the 1975 European Super Cup. Victory in Europe publicized a number of Dynamo's star players, notably Oleg Blokhin, who scored all three of his side's goals against Bayern. Blokhin, who had also scored against Ferencváros in the Cup Winners Cup Final, was awarded the title of European Footballer of the Year in 1975.

A second Cup Winners Cup victory was achieved under the guidance of long-serving coach Valerii Lobanovsky

*Above: The prolific scorer Sergei Rebrov, star of the 1990s for Dynamo.*

in 1986, Dynamo overcoming Atlético Madrid 3–0 in the final. Veteran forward Blokhin was again among the Dynamo goalscorers, but this time the team's star player was right-winger Igor Belanov. Like Blokhin, Belanov was also voted European Footballer of the Year.

In 1988, seven Dynamo players appeared for the Soviet Union in the final of the European Championships in Germany. The Soviet team, which was coached by Lobanovsky, finished runners-up to Holland but earned much credit for beating Italy in the semi-finals. In the early 1990s, however, the Ukraine set up its own league and national team, which have, predictably, been dominated by Kiev Dynamo. Ten of the first 12 Ukraine Championships went to Dynamo and they won two more in 2004 and 2007. The team's greatest moments in recent years have come in the Champions League, notably in 1998–99, when Dynamo progressed to the quarter-finals with home and away victories over Barcelona.

# Lazio

**Year formed:** *1900*
**Country:** *Italy*
**Stadium:** *Olimpico (73,000)*
**Colours:** *Light blue with white trim*
**Domestic Honours:**
*Championships: 2;*
*Domestic Cups: 4*
**International Honours:** *European Cup Winners Cup: 1 (1999); European Super Cup: 1 (1999)*

If ever the story of a football club was tailor-made for a sporting biopic, it is that of SS Lazio. The Rome club may not have the largest collection of prizes in Italian football, but its colourful history has seen relegations, bribery scandals, UEFA bans and financial problems along with occasional trophies. It was therefore fitting that Lazio began its 1999–2000 centenary season by selling a player for a then-world record fee (Christian Vieri to Internazionale for £30m), and ended it with a first League and Cup "double".

It took Lazio 58 years to win its first major trophy, the 1958 *Coppa Italia*, with a 1–0 victory over Fiorentina. However, three years later the club was relegated to *Serie B*. Demotion became all too familiar to Lazio fans during the 1960s, with the club yo-yoing between Italy's top two divisions that decade.

*Below: Croatia's Alen Boksic, one of several expensive signings in the 1990s.*

*Above: Lazio skipper Alessandro Nesta holds aloft the UEFA Super Cup in 1999.*

In the early 1970s, it seemed that Lazio had established itself among Italy's elite, and in 1974, just two seasons after winning promotion back to *Serie A*, the club celebrated its first *Scudetto* (Italian championship). However, the champions were excluded from the European Cup the following season after being banned from Europe, following crowd trouble during a UEFA Cup match against Ipswich Town, in 1973. A gradual decline set in, and in 1980 the club was relegated to *Serie B* as a result of a bribery scandal.

For Lazio, the 1980s were spent in obscurity but, following the election of Sergio Cragnotti as club president, the club enjoyed a renaissance during the 1990s. Buoyed by Cragnotti's millions, Lazio invested heavily in players, signing a series of expensive foreign talent, most notably England's Paul Gascoigne, Germany's Karlheinz Riedle, Croatia's Alen Boksic and Chile's Marcelo Salas. The following year, led by coach Sven-Göran Eriksson, Lazio defeated Marseille to win the Cup Winners Cup Final but failed to win the *Scudetto* by one point. In 2000 they got the domestic "double".

However, the club's form slumped and Eriksson left in 2001 to manage England. Dino Zoff, then Alberto Zaccheroni followed by Roberto Mancini took over the team. Mancini left for Inter in 2004. A match-fixing scandal in 2006 led to a points reduction, and the club finished in 12th place in *Serie A* in 2008.

# Leeds United

**Year formed:** *1919*
**Country:** *England*
**Stadium:** *Elland Road (40,000)*
**Colours:** *White*
**Domestic Honours:**
*Championships: 3; Domestic (FA)
Cups: 1*
**International Honours:** *Fairs Cup: 2
(1968, 71)*

In the early 1960s, Leeds were a Second Division team. They had won nothing and their biggest headlines concerned an illegal payments scandal that had brought down the club's predecessors, Leeds City, in 1919. However, the arrival of Don Revie as manager, in 1961, initiated a change that propelled the club to the top of English football.

It is difficult to exaggerate Revie's influence at Elland Road. A skilled man-manager, shrewd tactician and expert judge of players, he instigated a new tactical system for the club, and he was even responsible for the switch to a Real Madrid-style all-white kit.

*Below: Peter Lorimer lets fly with his left foot against Liverpool.*

By the mid-1960s, Revie's efforts were beginning to bear fruit. A team built around the energy and skill of midfielders John Giles and Billy Bremner was taking shape, and in 1964, Leeds won promotion to the First Division. A year later the club finished as runners-up in the league, and made its first appearance at Wembley, taking on Liverpool in the FA Cup Final, but losing 2–1 in extra time. In each of the next ten seasons Leeds were either winners or runners-up in at least one

*Above: "We are Leeds." United celebrate the Championship in 1974.*

major competition, claiming two league titles, one FA Cup, one League Cup and the Fairs Cup twice. The final success of Revie's Elland Road tenure came in 1973–74, when his ageing team claimed their second league title.

The post-Revie era at Leeds saw a decline into the Second Division. Seven managers came and went, before Howard Wilkinson assembled an enterprising team in which veteran Scottish midfielder Gordon Strachan was the pivotal figure. Leeds won promotion in 1989–90, and two seasons later Elland Road celebrated its first league title for 17 seasons.

However, despite a new board, and, in 1998, a new young manager, David O'Leary, who spent heavily on new players, further success failed to follow. In the summer of 2002 O'Leary was sacked. Severe financial difficulties then came to a head, and most of Leeds' best players had to be sold to keep the club afloat, leading to their relegation from the Premiership in 2003–04, and then to the third tier division, accompanied by a 15-point deduction. Despite this, coach Dennis Wise, and then Gary McAllister guided Leeds to a play-off place in 2008, only to lose to Doncaster Rovers.

# Liverpool

**Year formed:** *1892*
**Country:** *England*
**Stadium:** *Anfield (45,000)*
**Colours:** *Red*
**Domestic Honours:**
*Championships: 18;*
*Domestic (FA) Cups: 7*
**International Honours:** *European Champions Cup: 5 (1977, 78, 81, 84, 2005); UEFA Cup: 3 (1973, 76, 2001); European Super Cup: 3 (1977, 2001, 2005)*

According to the record books, Liverpool FC is the most successful club in English football. Eighteen League Championships and numerous Cup successes are irrefutable proof of the Merseysiders' status, but still fail to reveal the scale of the club's feats during the 1970s and 1980s.

The architect of Liverpool's modern glories was undoubtedly Bill Shankly. Appointed manager in 1959, the Scotsman took charge of a club languishing in the Second Division, having won five League titles in better

*Below: John Barnes, a key figure in Liverpool's successful team of the 1980s.*

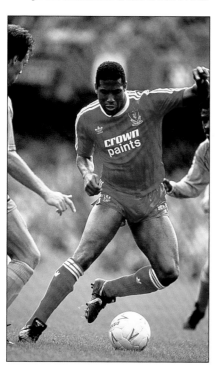

times. Promotion was secured in 1961–62 and Liverpool claimed the League Championship in 1963–64. They soon established a reputation for a controlled style of football that was entertaining though not flamboyant, and for players who were skilful and committed.

When Shankly retired in 1974, Liverpool appointed assistant manager Bob Paisley as his successor. He exceeded all expectations, winning nine domestic trophies, three European Cups and a UEFA Cup. No other manager of an English club has won such an impressive collection of silverware. In 1983, Paisley retired and once more the Liverpool board looked behind the scenes for a new manager, promoting assistant Joe Fagan to the top job. Joe, like his predecessor, was tipped to fail, but instead collected a "treble" of League Championship, League Cup and European Cup in his first season in 1983–84. Fagan's second and final season in charge ended in devastating tragedy at the Heysel Stadium in Belgium, in May 1985.

Liverpool appointed another internal candidate to the manager's job. The man chosen was Kenny Dalglish, who

*Above: Liverpool's inspirational captain Steven Gerrard raises the European Cup in Istanbul after beating AC Milan.*

became player-manager and led the Reds to the League and FA Cup "double" in his first season in charge. Dalglish helped Liverpool to two more league championships during his five-year stint, but his tenure also included the disaster at Hillsborough in 1989, which claimed the lives of 96 fans and shook the club to its core. The 1990s brought Liverpool little success, and after two old boys, Graeme Souness and Roy Evans, failed to restore past glories, the Anfield club brought in outsider Gerard Houllier as manager. In 2000–01, he led the team to the "treble" of the League Cup, FA Cup and UEFA Cup, the last in a thrilling 5–4 victory over Alaves, but was replaced at the end of the 2003–04 season by Rafa Benitez.

In his first season in charge, Benitez defied all predictions by deftly steering Liverpool to their fifth European Cup triumph after a sensational final against AC Milan in Istanbul in 2005. They were to meet AC Milan again in 2007's final, this time losing 2–1.

# Manchester United

**Year formed:** *1878*
**Country:** *England*
**Stadium:** *Old Trafford (69,000)*
**Colours:** *Red with black trim*
**Domestic Honours:**
*Championships: 17; Domestic (FA) Cups: 11*
**International Honours:** *European Champions Cup: 3 (1968, 99, 2008); European Cup Winners Cup: 1 (1991); European Super Cup: 1 (1991); World Club Cup 2 (1999, 2008)*

Adored by their widespread fans and, predictably, loathed by the rest, Manchester United are undeniably one of world football's elite clubs. By the start of the third millennium, Manchester United were a team without equal in England, with an impressive haul of silverware, including the "treble" of the English League and FA Cup and Europe's Champions League in 1998–99.

United are not only a successful club,

*Below: United regain the European Cup to complete the 2008 "double".*

they are also a club with a reputation for entertaining football, and for a cavalier style of play that would be foolhardy with players of lesser ability. The United approach can be attributed to one man above all others, Sir Matt Busby. As manager from 1945–69, Sir Matt elevated the Old Trafford club from the middle ground of English football to the pinnacle of the European game. United had won just three major trophies prior to Busby's arrival, but by the time he became general manager in 1969, that total had grown to 13.

The success of the Busby era, however, was blighted by the tragedy of the Munich air disaster in February 1958. United's youthful and highly talented team, which included Duncan Edwards, Bobby Charlton and Roger Byrne, was all but wiped out at Munich. Busby built again, and in 1965 a new-look United won the league championship. This was the Manchester United team that set the benchmark for the rest. The legendary attacking triumvirate of George Best, Denis Law and Bobby Charlton were

*Above: Alex Ferguson turned United into England's top team in the 1990s.*

responsible for goals, victories, and thousands of new fans. The zenith of the Busby years came in 1968 when the Reds defeated Benfica 4–1 in an epic European Cup Final at Wembley.

The job of succeeding Busby proved immense, and 17 years of struggle followed, taking in the reigns of five managers and relegation to the Second Division in 1974. United's pre-eminent status was eventually restored by Alex Ferguson, who was appointed manager in 1986. United's problems were so deep-seated that it took Ferguson until 1990 to win his first trophy (the FA Cup). It proved to be the first of many.

The Premier League was dominated by United, who claimed 8 of its first 12 championships. Throughout the 1990s, Ferguson expertly constructed his teams, combining home-grown talent such as Ryan Giggs, David Beckham and Paul Scholes, with overseas signings. Ferguson then began to build a new team around such players as Wayne Rooney, Christiano Ronaldo and Rio Ferdinand, and was rewarded by securing four league titles in the first decade of the 21st century, as well as a third European Cup in 2008, defeating Chelsea on penalties in Moscow.

# Marseille

**Year formed:** *1899*
**Country:** *France*
**Stadium:** *Vélodrome (60,000)*
**Colours:** *White with blue trim*
**Domestic Honours:**
*Championships: 8; Domestic Cups: 10*

In 1993, Marseille became the first French club to win the European Cup, defeating Fabio Capello's AC Milan 1–0 in Munich. However, the euphoria of this historic victory was to be short-lived. Within weeks of skipper Didier Deschamps lifting European football's greatest prize, allegations of match fixing were levelled against Marseille. Charges were duly brought and, once proven, the club was stripped of its European crown and relegated to the French Second Division. Alas, the shockwaves did not end there, and the club's controversial president, Bernard Tapie, was later sentenced to two years in prison for his part in the match-fixing scandal. Unsurprisingly, Marseille

*Below: Marseille's success in the 1980s owed much to the goals of Papin.*

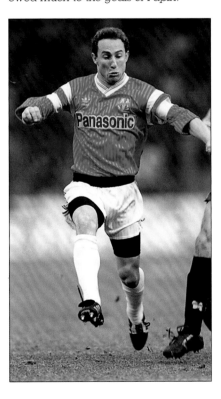

*Above: Marseille achieved their zenith with European Cup success in 1993, but they were later stripped of the title for match-fixing.*

soon found themselves in financial crisis too and, with debts of around 250 million French francs, the club entered receivership.

Marseille's fall from grace had come completely out of leftfield, but then the club's rise to the top of continental football in the early 1990s had also been somewhat unexpected. Formed in 1899, Olympique de Marseille is one of the oldest and richest football clubs in France. However, despite its much-envied wealth, Marseille won just four titles in its first 89 years. The arrival of Bernard Tapie in 1985, and the injection of new money thereafter, proved the turning point for the Riviera's favourite team. Millions of pounds were spent on the purchase of high-profile players, among them Chris Waddle, Deschamps, Marcel Desailly and Jean-Pierre Papin, as Marseille went in search of success. The trophies soon began to accumulate, with the first of four consecutive League titles arriving in 1989.

By the start of the 1990s, Marseille had become the dominant name in French football and, under Belgian coach Raymond Goethals, the club reached its first European final in

1991. Red Star Belgrade provided the opposition, but the match proved a dour encounter and the Yugoslavs claimed victory in a penalty shoot-out. Two years later, Marseille, with a much-changed team that included just three of the 1991 line-up, were back in the final and this time the entertainment would be of a more intense and long-lasting nature.

After the highs and lows of the Tapie-era, Marseille found much-needed stability under new owners in the mid-1990s. Top-flight status was reattained in 1996 and, with a fresh crop of expensive purchases wearing the white and blue jersey, the club challenged for honours once more. In 1999, Marseille served notice of their successful rehabilitation by reaching the UEFA Cup Final. The French team lost 3–0 to Parma in Moscow, but had proved their strength with victories over Blackburn Rovers, AS Monaco, Celta Vigo and Bologna en route to the final.

# AC Milan

**Year formed:** *1899*

**Country:** *Italy*

**Stadium:** *Giuseppe Meazza (San Siro) (85,000)*

**Colours:** *Red and black stripes*

**Domestic Honours:**
*Championships: 17; Domestic Cups: 5*

**International Honours:** *European Champions Cup: 7 (1963, 69, 89, 90, 94, 2003, 07); European Cup Winners Cup: 2 (1968, 73); World Club Cup: 3 (1969, 89, 90)*

*Above: Arrigo Sacchi (centre), the brains behind Milan's renaissance in the 1980s.*

It is hard to imagine a more assured, and talented football team than the AC Milan side that brushed aside Barcelona 4–0 in the 1994 European Cup Final. The "*Rossonieri*", as Milan are nicknamed, were a team packed with fine footballers, from the unsurpassable Marcel Dessaily and Paolo Maldini in defence to the transcendent Dejan Savicevic and energetic Daniele Massaro in attack.

Formed in 1899 as the Milan Cricket and Football Club, Milan were crowned Italian champions two years later, and winning quickly became a habit. The

*Below: Paulo Maldini holds the record for most appaearences for AC Milan and the Italian national side.*

club won two more *Scudetti* (Italian championships) in the first ten years of the 20th century, although Milan then spent several decades in the shade of their city rivals, Inter. A post-war revival came in the 1950s, courtesy of a string of high-profile foreign signings, most notably the Swedish trio of Gunnar Gren, Gunnar Nordahl and Nils Liedholm, and the Uruguayan World Cup-winning striker Juan Schiaffino. It was an unprecedented investment for an Italian team, and led to a period of sustained success throughout the 1950s and 1960s.

Milan's resurgence at domestic level was mirrored in European competition, and they soon established themselves as a significant threat to Real Madrid's European Cup monopoly. The Italian giants ran Madrid close in the 1958 final, losing 3–2 in extra time, and five years later they claimed European football's greatest prize with a 2–1 victory over Benfica. A second European Cup victory followed in 1969 with a 4–1 win against Ajax, but soon afterwards came a series

of financial problems, and a steady decline set in.

Just as the success of the post-war era owed much to imported talent, so too did Milan's triumphs of the 1980s and 1990s. This time, the foreign legion came because the club had been buoyed by the millions of president Silvio Berlusconi. Arrigo Sacchi was the first manager to benefit from Berlusconi's wealth, signing the Dutch duo of Marco Van Basten and Ruud Gullit in 1987. The effect was instant, and in 1988 Milan won their first title for nine years. Carlo Ancelotti took over as manager in 2001, and in 2003 Milan beat rivals Juventus in a penalty shoot-out in the Champions League Final at Old Trafford. In 2005, they lost in the final to Liverpool on penalties after taking a 3-0 first half lead; they gained revenge, however, in 2007, beating Liverpool 2-1 in the final of the same competition to win their seventh European Cup.

# Moscow Spartak

**Year formed:** *1922*
**Country:** *Russia*
**Stadium:** *Dinamo (38,000) and Lokomotiv (29,000)*
**Colours:** *Red and white*
**Domestic Honours:** *(USSR and Russia) Championships: 21; Domestic Cups: 13*

Moscow Spartak were one of the leading teams in the former USSR, so it was no surprise that, following the demise of the old Soviet league in 1991, Spartak became the dominant force in the fledgling Russian Championship. In six of the competition's first seven seasons they were champions.

Success at home has provided Spartak with a regular passport into European competition, although this may be regarded as a mixed blessing. The Russian club have benefited financially from their continental campaigns but, with their players enjoying increased media exposure, several of their brightest stars have been lured to richer

*Below: Soviet superstar, Igor Netto. Spartak's left-half was a consistent performer through the 1950s and 1960s.*

*Above: Spartak's Sergei Yuran takes on Blackburn Rovers' Graeme Le Saux in the Champions League, 1995.*

clubs abroad. Prior to the late 1980s, restrictions on foreign transfers meant that it was extremely difficult for Russian footballers to move abroad, but in recent years Spartak have seen the likes of Alexandre Mostovoi (to Celta Vigo), Igor Shalimov (Bologna), and Dmitriy Alenichev (AS Roma) all go West.

Despite the sale of the club's most talented players, Spartak enjoyed their greatest successes in Europe during the 1990s. In 1990–91, with a team that still included both Shalimov and Mostovoi, the Soviet champions progressed to the semi-finals of the European Cup. The run included memorable victories over Napoli, and a 3–1 triumph before a crowd of 91,000 in the Bernabau against Real Madrid, but was brought to an end by Marseille. Two years later, Spartak fought through to the last four of the Cup Winners Cup, before succumbing to eventual runners-up Royal Antwerp. A third European semi-final came in

1998, with Spartak beating both Karlsruhe and Ajax en route to a meeting with Inter Milan. The Italian giants went on to win both the match and the competition, but they needed two second-leg goals from Ronaldo to win 4–2 on aggregate.

Despite the successes of the 1990s, Spartak remain one of the biggest clubs that have still to win a major European trophy. Many among the club's large fan base believe that Spartak's best chance of European glory came with the team that won four league titles in the 1950s. However, this successful team, which included the great Igor Netto, peaked before European club competition began. It seems unlikely that in the modern, money-dominated game Spartak will be able to compete successfully for any of the major European prizes.

# Nacional

**Year formed:** *1891*

**Country:** *Uruguay*

**Stadium:** *Estadio Centenario (73,000) and Estadio Las Acacias (15,000)*

**Colours:** *White with blue and red trim*

**Domestic Honours:**
*Championships: 41*

**International Honours:** *Copa Libertadores: 3 (1971, 80, 88); World Club Cup: 3 (1971, 80, 88)*

The rivalry between Montevideo's two great clubs, Nacional and Penarol, dominates Uruguayan football. From the birth of the country's professional league, in 1932, until 1975 these two teams were the only champions of Uruguay. Nacional are, by eight years, the younger of the two clubs, having been founded by members of the Uruguayan Athletic Club and the Albion Football Club in 1891.

Nacional has a large and passionate fan base, and its supporters take great

*Below: Nacional take on First Division Liverpool in a Uruguay league game.*

pride from the fact that their club was the first to be formed by indigenous Uruguayans rather than European immigrants. Nacional fans can also be rightly proud of their team's achievements on the pitch, with the team in white, red and blue jerseys claiming 37 league championships during the 20th century. The first of these titles arrived in 1902, and a year later Nacional players were exclusively selected for an Uruguayan XI to play Argentina in Buenos Aires. The match against Uruguay's great rivals from across the River Plate was won 3–2, and victory added further weight to Nacional's growing reputation.

In the late 1930s and early 1940s, Nacional enjoyed their most sustained period of dominance in the domestic game. From 1939 to 1943, the "Five Golden Years", the club claimed consecutive championships during a spell that included a much-celebrated 8–0 victory over neighbours Peñarol. The 1950s and 1960s brought further successes, but it was in 1969 that Nacional returned to a position of undoubted pre-eminence in Uruguayan

*Above: Argentinian international Luis Artime scored the goals that took Nacional to success in the Copa Libertadores in 1971.*

football. The Argentina striker Luis Artime proved the hero of this second great era, scoring 60 goals to help Nacional to three successive league titles from 1969 to 1971.

The early 1970s also brought Nacional its first success in the *Copa Libertadores*. Fittingly, it was a goal from the prolific Artime that capped victory over Argentina's Estudiantes in the 1971 final, thus ending a run that had seen Nacional lose three *Libertadores* finals during the 1960s. A World Club Cup was duly won against Greek side Panathinaikos, with Artime scoring all three goals in a 3–2 aggregate victory, and the combination of World and South American titles was claimed again in both 1980 and 1988.

Nacional remain a significant force in Uruguayan football, with international striker Gabriel Alvez the club's most recent hero, but in the 1990s and beyond, the team from the Estadio Centenario has failed to add to their list of international prizes.

# Paris Saint-Germain

**Year formed:** *1970*

**Country:** *France*

**Stadium:** *Parc des Princes (48,000)*

**Colours:** *White with red panel*

**Domestic Honours:**
*Championships: 2; Domestic Cups: 7*

**International Honours:** *European Cup Winners Cup: 1 (1996)*

In 1996, and at just 26, Paris Saint-Germain defeated Rapid Vienna in the Cup Winners Cup Final to become the youngest club to lift a major European trophy. Victory in Europe was an immense achievement for a club that had only been formed as an attempt to create a Parisian team to fill the void left by the demise of Racing Club Paris.

For PSG, the route to European success may have been short but it was winding. The club began life in association with Saint Germain-en-Laye in 1970, but its ambition was clear and by 1973 it was a separate profesional outfit. Promotion to the French First Division came under the stewardship of Robert Vicot and Just Fontaine in 1974, and PSG have remained in France's top flight ever since.

*Below: PSG celebrate their Cup Winners Cup victory over Rapid Vienna in 1996.*

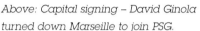

In the late 1970s, PSG president Daniel Hechter attempted to accelerate the club's development by signing a host of stars, notably Yugoslav playmaker Safet Susic and French international Luis Fernandez. Hechter's investment proved sound, and in 1982, the club's first silverware arrived in the shape of the French Cup. A second Cup came in 1983, and three years later the club, coached by Gerard Houllier, had its first triumph in the championship.

*Above: Capital signing – David Ginola turned down Marseille to join PSG.*

In the early 1990s, PSG's ascendancy took a temporary dip due to financial difficulties. A saviour was eventually found in the form of French television company *CanalPlus* who, together with the Paris municipal council, provided a solid foundation on which PSG were able to rebuild. On the field, Portuguese coach Artur Jorge directed PSG's resurgence with a run to the semi-final of the UEFA Cup, and victory in the French Cup in 1992–93. A second domestic championship arrived in 1993–94 and, like the first league title, it was achieved after much investment in Δplayers. PSG's most famous signings were Liberian George Weah and the Brazilian midfielder Raí.

The spending and success continued throughout the 1990s, and after a run to the semi-final of the Champions League in 1995, they won the following season's Cup Winners Cup. A second appearance in the Cup Winners Cup Final followed in 1997, but this time PSG suffered defeat by a Ronaldo-inspired Barcelona.

# Penarol

**Year formed:** *1891*

**Country:** *Uruguay*

**Stadium:** *Estadio Centenario (73,000) and Estadio Las Acacias (15,000)*

**Colours:** *Black and yellow stripes*

**Domestic Honours:**

*Championships: 45*

**International Honours:** *Copa Libertadores: 5 (1960, 61, 66, 82, 87); World Club Cup: 3 (1961, 66, 82)*

Penarol is the most successful football team in Uruguay. A total of 45 league championships in the 20th century do not lie and, despite the protestations of Nacional's supporters, the team from the Pignarolo district of Montevideo are the ones to beat. Penarol has its origins in

*Below: Midfielder Marcel Cleber Romero, a regular in Penarol's first team.*

the works team of the British-run Uruguayan Railway Company, which was formed in 1891, and in that guise the club won its first Uruguayan Championship in 1900. By the time the name Club Atlético Penarol was assumed in 1913, the team had collected five league titles and was already the pre-eminent force in Uruguayan football. Penarol also played a key role in the success of Uruguay's national team, most notably in 1950 when the club provided the backbone of the team that won the World Cup against Brazil. Among Penarol's World Cup-winning stars was the country's greatest-ever player, Juan Schiaffino.

In the 1960s Penarol were given the chance to test their mettle against foreign opposition in the new *Copa Libertadores*, and the Uruguayans did not waste the opportunity. The first

*Above: The experienced Pablo Bengoechea on the attack for Penarol.*

*Libertadores* was held in 1960 and found Penarol with a strong team in the midst of a run of four consecutive League titles (1959–1962). The jewel in Penarol's crown was Ecuadorian striker Pedro Spencer, and it was Spencer who struck the first goal of the final against Olimpia of Paraguay. A successful defence of the South American title followed in 1961, and afterwards came victory in the World Club Cup against Benfica. Penarol had been thrashed 5–1 by the mighty Real Madrid in the first World Club Cup the previous season, but this time the Uruguayan champions came out on the right end of the same scoreline.

Penarol, still buoyed by the goals of Spencer, again completed the "double" of the *Libertadores* and World Club Cup titles in 1966. However, 16 barren years followed until more trophies were won with victories in the *Copa Libertadores* in 1982 and 1987, and a third World Club Cup in 1982. These were the last of Penarol's international triumphs. With many Uruguayans now playing in Europe, there were only two Penarol players in Uruguay's World Cup squad of 2002 in Korea/Japan. Uruguay did not qualify for World Cup 2006.

# FC Porto

**Year formed:** *1893*
**Country:** *Portugal*
**Stadium:** *Estadio Do Drago (52,000)*
**Colours:** *Blue and white stripes*
**Domestic Honours:** *Championships: 23; Domestic Cups: 17*
**International Honours:** *European Champions Cup: 2 (1987, 2004); European Super Cup: 1 (1987); UEFA Cup: 1 (2003) World Club Cup: 1 (1987)*

FC Porto is reputed to be the oldest football team in Portugal, but until the 1980s the club lived in the shade of Lisbon rivals Sporting and Benfica. However, following Porto's famous victory against Bayern Munich in the 1987 European Cup Final, the country's footballing power base shifted from the capital to Oporto.
FC Porto's ascendancy continued throughout the 1990s, a decade that brought the club eight league championships, and into the 21st century, with more European success.

Porto enjoyed occasional and, all too often, brief periods of success prior to the 1980s. The most celebrated of these triumphs came in 1956 when the club

*Below: Striker Mario Jardel scored 129 goals for Porto between 1996 and 2000.*

claimed the League and Cup "double" to end 16 years of Lisbon domination. However, during the 1960s, Porto was forced to watch as the Eusebio-inspired Benfica team joined Europe's elite. Though the 1970s brought some respite with league success in 1978 and 1979, it was not until the 1980s that the club's resurgence began.

The appointment of Jorge Nuno Pinto da Costa as club president in 1982, signalled the start of a new era. Da Costa immediately oversaw the return of coach Pedroto, the man who had led Porto to league titles in 1978 and 1979, and in 1984 Porto went on to their first European final. Juventus

*Above: Porto celebrate beating Monaco to win the 2004 Champions League.*

provided the opposition in the 1984 Cup Winners Cup Final but, despite taking the lead, Porto were beaten 2–1. Artur Jorge replaced Pedroto as coach and, following league championship successes in 1985 and 1986, Porto made it to the European Cup Final and a classic 2–1 win against Bayern.

In a purple patch under coach Jose Mourinho, Porto won the Portuguese Championship in 2003 and 2004, the UEFA Cup in 2003, and the Champions League in 2004. Mourinho then left for England to coach Chelsea.

# PSV Eindhoven

**Year formed:** *1913*
**Country:** *Holland*
**Stadium:** *Philips (30,000)*
**Colours:** *Red and white stripes*
**Domestic Honours:**
*Championships: 21;*
*Domestic Cups: 8*
**International Honours:** *European Champions Cup: 1 (1988); UEFA Cup: 1 (1978)*

PSV began life as the athletic club of the Philips electrical factory, based in Eindhoven, Holland. The Philips association continues to this day and, over the years, it has provided PSV with financial security in return for publicity. For many years PSV was regarded as Holland's "third club", but today Dutch

*Below: A penalty shoot-out victory earned PSV the 1988 European Cup.*

football has a rather different pecking order. By the start of the third millennium, PSV had reached the pinnacle of the Dutch game at a time when great rivals Ajax and Feyenoord were struggling. PSV's growing status was largely due to the efforts of the club's 1999–2000 championship-winning team, which included the highly rated international striker, Ruud Van Nistelrooy.

Only a serious knee injury had prevented Van Nistelrooy from signing for Manchester United, a deal that was later completed in 2001. To the supporters of PSV, who had also seen the sale of Ruud Gullit and Brazilian legends Romario and Ronaldo during the past 15 years, the Van Nistelrooy situation was all too familiar. However, the fans also knew that selling big names had not stopped the club from doing extremely well. In 1987 the club

*Above: Striker Wim Kieft played a key role in the 1988 European Cup success.*

sold Ruud Gullit to AC Milan for a then-world record fee of over £5 million, but at the end of the first Gullit-less season, it had bagged the "treble" of League, Cup and European Cup.

Victory in the 1988 European Cup came via a penalty shoot-out against Benfica, and is the peak of PSV's achievements. The key players in the club's European Cup-winning team were goalkeeper Hans Van Breukelen, defender Ronald Koeman and forward Wim Kieft. Both Van Breukelen and Koeman also played key roles in Holland's triumph at the 1988 European Championships.

PSV have also enjoyed success in the UEFA Cup, winning the competition in 1978 under coach Kees Rijvers. Bastia provided the opposition for PSV's first appearance in a European final, but the Corsican team were unable to contend with the attacking invention of the Van der Kerkhof twins, and PSV ran out the winners. In the Dutch league they won the title four years in succession between 2005 and 2008 and are currently Holland's most dominant club.

# Rangers

**Year formed:** *1872*
**Country:** *Scotland*
**Stadium:** *Ibrox (50,000)*
**Colours:** *Blue with white and red trim*
**Domestic Honours:**
*Championships: 51; Domestic Cups: 32*
**International Honours:** *European Cup Winners Cup: 1 (1972)*

By the year 2000, Rangers had become the pre-eminent force in Scottish football. Nine league titles in the 1990s, together with nine successes in Scotland's two cup competitions, had left them with little to prove. But then Celtic struck back.

Football in Glasgow is divided along sectarian lines. Rangers fans are predominantly Protestant, while the Catholics support Celtic. So deep-rooted was the religious divide that for 44 years, after the end of World War Two, no Roman Catholic wore the blue jersey of Rangers.

*Above: Prolific goalscorer Ally McCoist spent 15 years with Rangers.*

*Below: The sublimely skilful Jim Baxter, one of Rangers' great entertainers.*

In 1989 everything changed with the much-publicized signing of the former Celtic striker Maurice Johnston. Ironically, Johnston was an immediate hit with the Ibrox faithful; the fans could hardly turn against a player who scored 51 goals in his first 110 games.

Johnston's signing was the result of the foresight and single-mindedness of manager Graeme Souness, and the financial backing of club owner David Murray. Souness had taken charge of a club that was in Celtic's shadow, having failed to win the league in eight seasons, but, with Murray's support, he built a team that soon emulated the achievements of the great Rangers teams of the 1920s and 1930s. This time, they swept all before them with a backbone of players plucked from England's First Division. Englishmen such as Graham Roberts, Mark Hateley, Terry Butcher and Trevor Steven were the new heroes, just as Scots such as

David Meiklejon, Alan Morton and Bob McPhail had starred for the inter-war teams of Willie Struth.

By the turn of the millennium, Rangers had amassed 97 successes in Scotland's three major competitions, but in Europe the club's record is far from impressive. Despite their domestic dominance, the Glasgow club has made it to just three European finals (each in the now defunct Cup Winners Cup), winning just one. That success came in 1972 when they triumphed over Moscow Dynamo 3–2 in Barcelona.

At the turn of the century the Scottish pendulum of power swung back to Celtic, despite Rangers winning the Cup in 2002. Then new manager Alex McLeish's team took the League and Cup in 2003, and won the League on the final day in 2005.

# Real Madrid

**Year formed:** *1902*

**Country:** *Spain*

**Stadium:** *Santiago Bernabeu (80,000)*

**Colours:** *White*

**Domestic Honours:**
*Championships: 31;*
*Domestic Cups: 17*

**International Honours:** *European Champions Cup: 9 (1956, 57, 58, 59, 60, 66, 98, 2000, 02); UEFA Cup: 2 (1985, 86); World Club Cup: 3 (1960, 98, 2002)*

*Above: Raúl rounds the Valéncia keeper during the 2000 Champions League Final.*

There is no bigger team in the world than Real Madrid. The Bernabeu club was the first to win the European Cup in 1956, and it has been crowned continental champions on eight further occasions. If more evidence of Real's stature were needed, just look at its 31 Spanish League Championship titles. Real Madrid is a club that invites hyperbole: it is rich, successful, stylish and passionately supported – Real fans, during a slump in 1999, threatened the players: "We will burn your Ferraris!".

The club was formed as Madrid FC in 1902, acquiring its "Real" tag some

*Below: True champions – Real Madrid celebrate the 2000 European Cup win.*

years later, after permission was granted by King Alfonso XIII, and a first Spanish championship was won in 1932. But it was in the 1950s that Real established itself among Spanish football's elite. The catalyst for the club's upward mobility was president and former player Santiago Bernabeu. Under Bernabeu, Real grew from a club that had a dilapidated ground and was virtually penniless, to become Europe's first superteam. Fittingly, Real's current home, the magnificent 80,000-seater Bernabeu stadium, is named after the club's saviour.

Real was one of the first teams to see the importance of international club football. Its committed approach to the fledgling European Cup was rewarded with successive victories in the first five seasons. Real's early dominance of the European Cup was achieved with a team of immense talent, which included the legendary forward line of Paco Gento, Alfredo Di Stefano, Ferenc Puskas and Luis Del Sol. It was a line-up that became the benchmark for future Real

Madrid teams but, although a sixth European Cup was claimed in 1966, expectation outweighed achievement.

Near the end of the century, however, Real again began a period of ascendancy. With players like Roberto Carlos, Raul, Morientes and Hierro they won the Champions League three more times in five years, beating in the finals Bayern Munich in 1998, Valéncia in 2000 and Bayer Leverkusen in 2002. They were voted the team of the 20th century, and a record ninth Champions League plus the World Club Cup came in their centenary year, after record fees had bought Luis Figo and Zinedine Zidane to the club. Ronaldo joined in 2002 and David Beckham in 2003, but the 2003–04 and 2004–05 seasons saw a decline in both performance and achievement. In 2007 and 2008 they reasserted themselves by winning the league and are currently managed temporarily by Juande Ramos.

# Red Star Belgrade

**Year formed:** *1945*

**Country:** *Serbia*

**Stadium:** *Crvena Zvezda (55,000)*

**Colours:** *White and red stripes*

**Domestic Honours:** *(Yugoslavia, Serbia-Montenegro and Serbia) Championships: 25; Domestic Cups: 22*

**International Honours:** *European Champions Cup: 1 (1991); World Club Cup: 1 (1991)*

At the start of the 1990s, Red Star Belgrade was on the brink of greatness. The club had assembled the most talented line-up in the history of Yugoslavian football, boasting the likes of Dejan Savicevic, Robert Prosinecki, Miodrag Belodedici, Darko Pancev and Ljubko Petrovic in their squad. In 1991 they had won the European Cup and, with their players making up the bulk of Yugoslavia's highly fancied international team, the future looked promising. However, the outbreak of civil war in the Balkans in 1992 took its toll on Red Star. The club's talented players were lured away to Spain and Italy, although

*Below: Dejan Savicevic is thwarted by a Marseille defender in 1991.*

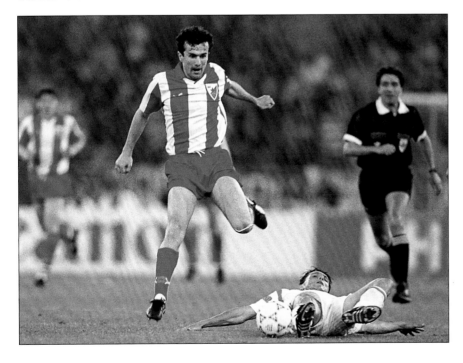

transfer fees were not always forthcoming. By 1993, the European Cup-winning team had all but disappeared and, despite continued domestic success, Red Star has yet to recover fully from its dramatic decline. Red Star Belgrade, or *Crvena Zvezda Beograd* to use its Serbian name, is a relatively young club. It was formed by Belgrade University students in 1945, but grew quickly and by the early 1950s had become the dominant force in

*Above: Red Star enjoy the moment after victory in the 1991 European Cup.*

Yugoslavian football. Red Star hinted of their potential by reaching the semi-final of the European Cup in 1957, a feat they repeated in 1971 when they lost to Panathinaikos on away goals. By 1978, Red Star were no longer underestimated in Europe, and following an away-goals victory over Hertha Berlin in the semi-final of the UEFA Cup, Red Star reached its first European final. However, Borussia Mönchengladbach proved too experienced, and won the game 2–1 on aggregate.

With the emergence of the great team of the early 1990s, Red Star mounted its next campaign in Europe. After overcoming Bayern Munich with a superb performance in the semi-final, the Yugoslavs became the favourites to beat Marseille in the 1991 European Cup Final The Yugoslavs' usual attacking football was replaced by a cagey approach. After 120 minutes of tedium, Red Star won a penalty shoot-out. After the Balkan civil war in the 1990s, Belgrade became the capital of Serbia and Montenegro and, after the secession of Montenegro in 2006, of Serbia alone.

# Santos

**Year formed:** *1912*
**Country:** *Brazil*
**Stadium:** *Vila Belmiro (25,000)*
**Colours:** *White*
**Domestic Honours:**
**International Honours:** *Copa Libertadores: 2 (1962, 63); World Club Cup: 2 (1962, 63)*

The story of Santos FC revolves around one man, the incomparable Pelé. Prior to his arrival in 1956 Santos had won little, but by the time Brazil's finest player departed for the North American Soccer League in 1974, the club had become one of the most famous in world football.

Santos was founded by three members of the Americano club in 1912, and four years later the club made its debut in the Sao Paulo State Championship. In 1935 Santos were crowned champions for the first time, just two years after the club had turned professional. However, 21 trophyless years followed, and it was not until the mid-1950s that the club began to be anything more than mediocre. The change in Santos's fortunes will, of course, always be credited to the signing of Pelé in 1956 but, in truth

*Below: Santos' squad in the 1950s included Brazil international Zito.*

the assent had already begun by the time the young genius arrived.

In 1955 and 1956 a Santos line-up that included future World Cup winners Pepe, Zito and Dorval, won consecutive State Championships. The 15-year-old Pelé arrived soon after the second of these successes and, during his 18-year stay, he helped Santos to nine championships andfive consecutive Brazilian Cups (1961–65). By the early 1960s, Pelé, who at 17 had won the World Cup with Brazil, had become *the* player to watch and Santos were *the* team. Lucrative friendlies and foreign tours dominated the Santos schedule throughout the 1960s. Despite these distractions Santos still proved themselves a team of substance and style, and in 1962 became the first Brazilian team to win the *Copa Libertadores*. As South American

*Above: The name "Santos" still remains synonomous with the legendary Pelé.*

Champions, Santos now gained the right to test themselves against their European counterparts, Benfica, in the final of the World Club Cup. The Portuguese side, which included Eusebio and Coluna, were no match for Santos, and five goals from Pelé secured an 8–4 aggregate victory.

Santos successfully defended their World and South American titles in 1963, and continued to collect trophies throughout the 1960s, but the club had reached its zenith. Pelé left for America in 1974, leaving a club in decline that collected just two Sao Paulo State Championships during the rest of the 20th century. However, the new century saw a revival, with the team winning the championship in 2002 and 2004.

# Sao Paulo

**Year formed:** *1935*
**Country:** *Brazil*
**Stadium:** *Morumbi (80,000)*
**Colours:** *White with a red and black hoop*
**Domestic Honours:** *National Championships: 5*
**International Honours:** *Copa Libertadores: 3 (1992, 93, 2005); World Club Cup: 3 (1992, 93, 2005)*

The formation of the Sao Paulo football club is a tale that seems to involve the foundation and absorption of more than a dozen smaller clubs. The fact is, though, that in December 1935 one of the most famous names

*Below: Sao Paolo's players celebrate their 2–1 victory over Barcelona in the 1992 World Club Cup.*

in Brazilian club football was born. Sao Paulo quickly made up ground on their established rivals, and by the end of the century the club had won 20 championships. Success in Brazil is measured by more than just silverware, and the followers of Sao Paulo have enjoyed a series of exciting teams featuring stars from the national team, such as Ricardo Rocha, Cafu, Leonardo, Raí, Serginho and, most recently, Denilson and Juninho.

Sao Paulo's first silverware was the 1943 State Championship, and they followed it with four further victories in the same competition during the 1940s. The following decade brought further success but, shortly after moving to the massive Morumbi stadium in 1960, Sao Paulo were cast in the shade of rivals Santos.

*Above: The powerful and versatile Raí starred for Sao Paulo in the early 1990s.*

In 1977, propelled by the goals of Serginho, the club won the National Championship. A second title was claimed in 1986, with Careca now the goalscoring hero for the club. During the early 1990s Sao Paulo, coached by former national team manager Telê Santana, enjoyed their greatest success. In 1991 Santana led Sao Paulo to their third national title and, a year later, with a team including Cafu, Rocha and Raí, the club beat Newell's Old Boys of Argentina to take its first ever *Copa Libertadores*.

The World Club Cup provided Sao Paulo's next challenge and, against European Cup holders Barcelona, Santana's team won again. Both Raí and Rocha soon departed to develop their careers with European clubs but, with a new intake of players that included Juninho and Leonardo, Sao Paulo successfully defended their South American and World crowns in 1993 and repeated the feat in 2005. They also won the Brazilian league in 2006 and 2007.

# Sparta Prague

**Year formed:** *1893*
**Country:** *Czech Republic*
**Stadium:** *AXA Arena (22,000)*
**Colours:** *Red and white*
**Domestic Honours:** *League champions: 34; Cup: 17*

The most popular club in the Czech Republic, Sparta Prague possess a proud tradition dating back more than a century. Founded in 1893 as Athletic Club Kralovske Vonobrady ("King's Vineyard"), they took their present name the following year. They won their first Czech league title in 1912 and by 1927 they had won the competition a further eight times. In 1927 they won the first Mitropa Cup, a Central European international tournament, and won it again in 1935, beating Hungary's Ferencvaros. Inside-left Oldrich Nejedly was the club's star player in the 1930s and his 170 league goals helped Sparta to three league titles that decade. He also won the 1934 World Cup Golden Boot with five goals for his country.

After World War Two, the Communist authorities forced Sparta into a number of name changes but they readopted their current name in 1965, the year

*Below: Ivan Hasek, ex-captain of Sparta, returned to coach the team in 1999.*

*Above: Czech international Tomas Skuhravy made his name with Sparta, before moving to Italian team Genoa.*

that they won their first league title, which had been monopolized by arch-rivals Dukla Prague for ten years. They took the league title again two years later but were briefly relegated in the mid-1970s when Slovan Bratislava ruled. Between 1984 and 1999, however, Sparta imposed their dominance, winning the league no less than 13 times. Since then they have won the league five times and the cup on four occasions.

In recent years, they have performed well in Europe, and, with the exception of 1996, they have been regular competitors in the Champions League since its formation in 1992. Sparta continue to dominate Czech football and will surely continue to represent their country in Europe's most prestigious tournament. Despite a takeover by wealthy German publishing group Vitava-Labe-Press, major successes in Europe are unlikely as long as the club have to sell their best players to richer sides abroad.

# Steaua Bucharest

**Year formed:** *1947*

**Country:** *Romania*

**Stadium:** *Steaua (30,000)*

**Colours:** *Red*

**Domestic Honours:**

*Championships: 23; Domestic Cups: 20*

**International Honours:** *European Champions Cup: 1 (1986); European Super Cup: 1 (1986)*

In 1986 Steaua Bucharest defeated Barcelona in a penalty shoot-out to become the first East European team to win the European Cup. Steaua was formed in 1947 and, like Dukla Prague in Czechoslovakia and CSKA Sofia in

*Below: Steaua celebrate beating Barça to the European Cup in 1986.*

Bulgaria, enjoyed a formal association with the army. By the mid-1950s Steaua had become the leading team in Romanian football, winning four league titles from 1951–56. However, in the 1960s and 1970s, Dinamo (the secret police team) became Romania's dominant club side. The balance of power switched once again between Bucharest's leading clubs in the 1980s, with Steaua benefiting from the influence of its most famous supporter, Valentin Ceauscescu, son of Romania's tyrannical dictator, Nicolae.

Opposing supporters still dismiss Steaua as "Ceauscescu's kids", a reference to the fact that Ceauscescu pressganged star players of rival teams into signing for Steaua in the 1980s. Ceauscescu's recruitment drive was

*Above: Marius Lacatus, star of Steaua's all-conquering team of 1986.*

cynical but it was successful, and in 1985 the controversially assembled all-star line-up won the "double". The following season, the club set its sights on European glory, and Steaua slipped almost unnoticed past Rangers and Anderlecht en route to the European Cup Final against Barcelona.

Barcelona were urged on by a crowd of 70,000 Catalans in Valéncia. But Steaua were unfazed by the partisan crowd and, with the steady Miodrag Belodedici in defence and Anghel Iordanescu in midfield, the Romanian champions took the game to a penalty shoot-out. It was a calculated risk, but one which paid off. Barcelona missed each of their spot kicks, while both Marius Lacatus and Gavril Balint converted theirs to secure victory.

In 1986, Steaua signed Gheorghe Hagi, arguably Romania's greatest-ever player, and the club swept to successive League and Cup "doubles" in the next three seasons. In 1989, Steaua made it to a second European Cup Final. This time the Romanians crashed to a 4–0 defeat against AC Milan.

After the end of Ceauscescu's regime, Steaua's demise was widely predicted. However, Steaua have continued to dominate the game in Romania, even if success on a wider stage is unlikely.

# Tottenham Hotspur

**Year formed:** *1882*

**Country:** *England*

**Stadium:** *White Hart Lane (36,000)*

**Colours:** *White with blue trim*

**Domestic Honours:**

*Championships: 2; Domestic (FA) Cups: 8*

**International Honours:** *European Cup Winners Cup: 1 (1963); UEFA Cup: 2 (1972, 84)*

In 1961 Tottenham Hotspur achieved what was widely believed to be the impossible; they defeated Leicester City to complete the League and FA Cup "double". Not since 1897 had a team won both major honours, but under the guidance of manager Bill Nicholson, assisted by his talented skipper Danny Blanchflower, Spurs swept the board. What is more, it was a feat attained through a rare blend of confidence and ability. Spurs did it with style.

In fact, style is a word that is often associated with Spurs – a club where the supporters share the view of their "double"-winning captain that "Football is not really about winning, or goals, or saves... it's about glory. This philosophy brought some of the world's most gifted players to White Hart Lane and, at one time or another, Jimmy Greaves, Glenn Hoddle, Osvaldo Ardiles, Chris Waddle, Paul Gascoigne, Jürgen Klinsmann, David Ginola and Sergei Rebrov have all worn the famous white shirt.

It would, however, be wrong to portray Tottenham Hotspur as a triumph of style over substance, for the White Hart Lane faithful have also been treated to their fair share of silverware. Spurs' earliest success came in 1901 when the club became the first non-league side to win the FA Cup. The North Londoners won the Cup again in 1921, but they had to wait until 1951 for their first success in the league. Then came the "double", and after successfully defending the FA

Cup, came their first European success in the Cup Winners Cup of 1963. The previous season, Spurs had entered the European Cup, losing to reigning champions Benfica at the semi-final stage but, second time around, Bill Nicholson's team made no mistake, defeating Atletico Madrid 5–1 to become the first English team to win a European trophy.

During the 1970s and 1980s, Spurs got a reputation as a cup team, twice winning the League Cup, the FA Cup and UEFA Cup. However, as the 1980s

*Above: The team of 1961 with the FA Cup that won them the "double".*

drew to a close, the club found itself in dire financial straits and, despite winning the FA Cup in 1991, Spurs were forced to sell their prize asset, Paul Gascoigne, to Lazio. Shortly afterwards, businessman Alan Sugar took over in 2001 and restored financial stability before selling to Daniel Levy, but success on the field remains hindered by unsettled management at the club between 2001 and 2008.

# Valéncia

**Year formed:** *1903*
**Country:** *Spain*
**Stadium:** *Mestalla Camp (55,000)*
**Colours:** *White*
**Domestic Honours:**
*Championships: 6; Domestic Cups: 7*
**International Honours:** *European Cup Winners Cup: 1 (1980); Fairs Cup: 2 (1962, 63); UEFA Cup 1 (2004); European Super Cup: 2 (1980, 2004)*

Valéncia have only ever enjoyed intermittent success during their hundred year history, but the team from the Luis Casanova stadium are currently basking in the glory of a well-timed resurgence. Two-time winners of the Fairs Cup and champions in the Cup Winners Cup, Valéncia regained "contender" status after a series of eyecatching displays took them to successive Champions League Finals in 2000 and 2001. Sadly they lost to Real Madrid and Bayern Munich (on penalties). However, Spanish Championships in 2002 and 2004, and

*Below: Valéncia celebrate victory in the Copa del Rey, 1999.*

the 2004 UEFA Cup, have established Valéncia as second to none in Europe.

Valéncia's first taste of success, and also their only sustained period of domestic dominance, arrived in the 1940s, when they won three League titles and twice lifted the *Copa del Rey*. The 1950s brought just one addition to the trophy collection at the Luis Casanova, and it was not until the 1960s that a return to former glories was achieved. This time Valéncia's success arrived in the Fairs Cup, which they won in 1962 with a celebrated 7–3 aggregate victory over Barcelona. It was the first of three successive Fairs Cup Finals for Valéncia, who were inspired by the goals of Vincente Guillot in 1962. The following year Valéncia were too good for Dinamo Zagreb, whom they beat 4–1 on aggregate. A hat trick of titles proved elusive, and in 1964 Real Zaragoza wrestled the Fairs Cup from Valéncia's grip with a late goal in the final.

Sixteen years passed between Valéncia's third and fourth European finals, but in 1980, with an expensively assembled team that included Argentina's 1978 World Cup-winning striker Mario Kempes, success was achieved in the Cup Winners Cup Final. This time the

*Above: Spanish internationals David Villa (right) and David Silva (left) celebrate scoring for Valencia.*

vanquished team were Arsenal, although the Spaniards required a penalty shoot-out to win.

Valéncia's current renaissance began under the stewardship of Italian coach Claudio Ranieri, who attracted a number of South American superstars to the club in the late-1990s, among them Romario, Aerial Ortega and Claudio Lopez. Ranieri's efforts came to fruition in 1999 when he led Valéncia to victory in the *Copa del Rey* and to fourth place in the League. The Argentine coach left the club in the summer of 1999 and was replaced by the Argentine Hector Cuper. The European Champions Cup Final was reached in both 2000 and 2001 before Cuper left for Inter, and, under coach Rafa Benitez, Valéncia won the Spanish Championship in 2002 and 2004, and the UEFA Cup in 2004. Valencia are now managed by Unai Emery, following an unsuccessful spell under Ronald Koeman.

# The Great Teams

When gifted individual players with complementary skills work together, the result can be sublime. Here we look at some unforgettable dream teams.

## Italy, 1934–38

**Honours:** *World Cup winners 1934, 1938; Olympic Champions, 1936*

In 1934, Mussolini's Italy hosted the World Cup finals. Under manager Vittorio Pozzo, they had exploited the "Orundi" (Argentinians of Italian descent), and three of the team, including captain Luisito Monti, were technically Argentinian. Their great forwards Giuseppe Meazza and Giovanni Ferrari played in the finals, and the team defeated the USA 7–1, Spain 1–0 in a second-round replay and Austria 1–0 to reach the Final against Czechoslovakia. Although the Czechs took the lead, Angelo Schiavo's extra-time goal won the World Cup for the host nation. In 1936 they won the Olympics, beating Austria 2–1 in the final, and in 1938 they went to France for the World Cup finals. Of the 1934 team only Ferrari and Meazza played in the tournament. Silvio Paolo's late goal

*Below: Hungary celebrate another goal in their 1953 6–3 thrashing of England.*

*Above: Italy's captain Guiseppe Meazza is led off the pitch after Italy beat Spain in the World Cup finals of 1934.*

saw off Norway, and he scored two more against France to win 3–1. Against Brazil in the semi-final a penalty from Meazza proved the winner in a 2–1 victory. Italy took on Hungary in the final where a determined performance by Italy was too much for a Gyorgy Sarosi-inspired Hungary, and a Piola goal towards the end saw Italy claim the World Cup for the second time in succession.

## Hungary, 1952–56

**Honours:** *Olympic Champions, 1952, World Cup runners-up, 1954*

The "Mighty Magyars", featuring Zoltan Czibor, Sandor Kocsis, Nandor Hidegkuti and Ferenc Puskas were the most feared side in Europe in the early 1950s. They won the 1952 Olympics and came to Wembley to play England in a friendly match in 1953. They astonished England by giving them a 6–3 football lesson, England's first defeat by a foreign side at home; further humiliation followed six months later with a 7–1 hammering in Budapest. In the 1954 World Cup, Hungary won their quarter-final against Brazil 4–2. The game was known as the "Battle of Berne" as three players were sent off and a mass brawl occurred after the match. In the semi-final Hungary met Uruguay. The game was 2–2 in extra time until Kocsis scored twice for a 4–2 win. In the final against West Germany, the score was 2–2 after only 18 minutes. Hungary piled on the pressure, but Germany scored the winner with six minutes to go. Hungary had failed to win the trophy their talent demanded, and the side was to disintegrate in the wake of the Hungarian Revolution of 1956, as its key players left for the West.

## Benfica, 1960–69

**Honours:** *European Cup winners, 1961, 1962; Portuguese Champions 1959–60, 1960–1, 1962–3, 1963–4, 1964–5, 1966–7, 1968–9; Portuguese Cup winners 1962, 1964, 1969*

The Hungarian Bela Guttmann coached Benfica to outstanding success in Europe in the early 1960s. The club broke the stranglehold of Real Madrid and, with such players as midfielder Mario Coluña, striker José Aguas and goalkeeper Costa Pereira, they won the European Cup in 1961, beating Barcelona 3–2. With the brilliant Eusebio now leading the attack, Benfica won the trophy again in 1962, beating Real Madrid 5–3, with the two winning goals coming from Eusebio. Without Guttman, Benfica reached their third final in 1963 against Milan at Wembley. Eusebio scored in the eighteenth minute with a fine solo goal but Brazilian forward José Altafini pulled back two in the second half to give Milan a 2–1 victory. Two years later Benfica were again in the final, but a defensive performance by Inter Milan in the San Siro saw them defeated 1–0. The team, with Eusebio still in attack, played their fifth final of the decade in 1968 and lost again, this time to Manchester United and three extra-time goals. The Benfica team was now an ageing one and their glorious period had come to an end.

## England, 1966

**Honours:** *World Cup winners, 1966*

Alf Ramsey was appointed England manager in 1963 and appointed Bobby Moore as captain. Over the next three years he added Gordon Banks in goal, Ray Wilson and George Cohen as full-backs, with Jackie Charlton in the central defensive role. Alan Ball and Martin Peters controlled midfield with Bobby Charlton and his Manchester United teammate Nobby Stiles, while upfront toiled Jimmy Greaves and Roger Hunt. In the 1966 World Cup, England began with a disappointing 0–0 draw with Uruguay, but won their next two matches, against Mexico and France, 2–0. Geoff Hurst, who had replaced the injured Greaves, scored the winner in a bad-tempered quarter-final against Argentina, and in the semi-final, Bobby Charlton's two goals were too much for Eusebio's Portugal. Against West Germany in the final on 30 July at Wembley, where England had played all their games, Helmut Haller scored first but Hurst and then Peters made the score 2–1. In the last minute Wolfgang Weber scored to take the game into extra time, where a hotly disputed Hurst goal and then a 20-yard effort for his hat trick gave England their first and only World Cup triumph.

## Celtic, 1967

**Honours:** *European Cup winners, 1967*

Jock Stein had taken over as Celtic manager in 1965 and set about transforming the fortunes of the club. Rangers had been dominant in Scottish football since 1960 but Stein's fast,

*Above: English heroes Nobby Stiles, Bobby Moore, Geoff Hurst and Martin Peters with the 1966 World Cup trophy.*

exciting side had won the league title for the first time in 12 years. Big Billy McNeill was captain and centre-half, and Jimmy Johnstone chief tormentor on the right wing, while Bobby Murdoch and Bertie Auld schemed in midfield. Steve Chalmers and Bobby Lennox were the chief scorers. The club made its first appearance in the European Cup in 1966–67, knocking out FC Zürich 5–0, Nantes 6–2 and Vjvodina Novi Sad 2–1 in the quarter-final, thanks to a McNeill headed winner. Two goals from Chalmers helped finish off Dukla Prague 3–1 in the semi-final, and Celtic were through to meet Inter Milan in Lisbon in the final. Although Sandro Mazzola scored first for Inter, a screamer of a goal from attacking left-back Tommy Gemmell equalized. With seven minutes left, Chalmers touched in a Murdoch cross, and Celtic became the first British club to win the European Cup. Celtic went on to win a further eight league titles and seven Scottish Cups under Stein, but this was the club's finest moment.

## Manchester United, 1968

**Honours:** *European Cup winners, 1968*

Matt Busby's great Manchester United team, featuring George Best, Denis Law and Bobby Charlton, had reached the semi-final of the European Cup in 1966, only to lose 2–1 to Partizan Belgrade. They were back in 1968, having won the English League, and they dispatched Hibernians Malta and Sarajevo in the opening rounds. Best and a young Brian Kidd both scored against Gornik Zabrze at Old Trafford and Gornik could only score one in Poland. United now had to meet Real Madrid in the semi-final. A Best goal at Old Trafford gave them a 1–0 lead to take to the Bernabeu. With 18 minutes to go, Real were 3–1 ahead on the night but a David Sadler goal and Foulkes' conversion of a Best cross, with just five minutes remaining, scraped United through to face Benfica in the final at Wembley. Charlton opened the scoring and Graca equalized towards the end of normal time. In extra time, a goal from Best and one each from Kidd and Charlton made the final score 4–1. Manchester United were the first English team to lift the European Cup.

## Ajax, 1971–73

**Honours:** *European Cup winners 1971, 1972, 1973; Dutch league champions: 71–72, 72–73; Dutch Cup winners 1971, 1972*

The authoritarian Ajax manager Rinus Michels had discovered the brilliant young forward Johan Cruyff and had designed the philosophy of "total football" around him. Also in his exciting side were the midfielders Johan Neeskens and Arie Haan, winger Piet Keizer, attacking full-back Ruud Krol and the youngster Johnny Rep. The club had reached the 1969 European Cup Final, losing 4–1 to an experienced AC Milan team, but they were back in the final in 1971. Centre-forward Dick Van Dijk and Haan both scored in Ajax's 2–0 defeat of Panathinaikos. The next season, with Stefan Kovacs having taken over from Barcelona-bound Michels, they again reached the final, against Inter Milan. Cruyff scored after a defensive error and then made it 2–0 with a header, and only some stout goalkeeping saved Inter from a much higher scoreline. In 1972–3, a 4–0 thrashing of Bayern Munich in the quarter-final and two wins over Real Madrid in the semis took Ajax through to their third successive final, against Juventus. Johnny Rep scored the winning goal in the sixth minute in what proved a disappointing game, but Ajax had now won the European Cup three times in succession, the first team to do so since Real Madrid. The departure of Cruyff and Neeskens to Barcelona took the heart out of the side; they would not triumph in the European Cup again until 1995.

*Below: Ajax's Johhny Rep (front) celebrates after scoring against Juve in the 1973 European Cup Final.*

## Bayern Munich, 1974–76

**Honours:** *European Cup winners 1974, 1975, 1976; West German league champions 1973–74*

West German and Bayern Munich captain Franz Beckenbauer was the mastermind behind Bayern's three-year reign as European champions in the 1970s. The attacking sweeper led a team of German internationals, including Gerd Müller, Paul Breitner, Sepp Maier, Uli Hoeness and Georg Schwarzenbeck, and they were a formidable side in the European Cup. They claimed their first trophy in 1974, beating Atlético Madrid 4–1 in a replay. In 1975 they won a toughly contested final against Leeds United. In the 1975–76 tournament Müller scored twice in Bayern's 5–0 crushing of Benfica in the quarter-final, and twice in the semi-final against Real Madrid. Bayern, now with a young Karl-Heinz Rummenigge in the first team, faced Saint Etienne in the final, and a goal from Franz Roth gave Bayern their third European Cup. As with Ajax three years previously, the star players then began to leave. It took until 2001 for Bayern to regain the European Cup.

## Liverpool, 1974–83

**Honours:** *European Cup winners 1977, 1978, 1981; UEFA Cup winners 1976; League title winners 1975–76, 1976–77, 1978–79, 1979–80, 1981–2, 1982–3, 1983–4; FA Cup winners 1974; League Cup winners 1981, 1982, 1983*

The managership of Bob Paisley brought Liverpool more major honours than any other club in the British game. Inheriting Bill Shankly's squad, he shrewdly added to it with the acquisition of Kenny Dalglish, Graeme Souness and Alan Hansen, and he had the finest club in European football for almost a decade. Aside from their many domestic honours, Liverpool won three European Cups under his guidance. In 1977, they triumphed over Borussia Mönchengladbach 3–1 in a thrilling match; the next year, in a less than exciting final against Bruges, Dalglish's delicate chip proved the difference between the two sides; and in 1981 defender Alan Kennedy scored the only goal against Real Madrid. Liverpool won seven league titles during Paisley's reign, three in succession between 1982 and 1984, and they won the League Cup three times between 1981 and 1983. Paisley left the club before Liverpool's victory in the 1984 European Cup Final against Roma, but his astute buying of players included keeper Bruce Grobbelaar and Ian Rush, both of whom would play their parts in the 1984 European campaign.

## AC Milan, 1988–94

**Honours:** *European Cup winners 1989, 1990, 1994; Italian league champions 1987–88, 1991–92, 1992–93, 1993–94*

Millionaire-businessman Silvio Berlusconi bought the debt-ridden, sleeping giant AC Milan in 1986, and he had turned the club into the best in Europe within just three years.

*Above: Souness, Dalglish and Hansen, Liverpool's heroes of the 1970s and 80s.*

Berlusconi bought three hugely talented Dutchmen, Ruud Gullit, Marco Van Basten and Frank Rijkaard, who lined up alongside classy defenders Franco Baresi and Paolo Maldini, and Roberto Donadoni in midfield. Berlusconi also hired coach Arrigo Sacchi, and in 1988, Milan won their first *Serie A* title for nine years. The following season, they won the European Cup – Gullit and Van Basten both scoring twice in their 4–0 defeat of Steaua Bucharest. In 1990 they won again with a 1–0 victory over Benfica. Sacchi left to run the Italian national side and former player Fabio Capello took over. Milan won the *Serie A* three times from 1992 to 1994, but lost the 1993 European Cup Final 1–0 to Marseille. By 1994 Van Basten had retired but Capello had bought "the genius" Dejan Savicevic and Gianluigi Lentini. Milan reached the European Cup Final that year against Barcelona. In an outstanding performance from the Italians, they humbled Barcelona 4–0, with Daniele Massaro scoring a hat trick and Savicevic scoring one. However, a decline then set in, and Milan lost the 1995 final to a youthful Ajax side.

## Juventus, 1994–98

**Honours:** *European Cup winners 1996; Italian league champions 1994–95, 1996–97, 1997–98*

When coach Marcello Lippi took over the venerable old club Juventus in 1994, he already had in the side such quality players as Gianluca Vialli, Fabrizio Ravanelli, Roberto Baggio, the young Alessandro Del Piero, Paulo Sousa and Didier Deschamps. They won their first *Serie A* title for nine years in 1994–5, and reached the European Cup Final the following year to play Ajax. Ravanelli scored an early goal for Juventus, then Jari Litmanen equalized, but Juventus won in a penalty shoot-out. In 1996–7, now with Christian Vieri, Alen Boksic and French playmaker Zinedine Zidane, Juve won the *Serie A* title, but lost the European Cup Final 3–1 to an unfancied Borussia Dortmund. Lippi's team won the League again in 1997–8, with new striker Filippo Inzaghi and midfielder Edgar Davids, and they knocked out Kiev Dynamo and Monaco to reach their third European Cup Final, this time against Real Madrid. A Predrag Mijatovic-strike sealed the game for Real, and the next season Lippi was sacked. Juventus, however, remain a force to be reckoned with are sure to be back.

# The Great Games

"To say that these men paid their shillings to watch 22 hirelings kick a ball is merely to say that a violin is wood and catgut, that Hamlet is so much paper and ink." J.B. Priestley on the nature of football in *The Good Companions*, 1929.

Whether or not football is a game that has entertainment as its primary objective is something about which there is much disagreement. To some, it is "the beautiful game", a spectacle that should aim to lift the sprits of the dourest of souls, while to others, any pleasure derived by those watching is no more than a fortunate by-product of an activity that is essentially for the benefit of its participants. Whatever its driving force, and whether by accident or design, the game of football is undoubtedly capable of creating engaging drama of which any scriptwriter would be proud. To illustrate the round ball's ability to both surprise and entertain we have selected five of the most memorable matches in footballing history.

*Below: Real Madrid v Eintracht Frankfurt, arguably the most entertaining game ever played.*

## Great Upset

### United States 1 England 0
*29 June 1950, Belo Horizonte, World Cup finals*

A classic David and Goliath tale. England, with Finney, Mortensen, Mannion and Wright, took to the field with a record of 22 wins in their 28 games since World War Two. The USA had no international pedigree and their star player was captain Eddie McIlvenny, a Scotsman from Third Division Wrexham. A bumpy pitch, a hostile crowd, the effects of a long domestic season, a touch of arrogance and a headed goal from Eddie Gaetjens proved England's undoing. Walter Winterbottom's team had missed a hatful of chances, but there was no excuse for such an embarrassing result.

## Ten-goal Thriller

### Real Madrid 7
### Eintracht Frankfurt 3
*18 May 1960, Hampden Park, European Cup Final*

In the book of unlikely results, a chapter must surely be reserved for the highest-scoring European Cup Final in history. Ten-goal thrillers are infrequent fare at any level of football, so the fact that this festival of scoring came in a European Cup Final makes it all the more remarkable. The match saw the mighty Real Madrid claim their fifth successive continental crown, but it was Eintracht Frankfurt's commendable, though perhaps foolhardy, attacking approach that made it a memorable encounter and scoreline. Eintracht took the lead after 18 minutes but were soon pegged back by a goal from Alfredo Di Stefano. The Argentinian completed his hat trick in the second half – a feat exceeded by Puskas who scored four times. For the record, the other two Eintracht goals both came from veteran winger Kress. The 127,000-strong crowd at Hampden Park patiently waited behind to applaud Real off the field at the end of the game.

## Great Comeback

### North Korea 3 Portugal 5
*23 July 1966, Goodison Park, World Cup finals*

A meeting between North Korea and Portugal is not a match that would normally be expected to throw up a classic encounter. However, in 1966, on Merseyside, these two teams produced one of football's most memorable comebacks. North Korea, who had already caused a stir by beating Italy, took a first-minute lead and cruised 3–0 ahead after 30 minutes against Portugal, who had themselves already beaten holders Brazil. However, as every good cliché-wielding commentator knows, it only takes a minute to score a goal and, with an hour left on the clock, Portugal finally woke up. The great Eusebio took control of the match, scoring twice before half-time to bring the Koreans into range. Two more goals from Eusebio after the break took the Portuguese into the lead, before Augusto completed the scoring.

Above: Olé Gunnar Solskjaer scores the dramatic winner in the dying moments of the 1999 European Cup Final.

Below: Savo Milosevic was among Yugoslavia's scorers against Spain.

## Late, Late Show
**Manchester United 2**
**Bayern Munich 1**
*26 May 1999, Camp Nou, European Cup Final*

For 90 minutes, the 1999 European Cup Final was in no sense remarkable. Bayern Munich, the slight underdogs, had taken the lead in the ninth minute through Mario Basler and, although both teams had created chances, neither side had added to the scoreline as the match entered stoppage time. Teddy Sheringham was the first to strike for United, turning home a Ryan Giggs cross. Fellow substitute Olé Gunnar Solskjaer then struck the winner deep into added time, after a corner from David Beckham. The Germans were distraught, but for Alex Ferguson's team the frustrations of a stuttering performance were forgotten after a breathtaking three minutes, in which they secured the greatest prize in European club football.

## Thriller with a Late Twist
**Spain 4 Yugoslavia 3**
*21 June 2000, Jan Breydel Stadium, Bruges, European Championships*

It was the last game of the group stage. Spain had to win and Yugoslavia had only to draw to progress. By half-time Yugoslavia were 2–1 up. Munitis equalized in the second half, but a ten-man Yugoslavia delighted their fans by scoring with 15 minutes to go. On the stroke of normal time, Mendieta equalized with a penalty. Deep into injury time, with Spain pouring forward and Yugoslavia defending desperately, Alfonso sent a half-volley crashing into the Yugoslav net. The whistle went and the final score was 4–3 to Spain, who qualified. The dejected Yugoslav crowd filed out of the stadium, but then came the news that Norway had drawn with Slovenia: Yugoslavia would go through. The party continued late into the night.

# World Cup Results

## 1930 (Uruguay)

The tournament was divided into four groups, with the winners of each group proceeding to the semi-finals.

**Semi-finals**
Argentina 6 v United States 1
Uruguay 6 v Yugoslavia 1
**Final**
Uruguay 4 v Argentina 2. Montevideo, 90,000.
**Uruguay**: Ballesteros, Nasazzi, Mascheroni, Andrade, Fernandez, Gestido, Dorado (1), Scarone, Castro (1), Cea (1), Iriarte (1)
**Argentina**: Botazzo, Torre, Paternoster, J Evaristo, Monti, Suarez, Peucelle (1), Varallo, Stabile (1), Ferreira, M Evaristo

## 1934 (Italy)

The format was changed this year to straight knockout between 16 teams.

**Semi-finals**
Italy 1 v Austria 0
Czechoslovakia 3 v Germany 1

**Final**
Italy 2 v Czechoslovakia 1; after extra time. Rome, 55,000.
**Italy**: Combi, Monzeglio, Allemandi, Ferraris, Monti, Bertolini, Guaita, Meazza, Schiavio (1), Ferrari, Orsi (1)
**Czechoslovakia**: Planicka, Zenisek, Ctyrocky, Kostalek, Cambal, Krcil, Junek, Svoboda, Sobotka, Nejedly, Puc (1)

## 1938 (France)

Fifteen countries competed for this year's knockout, Sweden receiving a bye in the first round.

**Semi-finals**
Italy 2 v Brazil 1
Hungary 5 v Sweden 1

**Final**
Italy 4 v Hungary 2. Paris, 45,000.
**Italy**: Olivieri, Fona, Rava, Serantoni, Andreolo, Locatelli, Biavati, Meazza, Piola (2), Ferrari, Colaussi (2)
**Hungary**: Szabo, Polgar, Biro, Szalay, Szucs, Lazar, Sas, Vincze, Sarosi (1), Szengeller, Titkos (1)

## 1950 (Brazil)

For this year's competition, a league system replaced the knockout format. The authorities had neglected to schedule a final, but fortunately the last game in the league group, Uruguay v Brazil, was the deciding match.

**Final pool**

|         | P | W | D | L | F  | A  | Pts |
|---------|---|---|---|---|----|----|-----|
| Uruguay | 3 | 2 | 1 | 0 | 7  | 5  | 5   |
| Brazil  | 3 | 2 | 0 | 1 | 14 | 4  | 4   |
| Sweden  | 3 | 1 | 0 | 2 | 6  | 11 | 2   |
| Spain   | 3 | 0 | 1 | 2 | 4  | 11 | 1   |

**Final**
Uruguay 2 v Brazil 1. Rio de Janeiro, 199,854.
**Uruguay**: Maspoli, Gonzalez, Tejera, Gambetta, Varela, Andrade, Ghiggia (1), Perez, Miguez, Schiaffino (1), Moran
**Brazil**: Barbosa, Augusto, Juvenal, Bauer, Danilo, Bigode, Friaca (1), Zizinho, Ademir, Jair, Chico

## 1954 (Switzerland)

A knockout system was re-introduced after the group matches.

**Semi-finals**
Hungary 4 v Uruguay 2
West Germany 6 v Austria 1

**Final**
West Germany 3 v Hungary 2; after extra time. Berne, 60,000.
**West Germany**: Turek, Posipal, Kohlmeyer, Eckel, Liebrich, Mai, Rahn (2), Morlock (1), O Walter, F Walter, Schaefer
**Hungary**: Grosics, Buzansky, Lantos, Bozsik, Zakarias, Lorant, Czibor (1), Kocsis, Hidegkuti, Puskas (1), Toth

## 1958 (Sweden)

**Semi-finals**
Brazil 5 v France 2
Sweden 3 v West Germany 1

**Final**
Brazil 5 v Sweden 2. Stockholm, 47,937.
**Brazil**: Gilmar, D Santos, N Santos, Zito, Bellini, Orlando, Garrincha, Didi, Vava (2), Pelé (2), Zagallo (1)
**Sweden**: Svensson, Bergmark, Axbom, Borjesson, Gustavsson, Parling, Hamrin, Gren, Simonsson (1), Liedholm (1), Skoglund

## 1962 (Chile)

**Semi-finals**
Brazil 4 v Chile 2
Czechoslovakia 3 v Yugoslavia 1

**Final**
Brazil 3 v Czechoslovakia 1. Santiago, 68,679.
**Brazil**: Gilmar, D Santos, N Santos, Zito (1), Mauro, Zozimo, Garrincha, Didi, Vava (1), Amarildo (1), Zagallo
**Czechoslovakia**: Scroiff, Tichy, Novak, Pluskal, Popluhar, Masopust (1), Pospichal, Scherer, Kvasnak, Kadraba, Jelinek

## 1966 (England)

**Semi-finals**
England 2 v Portugal 1
West Germany 2 v USSR 1

**Final**
England 4 v West Germany 2; after extra time. London, 93,802.
**England**: Banks, Cohen, Wilson, Stiles, J Charlton, Moore, Ball, Hunt, Hurst (3), R Charlton, Peters (1)
**West Germany**: Tilkowski, Hottges, Schulz, Weber (1), Schnellinger, Haller (1), Beckenbauer, Overath, Seeler, Held, Emmerich

## 1970 (Mexico)

**Semi-finals**
Italy 4 v West Germany 3; after extra time
Brazil 3 v Uruguay 1

**Final**
Brazil 4 v Italy 1. Mexico City, 107,000.
**Brazil**: Felix, Carlos Alberto (1), Brito, Piazza, Everaldo, Clodoaldo, Gerson (1), Jairzinho (1), Tostao, Pelé (1), Rivelino
**Italy**: Albertosi, Burgnich, Cera, Rosato, Facchetti, Bertini (Juliano), Mazzola, De Sisti, Domenghini, Boninsegna (1) (Rivera), Riva

## 1974 (West Germany)

The winners and second-placed teams in the first four groups moved to a further two groups of four, with the two winners playing each other in the final.

**Group A**

|           | P | W | D | L | F | A | Pts |
|-----------|---|---|---|---|---|---|-----|
| Holland   | 3 | 3 | 0 | 0 | 8 | 0 | 6   |
| Brazil    | 3 | 2 | 0 | 1 | 3 | 3 | 4   |
| E Germany | 3 | 0 | 1 | 2 | 1 | 4 | 1   |
| Argentina | 3 | 0 | 1 | 2 | 2 | 7 | 1   |

**Group B**

|            | P | W | D | L | F | A | Pt |
|------------|---|---|---|---|---|---|----|
| W Germany  | 3 | 3 | 0 | 0 | 7 | 2 | 6  |
| Poland     | 3 | 2 | 0 | 1 | 3 | 2 | 4  |
| Sweden     | 3 | 1 | 0 | 2 | 4 | 6 | 2  |
| Yugoslavia | 3 | 0 | 0 | 3 | 2 | 6 | 0  |

## Final

West Germany 2 v Holland 1. Munich, 77,833.
**West Germany:** Maier, Vogts, Schwarzenbeck, Beckenbauer, Breitner (1 pen), Bonhof, Hoeness, Grabowski, Müller (1), Overath, Holzenbein
**Holland:** Jongbloed, Suurbier, Rijsbergen (De Jong), Haan, Krol, Jansen, Van Hanegem, Neeskens (1 pen), Rep, Cruyff, Rensenbrink (Van der Kerkhof)

# 1978 (Argentina)

### Group A

|          | P | W | D | L | F | A | Pts |
|----------|---|---|---|---|---|---|-----|
| Holland  | 3 | 2 | 1 | 0 | 9 | 4 | 5   |
| Italy    | 3 | 1 | 1 | 1 | 2 | 2 | 3   |
| W Germany| 3 | 0 | 2 | 1 | 4 | 5 | 2   |
| Austria  | 3 | 1 | 0 | 2 | 4 | 8 | 2   |

### Group B

|           | P | W | D | L | F | A  | Pts |
|-----------|---|---|---|---|---|----|-----|
| Argentina | 3 | 2 | 1 | 0 | 8 | 0  | 5   |
| Brazil    | 3 | 2 | 1 | 0 | 6 | 1  | 5   |
| Poland    | 3 | 1 | 0 | 2 | 2 | 5  | 2   |
| Peru      | 3 | 0 | 0 | 3 | 0 | 10 | 0   |

### Final

Argentina 3 v Holland 1; after extra time. Buenos Aires, 77,000.
**Argentina:** Fillol, Olguin, Galvan, Passarella, Tarantini, Ardiles (Larrosa), Gallego, Ortiz (Houseman), Bertoni (1), Luque, Kempes (2)
**Holland:** Jongbloed, Jansen (Suurbier), Krol, Brandts, Poortvliet, Haan, Neeskens, W Van der Kerkhov, Rep (Nanninga 1), R Van der Kerkhov, Rensenbrink

# 1982 (Spain)

The second round was expanded into four groups of three, with the winners proceeding to the semi-finals.

### Semi-finals

Italy 2 v Poland 0
West Germany 3 v France 3;
West Germany won 5–4 on penalties

### Final

Italy 3 West Germany 1. Madrid, 90,000.
**Italy:** Zoff, Cabrini, Scirea, Gentile, Collovati, Oriali, Bergomi, Tardelli (1), Conti, Rossi (1), Graziani (Altobelli 1)
**West Germany:** Schumacher, Kaltz, Stielike, K Forster, B Forster, Breitner (1), Breigel, Dremmler (Hrubesch), Rummenigge (Müller), Littbarski, Fischer

# 1986 (Mexico)

For this tournament, the league system was dropped for the second round and replaced by knock-outs.

### Semi-finals

West Germany 2 v France 0
Argentina 2 v Belgium 0

### Final

Argentina 3 v West Germany 2. Mexico City, attendance 115,000.
**Argentina:** Pumpido, Cuciuffo, Brown (1), Ruggeri, Olarticoechea, Batista, Giusti, Enrique, Burruchaga (1) (Trobbiani), Maradona, Valdano (1)
**West Germany:** Schumacher, Jakobs, K Forster, Briegel, Brehme, Eder, Berthold, Matthäus, Magath (Hoeness), Rummenigge (1), Allofs (Voller (1))

# 1990 (Italy)

### Semi-finals

Argentina 1 v Italy 1; Argentina won 4–3 on penalties
West Germany 1 v England 1; West Germany won 4–3 on penalties

### Final

West Germany 1 v Argentina 0. Rome, 73,603.
**West Germany:** Illgner, Berthold (Reuter), Kohler, Augenthaler, Buchwald, Brehme (1), Hassler, Matthäus, Littbarski, Voller, Klinsmann
**Argentina:** Goycochea, Ruggeri (Monzon), Simon, Serrizuela, Sensini, Basualdo, Burruchaga (Calderon), Troglio, Lorenzo, Maradona, Dezotti

# 1994 (USA)

### Semi-finals

Italy 2 v Bulgaria 1
Brazil 1 v Sweden 0

### Final

Brazil 0 v Italy 0; Brazil won 3–2 on penalties. Pasadena, 94,000.
**Brazil:** Taffarel, Jorghino (Cafu), Aldair, Marcio Santos, Branco, Mazinho, Mauro Silva, Dunga, Zinho (Viola), Romario, Bebeto
**Italy:** Pagliuca, Mussi (Apolloni), Baresi, Maldini, Benarrivo, Berti, Albertini, D Baggio (Evani), Donadoni, R Baggio, Massaro
**Penalty shoot-out:** Baresi misses, 0–0; Marcio Santos misses, 0–0; Albertini scores, 0–1; Romario scores, 1–1; Evani scores, 1–2; Branco scores, 2–2; Massaro misses, 2–2; Dunga scores, 3–2; R Baggio misses 3–2.

# 1998 (France)

### Semi-finals

Brazil 1 v Holland 1; Brazil won 4–2 on penalties
France 2 v Croatia 1

### Final

France 3 v Brazil 0. St Denis, Paris, 75,000.
**France:** Barthez, Thuram, Leboeuf, Desailly, Lizarazu, Karembeu (Boghossian), Deschamps, Zidane (2), Petit (1), Djorkaeff (Vieira), Guivarc'h (Dugarry)
**Brazil:** Taffarel, Cafu, Aldair, Baiano, Roberto Carlos, Leonardo (Denilson), Cesar Sampaio (Edmundo), Dunga, Rivaldo, Ronaldo, Bebeto

# 2002 (Japan and South Korea)

### Semi-finals

Brazil 1 v Turkey 0
Germany 1 v South Korea

### Final

Brazil 2 v Germany 0. Yokohama, 69,029.
**Brazil:** Marcos, Lucio, Roque Junior, Edmilson, Cafu, Kleberson, Gilberto Silva, Roberto Carlos, Rivaldo, Ronaldinho (Juninho), Ronaldo (2) (Denilson)
**Germany:** Kahn, Linke, Ramelow, Metzelder, Frings, Schneider, Hamann, Jeremies (Asamoah), Bode (Ziege), Neuville, Klose (Bierhoff)

# 2006 (Germany)

### Semi-finals

Italy 2 v Germany 0
France 2 v Portugal 0

### Final

Italy 1 v France 1. Italy won 5–3 on penalties. Berlin, 69,000.
**Italy:** Buffon, Zambrotta, Cannavaro, Materazzi (1), Grosso, Camoranesi (Del Piero), Pirlo, Gattuso, Perrotta (Iaquinta), Totti (De Rossi), Toni
**France:** Barthez, Sagnol, Thuram, Gallas, Abidal, Ribery (Trezeguet), Vieira (Diarra), Makelele, Zidane (1), Malouda, Henry (Wiltord)

# International Results

## EUROPEAN CHAMPIONSHIP

### 1960
USSR 2 v Yugoslavia 1. Paris, 18,000.
**USSR:** Yashin, Tchekeli, Kroutilov, Voinov, Maslenkin, Netto, Metreveli (1), Ivanov, Ponedelnik (1), Bubukin, Meshki
**Yugoslavia:** Vidinic, Durkovic, Zanetic, Jusufi, Miladinovic, Perusic, Sekularac, Jerkovic, Matus, Galic (1), Kostic

### 1964
Spain 2 v USSR 1. Madrid, 120,000.
**Spain:** Iribar, Olivella, Rivilla, Calleja, Fuste, Zoco, Pereda (1), Marcelino (1), Amancio, Suarez, Lapetra
**USSR:** Yashin, Chustikov, Mudrik, Voronin, Shesterniev, Chislenko, Anitchkin, Ivanov, Kornalev, Ponedelnik, Khusainov (1)

### 1968
Yugoslavia 1 v Italy 1; after extra time. Replay Italy 2 v Yugoslavia 0. Rome, 75,000.
**Italy:** Zoff, Burgnich, Rosato, Guarneri, Facchetti, Salvadore, Domenghini, Anastasi (1), Mazzola, De Sisti, Riva (1)
**Yugoslavia:** Pantelic, Fazlagic, Damjanovic, Pavlovic, Holcer, Hosic, Paunovic, Acimovic, Trivic, Musemic, Dzajic

### 1972
West Germany 3 v USSR 0. Brussels, 43,000.
**West Germany:** Maier, Hottges, Schwarzenbeck, Beckenbauer, Breitner, Wimmer (1), Netzer, Hoeness, Heynckes, Müller (2), Kremers
**USSR:** Rudakov, Dzodzuashvili, Khurtislava, Istomin, Troshkin, Kaplichny, Kolotov, Konkov (Dolmatov), Baidachini, Banishevsky (Kozinkievits), Oninshenko

### 1976
Czechoslovakia 2 v West Germany 2; Czechoslovakia won 5–3 on penalties. Belgrade, 45,000.
**Czechoslovakia:** Viktor, Dobias (1) (Vesely), Capkovic, Ondrus, Pivarnik, Gogh, Moder, Panenka, Svehlik (1) (Jurkemik), Masny, Nehoda
**West Germany:** Maier, Beckenbauer, Schwarzenbeck, Dietz, Voigts, Bonhof, Wimmer (Flohe), Müller (1), Beer (Bongartz), Hoeness, Holzenbein (1)

### 1980
West Germany 2 v Belgium 1. Rome, 48,000.
**West Germany:** Schumacher, Kalz, Forster, Stielike, Dietz, Briegel (Cullman), Schuster, Müller, Rummenigge, Hrubesch (2), Allofs
**Belgium:** Pfaff, Gerets, Millecamps, Meeuws, Renquin, Van Moer, Cools, Vandereycken (1), Van der Elst, Mommens, Ceulemans

### 1984
France 2 v Spain 0. Paris, 48,000.
**France:** Bats, Battiston (Amoros), Le Roux, Bossis, Domergue, Fernandez, Tigana, Giresse, Platini (1), Lacombe (Genghini), Bellone (1)
**Spain:** Arconada, Urquiaga, Salva (Roberto), Gallego, Julio Alberto (Sarabia), Senor, Victor, Camacho, Francisco, Santillana, Carrasco

### 1988
Holland 2 v Soviet Union 0. Munich, 72,000.
**Holland:** Van Breukelen, Van Aerle, Rijkaard, R Koeman, Van Tiggelen, Vanenburg, Wouters, Muhren, E Koeman, Gullit (1), Van Basten (1)

### 1992
Denmark 2 v Germany 0. Gothenburg, 38,000.
**Denmark:** Schmeichel, Piechnik, Olsen, Nielsen, Sivebaek (Christiansen), Vilfort (1), Jensen (1), Larsen, Christofte, Povlsen, Laudrup
**Germany:** Illgner, Reuter, Helmer, Buchwald, Kohler, Hassler, Effenberg (Thom), Sammer (Doll), Brehme, Klinsmann, Riedle

### 1996
Germany 2 v Czech Republic 1. London, 74,000.
**Germany:** Kopke, Helmer, Babbel, Struntz, Sammer, Scholl (Bierhof 2), Eilts (Bode), Hassler, Ziege, Kuntz, Klinsmann
**Czech Republic:** Kouba, Rada, Kadlec, Suchoparek, Bejbl, Hornak, Nedved, Nemec, Berger (1pen), Poborsky (Smicer), Kuka

### 2000
France 2 v Italy 1; "golden goal" in extra time. Rotterdam, 51,000.
**France:** Barthez, Thuram, Blanc, Desailly, Lizarazu (Pires), Dugarry (Wiltord 1), Vieira, Deschamps, Zidane, Djorkaeff (Trezeguet 1), Henry
**Italy:** Toldo, Maldini, Juliano, Nesta, Cannavaro, Flore (Del Piero), Albertini, Di Bagio (Ambrosini), Pessotto, Totti, Delvecchio (1)

### 2004
Greece 1 v Portugal 0; goal scored in 57th minute. Lisbon, 62,000.
**Greece:** Nikopolidis, Seitaridis, Dellas, Basinas, Zagorakis, Giannakopoulos, Charisteas (1), Fyssas, Vryzas, Kapsis, Katsouranis, Venetidis, Papadopoulos
**Portugal:** Ricardo, Jorge Andrade, Costinha, Figo, Pauleta, Miguel, Nuno Valente, Ricardo Carvalho, Ronaldo, Maniche, Deco, Paulo Ferreira, Rui Costa, Nuno Gomes

### 2008
Germany 0 v Spain 1. Vienna, 51,000.
**Germany:** Lehmann, Friedrich, Metzelder, Mertesacker, Lahm (Jansen), Hitzlsperger (Kuranyi), Frings, Podolski, Ballack, Schweinsteiger, Klose (Gomez)
**Spain:** Casillas, Sergio Ramos, Puyol, Marchena, Capdevila, Senna, Iniesta, Fabregas (Alonso), Xavi, Silva (Santi Cazorla), Torres (1) (Guiza)

## EUROPEAN CUP
### (from 1992–93 also called the Champions League)
**1956** Real Madrid 4 (Di Stefano, Rial 2, Marquitos) v Reims 3 (Le Blond, Templin, Hidalgo). Paris, 38,000.
**1957** Real Madrid 2 (Di Stefano, Gento) v Fiorentina 0. Madrid, 124,000.
**1958** Real Madrid 3 (Di Stefano, Rial, Gento) v AC Milan 2 (Schiffiano, Grillo); after extra time. Brussels, 70,000.
**1959** Real Madrid 2 (Matteos, Di Stefano) v Reims 0. Stuttgart, 72,000.
**1960** Real Madrid 7 (Di Stefano 3, Puskas 4) v Eintracht Frankfurt 3 (Kress, Stein 2). Glasgow, 127,000.
**1961** Benfica 3 (Aguas, Ramallets og, Coluna) v Barcelona 2 (Kocsis, Czibor). Berne, 27,000.
**1962** Benfica 5 (Aguas, Cavem, Coluna, Eusebio 3) v Real Madrid 3 (Puskas 3). Amsterdam, 61,000.
**1963** AC Milan 2 (Altafini 2) v Benfica 1 (Eusebio). London, 45,000.
**1964** Internazionale 3 (Mazzola 2, Milani) v Real Madrid 1 (Feola). Vienna, 71,000.
**1965** Internazionale 1 (Jair) v Benfica 0. Milan, 89,000.
**1966** Real Madrid 2 (Amancio, Serena) v Partizan Belgrade 1 (Vasovic). Brussels, 46,000.
**1967** Celtic 2 (Gemmell, Chalmers) v Internazionale 1 (Mazzola). Lisbon, 56,000.
**1968** Manchester United 4 (Charlton 2, Best, Kidd) v Benfica 1 (Graca); after extra time. London, 100,000.
**1969** AC Milan 4 (Prati 3, Sormani) v Ajax 1 (Vasovic). Madrid, 32,000.
**1970** Feyenoord 2 (Israel, Kindvaal) v Celtic 1 (Gemmell). Milan, 53,000.
**1971** Ajax 2 (Van Dijk, Haan) v Panathinaikos 0. London, 83,000.
**1972** Ajax 2 (Cruyff 2) v Internazionale 0. Rotterdam, 61,000.
**1973** Ajax 1 (Rep) v Juventus 0. Belgrade, 90,000.
**1974** Bayern Munich 1 (Schwarzenbeck) v Atlético Madrid 1 (Aragones). Brussels, 49,000.
**1974** (replay) Bayern Munich 4 (Hoeness 2, Müller 2) v Atlético Madrid 0. Brussels, 23,000.
**1975** Bayern Munich 2 (Roth, Müller) v Leeds United 0. Paris, 50,000.
**1976** Bayern Munich 1 (Roth) v Saint Etienne 0. Glasgow, 55,000.
**1977** Liverpool 3 (McDermott, Smith, Neal) v Borussia Mönchengladbach 1 (Simonsen). Rome, 52,000.
**1978** Liverpool 1 (Dalglish) v Bruges 0. London, 92,000.
**1979** Nottingham Forest 1 (Francis) v

Malmo 0. Munich, 57,000.

**1980** Nottingham Forest 1 (Robertson) v Hamburg 0. Madrid, 50,000.

**1981** Liverpool 1 (A Kennedy) v Real Madrid 0. Paris, 48,000.

**1982** Aston Villa 1 (Withe) v Bayern Munich 0. Rotterdam, 46,000.

**1983** Hamburg 1 (Magath) v Juventus 0. Athens, 75,000.

**1984** Liverpool 1 (Neal) v Roma 1 (Pruzzo); Liverpool won 4–2 on penalties. Rome, 70,000.

**1985** Juventus 1 (Platini) v Liverpool 0. Brussels, 50,000.

**1986** Steaua Bucharest 0 v Barcelona 0; Staeua won 2–0 on penalties. Seville, 50,000.

**1987** Porto 2 (Madjer, Jaury) v Bayern Munich 1 (Kogl). Vienna, 62,000.

**1988** PSV Eindhoven 0 v Benfica 0; PSV won 6–5 on penalties. Stuttgart, 70,000.

**1989** AC Milan 4 (Gullit 2, Van Basten 2) v Steaua Bucharest 0. Barcelona, 97,000.

**1990** AC Milan 1 (Rijkaard) v Benfica 0. Vienna, 57,000.

**1991** Red Star Belgrade 0 v Marseille 0; Red Star won 5–3 on penalties. Bari, 60,000.

**1992** Barcelona 1 (Koeman) v Sampdoria 0; after extra time. London, 70,000.

**1993** Marseille 1 (Boli) v AC Milan 0. Munich, 72,000.

**1994** AC Milan 4 (Massaro 2, Savicevic, Desailly) v Barcelona 0. Athens, 57,000.

**1995** Ajax 1 (Kluivert) v AC Milan 0. Vienna, 50,000.

**1996** Juventus 1 (Ravanelli) v Ajax 1 (Litmanen); Juventus won 4–2 on penalties. Rome, 70,000.

**1997** Borussia Dortmund 3 (Riedle 2, Ricken) v Juventus 1 (Del Piero). Munich, 60,000.

**1998** Real Madrid 1 (Mijatovic) v Juventus 0. Amsterdam, 48,500.

**1999** Manchester United 2 (Sheringham, Solskjaer) v Bayern Munich 1 (Basler). Barcelona, 90,000.

**2000** Real Madrid 3 (Morientes, McManaman, Raúl) v Valéncia 0. Paris, 78,500.

**2001** Bayern Munich 1 (Effenberg) v Valéncia 1 (Mendieta); Bayern won 5–4 on penalties. Milan, 71,500.

**2002** Real Madrid 2 (Raul, Zidane) v Bayer Leverkusen 1 (Lucio). Glasgow, 51,567.

**2003** AC Milan 0 v Juventus 0; AC Milan won 3–2 on penalties. Old Trafford, 66,500.

**2004** FC Porto 3 v Monaco 0. Arena Anfschalke, Germany, 60,000.

**2005** Liverpool 3 (Gerrard, Smicer, Alonso) v AC Milan 3 (Maldini, Crespo 2); Liverpool won 3-2 on penalties. Istanbul, 65,000.

**2006** Barcelona 2 (Eto'o, Belletti) v Arsenal 1 (Campbell). Paris, 79,000.

**2007** AC Milan 2 (Inzaghi 2) v Liverpool 1 (Kuyt). Athens, 74,000.

**2008** Manchester United 1 (Ronaldo) v Chelsea 1 (Lampard); Manchester United won 6–5 on penalties. Moscow 67,000.

**2009** Barcelona 2 v Manchester United 0 (Eto'o, Messi). Rome 62,000.

## EUROPEAN CUP WINNERS CUP

**1960–61** Fiorentina
**1961–62** Atlético Madrid
**1962–63** Tottenham Hotspur
**1963–64** Sporting Lisbon
**1964–65** West Ham United
**1965–66** Borussia Dortmund
**1966–67** Bayern Munich
**1967–68** AC Milan
**1968–69** Slovan Bratislava
**1969–70** Manchester City
**1970–71** Chelsea
**1971–72** Rangers
**1972–73** AC Milan
**1973–74** FC Magdeburg
**1974–75** Kiev Dynamo
**1975–76** Anderlecht
**1976–77** Hamburg
**1977–78** Anderlecht
**1978–79** Barcelona
**1979–80** Valéncia
**1980–81** Tbilisi Dynamo
**1981–82** Barcelona
**1982–83** Aberdeen
**1983–84** Juventus
**1984–85** Everton
**1985–86** Kiev Dynamo
**1986–87** Ajax
**1987–88** Mechelen
**1988–89** Barcelona
**1989–90** Sampdoria
**1990–91** Manchester United
**1991–92** Werder Bremen
**1992–93** Parma
**1993–94** Arsenal
**1994–95** Real Zaragoza
**1995–96** Paris Saint-Germain
**1996–97** Barcelona
**1997–98** Chelsea
**1998–99** Lazio
The competition ended in 1999

## FAIRS CUP/UEFA CUP

### Industrial Inter-Cities Fairs Cup

**1955–58** Barcelona
**1958–60** Barcelona
**1960–61** Roma
**1961–62** Valéncia
**1962–63** Valéncia
**1963–64** Real Zaragoza
**1964–65** Ferencvaros
**1965–66** Barcelona
**1966–67** Dinamo Zagreb
**1967–68** Leeds United
**1968–69** Newcastle United
**1969–70** Arsenal
**1970–71** Leeds United

### UEFA Cup

**1971–72** Tottenham Hotspur
**1972–73** Liverpool

**1973–74** Feyenoord
**1974–75** Borussia Mönchengladbach
**1975–76** Liverpool
**1976–77** Juventus
**1977–78** PSV Eindhoven
**1978–79** Borussia Mönchengladbach
**1979–80** Eintracht Frankfurt
**1980–81** Ipswich Town
**1981–82** IFK Gothenburg
**1982–83** Anderlecht
**1983–84** Tottenham Hotspur
**1984–85** Real Madrid
**1985–86** Real Madrid
**1986–87** IFK Gothenburg
**1987–88** Bayer Leverkusen
**1988–89** Napoli
**1989–90** Juventus
**1990–91** Internazionale
**1991–92** Ajax
**1992–93** Juventus
**1993–94** Internazionale
**1994–95** Parma
**1995–96** Bayern Munich
**1996–97** Schalke
**1997–98** Internazionale
**1998–99** Parma
**1999–2000** Galatasaray
**2000–2001** Liverpool
**2001–2002** Feyenoord
**2002–2003** FC Porto
**2003–2004** Valéncia
**2004–2005** CSKA Moskva
**2005–2006** Sevilla
**2006–2007** Espanyol
**2007–2008** Zenit St Petersburg
**2008–2009** Shakhtar Donetsk

## MITROPA CUP

**1927** Sparta
**1928** Ferencvaros
**1929** Ujpest
**1930** Rapid
**1931** 1st FC Vienna
**1932** Bologna (Slavia banned)
**1933** Austria
**1934** Bologna
**1935** Sparta
**1936** Sparta
**1937** Ferencvaros
**1938** Slavia
**1939** Ujpest
**1955** Voros Lobogo
**1956** Vasas
**1957** Vasas
**1958** Not contested
**1959** Honved
**1960** Hungary (based on clubs representation system)
**1961** Bologna
**1962** Vasas
**1963** MTK
**1964** Sparta
**1965** Vasas
**1966** Fiorentina
**1967** Trnava
**1968** Red Star Belgrade
**1969** Inter Bratislava

1970 Vasas
1971 Zenica
1972 Zenica
1973 Tatabanya
1974 Tatabanya
1975 Swarowski Wacker Innsbruck
1976 Swarowski Wacker Innsbruck
1977 Vojvodina Novisad
1978 Partizan Belgrade
1979 Not contested
1980 Udinese
1981 Tatran Presov
1982 AC Milan
1983 Vasas Budapest
1984 Eisenstadt
1985 Iskra
1986 Pisa
1987 Ascoli
1988 Pisa
1989 Banik Ostrava
1990 Bari
1991 Torino

## LATIN CUP

**First Series 1949–52**
1949 Barcelona
1950 Benfica
1951 AC Milan
1952 Barcelona
**Second Series 1953–57**
1953 Reims
1955 Real Madrid
1956 AC Milan
1957 Real Madrid

## COPA AMERICA

1910 Argentina
1916 Uruguay
1917 Uruguay
1919 Brazil
1920 Uruguay
1921 Argentina
1922 Brazil
1923 Uruguay
1924 Uruguay
1925 Argentina
1926 Uruguay
1927 Argentina
1929 Argentina
1935 Uruguay
1937 Argentina
1939 Peru
1941 Argentina
1942 Uruguay
1945 Argentina
1946 Argentina
1947 Argentina
1949 Brazil
1953 Paraguay
1955 Argentina
1956 Uruguay
1957 Argentina
1959 Argentina
1959 Uruguay
1963 Bolivia
1967 Uruguay
1975 Peru

1979 Paraguay
1983 Uruguay
1987 Uruguay
1989 Brazil
1991 Argentina
1993 Argentina
1995 Uruguay
1997 Brazil
1999 Brazil
2001 Colombia
2004 Brazil
2007 Brazil

## COPA LIBERTADORES

1960 Penarol (Uru)
1961 Penarol (Uru)
1962 Santos (Bra) )
1963 Santos (Bra)
1964 Independiente (Arg)
1965 Independiente (Arg)
1966 Penarol (Uru)
1967 Racing Club (Arg)
1968 Estudiantes de La Plata (Arg)
1969 Estudiantes de La Plata (Arg)
1970 Estudiantes de La Plata (Arg)
1971 Nacional (Uru)
1972 Independiente (Arg)
1973 Independiente (Arg)
1974 Independiente (Arg)
1975 Independiente (Arg)
1976 Cruzeiro (Bra)
1977 Boca Juniors (Arg)
1978 Boca Juniors (Arg)
1979 Olimpia (Par)
1980 Nacional (Uru)
1981 Flamengo (Bra)
1982 Penarol (Uru)
1983 Gremio (Bra)
1984 Independiente (Arg)
1985 Argentinos Juniors (Arg)
1986 River Plate (Arg)
1987 Penarol (Uru)
1988 Nacional (Uru)
1989 Atlético Nacional Medellin (Col)
1990 Olimpia (Par)
1991 Colo Colo (Chl)
1992 Sao Paulo (Bra)
1993 Sao Paulo (Bra)
1994 Velez Sarsfield (Arg)
1995 Gremio (Bra)
1996 River Plate (Arg)
1997 Cruzeiro (Bra)
1998 Vasco da Gama (Brz)
1999 Palmeiras (Brz)
2000 Boca Juniors (Arg)
2001 Boca Juniors (Arg)
2002 Olimpia (Par)
2003 Boca Juniors (Arg)
2004 Once Caldas (Col)
2005 Sao Paulo
2006 Internacional
2007 Boca Juniors
2008 LDU Quito

## CONCACAF CHAMPIONSHIP (GOLD CUP)

1941 Costa Rica
1943 El Salvador
1946 Costa Rica
1948 Costa Rica
1951 Panama
1953 Costa Rica
1955 Costa Rica
1957 Haiti
1960 Costa Rica
1961 Costa Rica
1963 Costa Rica
1965 Mexico
1967 Guatamala
1969 Costa Rica
1971 Mexico
1973 Haiti
1977 Mexico
1981 Honduras
1985 Canada
1989 Costa Rica
1991 United States of America
1993 Mexico
1996 Mexico
1998 Mexico
2000 Canada
2002 United States of America
2003 Mexico
2005 United States of America
2007 United States of America

## ASIAN GAMES

1951 India
1954 Taiwan
1958 Taiwan
1962 India
1966 Burma
1970 Title shared by Burma and South Korea
1974 Title shared by Iran and Israel
1978 Title shared by South Korea and North Korea
1982 Iraq
1986 South Korea
1990 Iran
1994 Uzbekistan
1998 Iran

## ASIAN CUP

1956 South Korea
1960 South Korea
1964 Israel
1968 Iran
1972 Iran
1976 Iran
1980 Kuwait
1984 Saudi Arabia
1988 Saudi Arabia
1992 Japan
1996 Saudi Arabia
2000 Japan
2004 Japan
2007 Iraq

## AFRICAN NATIONS CUP

| | |
|---|---|
| **1957** | Egypt |
| **1959** | Egypt, |
| **1962** | Ethiopia |
| **1963** | Ghana |
| **1965** | Ghana |
| **1968** | Congo Kinshasa |
| **1970** | Sudan |
| **1972** | Congo |
| **1974** | Zaire |
| **1976** | Morocco |
| **1978** | Ghana |
| **1980** | Nigeria |
| **1982** | Ghana |
| **1984** | Cameroon |
| **1986** | Egypt |
| **1988** | Cameroon |
| **1990** | Algeria |
| **1992** | Ghana |
| **1994** | Nigeria |
| **1996** | South Africa |
| **1998** | Egypt |
| **2000** | Cameroon |
| **2002** | Cameroon |
| **2004** | Tunisia |
| **2006** | Egypt |
| **2008** | Egypt |

## AFRICAN CHAMPIONS CUP

| | |
|---|---|
| **1964** | Oryx Douala (Cam) |
| **1965** | Not contested |
| **1966** | Stade Abidjan (IC) |
| **1967** | Tout Puissant Englebert (Zai) |
| **1968** | TP Englebert (Zai) |
| **1969** | Al Ismaili (Egy) |
| **1970** | Asante Kotoko (Gha) |
| **1971** | Asante Kotoko (Gha) |
| **1972** | Hafia Conakry (Gui) |
| **1973** | AS Vita (Zai) |
| **1974** | CARA Brazzaville (Con) |
| **1975** | Hafia Conakry (Gui) |
| **1976** | Mouloudia Chalia (Alg) |
| **1977** | Hafia Conakry (Gui) |
| **1978** | Canon (Cam) |
| **1979** | Union Douala (Cam) |
| **1980** | Canon (Cam) |
| **1981** | Jeunesse Electronique Tizi-Ouzou (Alg) |
| **1982** | Al Ahly (Egy) |
| **1983** | Asante Kotoko (Gha) |
| **1984** | Zamalek (Egy) |
| **1985** | Forces Armees Rabat (Mor) |
| **1986** | Zamalek (Egy) |
| **1987** | Al Ahly (Egy) |
| **1988** | Entente Plasticiens (Alg) |
| **1989** | Raja Casablanca (Mor) |
| **1990** | Jeunesse Sportive Kabyle (Alg) |
| **1991** | Club Africain (Tun) |
| **1992** | Wydad Casablanca (Mor) |
| **1993** | Zamalek (Egy) |
| **1994** | Esperance Sportive (Tun) |
| **1995** | Orlando Pirates (SA) |
| **1996** | Zamalek (Egy) |
| **1997** | Raja Casablanca (Mor) |
| **1998** | ASEC Abidjan (IC) |
| **1999** | Raja Casablanca (Mor) |
| **2000** | Hearts of Oak (Gha) |

| | |
|---|---|
| **2001** | Al Ahly (Egy) |
| **2002** | Zamalek (Egy) |
| **2003** | Enyimba (Nig) |
| **2004** | Enyimba (Nig) |
| **2005** | Al-Ahly (Egy) |
| **2006** | Al-Ahly (Egy) |
| **2007** | Etoile Sahel (Tun) |
| **2008** | Al-Ahly (Egy) |

## AFRICAN CUP WINNERS CUP

| | |
|---|---|
| **1975** | Tonnerre (Cam) |
| **1976** | Shooting Stars (Nig) |
| **1977** | Enugu Rangers (Nig) |
| **1978** | Horoya AC (Gui) |
| **1979** | Canon (Cam) |
| **1980** | Tout Puissant Mazembe (Zai) |
| **1981** | Union Douala (Cam) |
| **1982** | Arab Contractors (Egy) |
| **1983** | Arab Contractors (Egy) |
| **1984** | Al Ahly (Egy) |
| **1985** | Al Ahly (Egy) |
| **1986** | Al Ahly (Egy) |
| **1987** | Gor Mahia (Ken) |
| **1988** | CA Bizerte (Tun) |
| **1989** | Al Merreikh (Sud) |
| **1990** | BCC Lions (Nig) |
| **1991** | Power Dynamos (Zam) |
| **1992** | Africa Sports (IC) |
| **1993** | Al Ahly (Egy) |
| **1994** | Daring Club (Zai) |
| **1995** | JS Kabyle (Alg) |
| **1996** | Arab Contractors (Egy) |
| **1997** | Etoile Sahel (Tun) |
| **1998** | Esperance (Tun) |
| **1999** | Africa Sports (IC) |
| **2000** | Zamalek (Egy) |
| **2001** | Kaizer Chiefs (SA) |
| **2002** | Wydad Casablanca (Mor) |
| **2003** | Etoile Sahel (Tun) |

## OLYMPIC GAMES

| | |
|---|---|
| **1908** | England |
| **1912** | England |
| **1920** | Belgium |
| **1924** | Uruguay |
| **1928** | Uruguay |
| **1932** | Not contested |
| **1936** | Italy |
| **1948** | Sweden |
| **1952** | Hungary |
| **1956** | Soviet Union |
| **1960** | Yugoslavia |
| **1964** | Hungary |
| **1968** | Hungary |
| **1972** | Poland |
| **1976** | East Germany |
| **1980** | Czechoslovakia |
| **1984** | France |
| **1988** | Soviet Union |
| **1992** | Spain |
| **1996** | Nigeria |
| **2000** | Cameroon |
| **2004** | Argentina |
| **2004** | Argentina |
| **2008** | Argentina |

## WORLD CLUB CUP

| | |
|---|---|
| **1960** | Real Madrid |
| **1961** | Penarol |
| **1962** | Santos |
| **1963** | Santos |
| **1964** | Internazionale |
| **1965** | Internazionale |
| **1966** | Penarol |
| **1967** | Racing Club |
| **1968** | Estudiantes de La Plata |
| **1969** | AC Milan |
| **1970** | Feyenoord |
| **1971** | Nacional Montevideo |
| **1972** | Ajax |
| **1973** | Independiente |
| **1974** | Atlético Madrid |
| **1975** | Bayern Munich v Independiente |
| **1976** | Bayern Munich |
| **1977** | Boca Juniors |
| **1978** | Liverpool v Boca Juniors |
| **1979** | Olimpia |
| **1980** | Nacional |
| **1981** | Flamengo |
| **1982** | Penarol |
| **1983** | Gremio |
| **1984** | Independiente |
| **1985** | Juventus |
| **1986** | River Plate |
| **1987** | FC Porto |
| **1988** | Nacional |
| **1989** | AC Milan |
| **1990** | AC Milan |
| **1991** | Red Star Belgrade |
| **1992** | Sao Paulo |
| **1993** | Sao Paulo |
| **1994** | Velez Sarsfield |
| **1995** | Ajax |
| **1996** | Juventus |
| **1997** | Borussia Dortmund |
| **1998** | Real Madrid |
| **1999** | Manchester United |
| **2000** | Boca Juniors |
| **2001** | Bayern Munich |
| **2002** | Real Madrid |
| **2003** | Boca Juniors |
| **2004** | Porto |
| **2005** | Sao Paulo |
| **2006** | Internacional |
| **2007** | AC Milan |
| **2008** | Manchester United |

## WOMEN'S WORLD CHAMPIONSHIPS

| | |
|---|---|
| **1991** | United States of America |
| **1995** | Norway |
| **1999** | United States of America |
| **2003** | Germany |
| **2006** | Korea |
| **2008** | United States of America |

## WOMEN'S OLYMPIC GAMES

| | |
|---|---|
| **1996** | United States of America |
| **2000** | Norway |
| **2004** | United States of America |
| **2008** | United States of America |

# National Results

## ENGLAND

### Champions

1889 Preston NE
1890 Preston NE
1891 Everton
1892 Sunderland
1893 Sunderland
1894 Aston Villa
1895 Sunderland
1896 Aston Villa
1897 Aston Villa
1898 Sheffield U
1899 Aston Villa
1900 Aston Villa
1901 Liverpool
1902 Sunderland
1903 The Wednesday
1904 The Wednesday
1905 Newcastle U
1906 Liverpool
1907 Newcastle U
1908 Manchester U
1909 Newcastle U
1910 Aston Villa
1911 Manchester U
1912 Blackburn R
1913 Sunderland
1914 Blackburn R
1915 Everton
1916–19 Not contested
1920 West Bromwich A
1921 Burnley
1922 Liverpool
1923 Liverpool
1924 Huddersfield T
1925 Huddersfield T
1926 Huddersfield T
1927 Newcastle U
1928 Everton
1929 Sheffield W
1930 Sheffield W
1931 Arsenal
1932 Everton
1933 Arsenal
1934 Arsenal
1935 Arsenal
1936 Sunderland
1937 Manchester C
1938 Arsenal
1939 Everton
1940–46 Not contested
1947 Liverpool
1948 Arsenal
1949 Portsmouth
1950 Portsmouth
1951 Tottenham H
1952 Manchester U
1953 Arsenal
1954 Wolverhampton W
1955 Chelsea
1956 Manchester U
1957 Manchester U
1958 Wolverhampton W
1959 Wolverhampton W
1960 Burnley
1961 Tottenham H
1962 Ipswich T

1963 Everton
1964 Liverpool
1965 Manchester U
1966 Liverpool
1967 Manchester U
1968 Manchester C
1969 Leeds U
1970 Everton
1971 Arsenal
1972 Derby Co
1973 Liverpool
1974 Leeds U
1975 Derby Co
1976 Liverpool
1977 Liverpool
1978 Nottingham F
1979 Liverpool
1980 Liverpool
1981 Aston Villa
1982 Liverpool
1983 Liverpool
1984 Liverpool
1985 Everton
1986 Liverpool
1987 Everton
1988 Liverpool
1989 Arsenal
1990 Liverpool
1991 Arsenal
1992 Leeds U
1993 Manchester U
1994 Manchester U
1995 Blackburn R
1996 Manchester U
1997 Manchester U
1998 Arsenal
1999 Manchester U
2000 Manchester U
2001 Manchester U
2002 Arsenal
2003 Manchester U
2004 Arsenal
2005 Chelsea
2006 Chelsea
2007 Manchester U
2008 Manchester U
2009 Manchester U

### FA Cup Winners

1872 Wanderers
1873 Wanderers
1874 Oxford University
1875 Royal Engineers
1876 Wanderers
1877 Wanderers
1878 Wanderers
1879 Old Etonians
1880 Clapham R
1881 Old Carthusians
1882 Blackburn Olympic
1883 Blackburn R
1884 Blackburn R
1885 Blackburn R
1886 Blackburn R
1887 Aston Villa
1888 West Bromwich A
1889 Preston NE

1890 Blackburn R
1891 Blackburn R
1892 West Bromwich A
1893 Wolverhampton W
1894 Notts Co
1895 Aston Villa
1896 Sheffield W
1897 Aston Villa
1898 Nottingham F
1899 Sheffield U
1900 Bury
1901 Manchester C
1902 Aston Villa
1903 Bury
1904 Manchester C
1905 Aston Villa
1906 Everton
1907 Sheffield W
1908 Wolverhampton W
1909 Manchester U
1910 Newcastle U
1911 Bradford C
1912 Barnsley
1913 Aston Villa
1914 Burnley
1915 Sheffield U
1916–19 Not contested
1920 Aston Villa
1921 Tottenham H
1922 Huddersfield T
1923 Bolton W
1924 Newcastle U
1925 Sheffield U
1926 Bolton W
1927 Cardiff C
1928 Blackburn R
1929 Bolton W
1930 Arsenal
1931 West Bromwich A
1932 Newcastle U
1933 Everton
1934 Manchester C
1935 Sheffield W
1936 Arsenal
1937 Sunderland
1938 Preston NE
1939 Portsmouth
1940–45 Not contested
1946 Derby Co
1947 Charlton Ath
1948 Manchester U
1949 Wolverhampton W
1950 Arsenal
1951 Newcastle U
1952 Newcastle U
1953 Blackpool
1954 West Bromwich A
1955 Newcastle U
1956 Manchester C
1957 Aston Villa
1958 Bolton W
1959 Nottingham F
1960 Wolverhampton W
1961 Tottenham H
1962 Tottenham H
1963 Manchester U
1964 West Ham U

1965 Liverpool
1966 Everton
1967 Tottenham H
1968 West Bromwich A
1969 Manchester C
1970 Chelsea
1971 Arsenal
1972 Leeds U
1973 Sunderland
1974 Liverpool
1975 West Ham U
1976 Southampton
1977 Manchester U
1978 Ipswich T
1979 Arsenal
1980 West Ham U
1981 Tottenham H
1982 Tottenham H
1983 Manchester U
1984 Everton
1985 Manchester U
1986 Liverpool
1987 Coventry C
1988 Wimbledon
1989 Liverpool
1990 Manchester U
1991 Tottenham H
1992 Liverpool
1993 Arsenal
1994 Manchester U
1995 Everton
1996 Manchester U
1997 Chelsea
1998 Arsenal
1999 Manchester U
2000 Chelsea
2001 Liverpool
2002 Arsenal
2003 Arsenal
2004 Manchester U
2005 Arsenal
2006 Liverpool
2007 Chelsea
2008 Portsmouth
2009 Chelsea

## SCOTLAND

### Champions

1891 Dumbarton
1892 Dumbarton
1893 Celtic
1894 Celtic
1895 Heart of Midlothian
1896 Celtic
1897 Heart of Midlothian
1898 Celtic
1899 Rangers
1900 Rangers
1901 Rangers
1902 Rangers
1903 Hibernian
1904 Third Lanark
1905 Celtic
1906 Celtic
1907 Celtic
1908 Celtic
1909 Celtic
1910 Celtic
1911 Rangers
1912 Rangers
1913 Rangers
1914 Celtic
1915 Celtic
1916 Celtic
1917 Celtic
1918 Rangers
1919 Celtic
1920 Rangers
1921 Rangers
1922 Celtic
1923 Rangers
1924 Rangers
1925 Rangers
1926 Celtic
1927 Rangers
1928 Rangers
1929 Rangers
1930 Rangers
1931 Rangers
1932 Motherwell
1933 Rangers
1934 Rangers
1935 Rangers
1936 Celtic
1937 Rangers
1938 Celtic
1939 Rangers
1940–46 Not contested
1947 Rangers
1948 Hibernian
1949 Rangers
1950 Rangers
1951 Hibernian
1952 Hibernian
1953 Rangers
1954 Celtic
1955 Aberdeen
1956 Rangers
1957 Rangers
1958 Heart of Midlothian
1959 Rangers
1960 Heart of Midlothian
1961 Rangers

## SCOTLAND (continued)

1962 Dundee
1963 Rangers
1964 Rangers
1965 Kilmarnock
1966 Celtic
1967 Celtic
1968 Celtic
1969 Celtic
1970 Celtic
1971 Celtic
1972 Celtic
1973 Celtic
1974 Celtic
1975 Rangers
1976 Rangers
1977 Celtic
1978 Rangers
1979 Celtic
1980 Aberdeen
1981 Celtic
1982 Celtic
1983 Dundee U
1984 Aberdeen
1985 Aberdeen
1986 Celtic
1987 Rangers
1988 Celtic
1989 Rangers
1990 Rangers
1991 Rangers
1992 Rangers
1993 Rangers
1994 Rangers
1995 Rangers
1996 Rangers
1997 Rangers
1998 Celtic
1999 Rangers
2000 Rangers
2001 Celtic
2002 Celtic
2003 Rangers
2004 Celtic
2005 Rangers
2006 Celtic
2007 Celtic
2008 Celtic
2009 Rangers

### Cup Winners

1874 Queen's Park
1875 Queen's Park
1876 Queen's Park
1877 Vale of Leven
1878 Vale of Leven
1879 Vale of Leven
1880 Queen's Park
1881 Queen's Park
1882 Queen's Park
1883 Dumbarton
1884 Queen's Park
1885 Renton
1886 Queen's Park
1887 Hibernian
1888 Renton
1889 Third Lanark
1890 Queen's Park
1891 Heart of Midlothian
1892 Celtic
1893 Queen's Park
1894 Rangers
1895 St Bernard's
1896 Heart of Midlothian
1897 Rangers
1898 Rangers
1899 Celtic
1900 Celtic
1901 Heart of Midlothian
1902 Hibernian
1903 Rangers
1904 Celtic
1905 Third Lanark
1906 Heart of Midlothian
1907 Celtic
1908 Celtic
1909 Cup withheld
1910 Dundee
1911 Celtic
1912 Celtic
1913 Falkirk
1914 Celtic
1915–19 Not contested
1920 Kilmarnock
1921 Partick Thistle
1922 Morton
1923 Celtic
1924 Airdieonians
1925 Celtic
1926 St Mirren
1927 Celtic
1928 Rangers
1929 Kilmarnock
1930 Rangers
1931 Celtic
1932 Rangers
1933 Celtic
1934 Rangers
1935 Rangers
1936 Rangers
1937 Celtic
1938 East Fife
1939 Clyde
1940–46 Not contested
1947 Aberdeen
1948 Rangers
1949 Rangers
1950 Rangers
1951 Celtic
1952 Motherwell
1953 Rangers
1954 Celtic
1955 Clyde
1956 Heart of Midlothian
1957 Falkirk
1958 Clyde
1959 St Mirren
1960 Rangers
1961 Dumferline Athletic
1962 Rangers
1963 Rangers
1964 Rangers
1965 Celtic
1966 Rangers
1967 Celtic
1968 Dumferline Athletic
1969 Celtic
1970 Aberdeen
1971 Celtic
1972 Celtic
1973 Rangers
1974 Celtic
1975 Celtic
1976 Rangers
1977 Celtic
1978 Rangers
1979 Rangers
1980 Celtic
1981 Rangers
1982 Aberdeen
1983 Aberdeen
1984 Aberdeen
1985 Celtic
1986 Aberdeen
1987 St Mirren
1988 Celtic
1989 Celtic
1990 Aberdeen
1991 Motherwell
1992 Rangers
1993 Rangers
1994 Dundee U
1995 Celtic
1996 Rangers
1997 Kilmarnock
1998 Hearts
1999 Rangers
2000 Rangers
2001 Celtic
2002 Rangers
2003 Rangers
2004 Celtic
2005 Celtic
2006 Hearts
2007 Celtic
2008 Rangers
2009 Rangers

## NORTHERN IRELAND

### Champions

1891 Linfield
1892 Linfield
1893 Linfield
1894 Glentoran
1895 Linfield
1896 Distillery
1897 Glentoran
1898 Linfield
1899 Distillery
1900 Celtic
1901 Distillery
1902 Linfield
1903 Distillery
1904 Linfield
1905 Glentoran
1906 Cliftonville
1907 Linfield
1908 Linfield
1909 Linfield
1910 Cliftonville
1911 Linfield
1912 Glentoran
1913 Glentoran
1914 Linfield
1915 Celtic
1916–19 Not contested
1920 Celtic
1921 Glentoran
1922 Linfield
1923 Linfield
1924 Queen's Island
1925 Glentoran
1926 Celtic
1927 Celtic
1928 Celtic
1929 Celtic
1930 Linfield
1931 Glentoran
1932 Linfield
1933 Celtic
1934 Linfield
1935 Linfield
1936 Celtic
1937 Celtic
1938 Celtic
1939 Celtic
1940 Celtic
1941–47 Not contested
1948 Celtic
1949 Linfield
1950 Linfield
1951 Glentoran
1952 Glentoran
1953 Glentoran
1954 Linfield
1955 Linfield
1956 Linfield
1957 Glenavon
1958 Ards
1959 Linfield
1960 Glenavon
1961 Linfield
1962 Linfield
1963 Distillery
1964 Glentoran
1965 Derry City
1966 Linfield
1967 Glentoran
1968 Glentoran
1969 Linfield
1970 Glentoran
1971 Linfield
1972 Glentoran
1973 Crusaders
1974 Coleraine
1975 Linfield
1976 Crusaders
1977 Glentoran
1978 Linfield
1979 Linfield
1980 Linfield
1981 Glentoran
1982 Linfield
1983 Linfield
1984 Linfield
1985 Linfield
1986 Linfield
1987 Linfield
1988 Glentoran
1989 Linfield
1990 Portadown
1991 Portadown
1992 Glentoran
1993 Linfield
1994 Linfield
1995 Crusaders
1996 Portadown
1997 Crusaders
1998 Cliftonville
1999 Glentoran
2000 Linfield
2001 Linfield
2002 Portadown
2003 Glentoran
2004 Linfield
2005 Glentoran
2006 Linfield
2007 Linfield
2008 Linfield
2009 Glentoran

### Cup Winners

1881 Moyola Park
1882 Queen's Island
1883 Cliftonville
1884 Distillery
1885 Distillery
1886 Distillery
1887 Ulster
1888 Cliftonville
1889 Distillery
1890 Gordon Highlanders
1891 Linfield
1892 Linfield
1893 Linfield
1894 Distillery
1895 Linfield
1896 Distillery
1897 Cliftonville
1898 Linfield

1899 Linfield
1900 Cliftonville
1901 Cliftonville
1902 Linfield
1903 Distillery
1904 Linfield
1905 Distillery
1906 Shelbourne
1907 Cliftonville
1908 Bohemians
1909 Cliftonville
1910 Distillery
1911 Shelbourne
1912 Linfield
1913 Linfield
1914 Glentoran
1915 Linfield
1916 Linfield
1917 Glentoran
1918 Celtic
1919 Linfield
1920 Shelbourne
1921 Glentoran
1922 Linfield
1923 Linfield
1924 Queen's Island
1925 Distillery
1926 Celtic
1927 Ards
1928 Willowfield
1929 Ballymena U
1930 Linfield
1931 Linfield
1932 Glentoran
1933 Glentoran
1934 Linfield
1935 Glentoran
1936 Linfield
1937 Celtic
1938 Celtic
1939 Linfield
1940 Ballymena U
1941 Celtic
1942 Linfield
1943 Celtic
1944 Celtic
1945 Linfield
1946 Linfield
1947 Celtic
1948 Linfield
1949 Derry City
1950 Linfield
1951 Glentoran
1952 Ards
1953 Linfield
1954 Derry City
1955 Dundela
1956 Distillery
1957 Glenavon
1958 Ballymena U
1959 Glenavon
1960 Linfield
1961 Glenavon
1962 Linfield
1963 Linfield
1964 Derry City
1965 Coleraine
1966 Glentoran
1967 Crusaders
1968 Crusaders
1969 Ards
1970 Linfield
1971 Distillery
1972 Coleraine
1973 Glentoran
1974 Ards
1975 Coleraine
1976 Carrick Rangers
1977 Coleraine
1978 Linfield
1979 Cliftonville
1980 Linfield
1981 Ballymena U
1982 Linfield
1983 Glentoran
1984 Ballymena U
1985 Glentoran
1986 Glentoran
1987 Glentoran
1988 Glentoran
1989 Ballymena U
1990 Glentoran
1991 Portadown
1992 Glenavon
1993 Bangor
1994 Linfield
1995 Linfield
1996 Glentoran
1997 Glenavon
1998 Glentoran
1999 Portadown
2000 Glentoran
2001 Glentoran
2002 Linfield
2003 Coleraine
2004 Cliftonville
2005 Portadown
2006 Linfield
2007 Linfield
2008 Linfield
2009 Crusaders

## WALES

### Champions

1993 Cwmbran Town
1994 Bangor City
1995 Bangor City
1996 Barry Town
1997 Barry Town
1998 Barry Town
1999 Barry Town
2000 TNS Llansantffraid
2001 Barry Town
2002 Barry Town
2003 Barry Town
2004 Rhyl
2005 TNS Llansantffraid
2006 TNS Llansantffraid
2007 TNS Llansantffraid
2008 Llanelli
2009 Rhyl

### Cup Winners

1878 Wrexham
1879 Newtown
1880 Druids
1881 Druids
1882 Druids
1883 Wrexham
1884 Oswestry
1885 Druids
1886 Druids
1887 Chirk
1888 Chirk
1889 Bangor City
1890 Chirk
1891 Shrewsbury Town
1892 Chirk
1893 Wrexham
1894 Chirk
1895 Newtown
1896 Bangor City
1897 Wrexham
1898 Druids
1899 Druids
1900 Aberystwyth Town
1901 Oswestry
1902 Wellington
1903 Wrexham
1904 Druids
1905 Wrexham
1906 Wellington
1907 Oswestry
1908 Chester City
1909 Wrexham
1910 Wrexham
1911 Wrexham
1912 Cardiff City
1913 Swansea Town
1914 Wrexham
1915 Wrexham
1916–19 Not contested
1920 Cardiff City
1921 Wrexham
1922 Cardiff City
1923 Cardiff City
1924 Wrexham
1925 Wrexham
1926 Ebbw Vale
1927 Cardiff City
1928 Cardiff City
1929 Connah's Quay
1930 Cardiff City
1931 Wrexham
1932 Swansea Town
1933 Chester City
1934 Bristol City
1935 Tranmere Rovers
1936 Crewe Alexandra
1937 Crewe Alexandra
1938 Shrewsbury Town
1939 South Liverpool
1940–46 Not contested
1947 Chester City
1948 Lovell's Athletic
1949 Methyr Tydfil
1950 Swansea Town
1951 Methyr Tydfil
1952 Rhyl
1953 Rhyl
1954 Flint
1955 Barry Town
1956 Cardiff City
1957 Wrexham
1958 Wrexham
1959 Cardiff City
1960 Wrexham
1961 Swansea Town
1962 Bangor City
1963 Borough United
1964 Cardiff City
1965 Cardiff City
1966 Swansea Town
1967 Cardiff City
1968 Cardiff City
1969 Cardiff City
1970 Cardiff City
1971 Cardiff City
1972 Wrexham
1973 Cardiff City
1974 Cardiff City
1975 Wrexham
1976 Cardiff City
1977 Shrewsbury Town
1978 Wrexham
1979 Shrewsbury Town
1980 Newport County
1981 Swansea City
1982 Swansea City
1983 Swansea City
1984 Shrewsbury Town
1985 Shrewsbury Town
1986 Wrexham
1987 Methyr Tydfil
1988 Cardiff City
1989 Swansea City
1990 Hereford United
1991 Swansea City
1992 Cardiff City
1993 Cardiff City
1994 Barry Town
1995 Wrexham
1996 TNS Llansantffraid
1997 Barry Town
1998 Bangor City
1999 Inter Cable-Tel
2000 Bangor City
2001 Barry Town
2002 Barry Town
2003 Barry Town
2004 Rhyl
2005 Swansea City
2006 Swansea City
2007 New Saints
2008 Bangor City
2009 Bangor City

## NORTH AMERICA
### Champions
Western Soccer League
- **1985** San Jose Earthquakes
- **1986** Hollywood Kickers
- **1987** San Diego Nomads
- **1988** Seattle Storm
- **1989** San Diego Nomads
- **1990** San Francisco Bayhawks

American Soccer League
- **1988** Washington Diplomats
- **1989** Fort Lauderdale Strikers
- **1990** Maryland Bays

American Professional Soccer League
- **1989** Fort Lauderdale Strikers
- **1990** Maryland Bays
- **1991** San Francisco Bayhawks
- **1992** Colorado Foxes
- **1993** Colorado Foxes
- **1994** Montreal Impact

Major League Soccer
- **1996** DC United
- **1997** DC United
- **1998** Chicago Fire
- **1999** DC United
- **2000** Kansas City Wizards
- **2001** San Jose Earthquakes
- **2002** Los Angeles Galaxy
- **2003** San Jose Earthquakes
- **2004** Chicago Fire
- **2005** San Jose Earthquakes
- **2006** DC United
- **2007** DC United
- **2008** Columbus Crew

## CANADA
### Champions
- **1987** Calgary Kickers
- **1988** Vancouver 86ers
- **1989** Vancouver 86ers
- **1990** Vancouver 86ers
- **1991** Vancouver 86ers
- **1992** Winnipeg Fury
- **1998** St Catherine's Roma Wolves
- **1999** Calgary Celtic SFC
- **2000** Luciana Soccer Club
- **2001** Halifax King of Donair
- **2002** Sons of Italy, Manitola
- **2003** Calgary Callies

### Cup Winners
- **1913** Norwood Wanderers
- **1914** Norwood Wanderers
- **1915** Winnipeg Scots
- **1916–18** Not contested
- **1920** Westinghouse Ontario
- **1921** Toronto Scots
- **1922** Hillhurst Calgary
- **1923** Nanaimo
- **1924** Weston University
- **1925** Toronto Ulsters
- **1926** Weston University
- **1927** Nanaimo
- **1928** New Westminster Royals
- **1929** CNR Montreal
- **1930** New Westminster Royals
- **1931** New Westminster Royals
- **1932** Toronto Scots
- **1933** Toronto Scots
- **1934** Werduns Montrealo
- **1935** Aldreds Montreal
- **1936** New Westminster Royals
- **1937** Johnston Nationals
- **1938** North Shore Vancouver
- **1939** Radials Vancouver
- **1940–45** Not contested
- **1946** Toronto Ulsters
- **1947** St. Andrews Vancouver
- **1948** Carsteel Montreal
- **1949** North Shore Vancouver
- **1950** Vancouver City
- **1951** Ulster United Toronto
- **1952** Steelco Montreal
- **1953** New Westminster Royals
- **1954** Scottish Winnipeg
- **1955** New Westminster Royals
- **1956** Halecos Vancouver
- **1957** Ukrainia SC Montreal
- **1958** New Westminster Royals
- **1959** Alouetts Montreal
- **1960** New Westminster Royals
- **1961** Concordia Montreal
- **1962** Scottish Winnipeg
- **1963** Not contested
- **1964** Columbus Vancouver
- **1965** Vancouver Firefighters
- **1966** Vancouver Firefighters
- **1967** Toronto
- **1968** Toronto Royals
- **1969** Columbus Vancouver
- **1970** Manitoba Selects
- **1971** Eintracht Vancouver
- **1972** New Westminster Blues
- **1973** Vancouver Firefighters
- **1974** Calgary Springer Kickers
- **1975** London Boxing Club Victoria
- **1976** Victoria West SC
- **1977** Columbus Vancouver
- **1978** Columbus Vancouver
- **1979** Victoria West SC
- **1980** St. John Dry Dock
- **1981** Toronto Ciocario
- **1982** Victoria West SC
- **1983** Vancouver Firefighters
- **1984** Victoria West SC
- **1985** Vancouver Croatia
- **1986** Hamilton Steelers
- **1987** Lucania SC
- **1988** Holy Cross
- **1989** Scarborough Azzurri
- **1990** Vancouver Firefighters
- **1991** Norvan SC
- **1992** Norvan SC
- **1993** West Side Rino
- **1994** Edmonton Ital-Canadians
- **1995** Mistral-Estrie
- **1996** Westside CIBC
- **1997** Edmonton Ital-Canadians
- **1998** Toronto Olympians

## AUSTRALIA
### Champions
- **1977** Sydney City Hakoah
- **1978** West Adelaide Hellas
- **1979** Marconi
- **1980** Sydney City Hakoah
- **1981** Sydney City Hakoah
- **1982** Sydney City Hakoah
- **1983** St. George Budapest
- **1984** South Melbourne Hellas
- **1985** Brunswick Juventus
- **1986** Adelaide City Juventus
- **1987** APIA-Leichhardt
- **1988** Marconi
- **1989** Marconi
- **1990** Sydney Olympic
- **1991** South Melbourne Hellas
- **1992** Adelaide City Juventus
- **1993** Marconi
- **1994** Adelaide City
- **1995** Melbourne Knights
- **1996** Melbourne Knights
- **1997** Brisbane Strikers
- **1998** South Melbourne Lakers
- **1999** South Melbourne
- **2000** Wollongong City Wolves
- **2001** Wollongong City Wolves
- **2002** Sydney Olympic Sharks
- **2003** Perth Glory
- **2004** Perth Glory

### Cup Winners
- **1977** Brisbane City
- **1978** Brisbane City
- **1979** Adelaide City Juventus
- **1980** Marconi
- **1981** Brisbane Lions
- **1982** APIA Leichhardt
- **1983** Sydney Olympic
- **1984** Newcastle Rosebud
- **1985** Sydney Olympic
- **1986** Sydney City Hakoah
- **1987** Sydney Croatia
- **1988** APIA Leichhardt
- **1989** Adelaide City Juventus
- **1990** South Melbourne Hellas
- **1991** Parramatta Melita
- **1992** Adelaide City Juventus
- **1993** Heidelberg United
- **1994** Parramatta Eagles
- **1995** Melbourne Knights
- **1996** South Melbourne
- **1997** Collingwood Warriors
- **1998–** Not contested

# Index

Overath, Wolfgang 130
Overmars, Marc 116
Owen, Michael 55, 131, 163

Paisley, Bob 73–4
Palmeiras 48
Papin, Jean-Pierre 132, 221
Paris St-Germain 225
Parker, Tom 18
Parma 5, 47, 64
Passarella, Daniel 132
Pegg, David 27
Pelè 25, 35, 40–1, 55, 80, 88, 94, 110, 133, 232
Penarol 11, 30, 33, 43, 66, 226
Peru 184
Peters, Martin 35, 39, 239
Petit, Emmanuel 53
Piazza, Wilson 40
Piola, Silvio 17
Pirlo, Andrea 134
Platini, Michel 42, 43, 44, 56–7, 56, 75, 134, 164
Podolski, Lukas 55
Porto 11, 42–3, 47, 49, 64, 227
Portugal 171, 242
Pozzo, Vittorio 16, 99
Preston North End 11
professionalism 10–11, 34
Prosinecki, Robert 135
PSV Eindhoven 36, 42, 228
Puskas, Ferenc 22, 24, 29, 30, 33, 62–3, 67, 92, 95, 103, 135, 167

Racing Club 33
Radebe, Lucas 193
Rahn, Helmut 24–5, 55
Raja Casablanca 43, 48
Ramsey, Alf 23, 35, 74
Rangers 11, 37, 64, 229
Rapid Vienna 11, 21
Raul 63, 230
Ravelli, Thomas 136, 212
Real Madrid 4, 5, 20–1, 28–30, 33, 42, 46, 49, 62, 64–5, 67, 230, 242
Real Zaragoza 31, 64, 65
Rebrov, Sergei 216

Red Star Belgrade 49, 63, 231
Rensenbrink, Robbie 39, 55, 197
Rep, Johnny 36, 91, 117, 196, *240*
Revie, Don 31, 86, 104
Rial, Hector 28
Riedle, Karlheinz 64, 204
Riise, Hege 70
Rijkaard, Frank 42, 63, 136
Rimet, Jules 16, *23*, 54
Riva, Gigi 39
Rivaldo 51, 55, 116, 137
Riva, Luigi 136
Rivelino 40–1, 181
Rivera, Gianni 41, 137
River Plate 43, 48
Rix, Graham 64
Roberto 39
Roberts, Herbert 18
Robertson, John 42
Robinho 138
Robson, Bobby 146
Robson, Bryan 139
Rodriguez, Maxi 53
Roma 31, 73
Romania 173
Romario 52, 55, 79, 209
Romero, Cleber *226*
Ronaldinho 139
Ronaldo 4–5, 51, 53, 55, 64–5, 110, 140, 214
Ronaldo, Cristiano 5, 140, 171
Rooney, Wayne 53, 140, 141
Rosicky 161
Rossi, Paolo 43, 45, 55, 75, 138, 168
Roth, Franz 36
Rudakov 56
rules 10, 11, 13, 30, 68
Rummenigge, Karl-Heinz 45, 55, 141
Rush, Ian 142
Russia 174

Sacchi, Arrigo 46, 222
St John, Ian 74
Salas, Marcelo 182
Salenko, Oleg 55
Sammer, Matthias 142
Sanchez, Hugo 55, 87, 143, 186
Santamaria, Josè 28
Santos 33, 232
Santos, Djalma 35
Sao Paolo 48, 49, 233
Sarosi, Gyorgy 17, 143
Savicevic, Dejan 80, 144, 231
Schalke 47, 65
Schiaffino, Juan 21, 23, 28, 55, 120, 144
Schiavo, Angelo 16, 55

Schillaci, Salvatore 55
Schmeichel, Peter 73, 145, 162
Schön, Helmut 74
Schumacher, Harald 45
Scifo, Vicenzo 45, 145
Scirea, Gaetano 80, 103
Scotland 23, 175, 250–1
Scurry, Briana 70
Seeler, Uwe 39, 146
Senegal 4
Sevilla 48
Shankly, Bill 74
Shearer, Alan 146
Sheffield 11
Sheffield United 13
Shilton, Peter 45, 90, 147
Silva, David 237
Silva, Gilberto 4
Silva, Maurio 52
Sissi 69
Sivori, Omar 88, 147
Skuhravy, Tomas 55, 234
Slovan Bratislava 33
Socrates 148
Solskjaer, Ole Gunnar 170, 243
Song, Rigobert 190
Souness, Graeme 74, 148, 241
South Africa 193
South American Championship 22–3, 34, 38
South Korea 4, 5, 38
Soviet Union 34, 56
Spain *4*, 34, 56, 176, 243
Sparta Prague 11, 15, 31, 234
Spencer, Alberto 33
Stabile, Guillermo 55
Stade Abidjan 33
Stade de Reims 21
Steaua Bucharest 42, 63, 235
Stein, Jock 74–5, 112, 125
Stiles, Nobby 239
Stoichkov, Hristo 52, 55, 149, 159
Stoke City 11
Suarez, Luis 149
Suker, Davor 52, 55, 57, 149
Sundhage, Pia 69
Sun Wen 69, 70
Superga air crash 22
Swart 129
Sweden 22, 177
Switzerland 10, 11, 22
Szarmach 55
Szellenger 55

Taffarel, Cláudio 53
Tamudo, Raúl *58*
Tardelli, Marco 45
Taylor, Ernie 27

Taylor, Peter 72
Taylor, Tommy 26
Thuram, Lilian 52
Tibilisi Dinamo 43
Tigana, Jean 56
Tonni, Luca 53
Torino 22
Torres, Fernando 51, 55, 57, 150
Toshack, John 74, 114
Tostao 40
total football 36, 62, 73, 91, 117, 166
Tottenham Hotspur 32, 36, 42, 64, 65, 236
Totti, Francesco 53
Tout Puissant Engelbert 33, 37
Trapattoni, Giovanni 43, 75
Trezeguet, David 50
Troussier, Philippe 188
Turkey 4, 5

UEFA Cup 20, 36, 42, 47–8, 65, 247
Union Duoala 37
United States of America 187, 253
Uruguay 13, 22, 23, 185
Usuriaga, Albeiro 213

Valdano, Jorge 45
Valderrama, Carlos 151, 183
València 31, 43, 48, 64, 237
Van Basten, Marco 42–4, 56–7, 63, 80, 150, 166
Van Gaal, Louis 116
Van Hanegem, Wim 208
Van Himst, Paul 151, 197
Van Nistelrooy, Ruud 151
Van Tiggelen, Adri 56
Vasas Budapest 21, 31
Vasco da Gama 48, 66
Vassallo, Luciano 35
Vava 25, 35, 55, 94, *181*
Velez Sarsfield 48, 49

Venables, Terry 102
Vialli, Gianluca 152, 215
Vieira, Patrick 198
Vieri, Christian 55, 152
Villa, David 237
Villa, Ricky 79
Viollet, Dennis 26–7
Vita, AS 37
Vogts, Berti *37*
Voller, Rudi 45, 52

wages 10–11, 12, 31
Wales 178, 252
Wark, John 64
Weah, George 153
Weinert, Maren 71
Wenger, Arsene 75
West Bromwich Albion 11
West Germany 39, 52, 56
West Ham 32, 64
Whelan, Liam 27
Whittaker, Tom 19
Wiegamann, Bettina 70
Williams, Bert 23
Wimmer, Herbert 56
Winterbottom, Walter 22
Withe, Peter 42
WM formation 18
Wolverhampton Wanderers 11
women's football 68–71
Women's World Cup 70–1, 249
World Club Cup 33, 37, 43, 49, 67, 249
World Cup 4, 5, 16–17, 23–5, 35, 39, 40–1, 45, 52–3 54–5, 244–5
Wright, Billy 153
Wright, Ian 19
Wydad Casablanca 48

Xavier, Abel 50

Yashin, Lev 22, 34, 153
Yeats, Ron 74
Yugoslavia 22, 34, 179, 243
Yuran, Sergei 223

Zagallo 94
Zagalo, Mario 25, 75
Zagorakis, Theodoros 50
Zamalek 43, 48, 49
Zamorano, Ivan 47, 59, 182
Zenit St Petersburg 48
Zico 154, 209
Zidane, Zinedine 46, 50, 53, 55, 154, 164
Zito 35, 232
Zoff, Dino 155
Zola, Gianfranco 65
Zubizarreta, Andoni 155, 159